Law For The Common Man

Law For The Common Man

BY
Kush Kalra

LL.B., RGNUL, Punjab

Assisted by

Sonali Singh

LL.B., NLU, Delhi

Foreword by

Prof. M. Sridhar Acharyulu

Central Information Commissioner

Vij Books India Pvt Ltd

New Delhi (India)

Published by

Vij Books India Pvt Ltd
2/19, Ansari Road, Darya Ganj
New Delhi - 110002
Phones: 91-11- 43596460, 47340674
Fax: 91-11-47340674
e-mail : vijbooks@rediffmail.com
web : www.vijbooks.com

© 2014, *Kush Kalra*

First Published   : 2014

ISBN   : 978-93-82652-74-8

Price   : ₹ 495.00

Acknowledgement

My special thanks to Bhanu Tanwar (Law Student, NLU Delhi), Luv Kalra (Graduate in Public Policy) and Lalit Ajmani (Law Student, RGNUL Patiala, Punjab) for helping me in research work.

Contents

PROF. M.SRIDHAR ACHARYULU
CENTRAL INFORMATION COMMISSIONER
Phone: 011-26717352

Date: 22-05-2014

Foreword

A young Lawyer Mr. Kush Kalra, graduated from Punjab's Rajiv Gandhi National University of Law has already been the author of nine books and chooses to write another book for laymen.

The law that governs us is in a foreign language which most of our literates also do not properly understand. As a matter of fact, all the illiterates in their own mother tongue, if not in English, are denied access to law that was written, explained, interpreted and implemented (if at all) in English and English only. Those who know English language also find it difficult to demystify the mysterious legal English. They also need to be educated about the law in simple and plain English.

Thus because of the foreign language in which it is stored, most of our people are not in a position to read and understand it.

Strangely, the law mandates that ignorance of law is no defence quoting a Latin maxim, ignorantia juris non excusat. Another strange principle of law is that the State/law presumes that everyone knows the law. Once it is published in Gazette, the state believes strongly that everyone read, understood and ready to follow it. Most interestingly the State, the Constitution and entire legal mechanism would expect every person to abide by the law, without enabling them even to know it at least.

How can any person follow law when he cannot have access to it, capacity to read it, ability to understand it and especially when he does not know that law presumes that he knows the law?

Every person has a fundamental right to know within the right to life under Article 21, and another equally important right is right to information as part of right to freedom of speech and expression under Article 19(1). On one hand state presumes that you know the law, and on the other it says you have a right to know.

As the state is not engaged in educating the common man, much less imparting the legal knowledge, it is the duty of every law graduate to educate them. In fact, citizen is not empowered unless he knows his rights and has enough ability to enforce them.

I am happy to know that young Lawyer Mr. Kush Kalra understood this duty and started working very fast and published many books.

I had a cursory look at this work of the young author. He took varied subjects from the judicial decisions which are useful to common man and offered the essence for easy understanding. He chose English as the medium which means he is addressing the laymen of limited sphere. Unless someone ventures to write in the vernacular or local language other than English, along with simple English expressions, the mission of reaching every layman will not get completed. It is very difficult to explain English law in Indian Languages. Still one has to attempt. I wish the legal knowledge should reach the illiterate also, for which visual media is more useful.

Appreciating the sincere attempt of the author, I would like to suggest that there is a need to further simplify the language to fulfill his aim of reaching laymen. We the lawmen, should shed the legalese, Latin and complex expressions and use simple plain language to reach the common man of India.

The rights of the citizen, the author chose to explain are very relevant, useful and certainly improve legal awareness, if read.

The law is like a huge ocean of salt water, which is very much needed but not useful for drinking. The authors like Mr. Kush Kalra have to convert them into drinking water. I wish him all the best and hope that this book will take him to the people who suffered by law, lawlessness and lawmen.

(M.Sridhar Acharyulu)

List of Abbreviations

AIR	-	All India Reporter
Bom	-	Bombay
D.B.	-	Division Bench
Govt.	-	Government
ILR	-	Indian Law Reporter
IPC	-	Indian Penal Code
Lah	-	Lahore
LJ	-	Law Journal
LR	-	Law Reporter
Mah	-	Maharashtra
M.P.	-	Madhya Pradesh
P&H	-	Punjab and Haryana
Sec	-	Section
SC	-	Supreme Court
SCC	-	Supreme Court Cases
SCR	-	Supreme Court Reporter

"Everything has been said already, but as no one listens,
We must always begin again."

Andre Gide

French thinker and writer

Environment Law

"Earth provides enough to satisfy every man's needs, but not every man's greed"

Mahatma Gandhi

Earth has been described as "a jewel in space" but that jewel is passing through various catastrophic problems such as lifeless rivers, land sterilized by humans, carbon dioxide and other gases in the air resulting in climate change, deserts expand, the deforestation, diminution of forest wealth, disorderly and rapid growth of cities, custom built slums, abject poverty and affluent life styles of world's one fifth population of the developed countries. It is said that the Black Sea is on the verge of a catastrophe as all life could disappear from it due to chemical poisoning. Our own Ganga- the cradle of India's civilisation has become one of the highly polluted rivers in the world threatening human lives around. Many beautiful rivers which nourished and nurtured many human civilisations have become sewers endangering the oceans. Alarmingly deforestation is consuming reservoirs of centuries in a short time, soil erosion and peat depletion are exhausting reservoirs of millennia at a rapid pace. Environment and its protection are the subject assuming international dimensions. The world is shrinking. Any event in any part of the world having its impact on environment by way of pollution or protection has its ramifications in every other part of the world. The anxiety world over is displayed by including one or other aspect of environment in international conventions and conferences recognising the negative impact of the pollution of air, water and environment. Showing keen concern on the growing problems of environmental pollution, the United Nations convened an International Conference on the Human Environment at Stockholm in 1972 which is popularly known as "Stockholm Conference". This conference has become a significant event in the world because an international dialogue on the protection of the environment began with the convening of that conference. The proclamation adopted by the Stockholm Conference which took place at Stockholm from June 5 to 16, 1972 and in which the Indian delegation led by the Prime Minister of India took a leading role, reads :--

"1. Man is both creature and moulder of his environment which gives him physical sustenance and affords him the opportunity for intellectual, moral, social and spiritual growth. In the long and tortuous evolution of the human race on this planet, a stage has been reached when through the rapid acceleration of science and technology, man has acquired the power to transform his environment in countless ways and on an unprecedented scale. Both aspects of man's environment, the natural and the man-made, are essential to his well being and to the enjoyment of basic human rights - even the right to life itself.

2. The protection and improvement of the human environment is a major issue which affects the well being of peoples and economic development throughout the world. It is the urgent desire of the peoples of the whole world and the duty of all Governments.

3. Man has constantly to sum up experience and go on discovering, inventing, creating and advancing. In our time, man's capability to transform his surroundings, if used wisely, can bring to all peoples the benefits of development and the opportunity to enhance the quality of life, wrongly or heedlessly applied, the same power can do incalculable harm to human beings and the human environment. We see around us growing evidence of man-made harm in many regions of the earth; dangerous levels of pollution in water, air, earth and living beings; major and undesirable disturbances of the ecological balance of the biosphere; destruction and depletion of irreplaceable resources; and gross deficiencies harmful to the physical, mental and social health of man, in the man-made environment, particularly in the living and working environment.

A point has been reached in history when we must shape our actions throughout the world with a more prudent care for their environmental consequences. Through ignorance or indifference we can do massive and irreversible harm to the earthly environment on which our life and well being depend. Conversely, through fuller knowledge and wiser action, we can achieve for ourselves and our posterity a better life in an environment more in keeping with human needs and hopes. There are broad vistas for the enhancement of environmental quality and the creation of good life. What is needed is an enthusiastic but calm state of mind and intense but orderly work. For the purpose of attaining freedom in the world of nature, man must use knowledge to build in collaboration with nature a better environment. To defend and improve the human environment for present and future generations has become an imperative goal for mankind - a goal to be pursued together with, and in harmony with, the established and fundamental goals of peace and of worldwide economic and social development.

To achieve this, environmental goal will demand the acceptance of responsibility by citizens and communities and by enterprises and institutions at every level, all sharing equitably in common efforts. Individuals in all walks of life as well as organisations in many fields, by their values and the sum of their actions, will shape the world environment of the future. Local and National Governments will bear the greatest burden for large-scale environmental policy and action within their jurisdictions. International co-operation is also needed in order to raise resources to support the developing countries carrying out their responsibilities in this field. A growing class of environmental problems, because they are regional or global in extent or because they effect the common international realm, will require extensive co-operation among nations and action by international organisations in the common interest[1]"

The traditional concept that development and ecology are opposed to each other is no longer acceptable. Sustainable Development is the answer. In the International sphere "Sustainable Development" as a concept came to be known for the first time in the Stockholm Declaration of 1972. Thereafter, in 1987 the concept was given a definite shape by the World Commission on Environment and Development in its report called Court Common Future. Sustainable development has been defined in many ways but the most frequently quoted definition is from the Brundtland Report which states as follows:

"Sustainable development is development that meets the needs of the present without compromising the ability of future generations to meet their own needs. It contains within it two key concepts:

The concept of **needs**, in particular the essential needs of the world's poor, to which overriding priority should be given; and

The idea of **limitations** imposed by the state of technology and social organisation on the environment's ability to meet present and future needs."

---

1   Appellants: **T. Ramakrishna Rao Vs.** Respondent: **Chairman, Hyderabad Urban Development Authority, Hyd. and others,** 2001(4)ALD758, 2002(2)ALT193

The United Nations Commission on Environment and Development defined the 'sustainable development' as follows:

"Sustainable development is the development that meets the needs of the present without compromising the ability of future generations to meet their own needs[2]"

While applying the concept of sustainable development, one has to keep in mind the "principle of proportionality" based on the concept of balance. It is an exercise in which courts or tribunals have to balance the priorities of development on the one hand and environmental protection on the other. So sustainable development should also mean the type or extent of development that can take place and which can be sustained by nature/ecology with or without mitigation. Some of the salient principles of "Sustainable Development", as culled-out from Brundtland Report and other international documents, are Inter-Generational Equity, Use and Conservation of Nature Resources, Environmental Protection, the Precautionary Principle, Polluter Pays principle, Obligation to assist and cooperate, Eradication of Poverty and Financial Assistance to the developing countries. "The Precautionary Principle" and "The Polluter Pays" principle are essential features of "Sustainable Development". The "Precautionary Principle" - in the context of the municipal law - means.

(i) Environment measures - by the State Government and the statutory Authorities must anticipate, prevent and attack the causes of environmental degradation.

(ii) Where there are threats of serious and irreversible damage lack of scientific certainly should not be used as the reason for postponing, measures to prevent environmental depredation.

(iii)The "Onus of proof" is on the actor or the developer/industrial to show that his action is environmentally benign.

"The Polluter Pays" principle has been held to be a sound principle by Supreme Court in *Indian Council for Enviro- Legal Action vs. Union of India*[3] The "Polluter Pays" principle as interpreted by Court means that the absolute liability for harm to the environment extends not only to compensate the victims of pollution but also the cost of restoring the environmental degradation. Remediation of the damaged environment

2   (World Commission on Economic Development [WCED], 1987: 43)

3   (2011)8SCC161

is part of the process of "Sustainable Development" and as such polluter is liable to pay the cost to the individual sufferers as well as the cost of reversing the damaged ecology.

The precautionary principle and the polluter pays principle have been accepted as part of the law of the land. Article 21 of the Constitution of India guarantees protection of life and personal liberty. The Courts have consistently taken the view that right to life includes the right to a decent environment. The right to a clean environment is a guaranteed fundamental right. The Courts could even impose exemplary damages against the polluter. Proper and healthy environment enables people to enjoy a quality of life which is the essence of the right guaranteed under Article 21. The right to have congenial environment for human existence is the right to life. The State has a duty in that behalf and to shed its extravagant unbridled sovereign power and to forge in its policy to maintain ecological balance and hygienic environment. Though Government has power to give directions, that power should be used only to effectuate and further the goals of the approved scheme, zonal plans, etc. If without degrading the environment or minimizing adverse effects thereupon by applying stringent safeguards, it is not possible to carry on development activity applying the principle of sustainable development, in that eventuality, development has to go on because one cannot lose sight of the need for development of industries, irrigation resources, power projects, etc. including the need to improve the employment opportunities and the generation of revenue. So a balance has to be struck[4].

Rapid and unchecked development would adversely affect the environment. Protection of the vital resources is the need of hour. Gandhian postulation recognized the rules for sustainable development and described them as follows:

"1). CONSERVATION: Preservation and nurturing of the vital resources, that still remain, are the sine qua non for good environmental management. Conservation as an idea is not merely confined to retaining whatever that is left, but involves a whole range of activities aimed at rejuvenation and propagation.

2). PROTECTION: Securing the resource and insulating it from any

---

4   (*Durga Das Basu's "Shorter Constitution of India"*, 14th edition, LexisNexis Butterworths Wadhwa Nagpur)

shocks of destruction and degradation is in contemplation here.

3). NON-DEGRADATION: Ensuring the intrinsic quality of the resources is not lost, while putting the same to use, and constitutes the basic tenet of proper and scientific resource use.

4). ADMINISTRATION that is TRANSPARENT, ACCOUNTABLE and PARTICIPATORY is a major requirement. This acknowledges the fact that the resources cannot be managed from above and finding local solutions to environmental problems would ensure effective and efficient environmental management.

5). LAW, POLICY AND PRACTICE in environmental management should emerge from and evolve out of people's needs and compulsions and be the result of crystallized home spun wisdom.

6). EQUITABLE SHARING OF BENEFITS is another underlying principle of good environmental governance, and

7). CONFLICT AVOIDANCE AND CONSENSUS BUILDING THROUGH CONSULTATIVE PROCESSES in Environmental decision-making is the crowning aspect of the system of administration. The litmus test for the existence of a healthy and wholesome environment, in any system, depends upon the internalization of these principles in the legal ordering.

The neo-expansion of Article 21 of the Constitution of India guarantees two important fundamental rights, right to life and right to personal liberty. In the area of environmental justice, the right to live is most relevant. After Maneka Gandhi's case[5], the right to live has seen new dimensions and one of the new emerging facets is the right to live in a clean environment. In this wave length the Apex Court in *Chhetriya Pradushan Mukti Sangharsh Samiti's case*[6], once again reiterated that, "every citizen has a fundamental right to have the enjoyment of quality of life and living as contemplated by Article 21 of the Constitution of India." Thus anything that endangers or impairs the quality of life or living of the people, will attract the provision of Article 21 of Constitution of India. In the context of human rights, right to life and liberty, pollution free Air and Water is guaranteed by our Constitution by Articles 21, 48-A and 51-A (g).

---

5   AIR 1978 SC 597

6   AIR 1990 SC 2060

In *M.C. Mehta v. Union of India*[7] , the Supreme Court observed as under:

Articles 21, 47, 48-A and 51-A(g) of the Constitution of India give a clear mandate to the State to protect and improve the environment and to safeguard the forests and wildlife of the country. It is the duty of every citizen of India to protect and improve the natural environment including forests, lakes, rivers and wildlife and to have compassion for living creatures. The "Precautionary Principle" makes it mandatory for the State Government to anticipate, prevent and attack the cause of environment degradation. In a catena of cases, Supreme Court has reiterated right to clean environment is a guaranteed fundamental right. The right to development cannot be treated as a mere right to economic betterment or cannot be limited as a misnomer to simple construction activities. The right to development encompasses much more than economic well-being, and includes within its definition the guarantee of fundamental human rights. The "development" is not related only to the growth of GNP. In the classic work, Development As Freedom, the Nobel prize winner Amartya Sen pointed out that "the issue of development cannot be separated from the conceptual framework of human right". The right to development includes the whole spectrum of civil, cultural, economic, political and social process, for the improvement of peoples' well-being and realization of their full potential. It is an integral part of human rights.

In *Susetha v. State of Tamil Nadu*[8], the Supreme Court observed that the doctrine of sustainable development is not an empty slogan. It is required to be implemented taking the pragmatic view and not on *ipse dixit* of the Court. Following the same principle, it cannot more so be applied on an administrative authority or a Corporation vested with the statutory obligation of providing environmental protection to the residents under its jurisdiction. Sustainable development means that the richness of the earth's bio-diversity would be conserved for future generations by greatly slowing or if possible halting extinctions, habitat and ecosystem destruction, and also by not risking significant alterations of the global environment that might – by an increase in sea level or changing rainfall and vegetation patterns or increasing ultraviolet radiation – alter the opportunities available for future generations.

---

7 1997 (3) SCC 715

8 AIR 2006 SC 2893

People are a part of the environment closely linked to the area, water, soil, flora and fauna. This complex network of living and nonliving systems is under a perpetual state of flexibility and sustains the process of life. It is not a fragile fabric but a tough and dynamic system with a tremendous capacity for transformation or resurface in times of need. The environment provides the resource base for development. But how people use these resources would depend upon the technological capacity, on the social structure which govern the relationship and on the national or international views.

In the last century, a great German materialist philosopher warned mankind: "Let us not, however, flatter ourselves overmuch on account of our human victories over nature. For each such victory nature takes its revenge on us. Each victory, it is true, in the first place brings about the results we expected, but in the second and third places it has quite different, unforeseen effects which only too often cancel the first." Ecologists are of the opinion that the most important ecological and social problem is the wide-spread disappearance all over the world of certain species of living organisms. Biologists forecast the extinction of animal and plant species on a scale that is incomparably greater than their extinction over the course of millions of years. The International Association for the Protection of Nature and Natural Resources calculates that now, on an average, one species or sub-species is lost every year. It is said that approximately 1,000 bird and animal species are facing extinction at present. So it is that the environmental question has become urgent and it has to be properly understood and squarely met by man. Nature and history, it has been said, are two component parts of the environment is which we live, move and prove ourselves. An organized society right to live as a human being is not ensured by meeting only the animal needs of man, but secured only when he is assured of all facilities to develop himself and is freed from restrictions which inhibit his growth.

Where there is Righteousness in the heart, there is beauty in the character

When there is beauty in the character, there is harmony in the home

When there is harmony in the home, there is order in the nation

When there is order in the nation, there is peace in the world.

1

Duty of the state to provide clean drinking water[1]

Facts in Nutshell:

Public interest litigation[2] filed by one Hamid Khan, (who is a practising Advocate of Mandla[3]) for the apathy[4] of the State Government, or rather a gross negligence[5] on the part of the State Government in not taking proper measures before supplying drinking water from hand-pumps, which has resulted in colossal[6] damage to the population of Mandla District. The hand-pumps which have been sunk by the State Government for supply of drinking water had excessive fluoride[7] contents and on account of that, thousand of persons who consumed water have suffered major set-back

---

1   Appellants: **Hamid Khan Vs.** Respondent: **State of M.P. and Ors.**

   AIR1997MP191, ILR[1996]MP355

   Hon'ble Judges/Coram: A.K. Mathur, C.J. and Shahi Kant Kulshreshtha, Judge

2   **Public-Interest Litigation** is litigation for the protection of the public interest. In Indian law, **Article 32** of the Indian constitution contains a tool which directly joins the public with judiciary. A PIL may be introduced in a court of law by the court itself (*suo motu*), rather than the aggrieved party or another third party. For the exercise of the court's jurisdiction, it is not necessary for the victim of the violation of his or her rights to personally approach the court. In a PIL, the right to file suit is given to a member of the public by the courts through judicial activism. The member of the public may be a non-governmental organization (NGO), an institution or an individual.

3   District Mandla comprises 13,269 sq. kilometers and its population is about 12,91,000. According to the census of 1991, Mandla District has total number of 2160 rural villages

4   **Meaning of Apathy: Apathy** is most commonly defined as a lack of feeling, emotion, interest, or concern

5   **Gross negligence** is a legal concept which means serious carelessness. Negligence is the opposite of diligence, or being careful. The standard of ordinary negligence is what conduct one expects from the proverbial "reasonable person." By analogy, if somebody has been grossly negligent, that means they have fallen so far below the ordinary standard of care that one can expect, to warrant the label of being "gross."

6   **Meaning of Colossal:** Extremely large or great

7   **Fluoride** is an inorganic anion of fluorine. It contributes no color to fluoride salts. Fluoride is the main component of fluorite (apart from calcium ions; fluorite is roughly 49% fluoride by mass), and contributes a distinctive bitter taste, but no odor to fluoride salts. Its salts are mainly mined as a precursor to hydrogen fluoride. As it is classified as a weak base, concentrated fluoride solutions will cause skin irritation.

in their life either in terms of deformity of various nature, like skeletal fluorosis or dental fluorosis[8]. It was pointed out that for the last 25 years, Public Health Engineering Department of Madhya Pradesh, with the help of Central Government Rural Development Department, is providing drinking water by drilling tube-wells in the villages of Mandla District. When adverse reports were received, then an enquiry was conducted and the Assistant Surgeon posted at Primary Health Centre, Mohania Patpara in District Mandla submitted a report to the Chief Medical Officer Mandla on 10-2-1995 and on that basis a team of experts consisting of Child Specialist and Arthopaedic Specialist headed by Chief Medical and Health Officer Mandla was deputed and it was found that 29 children were suffering from bone diseases and were having deformity[9] in legs. The team of experts also examined their eating habits as well as drinking water and some treatment was given. Thereafter, the Chief Medical and Health Officer vide his letter dated 30th March, 1995 to I.C.M.R. Jabalpur reported this matter and the I.C.M.R. deputed a team of experts headed by Dr. Tapas Chakma who visited the village on 10th May, 1995 to 17th May 1995 and took water of five hand-pumps of village Talaipani and in that, it was found that fluoride contents were at a high level of 10 mg. per litre. The team of experts recommended that these hand-pumps, should be immediately closed and alternative arrangement for drinking water should be made. It was also found that water contained excessive fluoride. Consequently, hand-pumps were closed of the said village Talaipani. When reports regarding deformities of affected persons were received, then survey was undertaken in order to find out the cause for the same. It was found that the water of hand pumps had excessive fluoride.

Responsibility of the State to raise the level of nutrition and the standard of living of its people:

Under Article 47[10] of the Constitution of India, it is the responsibility of

---

8   **Dental fluorosis**, also called **mottling of tooth enamel**, is a developmental disturbance of dental enamel caused by excessive exposure to high concentrations of fluoride during tooth development.

9   **Meaning of Deformity:** A **deformity, dysmorphism**, or **dysmorphic feature** is a major difference in the shape of a body part or organ compared to the average shape of that part.

10   Article 47 in The Constitution Of India 1949

     Duty of the State to raise the level of nutrition and the standard of living and to improve public health: The State shall regard the raising of the level of nutrition and the standard of living of its people and the improvement of public health as among its primary duties and, in particular, the State shall endeavour to bring about prohibition of the consumption except for medicinal purposes of intoxicating drinks and of drugs which are injurious to health

the State to raise the level of nutrition and the standard of living of its people and the improvement of public health. It is incumbent[11] on State to improve the health of public providing unpolluted drinking water.

Right to Life includes Right to live properly:

It is the right of the citizens of India to have protection of life, to have pollution free air and pure water, as has been held by their Lordships of the Hon'ble Supreme Court in the case of *Subhash Kumar v. State of Bihar*[12] that right to life includes right to live properly and have the benefit of all natural resources i.e. unpolluted air and water. It was observed at page 424 of the case:

"Right to live is a fundamental right[13] under Article 21[14] of the Constitution and it includes the right of enjoyment of pollution free water and air for full enjoyment of life. If anything endangers[15] or impairs that quality of life in derogation[16] of laws, a citizen has right to have resource to Article 32[17]

---

11 **Meaning of Incumbent:**

  1. Imposed as an obligation or duty

  2. Currently holding a specified office

12 AIR 1991 SC 420

13 **Meaning of Fundamental Rights:** The Fundamental Rights are defined as basic human freedoms which every Indian citizen has the right to enjoy for a proper and harmonious development of personality. These rights universally apply to all citizens, irrespective of race, place of birth, religion, caste, creed, colour or gender. Aliens (persons who are not citizens) are also considered in matters like equality before law. They are enforceable by the courts, subject to certain restrictions

14 **Article 21 in The Constitution Of India 1949**

  Protection of life and personal liberty: No person shall be deprived of his life or personal liberty except according to procedure established by law

15 **Meaning of Endanger:**

  1. To expose to harm or danger; imperil

  2. To threaten with extinction

16 **Meaning of Derogation:**

  1. To take away

  2. To deviate from a standard or expectation; go astray

17 **Article 32 in The Constitution Of India 1949**

  32. Remedies for enforcement of rights conferred by this Part

  (1) The right to move the Supreme Court by appropriate proceedings for the enforcement of the rights conferred by this Part is guaranteed

  (2) The Supreme Court shall have power to issue directions or orders or writs, including writs in the nature of habeas corpus, mandamus, prohibition, quo warranto and certiorari, whichever may be appropriate, for the enforcement of any of the rights conferred by this Part

of the Constitution for removing the pollution of water or Air which may be detrimental[18] to the quality of life".

Decision by High Court:

Court held that it is the State which is responsible for not taking proper precaution to provide proper drinking water to the citizens. Court directed that free Medical treatment (whether, it be by way of surgery or by way of callipers and shoes) be made available to the affected persons (excessive flouride in water which has caused great damage to the population by way of deformities in hands, legs and dental problem) by state. Court further held that in case surgery is required, then, the same shall be undertaken at the expense of the State and each person whose surgery is done shall be paid Rs. 3,000/- (three thousand) over and above free medical treatment at the expense of the State. If persons even after the surgery, require necessary artificial appliances like limbs or callipers, the same should be provided by state.

---

(3) Without prejudice to the powers conferred on the Supreme Court by clause (1) and (2), Parliament may by law empower any other court to exercise within the local limits of its jurisdiction all or any of the powers exercisable by the Supreme Court under clause (2)

(4) The right guaranteed by this article shall not be suspended except as otherwise provided for by this Constitution

18   **Meaning of Detrimental:** Causing damage or harm; injurious

2

Right of using the ground water without any infiltration and without any pollution[1]

Facts in Nutshell:

The petitioner[2] approached High Court praying for the issuance of a writ[3] of certiorarified mandamus[4] to call for the records of the first respondent[5] (Madras Metropolitan Development Authority) who reclassified the land use of the vacant lands measuring about 7 acres comprised in Survey Nos. 46(part), 47 and 49 of Urur Village, Besant Nagar from primary residential zone to 'institutional zone' and to quash[6] the same and consequently direct the fourth respondent (Central Public Works Development (CPWD) not to proceed with the proposed construction of an office complex in the said land.

The petitioner association, a society registered under the Societies Registration Act, 1975 formed for the purposes of protecting the Welfare

---

1 Appellants: **Besant Nagar Residents Vs.** Respondent: **Madras Metropolitan Development Authority and Ors.** (1990)1MLJ445

   Hon'ble Judges/Coram: K.S. Bakthavatsalam, Judge

2 **Meaning of Petitioner:** A person who presents a Petition. (**Meaning of Petition:** A formal message requesting something that is submitted to an authority)

3 In common law, a **writ** is a formal written order issued by a body with administrative or judicial jurisdiction; in modern usage, this body is generally a court. Warrants, prerogative writs and subpoenas are common types of writs but there are many others

4 **Mandamus** is a judicial remedy in the form of an order from a superior court, to any government subordinate court, corporation, or public authority—to do (or forbear from doing) some specific act which that body is obliged under law to do (or refrain from doing)—and which is in the nature of public duty, and in certain cases one of a statutory duty. It cannot be issued to compel an authority to do something against statutory provision. For example, it cannot be used to force a lower court to reject or authorize applications that have been made, but if the court refuses to rule one way or the other then a mandamus can be used to order the court to rule on the applications.

5 **Meaning of Respondent:** A **respondent** is a person who is called upon to issue a response to a communication made by another. In legal usage, this specifically refers to the defendant in a legal proceeding commenced by a petition, or to an appellee, or the opposing party, in an appeal of a decision by an initial fact-finder

6 **Meaning of Quash:** To set aside or annul, especially by judicial action

of the residents in the Besant Nagar Kalakshetra colony area in Madras. The Besant Nagar and its vicinity[7] have been originally planned as a Primary residential locality and the Madras Metropolitan Development Authority, the first respondent, as well as the Corporation of Madras, the second respondent, have been sanctioning building plans on this basis. The infrastructure in that area such as sewerage, drinking water, public health facilities, shops and public establishments etc. have all been developed only on the basis of Besant Nagar being a primary residential locality. It was alleged in the affidavit[8] filed in support of the petition[9] that every inch of available space, except for a plot of land measuring about 7 acres comprised in Survey Nos. 46(part), 47 and 49 of Urur village has been built upon, that the plot of land was originally acquired by the Tamil Nadu Housing Board (TNHB) along with other lands in Besant Nagar area for the specific purpose of developing it into a residential locality. Subsequently, it was transferred to the Central Public Works Development (CPWD), the fourth respondent. It was also alleged in the affidavit that the classification of the land as 'primary residential zone' was done by the first respondent (Madras Metropolitan Development Authority) under the provisions of the Tamil Nadu Town and Country Planning Act.

The residents of Besant Nagar were entirely dependant on **ground water** for their needs. The rate of extraction of ground water is in excess of the replenishment[10] of ground water. In fact in August, 1985 the Besant Nagar Citizens Forum and Kalakshetra Colony Welfare Association, both affiliates of the Petitioner, at the request of the Tamil Nadu Prevention and Control of Water Pollution Board, conducted a survey of the rate of extraction of ground water in the Besant Nagar Area. It was established in the survey that from a dozen larger wells, approximately 4,50,000 gallons of water was extracted per day. Apart from this an estimated 1,000 private borewells, (1-1/2" dia) accounted for an additional 2,000 gallons per day.

---

7   **Meaning of Vicinity:**

   1. a surrounding, adjacent, or nearby area; neighbourhood

   2. the fact or condition of being close in space or relationship

8   **Meaning of Affidavit:** A written declaration made under oath before a notary public or other authorized officer

9   **Meaning of Petition:** A formal message requesting something that is submitted to an authority

10 **Meaning of Replenishment:**

   1. To fill or make complete again

   2. To inspire or nourish

The extraction of ground water on these lines at the rate of approximately 1.23 million gallons per day unless replenished would result in the incursion[11] of sea water from below. Once such an incursion takes place the process is irreversible and would lead to a catastrophic[12] situation where the entire ground water in the Besant Nagar Area would turn brackish[13] making it unfit for human consumption. It was also emphasised that the prospect of sea water incursion was very much a reality particularly since most of the, catchment area for Besant Nagar has been constructed upon with hardly any open area available for the rain water to percolate[14] into the ground. It was alleged in the affidavit that the petitioner association came to know that the first respondent (Madras Metropolitan Development Authority) has reclassified the land use of the subject land by the notification, that the said order does not give any reason whatsoever for the reclassification and that it does not take into account the objections raised by the petitioner association as well as by other associations. It was further alleged [15] in the affidavit that the petitioner association, representing the welfare of the residents of the locality is vitally affected by the said reclassification and as such they approached the High Court. It was further stated in the affidavit that due to over drawal of water, sea-water infiltration was taking place into the ground water, and that a study conducted by various welfare associations on the ground water revealed that the water is unfit for human consumption as per I.S.I, standards.

---

11 **Meaning of incursion:**

1. An aggressive entrance into foreign territory; a raid or invasion.

2. The act of entering another's territory or domain.

3. The act of entering or running into

12 **Meaning of catastrophic:**

1. Of, relating to, or involving a catastrophe.

2. Involving or resulting in substantial, often ruinous medical expens

13 **Meaning of Brackish:**

Having a somewhat salty taste, especially from containing a mixture of seawater and fresh water Distasteful; unpalatable

14 **Meaning of Percolate:**

1. To cause (liquid, for example) to pass through a porous substance or small holes; filter.

2. To pass or ooze through

15 **Meaning of Alleged:**

Represented as existing or as being as described but not so proved; supposed

Articles 21, 48A and 51 A of the Constitution of India:

Article 21 of the Constitution reads as follows:

No person shall be deprived of the life or personal liberty except according to procedure established by law.

Article 48A: Protection and improvement and safeguarding of forests and wild life:- The State shall endeavour[16] to protect and improve the environment and to safeguard the forests and wild life of the country.

Article 51A: Fundamental duties:- It shall be the duty of every citizen of India --

(a) to abide by the Constitution and respect its ideals and institutions, the National Flag and the National Anthem;

(b) to cherish and follow the noble ideals which inspired our national struggle for freedom;

(c) to uphold and protect the sovereignty unity and integrity of India;

(d) to defend the country and render national service when called upon to do so;

(e) to promote harmony and the spirit of common-brotherhood amongst all the people of India transcending religious, linguistic and regional or sectional diversities; to renounce practices derogatory to the dignity of women;

(f) to value and preserve the rich heritage of our composite culture;

(g) to protect and improve the natural environment including forests, lakes rivers and wild life, and to have compassion for living creatures;

(h) to develop the scientific temper, humanism and the spirit of inquiry and reform;

(i) to strive towards excellence in all sphere of individual and collective activity so that the nation constantly rises to higher reveals of endeavour and achievement.

---

16   **Meaning of endeavour:**

    1. To try (to do something)

    2. An effort to do or attain something

Water is the most important of the elements of the nature:

In *State of Himachal Pradesh v. Umed Ram Sharia*[17] the Supreme Court has held that every person is entitled to life as enjoined in Article 21[18] of the Constitution, that he has also the right under Article 21 to his life and that right under Article 21 embraces not only physical existence of life but also the quality of life.

Decision by High Court:

Court held that the residents of the locality have a right to object to imbalance due to more extraction of ground water. Simply because any building is going to be constructed for public purpose, it does not mean that it can take away the rights of the public in that locality. Court further held that the petitioner have the right of using the ground water without any infiltration and without any pollution due to the construction of a huge office complex. The denial for right to clean water would be denial of life as understood in its richness and fullness by the ambit of the Constitution.

---

17 [1986] 1 SCR 251

18 **Article 21 in The Constitution Of India 1949**

   Protection of life and personal liberty: No person shall be deprived of his life or personal liberty except according to procedure established by law

3

Forest Produce[1]

Facts in Nutshell:

Poor Adivasis[2] known as Kotwalias and Vansfodias preferred writ petitions[3] making a grievance[4] that they were being harassed by the officers of the Forest Department with a view to deprive them of the privileges conferred upon them by the State Government. The petitioners[5] have their residence in reserved forests[6] and they claim certain privileges in regard to the collection of forest produce, including bamboos[7]. According

---

1   Appellants: **Fatesang Gimba Vasava and Ors. Vs.** Respondent: **State of Gujarat and Ors.**

    AIR1987Guj9, (1987)1GLR219

    Hon'ble Judges/Coram: A.M. Ahmadi and R.A. Mehta, JJ.

2   **Adivasi** is an umbrella term for a heterogeneous set of ethnic and tribal groups claimed to be the aboriginal population of India. They comprise a substantial indigenous minority of the population of India

3   **Meaning of Writ Petition:** Under the Indian legal system, jurisdiction to issue 'prerogative writs' is given to the Supreme Court, and to the High Courts of Judicature of all Indian states. Parts of the law relating to writs are set forth in the Constitution of India. The Supreme Court, the highest in the country, may issue writs under Article 32 of the Constitution for enforcement of Fundamental Rights and under Articles 139 for enforcement of rights other than Fundamental Rights, while High Courts, the superior courts of the States, may issue writs under Articles 226. 'Writ' is eminently designed by the makers of the Constitution, and in the same way it is developed very widely and efficiently by the courts in India. The Constitution broadly provides for five kinds of "prerogative" writs, namely, Habeas Corpus, Certiorari, Mandamus, Quo Warranto and Prohibition

4   **Meaning of Grievance:**

    a. An actual or supposed circumstance regarded as just cause for complaint.

    b. A complaint or protestation based on such a circumstance

5   **Meaning of Petitioner:** A person who presents a Petition. (**Meaning of Petition:** A formal message requesting something that is submitted to an authority)

6   A **reserved forest** (also called **reserve forest**) or a protected forest in India are terms denoting forests accorded a certain degree of protection. The terms were first introduced in the Indian Forest Act, 1927 in British India, to refer to certain forests granted protection under the British crown in British India, but not associated suzerainties. After Indian independence, the Government of India retained the status of the existing reserved and protected forests, as well as incorporating new reserved and protected forests. A large number of forests which came under the jurisdiction of the Government of India during the political integration of India were initially granted such protection. The first Reserve Forest Of India was Satpura National Park.

7   Bamboos are some of the fastest-growing plants in the world, due to a unique rhizome-

to them, they were privileged to collect a certain quantity of bamboos per family from the reserved forests for the purpose of making toplas, supdas, palas, etc., for their hutments and livelihood.

The grievance of the petitioners, however, was that despite Government orders which confer certain privileges on the Adivasis - Kotwalias and Vansfodias -residing in forest areas the officers of the Forest Department do not permit them to remove bamboos from the reserved forest areas. According to the petitioners they were entitled to receive bamboos at the prescribed concessional rates for the purpose of making bamboo articles, such as, supdas, palas and toplas. It was the case of the petitioners that they prepared certain articles from bamboo chips and sell them in the market to earn their livelihood. Since the officers of the Forest Department have of late obstructed the removal of bamboos by the Adivasis- Kotwalias and Vansfodias - living in the reserved forest areas they have been deprived of their meagre income which they received or earned for their livelihood and were facing extreme economic hardship.

Writ petition was initiated by a businessman who was purchasing toplas, Supadas and Palas prepared from bamboos by the Adivasis. Since the officers of the Forest Department did not permit the removal of the articles from the forest area without pass or permit, the said merchant demanded a writ of mandamus[8] to restrain the officers of the Forest Department from interfering with the free transit of the articles prepared from bamboos from the forest area and for refund of the amount of Rs. 3,000/- taken as deposit from him by the officers of the Forest Department.

Decision by Learned Single Judge:

The writ petition was summarily rejected by P.D.Desai, Judge on July 24, 1981. According to the learned single Judge the expression 'forest produce' included trees and leaves, flowers and fruits and all other parts

---

dependent system. Bamboos are of notable economic and cultural significance in South Asia, Southeast Asia and East Asia, being used for building materials, as a food source, and as a versatile raw product. High-quality bamboo is stronger than steel, a property that has made it a choice in building materials and weaponry

8   **Mandamus** is a judicial remedy in the form of an order from a superior court, to any government subordinate court, corporation, or public authority—to do (or forbear from doing) some specific act which that body is obliged under law to do (or refrain from doing)—and which is in the nature of public duty, and in certain cases one of a statutory duty. It cannot be issued to compel an authority to do something against statutory provision. For example, it cannot be used to force a lower court to reject or authorize applications that have been made, but if the court refuses to rule one way or the other then a mandamus can be used to order the court to rule on the applications.

or produce of trees which include bamboos and, therefore, any produce of bamboos would be comprehended with the expression "forest produce" and hence removal of such forest produce without pass or permit would amount to an offence under Section 26 of the Indian Forest Act, 1927. It was against that order that the petitioner preferred the appeal[9] before the High Court.

Indian Forest Act, 1927 (hereinafter called 'the Act):

The Act was enacted inter alia[10] to consolidate[11] the law, relating to the transit[12] of forest produce and the duty leviable thereon. The term 'forest-produce' is defined in Section 2(4) as under:

"Forest-produce" includes-

(a) The following whether found in or brought from, a forest or not, that is to say :-

timber, charcoal, caoutchouc, catechu, wood-oil, resin, natural varnish, bark, lac, mahua flowers, mahua seeds, kuth, apta and temburni leaves, rosha grass, rauwolfia serpentina and myrabalans; and

(b) The following when found in, or brought from, a forest, that is to say : -

(i) trees and leaves, flowers and fruits, and all other parts or produce not hereinbefore mentioned, of trees,

(ii) plants not being trees (including grass, creepers; reeds, and moss), and all parts of produce of such plants,

(iii) wild animals and skins, tusks, horns, bones, silk, cocoons, honey, and wax and all other parts of produce of animals, and

---

9   **Meaning of Appeal:** In law, an **appeal** is a process for requesting a formal change to an official decision. Very broadly speaking there are appeals on the record and *de novo* appeals. In *de novo* appeals, a new decision maker re-hears the case without any reference to the prior decision maker. In appeals on the record, the decision of the prior decision maker is challenged by arguing that he or she misapplied the law, came to an incorrect factual finding, acted in excess of his jurisdiction, abused his powers, was biased, considered evidence which he should not have considered or failed to consider evidence that he should have considered.

10 **Meaning of Inter Alia:** Among other things

11 **Meaning of Consolidate:**

   1. To unite into one system or whole; combine

   2. To make strong or secure; strengthen

12   **Meaning of Transit:** The act of passing over, across, or through; passage.

(iv) peat, surface, soil, rock, and minerals (including limestone, laterite, mineral oils, and all products of mines or quarries);

The expression 'timber' includes trees when they have fallen or have been felled and all wood whether cut up or fashioned or hollowed out for any purpose or not; and the expression 'tree' includes palms, bamboos, stumps, brushwood and canes.

Section 26 of Indian Forest Act, 1927:

Acts prohibited in such forests:

(1) Any person who-

(a) makes any fresh clearing prohibited by Section 5[13], or

(b) sets fire to a reserved forest or to a forest in a land in respect of which a notification declaring the decision of the State Government to constitute it a reserved forest has been issued under Section 4[14], or in contravention of any rules made by the State Government in this behalf, kindles in such forest any fire or leaves any fire burning, in such manner as to endanger

---

13   Section 5 in The Indian Forest Act, 1927

   Bar of accrual of forest-rights.—After the issue of a notification under section 4, no right shall be acquired in or over the land comprised in such notification, except by succession or under a grant or contract in writing made or entered into by or on behalf of the [Government] or some person in whom such right was vested when the notification was issued; and no fresh clearings for cultivation or for any other purpose shall be made in such land except in accordance with such rules as may be made by the [State Government] in this behalf

14   Section 4 in The Indian Forest Act, 1927

   Notification by [State Government]—

   (1) Whenever it has been decided to constitute any land a reserved forest, the 1[State Government] shall issue a notification in the [Official Gazette]—

   (a) declaring that it has been decided to constitute such land a reserved forest;

   (b) specifying, as nearly as possible, the situation and limits of such land; and

   (c) appointing an officer (hereinafter called "the Forest Settlement-officer") to inquire into and determine the existence, nature and extent of any rights alleged to exist in favour of any person in or over any land comprised within such limits or in or over any forest-produce, and to deal with the same as provided in this Chapter. Explanation.—For the purpose of clause (b), it shall be sufficient to describe the limits of the forest by roads, rivers, ridges or other well-known or readily intelligible boundaries.

   (2) The officer appointed under clause (c) of sub-section (1) shall ordinarily be a person not holding any forest-office except that of Forest Settlement-officer.

   (3) Nothing in this section shall prevent the [State Government] from appointing any number of officers not exceeding three, not more than one of whom shall be a person holding any forest-office except as aforesaid, to perform the duties of a Forest Settlement-officer under this Act.

such a forest;

or who, in a reserved forest or a forest in a land notified as aforesaid under Section 4-

(c) kindles, keeps or carries any fire except at such seasons as the Forest Officer may notify in this behalf;

(d) trespasses or pastures cattle, or permits cattle to trespass;

(e) causes any damage by negligence in felling any tree or cutting or dragging any timber;

(f) fells, girdles, lops taps, or burns any tree or strips off the back or leaves from or otherwise damages, the same-

(g) quarries[15] stone, bums lime or charcoal, or collects, subjects to any manufacturing process or removes, any forest-produce;

(h) clears or breaks up any land for cultivation or any other purpose;

(i) in contravention of any rules made in this behalf by the State Government hunts, shoots, fishes, poisons water or seats traps or snares; or

(j) in any area in which the Elephants' Preservation Act, 1879, is not in force, kills or catches elephants in contravention of any rules so made;

shall be punishable with imprisonment for a term which may extend to six months, or with fine which may extend to five hundred rupees, or with both, in addition such compensation for damage done to the forest at the convicting Court may direct to be paid.

(2) Nothing in this section shall be deemed to prohibit-

(a) any act done by permission in writing of the Forest Officer, or under any rule made by the Government; or

(b) the exercise of any right continued under CL (c) of sub-section (2) of S. 15, or created by grant or contract in writing made by or on behalf of the Government under S. 23.

(3) Whenever fire is caused wilfully or by gross negligence in reserved

---

15 **Meaning of quarries:**

    a. A hunted animal; prey.

    b. Hunted animals considered as a group; game

forest, the State Government may notwithstanding that any penalty has been inflicted under this section, direct that in such forest or any portion thereof the exercise of all rights of pasture or of forest-produce shall be suspended for such period as it thinks fit.

Decision by High Court:

Court held that the purpose and object of granting certain special privileges is to provide to the residents of forest villages a source of livelihood. These Adivasis - kotwalias and Vansfodias who reside in forest areas are solely dependent on forest produce and if they were deprived of the same their source of livelihood would be totally cut. Realising the same the Government issued certain orders from time to time to ensure the supply of bamboos to these residents to enable them to prepare certain articles from bamboo chips which could be sold in the open market to earn a living. The petitioners prepare bamboo articles from bamboo chips and sell them to private contractors at an agreed price. These private contractors may be entering into contracts with outstation merchants. . They were transporting these bamboo articles purchased from the Adivasis to different stations by rail. The bamboo articles prepared from bamboo chips supplied to Kotwalias/Vansfodias at the stipulated price are sold to contractors at a price agreed upon between them. Therefore, Court held that the petitioners and purchasers will be allowed to remove the bamboo articles so purchased from the forest areas to non-forest areas without treating them as 'forest-produce' within the meaning of Section 2(4) of the Indian Forest Act, 1927. Court further held that the petitioners will also be permitted to sell their bamboo articles such as supdas, palas, toplas, etc., to dealers in bamboo articles of their choice at such price or prices as may be agreed upon by and between them.

4

No inherent or fundamental right[1] in a citizen to manufacture, sell and deal with fire works which will create sound beyond permissible limit[2]

Facts in Nutshell:

Application filed by Mohan Fire Works and Chandan Golcha carrying on the business under the name and style of Chandan Mal Golcha to permit or allow manufacture, sell, dealing and/or trading and storing of fire works without any restriction and also to permit or allow bursting of fire works/caters of less than 90 dB[3] at 5 kilo metre distance from the site of bursting without any restriction whatsoever. The other application filed by Burrabazar Fire Works Dealers' Association against the imposition of ban on certain items of noisy fire works on the ground that the same violates the fundamental rights of the fire works Dealers to carry on trade and business guaranteed under Article 19(1)(g)[4] of the Constitution of

---

1   **Meaning of Fundamental Rights:** The Fundamental Rights are defined as basic human freedoms which every Indian citizen has the right to enjoy for a proper and harmonious development of personality. These rights universally apply to all citizens, irrespective of race, place of birth, religion, caste, creed, colour or gender. Aliens (persons who are not citizens) are also considered in matters like equality before law. They are enforceable by the courts, subject to certain restrictions

2   Appellants: **Burrabazar Fire Works Dealers Association and Ors. Vs.** Respondent: **The Commissioner of Police and Ors.**

      AIR1998Cal121

      Hon'ble Judges/Coram: Bhagabati Prosad Banerjee and Asis Baran Mukherjee, JJ.

3   The **decibel (dB)** is a logarithmic unit used to express the ratio between two values of a physical quantity, oftenpower or intensity. One of these quantities is often a reference value, and in this case the decibel can be used to express the absolute level of the physical quantity. A common use of the decibel unit is to measure sound pressure.

4   **Article 19 in The Constitution Of India 1949**

      19. Protection of certain rights regarding freedom of speech etc

      (1) All citizens shall have the right

      (a) to freedom of speech and expression;

India.

Every citizen has a right but his right comes to an end when it tends to interfere with others right:

In *Om Biraugana Religious Society v. State*[5] where the Court explained the provision of Article 19(1)(a) of the Constitution of India and it was held that within the scope and ambit of the provisions of Article 19(1) (a) of the Constitution of India which provides Fundamental Rights of Citizens to Freedom of Speech and Expression and this right was only subject to restriction under Article 19(2)[6] of the Constitution. It was held that freedom of speech and expression guaranteed under Article 19(1)(a) of the Constitution of India by necessary implication, includes right not to listen and/or to remain silent. This right includes right to leisure, **right to sleep,** right to read and speak with others and even right to worship in his own way and that it has been held that sound is a known source of pollution and by means of sound through loud-speaker or others, citizens cannot be made captive listeners and which forced to hear something which his body or system cannot hear and which he does not like to hear

---

(b) to assemble peaceably and without arms;

(c) to form associations or unions;

(d) to move freely throughout the territory of India;

(e) to reside and settle in any part of the territory of India; and

(f) omitted

(g) to practise any profession, or to carry on any occupation, trade or business

5   (1996)2CALLT474(HC)

6   **Article 19 in The Constitution Of India 1949**

19. Protection of certain rights regarding freedom of speech etc

(1) All citizens shall have the right

(a) to freedom of speech and expression;

(b) to assemble peaceably and without arms;

(c) to form associations or unions;

(d) to move freely throughout the territory of India;

(e) to reside and settle in any part of the territory of India; and

(f) omitted

(g) to practise any profession, or to carry on any occupation, trade or business

(2) Nothing in sub clause (a) of clause (1) shall affect the operation of any existing law, or prevent the State from making any law, in so far as such law imposes reasonable restrictions on the exercise of the right conferred by the said sub clause in the interests of the sovereignty and integrity of India, the security of the State, friendly relations with foreign States, public order, decency or morality or in relation to contempt of court, defamation or incitement to an offence

or likes to tolerate but he has to bear the tremendous effect of sound which had the effect of silencing him and have the chilling effect on all of his rights because of the tremendous sound and noise, the citizens cannot exercise all these fundamental rights. Every citizen has a right but his right comes to an end when it tends to interfere with others right. Nobody can enjoy an exclusive right of his at the cost of/or suspending the rights of others. In that judgment, it was held that the Police Authorities and/ or Administrations have no right to grant permission to use microphone without any restriction with regard to the noise level and accordingly, directed that the Pollution Control Board should maintain Noise Level Register for measuring the level of noise and the said Authority shall indicate the level of noise, which could be permitted by use of microphone on any occasion.

Law must constantly be on the move adopting itself to the fast changing society:

In *M. C. Mehta v. Union of India*[7], it was held that where a law of the past does not fit in the present context, the Court should evolve a new law and in *National Workers' Union v. P. R. Ramkrishnan*[8], it was held, if the law fails to respond, to the needs of the changing society, then either stifle[9] the growth of the society and choke its progress or if the society is vigorous[10] enough it will cast away the law which stands in the way of its growth. Law must therefore, constantly be on the move adopting itself to the fast changing society and not lag behind. It must shake off the inhibiting legacy of its colonial past and assume a dynamic role in the process of social transformation. "The truth is that the law is uncertain. It does not cover all the situations that may arise. Time and again practitioners are faced with new situations, where the decision may go either way. No one can tell what the law is until the Courts decide it. The Judges do every day make law, though it is almost hearsay to say so. If

---

7   [1987]1SCR819

8   (1983)ILLJ45SC

9   **Meaning of Stifle:**

    1. To interrupt or cut off (the voice, for example).

    2. To keep in or hold back; repress

    3. To kill by preventing respiration; smother or suffocate

10   **Meaning of vigorous:**

    1. Strong, energetic, and active in mind or body; robust

    2. Marked by or done with force and energy

the truth is recognized then we may hope to escape from the dead hand of the past and consciously mould new principles to meet the needs of the present."[11]

The right of every citizen to pursue any lawful trade or business is obviously subject to such reasonable conditions as may be deemed by the Governing Authority:

Supreme Court in the case of *Cooverjee v. Excise Commissioner and the Chief Commissioner, Ajmer[12]*, have held that there is no inherent right in a citizen to sell intoxicating liqueurs by retail; it is not a privilege of a citizen. As it is a business attended with the danger to the community, it may be entirely prohibited and/or be permitted under such conditions as will limit to the utmost its evils. The manner and extent of regulation rest in the discretion of Governing Authority. It was further held, in order to determine the reasonableness of the restrictions regard must be had to the nature of the business and the condition prevailing in the trade. It is obvious that these factors must differ from trade to trade and no hard and fast rules concerning all traders can be laid down. The right of every citizen to pursue any lawful trade or business is obviously subject to such reasonable conditions as may be deemed by the Governing Authority of the country essential to the safety, health, peace, order and morals of the community.

Noise:

Sounds created by fire works, loud speakers, air-crafts, railways are all the products of the technological age and high level of continuous sounds damages hearing and that there cannot be any two opinion about it. It is clearly evident that several millions of people in different parts of the world have had their hearing damages because of generating of sounds. The noise not only creates pollution but it is also a source of annoyance. Noise is also created by traffic and noise also disturbs sleep. In our country the people have a right to sleep peacefully. A citizen too have right to a decent environment as highlighted by the Supreme Court in various decisions which are all well-known in the field of pollution. The effect of bad night sleep includes mood change, reduce cardiovascular[13]

---

11 ("The Reform of Equity", in C. J. Hamson (ed.), Law Reform and Law-Making (1953), p. 31)

12 [1954]1SCR873

13 **Cardiovascular disease** (also called **heart disease**) is a class of diseases that involve the heart, the blood vessels(arteries, capillaries, and veins) or both

performance and poor performance at intellectual and mechanical tasks. Noise has been identified as a pollutant under Air (Prevention and Control) Act, 1981. Noise admittedly is a hazard to health.

There are sounds which create soothing effect on a living creature like vocal music or instrumental music, but noise created by machines, is a product of the technological age. Music also generates some sort of sound and the use of fire works and microphones also generate sound but there is a gulf of difference between the two types of sounds. Sound created by music or instrumental music is soothing for the human being but not a tremendous sound created by use of microphones and/or fire works which create sound all of a sudden and results in a serious impact on health which is a nuisance and punishable under the law.

Right to Sleep and Noise:

Under our Constitution, people have a right to sleep and leisure. Disruption or disturbance in sleeps creates mental stress, deficient in working efficiency and other things. Interference with rest or sleep and the factor associated with it -- lack of concentration, irritability reduced efficiency -- is one of the most obvious and annoying effects of noise. Sleep is a physiological[14] necessity and therefore, health may be adversely affected by insufficient sleep and Noise. Apart from health, apart from deafness[15] Noise affects the digestive system, cardiovascular system etc.

Decision by High Court:

High Court held that safety, health and peace are guaranteed to the citizens of India and none can carry on any trade or business which may seriously affect safety, health and peace of the Community. Accordingly, court held that Article 19(1)(g) of the Constitution of India does not guarantee the fundamental right to carry on trade or business which creates pollution or which takes away that communities' safety, health and peace. It cannot be said that a citizen have a fundamental right under Article 19(1)(g) of the Constitution of India to carry on trade or business and/or manufacture poison which may be used for killing of people. This right is negative as nobody has any right to carry on any trade or business

---

14 **Meaning of Physiological:**

    1. of or pertaining to physiology

    2. consistent with the normal functioning of an organism

15   **Meaning of Deafness:** Partially or completely lacking in the sense of hearing

in intoxicating liqueurs by virtue of the right conferred under Article 19(1) (g).

There is no inherent or fundamental right in a citizen to manufacture, sell and deal with fire works which will create sound beyond permissible limit and which will generate pollution which would endanger the health and the public order. A citizen or person cannot be made a captive listener to hear the tremendous sounds caused by bursting out from a noisy fire works. It may give pleasure to one or two persons who burst it but others have to be a captive listener whose fundamental rights guaranteed under Article 19(1)(a) and other provisions of the Constitution are taken away, suspended and made meaningless. A citizen of this country must be allowed to live in a society which is peaceful, free from mechanical and artificial sounds which creates a tremendous health hazards and adverse effect on the citizen. Citizens have a right to live in a society which is free from pollution. If pollutants are encouraged, in that event that would be the beginning of the end of the civilization.

5

Security of wild animals and preservation of sanctuary[1]

Facts in Nutshell:

Writ petitions[2] filed by Bombay Burmah Trading Corporation, Singampattl Group, Manjolal, Tirunelvell, aggrieved by the proceedings of Field Director (Project Tiger) & Conservator of Forest, Tirunelveli and passed by the Deputy Director, Mundanthurai, Kalakadu Sanctuary. Ambasamudaram, respectively. The proceedings are related to the usage of road inside the Mundanthurai Kalakadu Wild Life Sanctuary, which is included in the Tiger Project area. Admittedly, the estate of the petitioner[3] was located within the limits of the said sanctuary. The 'petitioner company have taken a tea estate of an extent of 3500 hectares (8373.57 acres) on lease[4], in Nellai Kattabomman District, under lease deed dated 12-2-1929 for ninety nine years. The said lease was taken over by the Government on 19-2-1952 under the Madras Estates (Abolition and Conversion into Ryotwari) Act, 1948. However, the erstwhile Board of Revenue, in the year 1958, allowed the petitioner to continue and keep the entire lease out area for the rest

---

1   Appellants: **Bombay Burmah Trading Corporation Vs.** Respondent: **Field Director (Project Tiger) and Conservator of Forests**

     AIR2000Mad163

     Hon'ble Judges/Coram: P.D. Dinakaran, Judge

2   **Meaning of Writ Petition:** Under the Indian legal system, jurisdiction to issue 'prerogative writs' is given to the Supreme Court, and to the High Courts of Judicature of all Indian states. Parts of the law relating to writs are set forth in the Constitution of India. The Supreme Court, the highest in the country, may issue writs under Article 32 of the Constitution for enforcement of Fundamental Rights and under Articles 139 for enforcement of rights other than Fundamental Rights, while High Courts, the superior courts of the States, may issue writs under Articles 226. 'Writ' is eminently designed by the makers of the Constitution, and in the same way it is developed very widely and efficiently by the courts in India. The Constitution broadly provides for five kinds of "prerogative" writs, namely, Habeas Corpus, Certiorari, Mandamus, Quo Warranto and Prohibition

3   **Meaning of Petitioner:** A person who presents a Petition. (**Meaning of Petition:** A formal message requesting something that is submitted to an authority)

4   A **lease** is a contractual arrangement calling for the lessee (user) to pay the lessor (owner) for use of an asset.

of the lease period, subject to certain additional conditions.

It was not in dispute that the entire extent of 3500 hectares leased out to the petitioner has been notified as a Reserve Forest[5] under the Tamil Nadu Forest Act, 1882. Similarly, it was also not disputed that the petitioner has provided quarters for about 2500 workers working in their estate, as required under the Plantation Labour Act, 1951 and have also provided basic amenities like hospitals etc.

The Wild Life Protection Act, 1972 came into effect in the State of Tamil Nadu from 1-1-1974. By proceedings dated 4-1-1991, the petitioner was directed not to use the road inside the sanctuary, during night time, viz. from 6 p.m. to 6 a.m., subject to the permission of the Forest Range Officer at Ambasamudaram, who shall exercise his discretion in exceptional case of emergency. Similarly when the petitioner sought for permission, by letter dated 10-10-1990 to ply about 86 vehicles inside the sanctuary area, the Deputy Director. Mundanthurai Kalakadu Sanctuary, by his proceedings dated 7-2-1991, gave permission to ply only 24 vehicles, subject to the following conditions, viz.

(i) The vehicle is liable to be examined at any time within the Forest limit by the Forest officials;

(ii) The vehicle should ply only between 6 a.m. to 6 p.m.;

(iii) They should not commit or connive[6] in any Forest and Wildlife offences;

(iv) They should abide by the Rules and Regulations laid down in the Tamil Nadu Forest Act. 1882 and Wildlife Protection Act, 1972;

(v) The permit is liable to be cancelled by the Deputy Director at any time at his discretion without assigning any reasons. The permit holder shall not be entitled to any compensation for such cancellation;

(vi) Every time the vehicle enter into the sanctuary area, the date and time should be got noted in the permit book;

(vii) Number plate of the vehicle should be legible; and

---

5   A **reserve forest** or a **reserved forest** is a specific term for designating forests and other natural areas which enjoy judicial and / or constitutional protection under the legal systems of many countries

6   **Meaning of connive:** To give assent or encouragement (to the commission of a wrong)

Aggrieved by the proceedings dated 4-1-1991 and condition Nos. (ii) and (v) in the proceedings, the petitioner filed the writ petitions in High Court.

The Wild Life (Protection) Act, 1972:

The Wild Life (Protection) Act which came into force in the State of Tamil Nadu from 1-1-1974, was enacted as a result of a compelling need to restore the catastrophic ecological imbalances introduced by the depredations[7] inflicted on nature by human beings. The matter of preservation of the wild life and the environment have become a matter of necessity to maintain the ecological balance, keeping in view the habit of grazing and movement of the live stock, the wild life in particular, and to provide adequate protection for the wild birds and animals. When an Act was thus enacted and brought into force for vowed and prudent object to provide for the protection of wild animals, birds and plants and of matters connected therein or ancillary or incidental thereto, any action or steps taken by the authorities concerned to ensure the security of the wild animals in the sanctuary, keeping the interest of the wild life as well as their habit like grazing movements into consideration, such step or measures taken by the authorities should be tested only in the light of the object sought to be achieved under the Act. Therefore, once a particular area is declared and notified as a wild life sanctuary, any private right of a person should be subjected to the object of the Act.

Section 27 of the Wild Life (Protection) Act, 1972, which reads as follows :

27. Restriction on entry in sanctuary

(1) No person other than,

(a) a public servant on duty;

(b) a person who has been permitted by the Chief Wild Life Warden or the authorised officer to reside within the limits of the sanctuary;

(c) a person who has any right over immovable property within the limits of the sanctuary;

(d) a person passing through the sanctuary along a public highway; and

---

7   **Meaning of depredations:**

    1. A predatory attack; a raid

    2. Damage or loss; ravage

(e) the dependants of the person referred to in Clause (a), Clause (b) or Clause (c), shall enter or reside in the sanctuary, except under and in accordance with the conditions of a permit granted under Section 28[8].

(2) Every person shall, so long as he resides in the sanctuary, be bound--

(a) To prevent the commission, in the sanctuary, of an offence against this Act;

(b) Where there is reason to believe that any such offence against this Act has been committed in such sanctuary, to help in discovering and arresting the offender[9];

(c) To report the death of any wild animal and to safeguard its remains until the Chief Wild Life Warden or the authorised officer takes charge thereof;

(d) To extinguish any fire in such sanctuary of which he has knowledge or information and to prevent from spreading, by any lawful means in his power, any fire within the vicinity of such sanctuary of which he has knowledge or information; and

(e) To assist any Forest Officer, Chief Wild Life Warden, Wild Life Warden or Police Officer demanding his aid for preventing the commission of any offence against this Act or in the investigation of any such offence.

(3) No person shall, with intent to cause damage to any boundary-mark of a sanctuary or to cause wrongful gain as defined in the Indian Penal Code, 1860 (45 of 1860), alter, destroy, move or deface such boundary-mark.

(4) No person shall tease or molest any wild animal or litter the grounds

---

8   Section 28 of the Wildlife (Protection) Act, 1972:

   28. Grant of permit – (1) The Chief Wildlife Warden may, on application, grant to any person a permit to enter or reside in a sanctuary for all or any of the following purposes, namely:

   (a) investigation or study of wildlife and purposes ancillary or incidental thereto;

   (b) photography;

   (c) scientific research;

   (d) tourism;

   (e) transaction of lawful business with any person residing in the sanctuary.

   (2) A permit to enter or reside in a sanctuary shall be issued subject to such conditions and on payment of such fee as may be prescribed

9   **Meaning of Offender:** One that offends, especially one that breaks a public law

of sanctuary.

Section 28 of the Wildlife Act, 1972 reads as follows:

28. Grant of permit

(1) The Chief Wild Life Warden may, on application, grant to any person a permit to enter or reside in a sanctuary for all or any of the following purposes, namely:--

(a) investigation[10] or study of wild life and purposes ancillary or incidental thereto;

(b) photography:

(c) Scientific research;

(d) tourism;

(e) transaction of lawful business with any person residing in the sanctuary.

(2) A permit to enter or reside in a sanctuary shall be issued subject to such conditions and on payment of such fee as may be prescribed.

Decision by High Court:

Court held that since the petitioner estate was located in the midst of Mudanthurai Kalakadu Sanctuary, even though the petitioner has any private right over the estate which is within the limits of the sanctuary, such private right of the petitioner was subject to the permission by the Chief Wild Life Warden or the officer authorised by him. Therefore, Sections 27 and 28 of the Wildlife Act, 1972 have to be read together; and in which case, even if the petitioner has got a right to reside in the estate, the same is permissible only subject to the permission of the competent authorities, as required under the Act, as the estate is located within the sanctuary. Consequently, the right to use the roads in the sanctuary area is subject to the conditions that could be imposed by the Chief Wild Life Warden or the officers authorised by him, as they are empowered to impose such reasonable restrictions and conditions in the matter of entry and use of roads in the sanctuary area, taking into consideration the

---

10 **Meaning of Investigation:**

  1. The act or process of investigating

  2. A detailed inquiry or systematic examination

security of the wild animal in the sanctuary, preservation of the sanctuary and wild animals therein and keeping the interest of wild life and their habits, such as grazing and movement into consideration. In which case, the restriction imposed that they should ply their vehicles between 6 a.m. to 6 p.m. in order to achieve the above object, cannot be complained as arbitrary, unreasonable or Innocuous[11].

Similarly, restricting the number of vehicles also cannot be complained as arbitrary and unreasonable, if the authorities concerned, under the Wildlife Act, 1972 who are expected to ensure security of wild life and preservation of sanctuary[12], is of opinion that granting permission for 84 vehicles, as claimed by the petitioner, may harm the wild life. Court cannot by exercising power under Article 226[13] of the Constitution of

---

11 **Meaning of Innocuous:**

   1. Having no adverse effect; harmless.

   2. Not likely to offend or provoke to strong emotion; insipid

12 **Meaning of sanctuary:** A reserved area in which birds and other animals, especially wild animals, are protected from hunting or molestation

13 **Article 226 in The Constitution Of India 1949**

   226. Power of High Courts to issue certain writs

   (1) Notwithstanding anything in Article 32 every High Court shall have powers, throughout the territories in relation to which it exercise jurisdiction, to issue to any person or authority, including in appropriate cases, any Government, within those territories directions, orders or writs, including writs in the nature of habeas corpus, mandamus, prohibitions, quo warranto and certiorari, or any of them, for the enforcement of any of the rights conferred by Part III and for any other purpose

   (2) The power conferred by clause (1) to issue directions, orders or writs to any Government, authority or person may also be exercised by any High Court exercising jurisdiction in relation to the territories within which the cause of action, wholly or in part, arises for the exercise of such power, notwithstanding that the seat of such Government or authority or the residence of such person is not within those territories

   (3) Where any party against whom an interim order, whether by way of injunction or stay or in any other manner, is made on, or in any proceedings relating to, a petition under clause (1), without

   (a) furnishing to such party copies of such petition and all documents in support of the plea for such interim order; and

   (b) giving such party an opportunity of being heard, makes an application to the High Court for the vacation of such order and furnishes a copy of such application to the party in whose favour such order has been made or the counsel of such party, the High Court shall dispose of the application within a period of two weeks from the date on which it is received or from the date on which the copy of such application is so furnished, whichever is later, or where the High Court is closed on the last day of that period, before the expiry of the next day afterwards on which the High Court is open; and if the application is not so disposed of, the interim order shall, on the expiry of that period, or, as the case may be, the expiry of the aid next day, stand vacated

   (4) The power conferred on a High Court by this article shall not be in derogation of the power

India, interfere with such expert opinion of the authorities, otherwise the vowed[14] object of the Wildlife Act, 1972 could not be achieved.

---

conferred on the Supreme court by clause (2) of Article 32

14 **Meaning of Vowed:**

　1. An earnest promise to perform a specified act or behave in a certain manner, especially a solemn promise to live and act in accordance with the rules of a religious order.

　2. A declaration or assertion.

6

Protection of environment is to be taken care in development scheme[1]

Facts in Nutshell:

A site near the Sankey's Tank in Rajmahal Vilas Extension in the City of Bangalore was reserved as an open space in an improvement scheme adopted under the City of Bangalore Improvement Act, 1945. This Act was repealed[2] by Section 76[3] of the Bangalore Development Authority Act, 1976 (Karnataka Act No. 12 of 1976) (hereinafter referred to as the "Act") which received the assent of the Governor on 2.3.1976 and is deemed to have come into force on 20.12.1975.

Accordingly, the scheme prepared under the repealed enactment is deemed to have been prepared and duly sanctioned by the Government in terms of the Act for the development of Rajmahal Vilas Extension. In the

---

1   Appellants: **Bangalore Medical Trust Vs.** Respondent: **B.S. Muddappa and others**

     AIR1991SC1902

     Hon'ble Judges/Coram: T.K. Thommen and R.M. Sahai, JJ.

2   **Meaning of Repeal:**

     1. To revoke or rescind, especially by an official or formal act

     2. *Obsolete* To summon back or recall, especially from exile

3   **Section 76. REPEAL AND SAVINGS** (1) On the issue of the notification under Sub-section (1) of Section 3 constituting the Bangalore Development Authority, the City of Bangalore Improvement Act, 1945 (Mysore Act 5 of 1945) shall stand repealed.

     (2) ...

     (3) ...

     Provided further that anything done or any action taken (including any appointment, notification, rule, regulation, order, *scheme* or bye-law made or issued, any permission granted) under the said Act shall be deemed to have been done or taken under the corresponding provisions *of this Act* and shall continue to be in force accordingly unless and until superseded by anything done or any action taken under this Act:

     Provided also that any reference in any enactment or in any instrument to any provision of the repealed Act shall unless a different intention appears be construed as a reference to the corresponding provision of this Act.

(4) ....

scheme so sanctioned the open space in question has been reserved for a **public park.** However, pursuant to the orders of the State Government dated 27.5.1976 and 11.6.1976 and by its resolution dated 14.7.1976, the Bangalore Development Authority (BDA) allotted the open space in favour of the appellant[4], a **medical trust**, for the purpose of constructing a hospital. This site is stated to be the only available space reserved in the scheme for a public park or play ground. This allotment has been challenged by the writ petitioners[5] who were residents of the locality on the ground that it was contrary to the provisions of the Act and the scheme sanctioned thereunder, and the legislative intent to protect and preserve the environment by reserving open space for 'ventilation', recreation and play grounds and parks for the general public. The writ petitioners, being aggrieved as members of the general public and residents of the locality challenged the diversion of the user and allotment of the site to private persons for construction of a hospital.

Decision by Learned Single Judge and Division Bench:

The learned Single Judge who heard the writ petition[6] found no merit in it and dismissed the same. He held that, a hospital being a civic amenity, the allotment of the site by the BDA in favour of the appellant *(Bangalore Medical Trust)* for the purpose of constructing a hospital was valid and in accordance with law. On appeal by the respondents[7] (the residents of the locality) the learned Judges of the Division Bench held that, the area having been reserved in the sanctioned scheme for a public park, its diversion from that object and allotment in favour of a private body was not permissible under the Act, even if the object of the allotment was the construction of a hospital. The learned Judges were not impressed by the argument that the proposed hospital being a civic amenity, the Act did not prohibit the abandonment of a public park for a private hospital. Accordingly, allowing the respondents' appeal and without prejudice to a fresh allotment by the BDA of any alternative site in favour of the

---

4   **Meaning of Appellant:** A person who dissatisfied with the judgment rendered in a lawsuit decided in a lower court or the findings from a proceeding before an Administrative Agency, asks a superior court to review the decision.

5   **Meaning of Petitioner:** A person who presents a Petition. (**Meaning of Petition:** A formal message requesting something that is submitted to an authority)

6   **Meaning of Petition:** A formal message requesting something that is submitted to an authority

7   **Meaning of Respondent:** A **respondent** is a person who is called upon to issue a response to a communication made by another. In legal usage, this specifically refers to the defendant in a legal proceeding commenced by a petition, or to an appellee, or the opposing party, in an appeal of a decision by an initial fact-finder

present appellant, according to law, the writ petition was allowed and the allotment of the site in question was set aside. Aggrieved by the decision appellants approached Supreme Court.

Question before the Supreme Court:

Whether an open space reserved for a park or play ground for the general public, in accordance with a formally approved and published development scheme in terms of the Bangalore Development Authority Act, 1976 can be allotted to a private person or a body of persons for the purpose of constructing a hospital?

Do the members of the public, being residents of the locality, have a right to object to such diversion of the user of the space and deprivation of a park meant for the general public and for the protection of the environment?

Are they in law aggrieved by such diversion and allotment?

Public Park as a place reserved for beauty and recreation was developed in 19th and 20th Century and is associated with growth of the concept of equality and recognition of importance of common man. Earlier it was a prerogative[8] of the aristocracy[9] and the affluent either as a result of royal grant or as a place reserved for private pleasure. Free and healthy air in beautiful surroundings was privilege of few. But now it is a, 'gift from people to themselves'. Its importance has multiplied with emphasis on environment and pollution. In modern planning and development it occupies an important place in social ecology. A private nursing home on the other hand is essentiality a commercial venture, a profit oriented industry. Service may be its moto but earning is the objective. Its utility may not be undermined but a park is a necessity not a mere amenity. A private nursing home cannot be a substitute for a public park. No town planner would prepare a blue print without reserving space for it. Emphasis on open air and greenery has multiplied and the city or town planning or

---

8 **Meaning of prerogative:**

   1. An exclusive right or privilege held by a person or group, especially a hereditary or official right

   2. The exclusive right and power to command, decide, rule, or judge

9 **Meaning of Aristocracy:**

   1. A hereditary ruling class; nobility

   2.a. Government by a ruling class

   b. A state or country having this form of government

development acts of different States require even private house-owners to leave open space in front and back for lawn and fresh air. Absence of open space and public park, in present day when urbanisation is on increase, rural exodus is on large scale and congested areas are coming up rapidly, may given rise to health hazard. May be that it may be taken care of by a nursing home. But it is axiomatic[10] that prevention is better than cure. What is lost by removal of a park cannot be gained by establishment of a nursing home.

Protection of the environment and open spaces for recreation are matters of great public concern:

Protection of the environment, open spaces for recreation and fresh air, play grounds for children, promenade[11] for the residents, and other conveniences[12] or amenities are matters of great public concern and of vital interest to be taken care of in a development scheme. It is that public interest which is sought to be promoted by Act by establishing the BDA (the Bangalore Development Authority). The public interest in the reservation and preservation of open spaces for parks and play grounds cannot be sacrificed by leasing or selling such sites to private persons for conversion to some other user. Any such act would be contrary to the legislative intent and inconsistent with the statutory requirements. Furthermore, it would be in direct conflict with the constitutional mandate to ensure that any State action is inspired by the basic values of individual freedom and dignity and addressed to the attainment of a quality of life which makes the guaranteed rights a reality for all the citizens[13].

Reservation of open spaces for parks and play grounds is universally recognised as a legitimate exercise of statutory power rationally related

---

10 **Meaning of axiomatic:**

    1. relating to or resembling an axiom; self-evident

    2. containing maxims; aphoristic

11 **Meaning of promenade:**

    a. A leisurely walk, especially one taken in a public place as a social activity.

    b. A public place for such walking

12 **Meaning of Conveniences:** Things that make you comfortable and at ease

13 See *Kharak Singh v. The Slate of U.P. and Ors.*, 1963CriLJ329 ; *Municipal Council, Ratlam v. Shri Vardhichand and Ors.*, 1980CriLJ1075 ; *Francis Coralie Mullin v. The Administrator, Union Territory of Delhi and Ors.* ,1981CriLJ306 ; *Olga Tellis and Ors. v. Bombay Municipal Corporation and Ors.* ,AIR1986SC180 ; *State of Himachal Pradesh and Anr. v. Umed Ram Sharma and Ors.*,[1986]1SCR251 and *Vikram Deo Singh Tomar v. State of Bihar*, AIR1988SC1782

to the protection of the residents of the locality from the ill-effects of urbanisation[14]. The statutes[15] in force in India and abroad reserving open spaces for parks and play grounds are the legislative attempt to eliminate the misery of disreputable housing condition caused by urbanisation[16]. Crowded urban areas tend to spread disease, crime and immorality.

Decision by Supreme Court:

Court held that the residents of the locality are the persons intimately, vitally and adversely affected by any action of the Bangalore Development Authority (BDA) and the Government which is destructive of the environment and which deprives them of facilities reserved for the enjoyment and protection of the health of the public at large. The residents of the locality are naturally aggrieved by the orders of BDA and Government and they have, therefore, the necessary locus standi[17].

Court further held that the orders of the Government dated 27.5.1976 and 11.6.1976 and the consequent decision of the BDA dated 14.7.1976 are inconsistent with, and contrary to, the legislative intent to safeguard the health, safety and general welfare of the people of the locality. These orders evidence a colourable exercise of power, and are opposed to the statutory scheme. The impugned[18] orders and the consequent action of the BDA in allotting to private persons areas reserved for public parks and play grounds and permitting construction of buildings for hospital was declared to be null and void and of no effect by court.

---

14 See for e.g: Karnataka Town and Country Planning Act, 1961; Maharashtra Regional and Town Planning Act, 1966; Bombay Town Planning Act, 1954; The Travancore Town and Country Planning Act, 1120; The Madras Town Planning Act, 1920; and the Rules framed under these Statutes; Town & Country Planning Act, 1971 (England & Wales); Encyclopaedia Americana, Volume 22, page 240; Encyclopaedia of the Social Sciences, Volume XII at page 161; Town Improvement Trusts in India, 1945 by Rai Sahib Om Prakash Aggarawala, p. 35; et. seq.; Halsbury's Statutes, Fourth Edition, p. 17 et. seq. and Journal of Planning & Environment Law, 1973, p. 130 et. seq.

15 A **statute** is a formal written enactment of a legislative authority that governs a state, city, or country

16 **Urbanization** (or **urbanisation**) is the increasing number of people that live in urban areas. It predominantly results in the physical growth of urban areas, be it horizontal or vertical.

17 **Meaning of Locus Standi**; The right of a party to appear and be heard before a court

18 **Meaning of Impugned**: To attack as false or questionable; challenge in argument

7

Importance of Wetland [1]

Ratio Decidendi[2]: "Socio-economic condition of country cannot be ignored by Court of law"

Facts in Nutshell:

Population growth and modern technological developments by themselves pose a great threat to the very existence of living and non-living organisms -- this is not confined to a particular region, but it has crossed trans-national frontiers. In 1972 the Stockholm Conference[3] under the auspices of the United Nations did deliberate upon the issues of protection of human environment. The Habitat Conference, Vancouver, British Columbia, 1976 and the World Water Conference at Argentina in 1977 recorded a detailed discussion as regards the **water pollution**. It is not out of place to mention that water pollution along with the pollution in the air and the noise pollution are in a much higher degree in the metropolitan centres than in the rural sectors and as such population influx and technological developments can be ascribed to be the two basic factors for such environmental degradation[4]. The National Environmental Engineering Research Institute has confirmed that levels of sulphur dioxide and other particulate matters in big cities have exceeded

---

1   Appellants: **People United for Better Living in Calcutta-Public and another Vs.** Respondent: **State of West Bengal and others**

     AIR1993Cal215

     Hon'ble Judges/Coram: Umesh Chandra Benerjee, Judge

2   **Meaning of Ration Decidendi:** *Ratio decidendi* is a Latin phrase meaning "the reason" or "the rationale for the decision." The *ratio decidendi* is "the point in a case which determines the judgment" or "the principle which the case establishes."

3   The United Nations Conference on the Human Environment, having met at Stockholm from 5 to 16 June 1972,having considered the need for a common outlook and for common principles to inspire and guide the peoples of the world in the preservation and enhancement of the human environment.

4   **Environmental degradation** is the deterioration of the environment through depletion of resources such as air, water and soil; the destruction of ecosystems and the extinction of wildlife. It is defined as any change or disturbance to the environment perceived to be deleterious or undesirable

the permissible limits as prescribed by the World Health Organisation (W.H.O.).

While it is true that in a developing country there shall have to be developments, but that development shall have to be in closest possible harmony with the environment, as otherwise there would be development but no environment, which would result in total devastation, though, however, may not be felt in present but at some future point of time, but then it would be too late in the day, however, to control and improve the environment. Nature will not tolerate us after a certain degree of its destruction and it will in any event, have its toil[5] on the lives of the people. Can the present-day society afford to have such a state and allow the nature to have its toll in future - the answer shall have to be in the negative. The present day society has a responsibility towards the posterity[6] for their proper growth and development so as to allow the posterity to breathe normally and live in a cleaner environment and have a consequent fuller development. Time has now come therefore, to check and control the degradation of the environment and since the Law Courts also have a duty towards the society for its proper growth and further development and more so by reason of definite legislations in regard thereto as noted hereinafter, it is a plain exercise of the judicial power to see that there is no such degradation of the society and there ought not to be any hesitation in regard thereto -- but does that mean and imply stoppage of every developmental programme -- the answer is again 'no' : There shall have to be a proper balance between the development and the environment so that both can co-exist without affecting the other. On the wake of the 21st century, it is neither feasible[7] not practicable to have a negative approach to the development process of the country or of the society, but that does not mean, without any consideration for the environment. There should be a proper balance between the protection of environment and the development process. The society shall have to prosper, but not at the cost of the environment and in the similar vein,

---

5   **Meaning of Toil:**

    1. To labor continuously; work strenuously.

    2. To proceed with difficulty

6   **Meaning of posterity:**

    1. Future or succeeding generations

    2. All of one's descendants

7   **Meaning of Feasible:** Capable of being accomplished or brought about; possible

the environment shall have to be protected but not at the cost of the development of the society. There shall have to be both development and proper environment and as such, a balance has to be found out and administrative actions ought to proceed in accordance therewith. Environmental conditions get substantially influenced by local factors; Factors like regular recurrence of natural calamities, i.e. floods, drought, land subsidence and the like or features like intensive exploitation of natural resources, e.g., mining, deforestation or a highly effective health phenomenon in the form of predominance of an endemic[8] disease or a typical socio-economic condition engulfing a large percentage of local population -- all exert profound influences of different nature and dimensions on the environment that revolve in a particular area.

The writ petition[9] in High court was filed and the entire thrust of challenge in the petition[10] was with regard to the maintenance of wetlands in the eastern fringe of the city of Calcutta.

Meaning and Importance of Wetland:

The Water Board of the New South Wales Government, Australia in its Secondary Poster 2 'Protecting our Wetlands' records the following:

"Wetlands, often called bogs, swamps, marshes, billabongs and a host of other names, are areas of wetland. The amount of water in them varies depending on the weather and the time of year. Sometimes they can be quite dry. Special plants, such as reeds, grow in wetland areas. Wetlands also provide a home for a host of different wildlife rainging from migratory and local birds to fish, reptiles, amphibians and insects. All these living things depend on wetlands for their existence. Eastuarine wetlands are found where rivers start to join the sea. Their water is brackish (a mixture of salt and fresh water) and it rises and falls along with the tide. Mangroves grow in estuarine wetlands. Billabongs are old river beds that

---

8   **Meaning of Endemic:** Prevalent in or peculiar to a particular locality, region, or people

9   **Meaning of Writ Petition:** Under the Indian legal system, jurisdiction to issue 'prerogative writs' is given to the Supreme Court, and to the High Courts of Judicature of all Indian states. Parts of the law relating to writs are set forth in the Constitution of India. The Supreme Court, the highest in the country, may issue writs under Article 32 of the Constitution for enforcement of Fundamental Rights and under Articles 139 for enforcement of rights other than Fundamental Rights, while High Courts, the superior courts of the States, may issue writs under Articles 226. 'Writ' is eminently designed by the makers of the Constitution, and in the same way it is developed very widely and efficiently by the courts in India. The Constitution broadly provides for five kinds of "prerogative" writs, namely, Habeas Corpus, Certiorari, Mandamus, Quo Warranto and Prohibition

10 **Meaning of Petition:** A formal message requesting something that is submitted to an authority

are left when the river takes a different direction. When the new river floods or there is heavy rain, the billabongs fill with water. Marshes and swamps can be found in many places. They are shallow, low lying areas of ground, filled with reeds and wildlife".

"Each wetland functions as an ecosystem that is, a system where all the parts (land, plants, animals, water, solar energy) depend on each other. If one part of the system, the amount of sunlight for instance, is changed, ail the other parts will be affected too. Often change to one element of an ecosystem results in the destruction of the whole. Not only are the wetlands fragile[11] ecosystems in themselves, but they form a vital part of the world's ecosystem as well. Wetlands rely on established water drainage pattern. Any population nearby, with its paved streets, gardens, stormwater waste etc. inevitably alters water drainage patterns and affects the wetland".

Wetlands provide a haven for vast numbers of living creatures which rely on them for food, shelter and as a breeding place. While they may not live permanently in the area, huge numbers of birds, animals, reptiles[12], fish, amphibians[13] and insects regularly visit and use wetlands. Disappearance of wetlands threatens their very existence. Migratory birds, some from as far away as Siberia and Japan, travel to Australian wetlands every year to escape the cold winter. Many of these migratory birds are rare and endangered species.

Many kinds of fish hatch and grow to maturity in the safety of the wetland mangrove swamps. When they are adults they move into the ocean. Most of the fish we eat depend on these mangrove 'nurseries' for hatching their young and for the survival of the species. Many species of plants survive only in the special environment of the wetlands. Loss of wetlands threatens their survival. Wetlands play an important role in the water

---

11 **Meaning of Fragile:**

1. Easily broken, damaged, or destroyed; frail.

2. Lacking physical or emotional strength; delicate

12 **Reptiles**, the class **Reptilia**, are an evolutionary grade of animals, comprising today's turtles, crocodilians,snakes, lizards and tuatara, as well as many extinct groups. A reptile is any amniote (a tetrapod whose egg has an additional membrane, originally to allow them to lay eggs on land) that is neither a mammal nor a bird.

13 **Amphibians** are ectothermic, tetrapod vertebrates of the class **Amphibia**. They inhabit a wide variety of habitats with most species living within terrestrial, fossorial, arboreal or freshwater aquaticecosystems. Amphibians typically start out as larva living in water, but some species have developed behavioural adaptations to bypass this.

cycle, cleaning and purifying water as it passes through them. They can also help control flood water by stopping and releasing it slowly through the ground.

There is growing evidence that wetlands are a vital link in the food chain, 'processing' food for some species, and also play a part in nitrogen fixing, a process which alters nitrogen to a form where it can be used by living creatures. Wetlands are also important for people, as areas where environmental scientists can learn more about our total environment, and as areas for relaxation where people can enjoy canoeing[14], fishing, picnics, photography, walking, bird watching and sometimes, just sitting in a quiet and beautiful place".

According to the American environmentalists, the following can be ascribed to be the contribution of the wetlands:--

(i) Wetlands act as water purifier;

(ii) They help maintain surface moisture;

(iii) They help curb soil erosion;

(iv) They lessen the impact of both floods as well as droughts;

(v) They contribute pure water to wells;

(vi) They preserve the wildlife; and

(vii) They support the fishing industry.

Wetlands being an unseen storehouse of nature's bounty and a gift of nature to mankind act as regulators and reservoirs for rivers. The marshes slow down the speed of the water flowing from the streams to the rivers, this delay gives the river the much required time to adjust to the various tides, but with the removal of the wetlands, the water from the streams will start flowing faster onto the rivers and the rivers, not being able to adjust, will flood the surrounding areas.

It is to be noted that India is a contracting party to the Ramsar Convention[15], an Inter Governmental Treaty on Wetlands under which she is obliged

---

14 **Meaning of canoeing:** A light, open, slender boat that has pointed ends and is propelled by paddles

15 The Convention on Wetlands (Ramsar, Iran, 1971) -- called the "Ramsar Convention" -- is an intergovernmental treaty that embodies the commitments of its member countries to maintain the ecological character of their Wetlands of International Importance and to plan for the "wise use", or sustainable use, of all of the wetlands in their territories.

to promote the conservation of wetlands habitat in her territory. The Salt Lake Swamp is acknowledged as an important wetland by virtue of its socio-economic and ecological values. As a matter of fact, it is in the Directory of Asian Wetlands and a wetland of international importance -- it meets all accepted criteria for identification of an internationally important wetland. The usefulness of a wetland can be determined from the point of view of flora[16] and fauna[17] it sustains, its ecosystem values, and contribution of wetlands for maintaining global air and water cycles[18]. The populations which are benefited from or thrive on wetlands range from man, animal, waterfowl, fish, plant to a host of other micro organisms. Wetlands are used by man for a multitude of need from food to disposal to waste. One can cite a long list of uses which man gets from wetlands both directly and indirectly. Wetland animals and birds provide food, fur, skin and other items. Plants provide food, shelter, timber, medicine and a host of other non-edible uses. Wetlands are habitat, for endangered and rare species of birds and animals. Wetland ecosystem is especially important for migratory birds and waders. They are habitats for different endemic, relict, regional varieties of subspecies of plants, insects and Other invertebrates and wildlife even in otherwise, congested industrial region.

When considered as an ecosystem, the wetlands are useful for a nutrient recovery and cycling, releasing excess nitrogen, inactivation of phosphates, removing toxins, chemicals, heavy metals through absorption by plants, arid also in treating waste water. Removal of suspended solids from flowing water by reducing the flow also benefits the retention of water for sometime whereby biological, physical and chemical changes are made possible. Retention of sediments by wetlands also reduces siltation in the rivers. Wetlands also help in mitigating floods, recharging acqui-fers and in reducing surface run off and consequent erosion. Mangrove wetlands on India and Bangladesh act as buffers[19] against devasting stroms of the Bay of Bengal. Wetlands also influence microclimate of a locality. Besides these, they are also valued for their aesthetic qualities and recreational opportunities. A fresh water wetland checks underground

16 **Flora** is the plant life occurring in a particular region or time, generally the naturally occurring or indigenous—native plant life

17 **Fauna** is all of the animal life of any particular region or time.

18 (Mitsch and Gosselink, 1986)

19 **Meaning of Buffers:**

   1. One that buffs, especially a piece of soft leather or cloth used to shine or polish.

   2. A buffing wheel.

salt water intrusion of an adjacent brackish water environment through interface pressure. On a global scale the wetlands function significantly in maintaining air and water quality including nitrogen, sulphur, methane and carbondioxide cycles.

Decision by High Court:

Court held that there is no manner of doubt, therefore, that wetland being a bounty of nature do have a significant role to play in the proper development of the society -- be it from environmental perspective or from economic perspective. Polluttion wise, metropolitan city of Calcutta tops the list in the country. Wetland acts as a benefactor to the society and there cannot be any manner of doubt in regard thereto and as such encroachment thereof would be detrimental to the society which the Law Courts cannot permit. This benefit to the society cannot be weighed on mathematical nicety so as to take note of the requirement of the society -- what is required today may not be a relevant consideration in the immediate future, therefore, it cannot really be assessed to what amount of nature's bounty is required for the proper maintenance of environmental equilibrium. It cannot be measured in terms of requirement and as such, the Court of Law cannot, in fact, decry the opinion of the environmentalist in that direction. Law Courts exists for the benefit of the society. Law Courts exists for the purpose of giving redress to the society when called for and it must rise above all levels so that justice is meted out and the society thrives thereunder.

Court restrained the State Respondents[20] from reclaiming any further wetland and prohibited the respondents from granting any permission to any person whatsoever for the purpose of changing the use of the land from agricultural to residential or commercial in the area of wetland. The State-Respondents were further directed to maintain the nature and character of the wetlands in their present form and to stop all encroachment[21] of the wetland area. The State- Respondents were further directed by court to take steps so as to stop private alienation[22] of wetlands.

20　**Meaning of Respondent:** A **respondent** is a person who is called upon to issue a response to a communication made by another. In legal usage, this specifically refers to the defendant in a legal proceeding commenced by a petition, or to an appellee, or the opposing party, in an appeal of a decision by an initial fact-finder

21　**Meaning of Encroachment:**　Any entry into an area not previously occupied; "an invasion of tourists"; "an invasion of locusts"

22　**Meaning of Alienation:** The act of transferring property or title to it to another

8

No one has right to carry on business so as to cause nuisance to society[1]

Facts in Nutshell:

Petitioners[2] who were conducting the business of dyeing and printing works at different places in the city of Rajkot challenged the notice issued by the respondent[3]- Municipal Commissioner. In the notice it was stated that at the place mentioned, the petitioners are discharging dirty water from the factory on public roads public drainage without purifying the same, thereby causing damage to the public health. Moreover, it was stated that on November 11, 1986 when the place was visited by the Commissioner himself it was found that by discharging dirty water nuisance[4] was being created. Hence each petitioners were called upon to prevent the discharge of dirty water and they were also directed to inform the Commissioner regarding compliance. It was further stated that if there is failure to comply with the notice than under the powers conferred upon the Municipal Commissioner, shall have to take steps to close the factory with a view to prevent the illegal discharge of dirty water.

The petitioners contended that they were carrying on the business for last about 20 to, 25 years and the industry is providing employment to twenty to thirty thousand families; the proposed action as stated-in the notice will have harsh consequences and the petitioners may have to

---

1   Appellants: **Abhilash Textile and Ors. etc. Vs.** Respondent: **The Rajkot Municipal Corporation**

     AIR1988Guj57

     Hon'ble Judges/Coram: A.P. Ravani, Judge

2   **Meaning of Petitioner:** A person who presents a Petition. (**Meaning of Petition:** A formal message requesting something that is submitted to an authority)

3   **Meaning of Respondent:** A **respondent** is a person who is called upon to issue a response to a communication made by another. In legal usage, this specifically refers to the defendant in a legal proceeding commenced by a petition, or to an appellee, or the opposing party, in an appeal of a decision by an initial fact-finder

4   **Nuisance** is a common law tort. It means that which causes offence, annoyance, trouble or injury. A nuisance can be either public (also "common") or private.

close down their business.

Question before the High Court:

Is there any right to carry on business or trade in unregulated manner and cause nuisance to the public and to the society at large?

To practice any profession or to carry on any occupation:

Article 19(1)(g)[5] of the Constitution confers right upon every citizen to practice any profession or to carry on any occupation, trade or business. But this fundamental right[6] is subject to reasonable restrictions which may be placed in the interest of the general public as provided for in sub-clause (6)[7] of Article 19 itself. No one has a right to carry on business so

---

5   **Article 19 in The Constitution Of India 1949**

   19. Protection of certain rights regarding freedom of speech etc

   (1) All citizens shall have the right

   (a) to freedom of speech and expression;

   (b) to assemble peaceably and without arms;

   (c) to form associations or unions;

   (d) to move freely throughout the territory of India;

   (e) to reside and settle in any part of the territory of India; and

   (f) omitted

   (g) to practise any profession, or to carry on any occupation, trade or business

6   **Meaning of Fundamental Rights:** The Fundamental Rights are defined as basic human freedoms which every Indian citizen has the right to enjoy for a proper and harmonious development of personality. These rights universally apply to all citizens, irrespective of race, place of birth, religion, caste, creed, colour or gender. Aliens (persons who are not citizens) are also considered in matters like equality before law. They are enforceable by the courts, subject to certain restrictions

7   **Article 19 in The Constitution Of India 1949**

   19. Protection of certain rights regarding freedom of speech etc

   (1) All citizens shall have the right

   (a) to freedom of speech and expression;

   (b) to assemble peaceably and without arms;

   (c) to form associations or unions;

   (d) to move freely throughout the territory of India;

   (e) to reside and settle in any part of the territory of India; and

   (f) omitted

   (g) to practise any profession, or to carry on any occupation, trade or business

   (2) Nothing in sub clause (a) of clause (1) shall affect the operation of any existing law, or prevent the State from making any law, in so far as such law imposes reasonable restrictions on the exercise of the right conferred by the said sub clause in the interests of the sovereignty and

as to cause nuisance to the society. One cannot carry on the business in the manner by which the business activity becomes a health hazard to the entire society. The fundamental right to carry on trade or business is subject to reasonable restrictions and regulations that may be placed in the interest of the general public.

Fundamental Duties[8]:

The provisions regarding fundamental duties of the citizens contained in Article 51A(g)[9] of the Constitution enjoins upon all the citizens to

---

integrity of India, the security of the State, friendly relations with foreign States, public order, decency or morality or in relation to contempt of court, defamation or incitement to an offence

(3) Nothing in sub clause (b) of the said clause shall affect the operation of any existing law in so far as it imposes, or prevent the State from making any law imposing, in the interests of the sovereignty and integrity of India or public order, reasonable restrictions on the exercise of the right conferred by the said sub clause

(4) Nothing in sub clause (c) of the said clause shall affect the operation of any existing law in so far as it imposes, or prevent the State from making any law imposing, in the interests of the sovereignty and integrity of India or public order or morality, reasonable restrictions on the exercise of the right conferred by the said sub clause

(5) Nothing in sub clauses (d) and (e) of the said clause shall affect the operation of any existing law in so far as it imposes, or prevent the State from making any law imposing, reasonable restrictions on the exercise of any of the rights conferred by the said sub clauses either in the interests of the general public or for the protection of the interests of any Scheduled Tribe

(6) Nothing in sub clause (g) of the said clause shall affect the operation of any existing law in so far as it imposes, or prevent the State from making any law imposing, in the interests of the general public, reasonable restrictions on the exercise of the right conferred by the said sub clause, and, in particular, nothing in the said sub clause shall affect the operation of any existing law in so far as it relates to, or prevent the State from making any law relating to,

(i) the professional or technical qualifications necessary for practising any profession or carrying on any occupation, trade or business, or

(ii) the carrying on by the State, or by a corporation owned or controlled by the State, of any trade, business, industry or service, whether to the exclusion, complete or partial, of citizens or otherwise

8   The *Fundamental Duties* are defined as the moral obligations of all citizens to help promote a spirit of patriotism and to uphold the unity of India. These duties, set out in Part IV–A of the Constitution concern individuals and the nation. Like the Directive Principles, they are not legally enforceable

9   **Article 51A in The Constitution Of India 1949**

51A. Fundamental duties It shall be the duty of every citizen of India

(a) to abide by the Constitution and respect its ideals and institutions, the national Flag and the National Anthem;

(b) to cherish and follow the noble ideals which inspired our national struggle for freedom;

(c) to uphold and protect the sovereignty, unity and integrity of India;

(d) to defend the country and render national service when called upon to do so;

(e) to promote harmony and the spirit of common brotherhood amongst all the people of India transcending religious, linguistic and regional or sectional diversities; to renounce practices

protect and improve the natural environment. The Article 51-A regarding fundamental duties of citizens has been inserted in the Constitution by Forty Second Amendment[10] and it has come into force with effect from January 3, 1977.

Case Laws Referred:

In the case of *T. B. Ibrahim v. The Regional Transport Authority*[11] the petitioner claimed his right to have a bus stand at a particular place, which he was using for last many years. The Regional Transport Authority, for the convenience of the traveling public, resolved to alter the starting place and termini of all public vehicles and the existing bus-stand owned by the petitioner was ordered to be discontinued. This action of the Regional Transport Authority was challenged by the petitioner. In Para 13 of the judgment the Supreme Court has observed as follows.

"There is no fundamental right in a citizen to carry on business wherever he chooses and his right must be subject to any reasonable restriction imposed by the executive authority in the interest of public convenience. The restriction may have the effect of eliminating the use to which the stand has been put hitherto but the restriction cannot be regarded as being unreasonable if the authority imposing such restriction had the power to dose. Whether the abolition of the stand was conductive to public convenience or not is a matter entirely for the Transport Authority to judge, and it. is not open to the Court substitute its own opinion for the opinion of the Authority, which is in the best position, having regard to its knowledge of local conditions, to appraise the situation."

---

derogatory to the dignity of women;

(f) to value and preserve the rich heritage of our composite culture;

(g) to protect and improve the natural environment including forests, lakes, rivers and wild life, and to have compassion for living creatures;

(h) to develop the scientific temper, humanism and the spirit of inquiry and reform;

(i) to safeguard public property and to abjure violence

10   The 42nd Amendment is regarded as the most controversial constitutional amendment in Indian history. It attempted to reduce the power of the Supreme Court and High Courts to pronounce upon the constitutional validity of laws. It laid down the Fundamental Duties of Indian citizens to the nation. This amendment brought about the most widespread changes to the Constitution in its history, and is sometimes called a "mini-Constitution" or the "Constitution of India"

11   AIR 1953 SC 79

In the case of *Covered B. Bharucha v. Excise Comair, Ajmer*[12] in Para 7 of the judgment the Supreme Court has observed as follows :

"The right of every citizen to pursue any lawful trade or business is obviously subject to such reasonable conditions as may be deemed by the governing authority of the country essential to the safety, health, peace, order and morals of the community. Some occupations by the noise made in their pursuit, some by the odors they engender, and some by the dangers accompanying them, require regulations as to the locality y in which they may be conducted. Some, by the dangerous character of the articles used, manufactured or sold require also special qualifications in the parties permitted to use, manufacture or sell them."

Decision by High Court:

Court held that if the petitioners wish to carry on the business they may have to incur expenditure and they must provide for purification-plant before discharging, the effluent water on public road or in the public drainage system. This is the minimum requirement for carrying on the business which they must comply with. If they have to incur expenditure for the purification-plant the same must be considered as part of the cost of the business. The petitioners cannot be allowed to reap profit at the cost of the public health. This is the mandate of the law.

---

12 AIR 1954 SC 220

9

Anything that affects or is likely to affect 'public health', 'hygiene' and tranquility[1] has to be abhorred[2]

Facts in Nutshell:

Application under Article 226[3] of the Constitution of India was filed by

---

1   **Meaning of Tranquility:** A disposition free from stress or emotion

2   Appellants: **Wing Commander Utpal Barbara and Ors. Vs.** Respondent: **State of Assam and Ors.**

    AIR1999Gau78

    Hon'ble Judges/Coram: B. Biswas, Judge

3   **Article 226 in The Constitution Of India 1949**

    226. Power of High Courts to issue certain writs

    (1) Notwithstanding anything in Article 32 every High Court shall have powers, throughout the territories in relation to which it exercise jurisdiction, to issue to any person or authority, including in appropriate cases, any Government, within those territories directions, orders or writs, including writs in the nature of habeas corpus, mandamus, prohibitions, quo warranto and certiorari, or any of them, for the enforcement of any of the rights conferred by Part III and for any other purpose

    (2) The power conferred by clause (1) to issue directions, orders or writs to any Government, authority or person may also be exercised by any High Court exercising jurisdiction in relation to the territories within which the cause of action, wholly or in part, arises for the exercise of such power, notwithstanding that the seat of such Government or authority or the residence of such person is not within those territories

    (3) Where any party against whom an interim order, whether by way of injunction or stay or in any other manner, is made on, or in any proceedings relating to, a petition under clause (1), without

    (a) furnishing to such party copies of such petition and all documents in support of the plea for such interim order; and

    (b) giving such party an opportunity of being heard, makes an application to the High Court for the vacation of such order and furnishes a copy of such application to the party in whose favour such order has been made or the counsel of such party, the High Court shall dispose of the application within a period of two weeks from the date on which it is received or from the date on which the copy of such application is so furnished, whichever is later, or where the High Court is closed on the last day of that period, before the expiry of the next day afterwards on which the High Court is open; and if the application is not so disposed of, the interim order shall, on the expiry of that period, or, as the case may be, the expiry of the aid next day, stand vacated

    (4) The power conferred on a High Court by this article shall not be in derogation of the power conferred on the Supreme court by clause (2) of Article 32

the petitioners[4] for issuance of writ[5] to quash[6] the order dated 5-6-1998 by the Additional District Magistrate, Kamrup, Guwahati in exercise of powers under Section 144[7] of the Code of Criminal Procedure banning the use of polythene bags[8] throughout the District of Kamrup. The improper disposal of the used polythene bags by the members of the public has blocked normal flow of drain water causing serious water

---

4   **Meaning of Petitioner:** A person who presents a Petition. (**Meaning of Petition:** A formal message requesting something that is submitted to an authority)

5   **Meaning of Writ:** A written order issued by a court, commanding the party to whom it is addressed to perform or cease performing a specified act

6   **Meaning of Quash:** To set aside or annul, especially by judicial action.

7   **Section 144 in The Code Of Criminal Procedure, 1973**

   144. Power to issue order in urgent cases of nuisance of apprehended danger.

   (1) In cases where, in the opinion of a District Magistrate, a Sub- divisional Magistrate or any other Executive Magistrate specially empowered by the State Government in this behalf, there is sufficient ground for proceeding under this section and immediate prevention or speedy remedy is desirable, such Magistrate may, by a written order stating the material facts of the case and served in the manner provided by section 134, direct any person to abstain from a certain act or to take certain order with respect to certain property in his possession or under his management, if such Magistrate considers that such direction is likely to prevent, or tends to prevent, obstruction, annoyance or injury to any person lawfully employed, or danger to human life, health or safety, or a disturbance of the public tranquility, or a riot, of an affray.

   (2) An order under this section may, in cases of emergency or in cases where the circumstances do not admit of the serving in due time of a notice upon the person against whom the order is directed, be passed ex parte.

   (3) An order under this section may be directed to a particular individual, or to persons residing in a particular place or area, or to the public generally when frequenting or visiting a particular place or area.

   (4) No order under this section shall remain in force for more than two months from the making thereof: Provided that, if the State Government considers it necessary so to do for preventing danger to human life, health or safety or for preventing a riot or any affray, it may, by notification, direct that an order made by a Magistrate under this section shall remain in force for such further period not exceeding six months from the date on which the order made by the Magistrate would have, but for such order, expired, as it may specify in the said notification.

   (5) Any Magistrate may, either on his own motion or on the application of any person aggrieved, rescind or alter any order made under this section, by himself or any Magistrate subordinate to him or by his predecessor- in- office.

   (6) The State Government may, either on its own motion or on the application of any person aggrieved, rescind or alter any order made by it under the proviso to sub- section (4).

   (7) Where an application under sub- section (5) or sub- section (6) is received, the Magistrate, or the State Government, as the case may be, shall afford to the applicant an early opportunity of appearing before him or it, either in person or by pleader and showing cause against the order; and if the Magistrate or the State Government, as the case may be, rejects the application wholly or in part, he or it shall record in writing the reasons for so doing. D.- Disputes as to immovable property

8   A **plastic bag, polybag,** or **pouch** is a type of packaging made of thin, flexible, plastic film, nonwoven fabric, or plastic textile. Plastic bags are used for containing and transporting goods such as foods, produce, powders, ice, magazines, chemicals and waste.

logging problem and resultant environmental pollution. According to the petitioners, they were proprietors of different firms operating factories for manufacture and supply of polythene bags throughout the State of Assam after obtaining licences/ No Objection Certificate from the competent authorities, namely, Gauhati Municipal Corporation, District Industries Centre and Assam Pollution Control Board. The order imposing ban on the use of polythene bags adversely affected the business of the petitioners infringing upon the right of the petitioners to carry on trade and business.

Question before the High Court:

Whether the Additional District Magistrate exceeded his jurisdiction[9] under Section 144 of the Code of Criminal Procedure in passing the order for banning the use of polythene bags?

Decision by High Court:

Court held that anything that affects or is likely to affect 'public health', 'hygiene' and tranquility has to be abhorred[10]. Use of polythene bags containing lead[11] (toxic element) because of dye used as an ingredient may be dealt with under Section 144 of the Code of Criminal Procedure for a short period, but not in perpetuity[12]. The 'legislative intent' embodied in the language of Section 144 suggests that this power is available only to meet an 'imminent situation'. Court was of the opinion that the 'satisfaction' arrived at by the learned Additional District Magistrate in issuing the order for banning the use of polythene bags was not justified. The order issued in exercise of powers under Section 144, Cr.P.C. being ex facie[13] illegal was set aside by court.

---

9   **Meaning of Jurisdiction:** The right and power to interpret and apply the law:

10 **Meaning of abhorred:** To detest vehemently; find repugnant; reject

11 **Lead** is a chemical element in the carbon group with symbol **Pb** (from Latin: *plumbum*) and atomic number 82. Lead is a soft and malleable metal, which is regarded as a heavy metal and an other metal. Metallic lead has a bluish-white color after being freshly cut, but it soon tarnishes to a dull grayish color when exposed to air. Lead has a shiny chrome-silver luster when it is melted into a liquid. It is also the heaviest non-radioactive element.

12 **Meaning of Perpetuity;**

    a. The condition of an estate that is limited so as to be inalienable either perpetually or longer than the period determined by law

    b. An estate so limited

13 **Ex facie** is a legal term typically used to note that a document's explicit terms are defective without further investigation

10

Polluter Pay Principle[1]

Ratio Decidendi[2]: *The "Polluter Pays" principle as interpreted by this Court means that the absolute liability for harm to the environment extends not only to compensate the victims of pollution but also the cost of restoring the environmental degradation. Remediation of the damaged environment is part of the process of "Sustainable Development" and as such polluter is liable to pay the cost to the individual sufferers as well as the cost of reversing the damaged ecology.*

Facts in Nutshell:

Public interest petition[3] under Article 32[4] of the Constitution of India was filed by Vellore Citizens Welfare Forum and was directed against the pollution which is being caused by enormous discharge of untreated effluent by the tanneries[5] and other industries in the State of Tamil Nadu. It was stated that the tanneries are discharging untreated effluent into

---

1   Appellants: **Vellore Citizens Welfare Forum Vs.** Respondent: **Union of India and others**

AIR1996SC2715

Hon'ble Judges/Coram: Kuldip Singh, Faizan Uddin and K. Venkataswami, JJ.

2   **Meaning of Ration Decidendi:** *Ratio decidendi* is a Latin phrase meaning "the reason" or "the rationale for the decision." The *ratio decidendi* is "the point in a case which determines the judgment" or "the principle which the case establishes."

3   **Meaning of Petition:** A formal message requesting something that is submitted to an authority

4   **Article 32 in The Constitution Of India 1949**

Remedies for enforcement of rights conferred by this Part

(1) The right to move the Supreme Court by appropriate proceedings for the enforcement of the rights conferred by this Part is guaranteed

(2) The Supreme Court shall have power to issue directions or orders or writs, including writs in the nature of habeas corpus, mandamus, prohibition, quo warranto and certiorari, whichever may be appropriate, for the enforcement of any of the rights conferred by this Part

(3) Without prejudice to the powers conferred on the Supreme Court by clause (1) and (2), Parliament may by law empower any other court to exercise within the local limits of its jurisdiction all or any of the powers exercisable by the Supreme Court under clause (2)

(4) The right guaranteed by this article shall not be suspended except as otherwise provided for by this Constitution

5   **Meaning of Tannery:** A place or building where skins and hides are tanned

agricultural fields, road-sides, waterways and open lands. The untreated effluent is finally discharged in river Palar[6] which is the main source of water supply to the residents of the area. According to the petitioner[7] the entire surface and sub-soil water of river Palar has been polluted resulting in non-availability of potable water to the residents of the area. It was stated that the tanneries in the State of Tamil Nadu have caused environmental degradation in the area. According to the preliminary survey made by the Tamil Nadu Agricultural University Research center Vellore nearly 35,000 hectares of agricultural land in the Tanneries Belt, has become either partially or totally unfit for cultivation. It has been further stated in the petition that the tanneries used about 170 types of chemicals in the chrome tanning processes. The said chemicals include sodium chloride[8], lime[9], sodium sulphate[10], chlorium sulphate[11], fat liquor Amonia[12] and sulphuric acid[13] besides dyes which are used in large quantities. Nearly 35 litres of water is used for processing one kilogram of finished leather, resulting in dangerously enormous quantities of toxic effluents being let out in the open by the tanning industry. These effluents have spoiled the physico-chemical properties of the soil, and have contaminated ground water by percolation[14].

---

6   **Palar** is a river of southern India. It rises in Nandi Hills, India in Kolar district of Karnataka state, and flows 93 km in Karnataka, 33 km in Andhra Pradesh and 222 km in Tamil Nadu before its confluence into the Bay of Bengal at Vayalur about 100 km south of Chennai.

7   **Meaning of Petitioner:** A person who presents a Petition. (**Meaning of Petition:** A formal message requesting something that is submitted to an authority)

8   **Sodium chloride**, also known as **salt**, **common salt**, **table salt** or **halite**, is an ionic compound with the formula NaCl, representing equal proportions of sodium and chlorine. Sodium chloride is the salt most responsible for the salinity of the ocean and of theextracellular fluid of many multicellular organisms.

9   **Lime** is a term referring to a citrus fruit which is typically round, green, 3⬚6 cm in diameter, and containing sour (acidic) pulp.

10 Sodium sulfate is mainly used for the manufacture of <u>detergents</u> and in the <u>Kraft process</u> of paper <u>pulping</u>.

11 **Chromium(III) sulfate** usually refers to the inorganic compound. This consists of the hydratedsulfate salt of the metal aquo complex, which is responsible for the purple color of this salt. It is widely used in the tanning of leather, with associated environmental damage.

12 **Ammonia**, or **azane**, is a compound of nitrogen and hydrogen. It is a colourless gas with a characteristic pungent smell.

13 **Sulfuric acid** (alternative spelling **sulphuric acid**) is a highly corrosive strong mineral acid. It is a pungent-ethereal, colorless to slightly yellow viscous liquid which is soluble in water at all concentrations. Sometimes, it is dyed dark brown during production to alert people to its hazards.

14 In physics, chemistry and materials science, **percolation** refers to the movement and filtering of fluids through porous materials.

Sustainable Development:

The traditional concept that development and ecology are opposed to each other, is no longer acceptable. "Sustainable Development" is the answer. In the International sphere "Sustainable Development" as a concept came to be known for the first time in the Stockholm Declaration of 1972. Thereafter, in 1987 the concept was given a definite shape by the World Commission on Environment and Development in its report called "Our Common Future". The Commission was chaired by the then Prime Minister of Norway Ms. G.N. Brundtland and as such the report is popularly known as "Brundtland Report". In 1991 the World Conservation Union, United Nations Environment Programme and World Wide Fund for Nature, jointly came out with a document called "Caring for the Earth" which is a strategy for sustainable living. Finally, came the Earth Summit held in June, 1992 at Rio which saw the largest gathering of world leaders ever in the history - deliberating and chalking out a blue pring for the survival of the planet. Among the tangible achievements of the Rio Conference was the signing of two conventions, one on biological diversity and another on climate change. These conventions were signed by 153 nations. The delegates also approved by consensus three non binding documents namely, a Statement on Forestry Principles, a declaration of principles on environmental policy and development initiatives and Agenda 21, a programme of action into the next century in areas like poverty, population and pollution. During the two decades from Stockholm to Rio "Sustainable Development" has come to be accepted as a viable concept to eradicate poverty and improve the quality of human life while living within the carrying capacity of the supporting eco-systems. "Sustainable Development" as defined by the Brundtland Report means "development that meets the needs of the present without compromising the ability of the future generations to meet their won needs". Some of the salient principles of "Sustainable Development", as culled-out from Brundtland Report and other international documents, are Inter-Generational Equity, Use and Conservation of Natural Resources, Environmental Protection, the Precautionary Principle, Polluter Pays principle, Obligation to assist and cooperate, Eradication of Poverty and Financial Assistance to the developing countries. The Precautionary Principle and The Polluter Pays principle are essential features of "Sustainable Development".

The "Precautionary Principle" in the context of the municipal law[15] means :

(i) Environmental measures - by the State Government and the statutory authorities - must anticipate, prevent and attack the causes of environmental degradation.

(ii) Where there are threats of serious and irreversible damage, lack of scientific certainty should not be used as a reason for postponing measures to prevent environmental degradation.

(iii) The "Onus of proof is on the actor or the developer/industrialist to show that his action is environmentally benign.

"The Polluter Pays" principle has been held to be a sound principle by Supreme Court in *Indian Council for Enviro - Legal Action v. Union of India*[16]. The Court ruled that "Once the activity carried on is hazardous[17] or inherently dangerous, the person carrying on such activity is liable to make good the loss caused to any other person by his activity irrespective of the fact whether he took reasonable care while carrying on his activity. The rule is premised upon the very nature of the activity carried on". Consequently the polluting industries are "absolutely liable to compensate for the harm caused by them to villagers in the affected area, to the soil and to the underground water and hence, they are bound to take all necessary measures to remove sludge and other pollutants lying in the affected areas". The "Polluter Pays" principle as interpreted by Supreme Court means that the absolute liability for harm to the environment extends not only to compensate the victims of pollution but also the cost of restoring the environmental degradation. Remediation of the damaged environment is part of the process of "Sustainable Development" and as such polluter is liable to pay the cost to the individual sufferers as well as the cost of reversing the damaged ecology.

The precautionary principle and the polluter pays principle have been

---

15 **Municipal law** is the national, domestic, or internal law of a sovereign state defined in opposition to international law. Municipal law includes not only law at the national level, but law at the state, provincial, territorial, regional or local levels. While, as far as the law of the state is concerned, these may be distinct categories of law, international law is largely uninterested in this distinction and treats them all as one. Similarly, international law makes no distinction between the ordinary law of the state and its constitutional law.

16 J.T. (1996) 2 196

17 **Meaning of Hazardous:** Involving great risk

accepted as part of the law of the land. Article 21[18] of the Constitution of India guarantees protection of life and personal liberty. Article 47 48A and 51A(g) of the Constitutional are as under :

47. Duty of the State to raise the level of nutrition and the standard of living and to improve public health. - The State shall regard the raising of the level of nutrition and the standard of living of its people and the improvement of public health as among its primary duties and in particular, the State shall endeavour to bring about prohibition of the consumption except from medicinal purposes of intoxicating drinks and of drugs which are injurious to health.

48A. Protection and improvement of environment and safeguarding of forests and wild life. - The State shall endeavour to protect and improve the environment and to safeguard the forests and wild life of the country.

51A(g). To protect and improve the natural environment including forests, lakes, rivers and wild life, and to have compassion for living creatures.

Apart from the constitutional mandate to protect and improve the environment there are plenty of post independence legislations on the subject but more relevant enactments for our purpose are : The Water (Prevention and Control of Pollution) Act, 1974 (the Water Act), The Air (Prevention and Control of Pollution) Act, 1981 (the Air Act) and the Environment Protection Act 1986 (the Environment Act). The Water Act provides for the Constitution of the Central Pollution Control Board by the Central Government and the Constitution of the State Pollution Control Boards by various State Governments in the country. The Boards function under the control of the Governments concerned. The Water Act prohibits the use of streams and wells for disposal of polluting matters. Also provides for restrictions on outlets and discharge of effluents without obtaining consent from the Board. Prosecution and penalties have been provided which include sentence of imprisonment. The Air Act provides that the Central Pollution Control Board and the State Pollution Control Boards constituted under the Water Act shall also perform the powers and functions under the Air Act. The main function of the Boards, under the Air Act, is to improve the quality of the air and to prevent, control and abate air pollution in the country.

---

18 Article 21 in The Constitution Of India 1949

  Protection of life and personal liberty: No person shall be deprived of his life or personal liberty except according to procedure established by law

Observation by Supreme Court:

It is no doubt correct that the leather industry in India has become a major foreign exchange earner and at present Tamil Nadu is the leading exporter of finished leather accounting for approximately 80% of the country's export. Though the leather industry is of vital importance to the country as it generates foreign exchange and provides employment avenues it has no right to destroy the ecology[19], degrade the environment and pose as a health hazard. It cannot be permitted to expand or even to continue with the present production unless it tackles by itself the problem of pollution created by the said industry.

Decision by Supreme Court:

Court held that the precautionary principle and the polluter pays principle are part of the environmental law of the country. Our legal system having been founded on the British Common Law[20] the right of a person to pollution free environment is a part of the basic jurisprudence of the land.

Directions by Supreme Court:

Court directed as under:

1. The Central Government shall constitute an authority under Section 3(3)[21] of the Environment (Protection) Act, 1986 and shall confer on the said authority all the powers necessary to deal with the situation

---

19 **Ecology** is the scientific study of interactions among organisms and their environment, such as the interactions organisms have with each other and with their abiotic environment.

20 A **common law** legal system is a system of law characterized by **case law** which is law developed by judges through decisions of courts and similar tribunals. Common law systems also include statutes enacted by legislative bodies, though those statutes typically either codify judicial decisions or fill in areas of the law not covered by case law. In contrast to common law systems, civil law (codified/continental law) systems are founded on a set of legal codes, which are organized laws that attempt to cover exhaustively the various legal domains, and is characterized by an absence of precedent in the judicial application of those codes.

21 **Section 3(3) of the Environment (Protection) Act, 1986:**

Power of Central Government to take measures to protect and improve environment:

(3) The Central Government may, if it considers it necessary or expedient so to do for the purpose of this Act, by order, published in the Official Gazette, constitute an authority or authorities by such name or names as may be specified in the order for the purpose of exercising and performing such of the powers and functions (including the power to issue directions under section 5) of the Central Government under this Act and for taking measures with respect to such of the matters referred to in sub-section (2) as may be mentioned in the order and subject to the supervision and control of the Central Government and the provisions of such order, such authority or authorities may exercise and powers or perform the functions or take the measures so mentioned in the order as if such authority or authorities had been empowered by this Act to exercise those powers or perform those functions or take such measures.

created by the tanneries and other polluting industries in the State of Tamil Nadu. The Authority shall be headed by a retired judge of the High Court and it may have other members - preferably with expertise in the field of pollution control and environment protection - to be appointed by the Central Government. The Central Government shall confer on the said authority the powers to issue directions under Section 5[22] of the Environment Act, 1986.

2. The authority so constituted by the Central Government shall implement the "precautionary principle" and the "polluter pays" principle. The authority shall, with the help of expert opinion and after giving opportunity to the concerned polluters assess the loss to the ecology/ environment in the affected areas and shall also identify the individuals/ families who have suffered because of the pollution and shall assess the compensation to be paid to the said individuals/families. The authority shall further determine the compensation to be recovered from the polluters as cost of reversing the damaged environment. The authority shall lay down just and fair procedure for completing the exercise.

3. The authority shall compute the compensation under two heads namely, for reversing the ecology and for payment to individuals. A statement showing the total amount to be recovered, the names of the polluters from whom the amount is to be recovered, the amount to be recovered from each polluter, the persons to whom the compensation is to be paid and the amount payable to each of them shall be forwarded to the Collector/District Magistrate of the area concerned. The Collector/ District Magistrate shall recover the amount from the polluters, if necessary, as arrears of land revenue. He shall disburse the compensation awarded by the authority to the affected persons/families.

---

22 Section 5 of the Environment (Protection) Act, 1986:

Power to give Directions

Notwithstanding anything contained in any other law but subject to the provisions of this Act, the Central Government may, in the exercise of its powers and performance of its functions under this Act, issue directions in writing to any person, officer or any authority and such person, officer or authority shall be bound to comply with such directions.

Explanation--For the avoidance of doubts, it is hereby declared that the power to issue directions under this section includes the power to direct--

(a) the closure, prohibition or regulation of any industry, operation or process; or

(b) stoppage or regulation of the supply of electricity or water or any other service.

4. The authority shall direct the closure of the industry owned/managed by a polluter in case he evades or refuse to pay the compensation awarded against him. This shall be in addition to the recovery from him as arrears of land revenue.

5. An industry may have set up the necessary pollution control device at present but it shall be liable to pay for the past pollution generated by the said industry which has resulted in the environmental degradation and suffering to the residents of the area.

6. Court imposed pollution fine of Rs. 10,000 each on all the tanneries in the districts of North Arcot Ambedkar, Erode periyar, Dindigul Anna, Trichi and Chengai M.G.R.

7. Court directed the Superintendent of Police and the Collector/District Magistrate/Deputy Commissioner of the district concerned to close all those tanneries with immediate effect who fail to obtain the consent from the Board. Such tanneries shall not be reopened unless the authority permits them to do so. It would be open to the authority to close such tanneries permanently or to direct their relocation.

Curt directed the State of Tamil Nadu to pay Rs. 50,000 towards legal fees and other out of pocket expenses incurred by Mr. M.C. Mehta (Lawyer).

11

Right to life comprehends[1] right to a safe environment[2]

Facts in Nutshell:

Petitioner[3] belongs to a denomination[4] of Christianity, known as 'Knanaya' Christians[5]. Thomas of Cana came to India from Mesopottomia in 344 A.D. and organised the south eastern church of Syrian Christians, as St. Thomas organised the north eastern church in A.D. 52. The followers of Thomas of Cana, came to be known as 'Knanaya' Christians. Some of the Knanaya Christians follow the rites of the Catholic Church, while others follow the Marthomite rites. Members of 'Knanaya' denomination do not marry outside that denomination, it is said -- with a view to preserve the purity of stock. This practice is denounced by petitioner. In his view, a Knanaya Christian should be free to marry anyone, professing the faith of Christianity. To propagate his views in this regard, petitioner sought permission to hold meetings using sound amplifiers. Second respondent -- Sub-Inspector of Police, granted permission, but withdrew the permission later, apprehending that views of petitioner may incite to violence the conservatives in the Church. Petitioner submitted that freedom of speech and expression imply freedom to use amplifying devices.

---

1 **Meaning of Comprehend:**

   1. To take in as a part; include

2 Appellants: **P.A. Jacob Vs.** Respondent: **The Superintendent of Police, Kottayam and Anr.**

   AIR1993Ker1

   Hon'ble Judges/Coram: Chettur Sankaran Nair, Judge

3 **Meaning of Petitioner:** A person who presents a Petition. (**Meaning of Petition:** A formal message requesting something that is submitted to an authority)

4 **Meaning of denomination:**

   A large group of religious congregations united under a common faith and name and organized under a single administrative and legal hierarchy.

5 The **Knanaya**, also known as the **Southists** or **Tekkumbhagar**, are an endogamous group in the Saint Thomas Christian community of Kerala, India. They are differentiated from another part of the community, known in this context as the Northists. Today there are about 300,000 Knanaya in India and elsewhere.

Question before the High Court:

Whether the Constitution guarantees a right to use a sound amplifying device, or whether use of such a device is part of the right to freedom of speech.

Freedom of Speech and Expression:

Freedom of speech and expression are rights cherished by all free societies. That freedom implies not only freedom to express the thought we approve of, but freedom to express the thought, we hate. A debate of ideas is essential in any free society. No one can forbid legitimate efforts to change the mind of society by expression of views, or advocating different persuasions[6] or even by questioning the existing order. J.S. Mill said :

"If we never hear questions, we will forget the answers."

Maintenance of opportunity for free political discussion is thus a cardinal principle of our Constitutional system. History bears witness to this process. Debate, brought in its wake, new thoughts and new ethos. Time has upset many fighting faiths. What was once regarded blasphemy[7], became the truth of another generation.

Free speech does not protect sedition[8], libel[9] or obscenity[10]. It does not sanction intrusion into rights of others. To be let alone, is as much a freedom, as the freedom to be heard. Right to silence or solitude[11],

---

6   **Meaning of Persuasions:**

   A strongly held opinion; a conviction

7   **Meaning of blasphemy:**

   a. A contemptuous or profane act, utterance, or writing concerning God or a sacred entity.

   b. The act of claiming for oneself the attributes and rights of God

8   **Meaning of Sedition:**

   1. Conduct or language inciting rebellion against the authority of a state.

   2. Insurrection; rebellion

9   **Meaning of Libel:**

   a. A false publication, as in writing, print, signs, or pictures, that damages a person's reputation.

   b. The act of presenting such material to the public

10   **Meaning of Obscenity:**

   1. The state or quality of being obscene.

   2. Indecency, lewdness, or offensiveness in behavior, expression, or appearance

11   **Meaning of Solitude:**

is as much a right, as right to expression is. What is negatively the right to silence, is positively freedom from injury by noise. Freedom or right, is not an exclusive matter between the State and a citizen. One man's freedom, may destroy another man's freedom. A community of rights, not always synchronizing[12] with each other, have to be harmonised, if any freedom is to be real.

The right to speech implies, the right to silence. It implies freedom, not to listen, and not to be forced to listen. The right comprehends freedom to be free from what one desires to be free from. Justice Douglas articulated this freedom as:

".......right to be let alone is the beginning of all freedoms. When we force people to listen to another's ideas, we give the propagandist[13] a powerful weapon. One man's lyric may be another's vulgarity[14]"

A person can decline to read a publication, or switch off a radio or television set. But, he cannot prevent the sound from a loud speaker reaching him. He could be forced to hear what, he wishes not, to hear. That will be an invasion of his right to be let alone, to hear what he wants to hear, or not to hear, what he does not wish to hear. One may put his mind or hearing to his own uses, but not that of another. No one has a right to trespass on the mind or ear of another and commit auricular[15] or visual aggression. Limits, must be drawn for liberties, lest they turn into licence, and the antithesis[16] of liberty in its true sense.

---

1. The state or quality of being alone or remote from others.

2. A lonely or secluded place

12 **Meaning of synchronizing:**

1. To occur at the same time; be simultaneous.

2. To operate in unison

13 **Meaning of propagandist:** A person who disseminates messages calculated to assist some cause or some government

14 **Meaning of vulgarity:**

1. The quality or condition of being vulgar.

2. Something, such as an act or expression, that offends good taste or propriety

15 **Meaning of auricular:**

1. of or relating to the sense of hearing or the organs of hearing.

2. Perceived by or spoken into the ear

16 **Meaning of antithesis:**

1. the exact opposite

Decision by High Court:

Court held that the sound levels generally caused by loud speakers transgress[17] safe limits by a wide margin. Loud speakers have become part of political, social, religious and cultural life of this country. To allow advocates of various persuasions to commit unlimited aural aggression on unwilling listeners, would be to allow them to subjugate[18] the right of life of unwilling listeners, to their aggressions. Compulsory exposure of unwilling persons to dangerous and disastrous levels of noise, would amount to a clear infringement of their constitutional guarantee of right to life under Article 21[19] of the Constitution. Right to life, comprehends right to a safe environment, including safe air quality, safe from noise.

Court denied the permission to petitioner to use a loud speaker on the ground that holding of meetings with loud speakers would lead to a law and order situation, on account of the displeasure that it may cause to another group. If obstruction is offered unlawfully or unreasonably, the responsibility of Police is to remove it, instead of stopping someone from doing what he may legitimately do. Court further observed that while petitioner has no fundamental right[20] to use a loud speaker, he will be free to avail of the amenity of using a loud speaker in a reasonable manner. Second respondent[21] Sub-Inspector of Police, was directed by court to permit petitioner to hold meetings with the use of loud speakers

---

2. contrast or opposition

17 **Meaning of Transgress:**

   To go beyond or over (a limit or boundary); exceed or overstep

18 **Meaning of Subjugate:**

   1. To bring under control; conquer.

   2. To make subservient; enslave.

19 **Article 21 in The Constitution Of India 1949**

   21. Protection of life and personal liberty No person shall be deprived of his life or personal liberty except according to procedure established by law

20 **Meaning of Fundamental Rights:** The Fundamental Rights are defined as basic human freedoms which every Indian citizen has the right to enjoy for a proper and harmonious development of personality. These rights universally apply to all citizens, irrespective of race, place of birth, religion, caste, creed, colour or gender. Aliens (persons who are not citizens) are also considered in matters like equality before law. They are enforceable by the courts, subject to certain restrictions.

21 **Meaning of Respondent:** A **respondent** is a person who is called upon to issue a response to a communication made by another. In legal usage, this specifically refers to the defendant in a legal proceeding commenced by a petition, or to an appellee, or the opposing party, in an appeal of a decision by an initial fact-finder.

of a box type. But, the output from the loud speaker, shall not exceed the range, necessary to reach a willing audience, confined in a reasonable area. If it exceeds such limits, Police will be free to stop the use of loud speakers.

12

Preservation of ecology[1]

Facts in Nutshell:

Petition[2] by Om Prakash Bhatt and others was filed in High Court basically to bring to the notice of Court as the residents of the hills, particularly of Garhwal, and more particularly of the district of Chamoli[3], fell threatened by the invasion[4] of State organizations and the erosion of the sanctity[5] and the peace and tranquillity[6] of the Bugiyal. Bugiyal, in Garhwal basically means meadows[7] and pasture land[8] which exists above a certain altitude[9] in the mountains no different than the alpine meadows[10] of Switzerland

---

1   Appellants: **Om Prakash Bhatt and others Vs.** Respondent: **State of U.P. and others**

   AIR1997All259

   Hon'ble Judges/Coram: Ravi S. Dhavan and A.B. Srivastava, JJ.

2   **Meaning of Petition:** A formal message requesting something that is submitted to an authority

3   **Chamoli district** is the second largest district of Uttarakhand state of India. It is bounded by the Tibet region to the north, and by the Uttarakhand districts of Pithoragarh and Bageshwar to the east, Almora to the south, Garhwal to the southwest, Rudraprayag to the west, and Uttarkashi to the northwest. The administrative headquarters of the district is Gopeshwar

4   **Meaning of Invasion:**

   1. The act of invading, especially the entrance of an armed force into a territory to conquer.

   2. A large-scale onset of something injurious or harmful, such as a disease.

5   **Meaning of Sanctity:**

   1. Holiness of life or disposition; saintliness.

   2. The quality or condition of being considered sacred; inviolability.

   3. Something considered sacred.

6   **Meaning of tranquility:** The quality or state of being tranquil; serenity.

7   **Meaning of Meadow:** A tract of grassland, either in its natural state or used as pasture or for growing hay

8   **Meaning of Pasture Land:** Land suitable for grazing.

9   **Meaning of Altitude:**

   1. The height of a thing above a reference level, especially above sea level or above the earth's surface. See Synonyms at elevation.

   2. A high location or area.

10 Alpine Meadows encompasses approximately five square miles and serves a permanent

and Austria. The complaint to the Court was that these areas are pasture lands to the sheep and the shepherd[11]. The submission was that the Bugiyal is basically an ecosystem[12] in itself and this delicate balance between ecology and environment has to be understood and respected. The complaint was that the Garhwal Mandal Vikas Nigam (hereinafter, in short, the Nigam) had put up pre-fabricated lodging houses as a hotel for tourist on the slopes of a Bugiyal which is below the peak of the temple of Tungnath[13]. Tungnath incidentally, is accepted and reported even by the State administration as one of the highest temples in India. The next issue presented was that indiscriminate import of plastic and non bio-degradable[14] material was playing havoc[15] with the environment of the hills as each seasons plastic collects on the slopes of the hills to be covered by autumn leaves of one season and this exercise is repeated year by year with plastic being sandwiched between leaves preventing rain water from seeping and percolating into the hill slopes and causing another ecological disbalance leading to disappearance of little streams and water resources on which the hill people rely upon. Deposit of plastic materials also kills the green life on the mountains.

The third aspect is about the tourist and trekking[16] pilgrimage routes, where the tourist, the pilgrim and the trekker devoid of all civic sense with no respect of the environment throw non bio-degradable material on the slopes of the hills and the mountain routes were being littered[17]

---

population of approximately 500 residents. This includes four commercial centers, a 30-unit apartment complex, 462 single-family homes, and 130 condominiums

11 **Meaning of Shepherd:**

   1. One who herds, guards, and tends sheep.

   2. One who cares for and guides a group of people, as a minister or teacher

12 **Meaning of Ecosystem:** An ecological community together with its environment, functioning as a unit.

13 **Tungnath** is the highest Shiva temple in the world and is one of the five and the highest Panch Kedar temples located in the mountain range of Tunganath in Rudraprayag district, in the Indian state of Uttarakhand.

14 **Meaning of Biodegradable:** Capable of being decomposed by biological agents, especially bacteria

15 **Meaning of Havoc:**

   1. Widespread destruction; devastation.

   2. Disorder or chaos

16 **Meaning of Trekking:**

   A **trek** is a long, adventurous journey undertaken on foot in areas where common means of transport are generally not available. Trekking should not be confused with mountaineering

17 **Meaning of Litter:**

with indiscriminate evidence of deliberately created garbage. Court's attention was drawn to the garbage strewn on the slopes of the hills right up to the glacier of Gomukh[18] and of man made deposits of synthetic and non bio-degradable materials at the source of the river Ganga at above 14,000 feet. Environmentalists have voiced concern on the receding glacier at Gomukh, the source of the river Ganga. A leading news agency reported that the glacier at Gomukh was drying up.

Polluter Pays Principle:

The **polluter pays principle** has been held to be a sound principle by Supreme Court in *Indian Council for Enviro-Legal Action v. Union of India[19]*. The Court held that "Once the activity carried on is hazardous [20]or inherently dangerous, the person carrying on such activity is liable to make good the loss caused to party (other person) by his activity irrespective of the fact whether he took reasonable care while carrying on his activity". The "Polluter Pays" Principle as interpreted by Court means that the absolute liability for harm to the environment extends not only to compensate the victims of pollution but also the cost of restoring the environmental degradation. Remediation of the damaged environment is part of the process of "Sustainable Development" and as such polluter is liable to pay the cost to the individual sufferers as well as the cost of reversing the damaged ecology.

Decision by High Court:

Court held that the Bugiyal belongs to the people. It is an ecosystem in itself. Nature has tailored it. It is not for man to erode the sanctity of this area. It must be resumed to nature to provide for whom it was meant; the sheep, the shepherd, the wild flowers, the micro-organism and the plant and insect life below the turf and in the shrubs at that altitude. Clearly, putting a tourist lodging house on a Bugiyal was a mistake. Court further held that the State administration cannot run away from its obligation

---

a. A disorderly accumulation of objects; a pile.

b. Carelessly discarded refuse, such as wastepaper

18 **Gomukh**, the terminus or snout of the Gangotri Glacier, from where Bhagirathi River originates, is one of the primary sources of the Ganges River. The place is situated at a height of 13,200 ft. It is one of the largest in the Himalayas with an estimated volume of over 27 cubic kilometers.

19 AIR 1996 SC 1446

20 **Meaning of Hazardous:**

   1. Marked by danger; perilous.

   2. Depending on chance; risky

set in the Constitution of India, Part IVA[21], under Article 51A[22] for strict monitoring and protecting the environment.

Directions by High Court:

(i) Between Gangotri [23]and Bhojwasa public conveniences i.e. toilet facilities will be spread at periodic intervals of four kilometers.

(ii) Every kilometre of the Gangotri Gomukh-Tapovan route shall have containers, bins or receptables to receive throw away wastes of packaging. Each of the receptables or bins shall be marked in Hindi and English to signify biogradable and non-biogradable metal and glass. Each receptable with a distinctive but separate colour to identify the category of garbage, for example, may carry the message: **Save Himalayan Ecology, Do Not Litter/Insert Glass Bottles Here**.

(iii) The meadows and the pasture lands essentially that is what a Bugiyal is at the higher reaches of the mountains of Garhwal and Kumaon are only for the sheep and shepherd. This area should not be encroached upon.

---

21 The *Directive Principles of State Policy* are guidelines for the framing of laws by the government. These provisions, set out in Part IV of the Constitution, are not enforceable by the courts, but the principles on which they are based are fundamental guidelines for governance that the State is expected to apply in framing and passing laws.

22 **Article 51A in The Constitution Of India 1949**

   51A. Fundamental duties: It shall be the duty of every citizen of India (a) to abide by the Constitution and respect its ideals and institutions, the national Flag and the National Anthem;

   (b) to cherish and follow the noble ideals which inspired our national struggle for freedom;

   (c) to uphold and protect the sovereignty, unity and integrity of India;

   (d) to defend the country and render national service when called upon to do so;

   (e) to promote harmony and the spirit of common brotherhood amongst all the people of India transcending religious, linguistic and regional or sectional diversities; to renounce practices derogatory to the dignity of women;

   (f) to value and preserve the rich heritage of our composite culture;

   (g) to protect and improve the natural environment including forests, lakes, rivers and wild life, and to have compassion for living creatures;

   (h) to develop the scientific temper, humanism and the spirit of inquiry and reform;

   (i) to safeguard public property and to abjure violence;

   (j) to strive towards excellence in all spheres of individual and collective activity so that the nation constantly rises to higher levels of endeavour and achievement

23 **Gangotri** is a town and a *Nagar Panchayat* (municipality) in Uttarkashi district in the state ofUttarakhand, India. It is a Hindu pilgrim town on the banks of the river Bhagirathi and origin of River Ganges. It is on the Greater Himalayan Range, at a height of 3,100m.

13

Right to live includes the right of enjoyment of pollution free water and air[1]

Facts in Nutshell:

Court has to decide the effect of unplanned stone crushing activities being carried out in the State of Karnataka, upon the health of the people of the State. In their writ petition[2], the petitioners[3] had prayed for quashing[4] of the consent by Karnataka State Pollution Control Board (hereinafter called the 'Board') to respondents for carrying on the stone crushing operation. The petitioners who were agriculturists have alleged that with the carrying on of the proposed stone crushing business their crops would be adversely affected and that their health and the health of others in the area would be exposed to diseases on account of the pollution caused by the stone crushers. They apprehend that with the commissioning of the stone crushing unit, the water and air in the area would be polluted.

---

1 Appellants: **Obayya Pujary and Others Vs.** Respondent: **The Member Secretary, Karnataka State Pollution Control Board, Bangalore and Others**

   AIR1999Kant157

   Hon'ble Judges/Coram: R.P. Sethi, C.J. and V. Gopala Gowda, Judge

2 **Meaning of Writ Petition:** Under the Indian legal system, jurisdiction to issue 'prerogative writs' is given to the Supreme Court, and to the High Courts of Judicature of all Indian states. Parts of the law relating to writs are set forth in the Constitution of India. The Supreme Court, the highest in the country, may issue writs under Article 32 of the Constitution for enforcement of Fundamental Rights and under Articles 139 for enforcement of rights other than Fundamental Rights, while High Courts, the superior courts of the States, may issue writs under Articles 226. 'Writ' is eminently designed by the makers of the Constitution, and in the same way it is developed very widely and efficiently by the courts in India. The Constitution broadly provides for five kinds of "prerogative" writs, namely, Habeas Corpus, Certiorari, Mandamus, Quo Warranto and Prohibition

3 **Meaning of Petitioner:** A person who presents a Petition. (**Meaning of Petition:** A formal message requesting something that is submitted to an authority)

4 **Meaning of Quash:** To set aside or annul, especially by judicial action.

Air Pollution:

The air we breathe is a mixture of nitrogen and oxygen with minor constituents like carbon dioxide and trap gases. Pollutants are substances which are not normally present in the air. Pollutants in the form of dust, smoke, industrial and automobile exhaust, gaseous and particulate matters, though not normally expected to be present, yet are found in the air. Nature and amount of such pollutants varies from place to place depending upon population, vehicular density and location of industrial units etc. Lungs are the major organs affected by the air pollution. The spectrum of functional and pathological reactions of the lungs to various exposures is wide. Chronic bronchitis[5] and airways obstruction is the result of long term exposure to air pollution. Organic matters including dust can cause the allergic reactions producing allergic alveolitis[6]. Inorganic dust may get deposited in the lungs and produce fibrosis. Exposure to dust may lower the lung defences and clearing mechanism, resulting in infections particularly tuberculosis[7]. Such occupational exposures may also lead to causing lung cancer as well. Such hazardous effects on health are likely to be caused on account of the air pollution which is caused due to stone crushing. By stone crushing a lot of thick dust is generated polluting the environment, visible dust contains particles more than 500 (sic) in diameter which settle down in the nose and pharynx[8]. Similar particles of 5-10 (sic) size remains suspended in air and are inhaled deeper. Such particles are deposited in the tracheobronchial tree and lung percenchyma which is likely to reduce fibrosis[9].

---

5   Chronic obstructive pulmonary disease (COPD), also known as chronic obstructive lung disease (COLD), andchronic obstructive airway disease (COAD), among others, is a type of obstructive lung disease characterized by chronically poor airflow. It typically worsens over time. The main symptoms include shortness of breath, cough, and sputum production

6   **Alveolitis** can refer to two inflammatory conditions. It can refer to inflammation of the alveoli in the lungs, or the dental alveolus in the jaw.

7   **Tuberculosis, MTB,** or **TB** (short for tubercle bacillus), in the past also called **phthisis, phthisis pulmonalis,** orconsumption, is a common, and in many cases fatal, infectious disease caused by various strains of mycobacteria, usually Mycobacterium tuberculosis. Tuberculosis typically attacks the lungs, but can also affect other parts of the body. It is spread through the air when people who have an active TB infection cough, sneeze, or otherwise transmit respiratory fluids through the air.

8   The **pharynx** (plural: *pharynges*) is an organ found in vertebrates and invertebrates, though the structure is not universally the same across the species. In humans the pharynx is part of the digestive system and also of the conducting zone of the respiratory system.

9   **Fibrosis** is the formation of excess fibrous connective tissue in an organ or tissue in a reparative or reactive process. This can be a reactive, benign, or pathological state. In response to injury this is called scarring and if fibrosis arises from a single cell line this is called a fibroma. Physiologically this acts to deposit connective tissue, which can obliterate the architecture and function of the

The above effects of air pollution caused due to stone crushing were noticed by high power committee appointed by the Environment Department, Government of Haryana. The committee had investigated[10] the health problems due to pollution caused by stone crushers scattered in various parts of Haryana. They examined the health status of 397 subjects working at the sites as well as the residents of the nearby areas and several stone crushers. They found significantly high prevalence of respiratory (46.60%) and gastrointestinal (30.20%) problems.

Right to Life and Environment:

The right to 'life' is the most fundamental right[11] as enshrined in Article 21[12] of the Constitution of India. Such right includes all attributes of the life. In *Kharak Singh v State of Uttar Pradesh and Others*[13] , the Supreme Court acknowledged that the term 'life' meant something more than mere animal existence. The inhibition against its deprivation extended to all those limbs and faculties by which the life is enjoyed. It equally prohibited the mutilation[14] of the body by the amputation[15] of an arm or leg, of putting out of an eye, or the destruction of any other organ by the body through which the soul communicates with the outer world. It postulates to be free from restrictions on the enjoyment of a decent, respectable and healthy life. Right of life under Article 21 of the Constitution is a right of a person to be free from restrictions or encroachment, whether imposed directly or indirectly brought about by calculated measures. In

---

underlying organ or tissue. Fibrosis can be used to describe the pathological state of excess deposition of fibrous tissue, as well as the process of connective tissue deposition in healing.

10 **Meaning of Investigated:** To observe or inquire into in detail; examine systematically

11 **Meaning of Fundamental Rights:** The Fundamental Rights are defined as basic human freedoms which every Indian citizen has the right to enjoy for a proper and harmonious development of personality. These rights universally apply to all citizens, irrespective of race, place of birth, religion, caste, creed, colour or gender. Aliens (persons who are not citizens) are also considered in matters like equality before law. They are enforceable by the courts, subject to certain restrictions

12 **Article 21 in The Constitution Of India 1949**

    Protection of life and personal liberty: No person shall be deprived of his life or personal liberty except according to procedure established by law

13 1963 AIR 1295, 1964 SCR (1) 332

14 **Mutilation** or **maiming** is an act of physical injury that degrades the appearance or function of any living body, sometimes causing death.

15 **Amputation** is the removal of a body extremity by trauma, prolonged constriction, or surgery. As a surgical measure, it is used to control pain or a disease process in the affected limb, such as malignancy or gangrene. In some cases, it is carried out on individuals as a preventative surgery for such problems.

Bandhua Mukti Morcha v Union of India and Others[16], it was held that it is a fundamental right of everybody to live with dignity[17]. Such right would include all those rights which ensure a person's life meaningful, complete and worth living. Right to life would also include right to live in peace, to sleep in peace, enjoy health free from pollution. In *Subhash Kumar v State of Bihar[18]*, the Apex Court held that enjoyment of pollution free atmosphere was included in the right to life under Article 21. The Court observed:-

"Right to live is a fundamental right under Article 21 of the Constitution and it includes the right of enjoyment of pollution free water and air for full enjoyment of life. If anything endangers or impairs that quality of life in derogation of laws, a citizen has right to have recourse to Article 32[19] of the Constitution for removing the pollution of water or air which may be determined to the quality of life".

However, such a right is not an absolute right and is obviously subject to reasonable restrictions. It is also controlled and regulated by needs of the society. It has to be kept in mind that rapid growth of the economy and the industrialisation is also the need of the mankind and attribute of and requirement of the decent, respectful and dignified life. While protecting the environment the industrial development cannot be completely ignored. The Supreme Court in *Rural Litigation and Entitlement Kendra and Others v State of Uttar Pradesh and Others[20]*, had observed:--

---

16 1984 AIR 802, 1984 SCR (2) 67

17 **Dignity** is a term used in moral, ethical, legal, and political discussions to signify that a being has an innate right to be valued and receive ethical treatment. It is an extension of the Enlightenment-era concepts of inherent, inalienable rights.

18 1991 AIR sc 420, 1991 SCR (1) 5

19 **Article 32 in The Constitution Of India 1949**

32. Remedies for enforcement of rights conferred by this Part

(1) The right to move the Supreme Court by appropriate proceedings for the enforcement of the rights conferred by this Part is guaranteed

(2) The Supreme Court shall have power to issue directions or orders or writs, including writs in the nature of habeas corpus, mandamus, prohibition, quo warranto and certiorari, whichever may be appropriate, for the enforcement of any of the rights conferred by this Part

(3) Without prejudice to the powers conferred on the Supreme Court by clause (1) and (2), Parliament may by law empower any other court to exercise within the local limits of its jurisdiction all or any of the powers exercisable by the Supreme Court under clause (2)

(4) The right guaranteed by this article shall not be suspended except as otherwise provided for by this Constitution

20 1989 AIR 594, 1989 SCC Supl. (1) 537

"Consciousness[21] for environmental protection is of recent origin. The United Nations Conference on World Environment held in Stockholm in June 1972 and the follow-up action thereafter is spreading the awareness. Over thousands of years men had been successfully exploiting the ecological system for his sustenance but with the growth of population the demand for land has increased and forest growth has decreased and forests are being cut down and man has started encroaching upon Nature and its assets. Scientific developments have made it possible and convenient for man to approach the places which were hitherto beyond his ken. The consequences of such interference with ecology and environment have now come to be realised ".

Again in *Sachidanand Pandey and Another v State of West Bengal and Others[22]*, the Supreme Court had held:--

"Today society's interaction with nature is so extensive that the environmental question has assumed proportions affecting all humanity. Industrialisation, urbanisation, explosion of population, over-exploitation of resources, depletion of traditional sources of energy and raw materials and the search for new sources of energy and raw materials, the disruption of natural ecological balances, the destruction of a multitude of animal and plant species for economic reasons and sometimes for no good reason at all are factors which have contributed to environmental deterioration. While the scientific and technological progress of man has invested him with immense power over nature, it has also resulted in the unthinking use of the power, encroaching endlessly on nature. If man is able to transform deserts into oasis he is also leaving behind deserts in the place of oasis. In the last century, a great German materialist philosopher warned mankind: 'Let us not, however, flatter ourselves over much on account of our human victories over nature. For each of such victory nature takes its revenge on us. Each victory, it is true, in the first place brings about the results we expected, but in the second and third places it has quite different unforeseen effects which only too often cancel the first'. Ecologists are of the opinion that the most important ecological and social problem is the widespread disappearance all over the world of certain species of living organisms, Biologists forecast the extinction of animal and plant species on a scale that is incomparably greater than their extinction over the course of millions of years. It is said

---

21 **Consciousness** is the quality or state of self-awareness, or, of being aware of an external object or something within oneself.

22 1987 AIR 1109, 1987 SCR (2) 223

that over half of the species which became extinct over the last 2,000 years did so after 1900. The International Association for the Protection of Nature and Natural Resources calculates that now, on average, one species or sub-species is lost every year. It is said that approximately 1,000 bird and animal species are facing extinction at present. So it is that the environmental question has become urgent and it has to be properly understood and squarely met by man. Nature and history, it has been said, are two component parts of the environment in which we live, move and prove ourselves".

The Supreme Court in *M.C. Mehta and Another v Union of India and Others*[23], has ruled that enterprise which has engaged in a hazardous or inherently dangerous industry which poses a potential threat to the health and safety of persons working in the industrial unit and residing in the surrounding areas owes an absolute obligation to the community to ensure that no harm results to any one on account of such hazardous or inherently dangerous nature of the activity. A person engaged in such industrial activity is under an obligation to conduct his commercial activities with the highest standards of safety. If the enterprise is permitted to carry on any hazardous or inherently dangerous activity for profit, the law must presume that such permission is conditional on the enterprise absorbing the cost of any accident arising on account of such activity as an appropriate item of its overheads. In case of loss on account of such activity the enterprise is even liable to indemnify and compensate the sufferer. No person, therefore, can claim to have a right of carrying on any commercial activity which admittedly affects the health of others. The State, under these circumstances is under a constitutional obligation to provide safeguards for protecting the life and health of the citizens. There is no absolute right vesting in any citizen to carry on commercial activities of trade or ovation without limitation. The experts on the subject are of the opinion that the theory which governs our environmental laws, is what may be called a 'Policing Society Theory' envisaging the Legislature and the administration would perform their task acting as vigilant policemen entrusted to detect crimes by bringing the culprits to the Court. Failure on the part of the Executive or the Legislature to perform their constitutional obligation would cast a duty upon the judiciary to react and come to the rescue of the people by providing remedial measures, issuance of appropriate direction protecting the environment for the safety of life, the health and property of the citizens.

---

23 AIR 1987 SC 1086

Decision by High Court:

Court held that it is not disputed that in the State of Karnataka, about 666 industries were involved in the business of crushing of the stones and allied matters. It was also not disputed that mushrooming of such industries is on the rise which is not effectively controlled by the State Executive. Such industries are scattered all over and not located within specified places. The pollution caused on account of the crushing of the stones can also not be disputed. The consequential effects of the dust, smoke and gases emitted from the conduct of the business are surely to affect the lungs and other major organs of the people involved in the business and living in the surrounding areas. Besides human beings, the animals and the vegetation including crops are likely to be affected unless protected. Court held that it was therefore, the duty of the **respondent**[24]-**State** to take measures and effective steps for regulating the conduct of the business (Stone Crushing) as has been done in many other States.

Directions by High Court to Respondent (State) :

(1) That the State shall immediately formulate a policy regulating the carrying on of the business related to the **crushing of stones** by prescribing reasonable conditions including guidelines and licences and their periodical renewals.

(2) Each stone crusher unit shall be located in a minimum area of one acre owned by the stone crusher, State or the Panchayat.

(3) All stone crushers shall be granted licences initially for a period of one year to be renewed every year on payment of such licence fee as may be prescribed.

(4) The licensing authority shall be under a legal obligation to inspect or get the inspection done of each stone crusher at least once a year.

(5) That out of the fee prescribed for the issuance of licence, a fund shall be created to be controlled and managed by the State Government which shall provide financial assistance including financial benefits for the protection of life, health, safety and education of the workmen employed in stone crusher units including their dependants.

---

24 **Meaning of Respondent:** A **respondent** is a person who is called upon to issue a response to a communication made by another. In legal usage, this specifically refers to the defendant in a legal proceeding commenced by a petition, or to an appellee, or the opposing party, in an appeal of a decision by an initial fact-finder

14

Human life is far more important than vehicular traffic[1]

Facts in Nutshell:

Shri Murali Purushothaman who was practicing in the High Court of Kerala filed petition[2] for espousing[3] a public cause of great moment. It is an undeniable reality that the air on and around most of the public roads in Kerala is saturated with carbon monoxide[4] emitted from fuel propelled automobiles. Petitioner has focussed attention on the consequences of air pollution created through uncontrolled and unmitigated automobile spitting and hence prayed for appropriate directions to be issued to the officials concerned for enforcing the statutory measures to reduce the gravity of the problem.

According to the petitioner, the gaseous pollutants emitted by vehicles plying through the streets of Kerala are highly harmful and hazardous to living creatures, particularly human-beings. Petitioner contended that inhalation of such pollutants leads to diseases like cancer and tuberculosis and points out that statutory[5] provision for reducing the density of such hazardous substances emitted by automobiles have not been implemented by the authorities. **Automobiles** can be ranked as one

---

1   Appellants: **Murali Purushothaman Vs.** Respondent: **Union of India (UOI) and Ors.**

AIR1993Ker297, ILR1993(2)Kerala728

Hon'ble Judges/Coram: K.T. Thomas, Judge

2   **Meaning of Petition:** A formal message requesting something that is submitted to an authority

3   **Meaning of Espousing:** To give one's loyalty or support to (a cause, for example)

4   **Carbon monoxide** (CO) is a colorless, odorless, and tasteless gas that is slightly less dense than air. It is toxic to humans and animals when encountered in higher concentrations, although it is also produced in normal animal metabolism in low quantities, and is thought to have some normal biological functions. In the atmosphere, it is spatially variable and short lived, having a role in the formation of ground-level ozone

5   **Meaning of Statutory:**

1. Of or relating to a statute.

2. Enacted, regulated, or authorized by statute

of the chief sources of air pollution. Vehicles pump out billows of carbon monoxide, hydrocarbons, and nitrogen oxides into the air by burning gasoline[6]. Problem of air pollution through automobiles plying on the roads in Kerala has been gradually snowballing into a dimension of threat to life.

Position in United States of America:

In United States, Environmental Protection Agency (EPA) was formed which has set some standards for restricting the amount of pollution produced by new vehicles. The Federal Clean Air Amendments Act of 1970 was passed requiring reduction of the carbon monoxide emission. In 1976 United States achieved reduction in carbon monoxide saturation in the air by a substantial degree. Automakers were compelled to install devices called "Catalytic Converters"[7] on the exhaust system of new cars for converting gases to harmless carbon dioxide and water. Later European automakers also adopted Catalytic Converters and fitted them with automobiles. But unfortunately, the progress achieved in India remained by and large poor.

Central Motor Vehicles Rules, 1989 and Air Pollution Act, 1981

Rules have been incorporated in the Central Motor Vehicles Rules, 1989 (for short 'the Rules') taking cue from Section 20[8] of Air (Prevention and Control of Pollution) Act, 1981 (for short Air Pollution Act). Rule 115 of the Rules provides for fixation of a standard for emission of smoke, vapour etc., from motor vehicles and directs that "every motor vehicle shall be manufactured and maintained in such condition and shall be so driven that smoke, visible vapour, grit, sparks, ashes, cinders or oily substance do not emit therefrom". Rule 116 of the Rules provides for adoption of tests

---

6   **Gasoline** is a transparent, petroleum-derived liquid that is used primarily as a fuel in internal combustion engines. It consists mostly of organic compounds obtained by the fractional distillation of petroleum, enhanced with a variety of additives

7   A **catalytic converter** is a vehicle emissions control device that converts toxic pollutants in exhaust gas to less toxic pollutants by catalyzing a redox reaction (oxidation or reduction)

8   **Section 20 of Air (Prevention and Control of Pollution) Act, 1981:**

     Power to give instructions for ensuring standards for emission from automobiles

     With a view to ensuring that the standards for emission of air pollutants from automobiles laid down by the State Board tinder clause (g) of sub-section (1) of section 17 are complied with, the State Government shall, in consultation with the State Board, give such instructions as may be deemed necessary to the concerned authority in charge of registration of motor vehicles under the Motor Vehicles Act, 1939 (Act 4 of 1939), and such authority shall, notwithstanding anything contained in that Act or the rules made thereunder be bound to comply with such instructions

for smoke as well as carbon monoxide level emitted from motor vehicles. The Rule also empowers officers not below the rank of Sub-Inspector of Police or Inspectors of motor vehicles to take action against drivers of those vehicles which emit smoke and/or other substances in excess of the emission limit.

Under Section 20 of the Air Pollution Act, 1981 State Government is under an obligation to give such instructions to the authorities in charge of registration of motor vehicles as are necessary to ensure compliance with the standards fixed by State Pollution Control Board regarding emission of air pollutants from automobiles. Rule 116 of the Rules deals with other duties of State Government in that regard. It reads thus:

116. Test for smoke emission level and carbon monoxide level for motor vehicles.

(1) Any officer not below the rank of a Sub-Inspector of Police or an Inspector of motor vehicles, who has reason to believe that a motor vehicles is, by virtue of the smoke emitted from it, or other pollutants like carbon monoxide emitted from it, is likely to cause environmental pollution endangering the health or safety of any other user of the road or the public, may direct the driver or any person in charge of the vehicle to submit the vehicle for undergoing a test to measure the standard of black smoke or the standard of any of the other pollutants.

(2) The driver or any person incharge of the vehicle shall, upon demand by any officer referred to in Sub-rule (1) submit the vehicle for testing for the purpose of measuring the standard of smoke or the levels of other pollutants or both.

(3) The measurement of standard of smoke shall be done with a smoke meter of a type approved by the State Government and the measurement of other pollutants like carbon monoxide, shall be done with instruments of a type approved by the State Government.

Decision by High Court:

Human life is far more important than vehicular traffic. The pristine adage that "Rules are for men and not men are for rules" assume contemporary relevance particularly in the area of environmental cleanliness. No authority, not even the State can be permitted to bide time without enforcing whatever provision is available and without exercising whatever power is commendable to protect human life.

Direction by High Court:

The State Government of Kerala shall provide, at least, one smoke meter and gas analyser (or any other approved instrument to measure carbon monoxide and other pollutants emitted by automobiles) each at all the major District Centres (Kozhikode, Palakkad, Thrissur, Ernakulam, Kottayam, Alapuzha, Kollam and Thiruvananthapuram).

The State Government shall expedite steps to provide such equipment at other places also as early as possible.

The State Government shall issue such instructions as are necessary to all authorities in charge of registration of motor vehicles to comply with the legislative mandate contained in Section 20 of the Air Pollution Act, 1981.

15

Right to religion guaranteed under the Constitution is subject to public order, morality and health[1]

Facts in Nutshell:

The writ[2] application was filed by Moulana Mufti Syed Md. Noorur Rehman Barkati, Imam and Khatib. Tipu Sultan; Shahi Masjid, Dharamtala and Chairman Gharib Nawaz Educational and Charitable Society, Calcutta and eight others for a declaration that Rule 3 of the Environmental (Protection) Rules, 1986 vis a vis[3] Schedule III[4] of the said Rule do not

---

1   Appellants: **Moulana Mufti Syed Md. Noorur Rehman Barkati and Ors. Vs.** Respondent: **State of West Bengal and Ors.**

    AIR1999Cal15

    Hon'ble Judges/Coram: Bhagabati Prosad Banerjee and Ronojit Kumar Mitra, JJ.

2   **Meaning of Writ:** A Written order issued by a court, commanding the party to whom it is addressed to perform or cease performing a specified act

3   **Meaning of vis a vis:** In relation to; with regard to

4   **Schedule III of the Environmental (Protection) Rules, 1986**

    3. Standards for emissions or discharge of environmental pollutants

    (1) For the purpose of protecting and improving the quality of the environment and preventing and abating environmental pollution, the standards for emission or discharge of environmental pollutants from the industries, operations or processes shall be as specified in [2][Schedule I to IV].

    (2) Notwithstanding anything contained in sub-rule (1),the Central Board or a State Board may specify more stringent standards from those provided in [3][Schedule I to IV] in respect of any specific industry, operation or process depending upon the quality of the recipient system and after recording reasons therefore in writing.

    [4](3) The standards for emission or discharge of environmental pollutants specified under sub-rule (1) or sub-rule (2) shall be complied with by an industry, operation or process within a period of one year of being so specified.

    [5][(3A)

    (i) Notwithstanding anything contained in sub-rules (1) and (2), on and from the 1st day of January, 1994, emission or discharge of environmental pollutants from the [6][industries, operations or processes other than those industries, operations or processes for which standards have been specified in Schedule-I] shall not exceed the relevant parameters and standards specified in schedule VI.

    Provided that the State Boards may specify more stringent standards for the relevant parameters

apply in case of Mosques more particularly at the time of call of Azan from the Mosques and for the further declaration that Schedule III of the Environmental (Protection) Rules, 1986 was ultra vires[5] Articles 14[6] and 25[7] of the Constitution. The petitioners case was that Namaz is the second

---

with respect to specific industry or locations after recording reasons therefore in writing;

(ii) The State Board shall while enforcing the standards specified in Schedule VI follow the guidelines specified in Annexure I and II in that Schedule].

[7][(3B)] The combined effect of emission or discharge of environmental pollutants in an area, from industries, operations, process, automobiles and domestic sources, shall not be permitted to exceed the relevant concentration in ambient air as specified against each pollutant in columns (3) to (5) of Schedule VII.]

(4) Notwithstanding anything contained in sub-rule (3)-

(a) the Central Board or a State Board, depending on the local conditions or nature of discharge of environmental pollutants, may, by order, specify a lesser period than a period specified under sub-rule (3) within which the compliance of standards shall be made by an industry, operation or process

(b) the Central Government in respect of any specific industry, operation or process, by order, may specify any period other than a period specified under sub-rule (3) within which the compliance of standards shall be made by such industry, operation or process.

(5) Notwithstanding anything contained in sub-rule (3) the standards for emission or discharge of environmental pollutants specified under sub-rule (I) or sub-rule (2) in respect of an industry, operation or process before the commencement of the Environment (Protection) Amendment Rules, 1991, shall be complied by such industry, operation or process by the 31st day of December 1991.

[8][(6) Notwithstanding anything contained in sub-rule (3), an industry, operation or process which has commenced production on or before 16th May, 1981 and has shown adequate proof of at least commencement of physical work for establishment of facilities to meet the specified standards within a time-bound programme, to the satisfaction of the concerned State Pollution Control Board, shall comply with such standards latest by the 31 st day of December, 1993.

(7) Notwithstanding anything contained in sub-rule (3) or sub-rule (6) an industry, operation or process which has commenced production after the 16th day of May, 1981 but before the 31st day of December 1991 and has shown adequate proof of at least commencement of physical work for establishment of facilities to meet the specified standards within a time-bound programme, to the satisfaction of the concerned State Pollution Control Board, shall comply with such standards latest by the 31st day of December, 1992.]

5   *Ultra vires* is a Latin phrase meaning literally "beyond powers", and slightly less literally (from interpolating the definite article "the", not found in Latin) "beyond [the] powers", although its standard legal translation and substitute is "beyond power". If an act requires legal authority and it is done with such authority, it is characterised in law as *intra vires* (nearly literally "within [the] powers", after interpolating "the"; standard legal translation and substitute, "within power").

6   **Article 14 in The Constitution Of India 1949**

   14. Equality before law: The State shall not deny to any person equality before the law or the equal protection of the laws within the territory of India Prohibition of discrimination on grounds of religion, race, caste, sex or place of birth

7   **Article 25 in The Constitution Of India 1949**

   25. Freedom of conscience and free profession, practice and propagation of religion

   (1) Subject to public order, morality and health and to the other provisions of this Part, all persons are equally entitled to freedom of conscience and the right freely to profess, practise

pillar of Islam and occupies a permanent position among the practical duties of the Muslims. Muslims offer obligatory prayers in congregation in Mosques five times a day and offer prayer in common (Jammat) to isolated prayers. Azan is essential for all obligatory prayers and is called by Muezzin[8] in loud voice to summon all Believers in Islam to prayers.

When Azan was introduced by Prophet Muhammed it was called by a person from mosque in loud voice but by reason of passage of time, it was felt that a system was required to be introduced to invite the Believers in Islam to the congregational prayers by calling Azan through any instrument because of increase in population, industries and environmental changes it was not possible to reach the voice of Azan to the Believers of Islam. Therefore, it was submitted that Azan was and/or is called through an electrical loud-speakers and/or microphones five times a day and it was claimed that use of microphones for the purpose of Azan is a part of the religious right guaranteed under Article 25 of the Constitution. In order to justify the use of microphones and the noise splitters, it was submitted by petitioners that it was the duty of the citizens to have a degree of tolerance, patience for the purpose of respecting other religion and custom.

Freedom of Speech and Expression:

Freedom of Speech and Expression of a citizen guaranteed under Article 19(1)(a)[9] of the Constitution cannot be interfered with save and except in

---

and propagate religion

(2) Nothing in this article shall affect the operation of any existing law or prevent the State from making any law

(a) regulating or restricting any economic, financial, political or other secular activity which may be associated with religious practice;

(b) providing for social welfare and reform or the throwing open of Hindu religious institutions of a public character to all classes and sections of Hindus Explanation I The wearing and carrying of kirpans shall be deemed to be included in the profession of the Sikh religion Explanation II In sub clause (b) of clause reference to Hindus shall be construed as including a reference to persons professing the Sikh, Jaina or Buddhist religion, and the reference to Hindu religious institutions shall be construed accordingly

8 A *muezzin* or *muzim*, is the person appointed at a mosque to lead, and recite, the call to prayer (*adhan*) for every event of prayer and worship in the mosque. The Muezzin's post is an important one, as he is the one responsible for each call to prayer. The community depends on him for accurate prayer schedules

9 **Article 19(1) in The Constitution Of India 1949**

(1) All citizens shall have the right

(a) to freedom of speech and expression;

accordance with the provisions of Article 19(2)[10] of the Constitution. Public cannot he made captive audience or listeners by the use of Microphones after obtaining permission from the police and persons who are otherwise unwilling to hear the sound and/or music or the communication made by the loudspeakers, but they are compelled to tolerate all these things against their will and at the cost of their health. If permission is granted to use microphones at a louder voice, such a course of action takes away the rights of a citizen to speak with others, the right to read or the right to know and the right to sleep and rest or to think any matter. Even if a citizen is ill and even if such a sound may create adverse effect on his physical and mental condition, yet he is made a captive audience or listener to listen sound from microphones. Freedom of speech and expression as guaranteed under Article 19(1)(a) of the Constitution of India includes by necessary implication, freedom not to listen and/or to remain silent. One cannot exercise his right at the cost and in total deprivation of others rights. A right cannot be conferred by the authorities concerned upon a person of a religious organisation to exercise their rights suspending and/or taking away the rights of others. It is well-settled that the right to propagate one's religion means the right to communicate a person's

---

(b) to assemble peaceably and without arms;

(c) to form associations or unions;

(d) to move freely throughout the territory of India;

(e) to reside and settle in any part of the territory of India; and

(f) omitted

(g) to practise any profession, or to carry on any occupation, trade or business

10 **Article 19 in The Constitution Of India 1949**

 19. Protection of certain rights regarding freedom of speech etc

(1) All citizens shall have the right

(a) to freedom of speech and expression;

(b) to assemble peaceably and without arms;

(c) to form associations or unions;

(d) to move freely throughout the territory of India;

(e) to reside and settle in any part of the territory of India; and

(f) omitted

(g) to practise any profession, or to carry on any occupation, trade or business

(2) Nothing in sub clause (a) of clause (1) shall affect the operation of any existing law, or prevent the State from making any law, in so far as such law imposes reasonable restrictions on the exercise of the right conferred by the said sub clause in the interests of the sovereignty and integrity of India, the security of the State, friendly relations with foreign States, public order, decency or morality or in relation to contempt of court, defamation or incitement to an offence

belief to another or to expose the tenets of that faith.

Freedom of speech is guaranteed to every citizen so that he may reach with the minds of willingness and not coerced unwillingness. There cannot be any dispute that sound is a known source of pollution. The adverse and ill effect of sound on human body is also known. It has a tremendous impact on the nerves system of human being.

A citizen has a right to leizure right to sleep, right not to hear and right to remain silent. He has also the right to read and speak with others. Use of microphones certainly takes away the right of the citizens to speak with others, their right to read or think or the right to sleep. There may he heart patients or patients suffering from nervous disorder and may be compelled to hear this serious impact of sound pollution which has had an adverse effect on them and it may create health problems.

Sounds created by fire works, loud-speakers, aircrafts, railways are all the products of the technological age and high level of continuous sounds damages hearing and that there cannot be any two opinion about it. The noise not only creates pollution but it is also a source of annoyance. Noise is also created by traffic and noise also disturbs sleep. In our country the people have a right to sleep peacefully. A citizen too have right to a decent. Noise has been identified as a pollutant under Air (Prevention and Control) Act, 1981. Noise admittedly is a hazard to health. A citizen of this country must be allowed to live in a society which is peaceful, free from mechanical and artificial sounds which creates a tremendous health hazards and adverse effect on the citizen. Citizens have a right to live in a society which is free from pollution. If pollutants are encouraged, in that event would be the beginning of the end of the civilisation.

Question before the High Court:

Whether the right to practise or propogate religion includes the right to use loud-speakers and microphones for the purpose of chanting religious tenets or religious texts and/or the indiscriminate use of microphones or loud-speakers during the religious performance in the society.

Decision by High Court:

Court held that Azan is certainly an essentially and integral part of Islam but use of microphone and loud-speakers are not an essential and an integral part thereof. Microphone is a gift of technological ages, its adverse effect is well felt all over the world. It is not only a source of pollution but it is also a source which cause several health hazardous. Use of microphone is not a integral of Azan. Court further held that if anybody is found violating the restrictions imposed on microphone/loud-speaker, the Police Authorities were directed to immediately seize and confiscate the microphone from whatever place it would be found and reported it to the Court for taking drastic action against the violators who are violating wilfully and deliberately. The Officer-in-Charge of all the Police Stations under the control of the Commissioner of Police, Calcutta and the Director General of Police of West Bengal were directed to confiscate[11] the microphones from any Mosques if it was found that the said Mosque Authorities are violating the time limit i.e., no Mosque should use loud-speaker before 7 a.m.

---

11 **Meaning of Confiscate:**

   1. To seize (private property) for the public treasury.

   2. To seize by or as if by authority

16

Protection of environment and keeping it free of pollution is an indispensable necessity[1]

Ratio Decidendi[2]: "*Protection of environment and keeping it free of pollution is an indispensable necessity for life to survive on earth*"

Facts in Nutshell:

Application filed in public interest by a practicing advocate of Supreme Court who has consistently been taking interest in matters relating to environment and pollution. The reliefs claimed in application under Article 32[3] of the Constitution are for issuing appropriate directions to cinema exhibition halls to exhibit slides containing information and messages on environment: free of cost; directions for spread of information relating to environment in national and regional languages and for broadcast thereof on the All India Radio and exposure thereof on the television in regular and short term programmes with a view to

---

1 Appellants: **M.C. Mehta Vs.** Respondent: **Union of India (UOI) and Ors.**

   AIR1992SC382, JT1991(4)SC531

   Hon'ble Judges/Coram: Ranganath Misra, C.J., G.N. Ray and Dr. A.S. Anand, JJ.

2 **Meaning of Ration Decidendi:** *Ratio decidendi* is a Latin phrase meaning "the reason" or "the rationale for the decision." The *ratio decidendi* is "the point in a case which determines the judgment" or "the principle which the case establishes."

3 **Article 32 in The Constitution Of India 1949**

   32. Remedies for enforcement of rights conferred by this Part

   (1) The right to move the Supreme Court by appropriate proceedings for the enforcement of the rights conferred by this Part is guaranteed

   (2) The Supreme Court shall have power to issue directions or orders or writs, including writs in the nature of habeas corpus, mandamus, prohibition, quo warranto and certiorari, whichever may be appropriate, for the enforcement of any of the rights conferred by this Part

   (3) Without prejudice to the powers conferred on the Supreme Court by clause (1) and (2), Parliament may by law empower any other court to exercise within the local limits of its jurisdiction all or any of the powers exercisable by the Supreme Court under clause (2)

   (4) The right guaranteed by this article shall not be suspended except as otherwise provided for by this Constitution

educating the people of India about their social obligation in the matter of the upkeep of the environment in proper shape and making them alive to their obligation not to act as polluting agencies or factors. There was also a prayer that environment should be made a compulsory subject in schools and colleges in a graded system so that there would be a general growth of awareness.

Importance of Environment:

Until 1972, general awareness of mankind to the importance of environment for the well being of mankind had not been appropriately appreciated though over the years for more than a century there was a growing realisation that mankind had to live in tune with nature if life was to be peaceful, happy and satisfied. In the name of scientific development, man started distancing himself from Nature and even developed an urge to conquer nature. Our ancestors had known that nature was riot subduable[4] and, therefore, had made it an obligation for man to surrender to nature and live in tune with it. Our Constitution underwent an amendment in 1976 by incorporating an Article (51A[5]) with the heading "Fundamental Duties[6]". Clause (g) thereof requires every citizen to protect and improve the natural environment including forests,

---

4   **Meaning of subduable:** Susceptible to being subjugated

5   **Article 51A in The Constitution Of India 1949**

   51A. Fundamental duties: It shall be the duty of every citizen of India (a) to abide by the Constitution and respect its ideals and institutions, the national Flag and the National Anthem;

   (b) to cherish and follow the noble ideals which inspired our national struggle for freedom;

   (c) to uphold and protect the sovereignty, unity and integrity of India;

   (d) to defend the country and render national service when called upon to do so;

   (e) to promote harmony and the spirit of common brotherhood amongst all the people of India transcending religious, linguistic and regional or sectional diversities; to renounce practices derogatory to the dignity of women;

   (f) to value and preserve the rich heritage of our composite culture;

   (g) to protect and improve the natural environment including forests, lakes, rivers and wild life, and to have compassion for living creatures;

   (h) to develop the scientific temper, humanism and the spirit of inquiry and reform;

   (i) to safeguard public property and to abjure violence;

   (j) to strive towards excellence in all spheres of individual and collective activity so that the nation constantly rises to higher levels of endeavour and achievement

6   The *Fundamental Duties* are defined as the moral obligations of all citizens to help promote a spirit of patriotism and to uphold the unity of India. These duties, set out in Part IV–A of the Constitution concern individuals and the nation. Like the Directive Principles, they are not legally enforceable.

lakes, rivers and wild life, and to have compassion for living creatures. Soon after the international conference on environment the Water Pollution Control Act of 1974 came on the statute book; the Air Pollution Control Act came in 1981 and finally came the Environment Protection Act of 1986.

Law is a regulator of human conduct as the professors of jurisprudence say, but no law can indeed effectively work unless there is an element of acceptance by the people in society. No law works out smoothly unless the interaction is voluntary. In order that human conduct may be in accordance with the prescription[7] of law it is necessary that there should be appropriate awareness about what the law requires and there is an element of acceptance that the requirement of law is grounded upon a philosophy which should be followed. This would be possible only when steps are taken in an adequate measure to make people aware of the indispensable necessity of their conduct being oriented in accordance with the requirements of law.

There has been an explosion of human population over the last 50 years. Life has become competitive. Sense of idealism in the living process has systematically eroded. As a consequence of this the age old norms of good living are no longer followed. The anxiety to do good to the needy or for the society in general has died out, today oblivious of the repercussions of one's actions on society, everyone is prepared to do whatever is easy and convenient for his own purpose. In this backdrop if the laws are to be enforced and the malaise of pollution has to be kept under control and the environment has to be protected in an unpolluted state it is necessary that people are aware of the vice of pollution and its evil consequences.

We are in a democratic polity where dissemination of information is the foundation of the system. Keeping the citizens informed is an obligation of the Government. It is equally the responsibility of society to adequately educate every component of it so that the social level is kept up.

Directions by Supreme Court:

(1) Union of India shall issue appropriate directions to the State Governments and Union Territories to invariably enforce as a condition of

---

7   **Meaning of Prescription:**

   a. The act of establishing official rules, laws, or directions.

   b. Something prescribed as a rule.

license of all cinema halls, touring cinemas and video parlours to exhibit free of cost at least two slides/messages on environment in each show undertaken by them. The material for the slides should be such that it would at once be impressive, striking and leave an impact on every one who sees the slide.

(2) The Ministry of Information and Broadcasting of the Government of India should without delay start producing information films of short duration on various aspects of environment and pollution bringing out the benefits for society on the environment being protected and the hazards involved in the environment being polluted. Mind catching aspects should be made the central theme of such short films. One such film should be shown, as far as practicable, in one show every day by the cinema halls and the Central Government and the State Governments were directed to ensure compliance of this condition from February 1, 1992.

(3) So far as education up to the college level is concerned, every State Government and every Education Board connected with education up to the matriculation stage or even intermediate colleges to immediately take steps to enforce compulsory education on environment in a graded way.

17

Right to profession not absolute - Reasonable restrictions can be imposed on profession[1]

Facts in Nutshell:

The petitioners[2] challenged certain amendments carried out in the Wild Life (Protection) Act, 1972 by the Amendment Act No. 44 of 1991 whereby the trade in *imported ivory[3] and articles made there from have been banned*. The grievance of the petitioners was that though they are not covered by the Wild Life (Protection) Act, 1972 and the Amendment Act No. 44 of 1991, the authorities were taking action against them for their being in possession of mammoth[4] ivory and articles made there from. The writ petitioners in writ petition[5] were mainly aggrieved by

---

1   Appellants: **M/s. Ivory Traders and Manufacturers Association and Other Vs.** Respondent: **Union of India and Others**

    AIR1997Delhi267

    Respondent: **Union of India and Others**

    Hon'ble Judges/Coram: M. Jagannadha Rao, C.J. A.D. Singh and Manmohan Sarin, JJ.

2   **Meaning of Petitioner:** A person who presents a Petition. (**Meaning of Petition:** A formal message requesting something that is submitted to an authority)

3   **Ivory** Is a hard, white material, derived from the tusks and teeth of animals, that is used in art or manufacturing. It consists ofdentine, a tissue that is similar to bone. It has been important since ancient times for making a range of items, from ivory carvings to false teeth, fans, and dominoes

4   A **mammoth** is any species of the extinct genus *Mammuthus*, proboscideans commonly equipped with long, curvedtusks and, in northern species, a covering of long hair. They lived from the Pliocene epoch (from around 5 million years ago) into the Holocene at about 4,500 years ago in Africa, Europe, Asia, and North America.

5   **Meaning of Writ Petition:** Under the Indian legal system, jurisdiction to issue 'prerogative writs' is given to the Supreme Court, and to the High Courts of Judicature of all Indian states. Parts of the law relating to writs are set forth in the Constitution of India. The Supreme Court, the highest in the country, may issue writs under Article 32 of the Constitution for enforcement of Fundamental Rights and under Articles 139 for enforcement of rights other than Fundamental Rights, while High Courts, the superior courts of the States, may issue writs under Articles 226. 'Writ' is eminently designed by the makers of the Constitution, and in the same way it is developed very widely and efficiently by the courts in India. The Constitution broadly provides for five kinds of "prerogative" writs, namely, Habeas Corpus, Certiorari, Mandamus, Quo Warranto and Prohibition.

the ban imposed by the Wild Life (Protection) Amendment Act, 1991, on the trade in ivory derived from the African elephant. It was asserted by them that they only deal with ivory imported before the coming into operation of Amendment Act No. 44 of 1991. It was claimed that the first petitioner, a Society registered under the Societies Registration Act, 1860 and is an Association of persons connected with the trade and business of Ivory, including persons manufacturing articles there from. The second petitioner to the fourteenth petitioner were dealers in ivory. They asserted that they were carrying on business and trade in ivory including the manufacture of articles derived from ivory lawfully imported into India prior to the ban.

In the Shorter Oxford Dictionary, the meaning of the ivory is given as under :

The hard, white, elastic and find grain substance (being dentine[6] of exceptional hardness) composing the main part of the tusks of the elephant.

The Wild Life (Protection) Act, 1972:

Birds were the first to get the attention of the British in India. The first legislation for protection of birds was enacted by the British in 1887 which was known as the Wild Birds Protection Act, 1887 (Act No. X of 1887). However, the purpose of this Act was limited as it prohibited the possession or sale of only certain kinds of wild birds during the breeding season. This Act did not have the desired effect as killing of birds was not prohibited. As a consequence of wanton killing of birds and animals a more comprehensive legislation.-was needed. In order, to remedy the situation the British enacted a legislation called the Wild Birds and Animals (Protection) Act, 1912 (Act No. VIII of 1912). Section 3 of that Act empowered the Provincial Government to declare the whole year or any part thereof, what may be called as close time, during which specified kind of wild birds or animals would not be killed and it was made unlawful to capture or kill or sell or buy or possess any such bird or animal. Section 4 made contravention of Section 3 punishable with fine. In the year 1935 the Act was amended by the Wild Birds and Animals (Protection) Act No. XXVII of 1935. By that Amendment Act, amongst other additions and alterations, section 11 was added by virtue of which

---

6   **Meaning of Dentine:** The calcified tissue surrounding the pulp cavity of a tooth and comprising the bulk of the tooth

the Provincial Government could declare any area to be a sanctuary for the birds or animals and their killing was made unlawful. Any violation of Section 11 was made punishable with fine. It is noteworthy that for the first time the concept of sanctuary[7] was introduced in India but the provisions of that Act also proved to be inadequate for protection of wild life and birds. For the next thirty-seven years nothing much was done to improve the situation. There was rapid depletion of wild life and birds and need was felt to enact a more comprehensive and effective legislation for protection of wild life. But there was a difficulty. The subject of wild life being a State subject falling in Entry 20, List 11 of Seventh Schedule of the Constitution, there was no way for the Parliament to enact a law in regard to the aforesaid subject except by invoking the provisions of Article 252[8] of the Constitution.

Having regard to the importance of the matter, the legislature of the States of Andhra Pradesh, Bihar, Gujarat, Haryana, Himachal Pradesh, Madhya Pradesh, Manipur, Punjab, Rajasthan, Uttar Pradesh and West Bengal passed resolutions in pursuance of Article 252 of the Constitution empowering the Parliament to pass the necessary legislation in regard to the protection of wild animals, birds and for all matters connected therewith. Thus armed with the resolutions, the Parliament enacted the Wild Life (Protection) Act, 1972. It came into effect from February 1, 1973.

The Statement of Objects and Reasons of the Wildlife Protection Act, 1972 which reads as follows :

---

7   A **sanctuary**, in its original meaning, is a sacred place, such as a shrine. By the use of such places as a safe haven, by extension the term has come to be used for any place of safety. This secondary use can be categorized into human sanctuary, a safe place for humans, such as a political sanctuary; and non-human sanctuary, such as an animal or plant sanctuary.

8   **Article 252 in The Constitution Of India 1949**

Power of Parliament to legislate for two or more States by consent and adoption of such legislation by any other State

(1) If it appears to the Legislatures of two or more States to be desirable that any of the matters with respect to which Parliament has no power to make laws for the States except as provided in Articles 249 and 250 should be regulated in such States by Parliament by law, and if resolutions to that effect are passed by all the House of the Legislatures of those States, it shall be lawful for Parliament to pass an Act for regulating that matter accordingly, and any Act so passed shall apply to such States and to any other State by which it is adopted afterwards by resolution passed in that behalf by the House or, where there are two Houses, by each of the Houses of the Legislature of that State

(2) Any Act so passed by Parliament may be amended or repealed by an Act of Parliament passed or adopted in like manner but shall not, as respects any State to which it applies, be amended or repealed by an Act of the Legislature of that State

The rapid decline of India's wild animals and birds, one of the richest and most varied in the world, has been a cause of grave concern. Some wild animals and birds have already become extinct[9] in this country and others are in the danger of being so. Areas which were once teeming[10] with wild life have become devoid of it and even in sanctuaries and National Parks the protection afforded to wild life needs to be improved. The Wild Birds and Animals Protection Act, 1912 (8 of 1912), has become completely outmoded[11]. The existing State laws are not only out-dated but provide punishments which are not commensurate with the offence and the financial benefits which accrue from poaching[12] and trade in wild life produce. Further, such laws mainly relate to control of hunting and do not emphasise the other factors which are also prime reasons for the decline of India's wild life, namely, taxidermy[13] and trade in wild life and products derived there from.

Having considered the relevant local provisions existing in the States, the Government came to the conclusion that these are neither adequate nor satisfactory. There is, therefore, an urgent need for introducing a comprehensive legislation, which would provide for the protection of wild animals and birds for all matters connected therewith or ancillary and incidental thereto.

The statement of objects and reasons of the Amendment Act of 1986 reads as follows:--

"The Wild Life (Protection) Act, 1972 provides for the protection of wild animals and birds and for matters connected therewith or

---

9   **Meaning of Extinct:**

  1. No longer existing or living

  2. No longer burning or active

10 **Meaning of Teeming:** To be full of things; abound or swarm

11 **Meaning of outmoded:**

  1. Not in fashion; unfashionable

  2. No longer usable or practical; obsolete

12 **Poaching** has traditionally been defined as the illegal hunting, killing or capturing of wild animals, usually associated with land use rights. Until the 20th century, mostly impoverished peasants poached for subsistence purposes, thus supplementing a scarce diet. By contrast, stealing domestic animals such as cattle raiding is considered theft, not poaching. Since the 1980s, the term poaching has also been used for the illegal harvest of wild plant species.

13 **Meaning of Taxidermy:** The art or operation of preparing, stuffing, and mounting the skins of dead animals for exhibition in a lifelike state

ancillary[14] thereto.

Poaching of wild animals and illegal trade of products derived there from together with degradiation and depletion, of habitats have seriously affected wild life population. In order to check this trend, it was proposed to prohibit hunting of all wild animals (other than vermin[15]). However, hunting of wild animals in exceptional circumstances, particularly for the purpose of protection of life and property and for education, research, scientific management and captive breeding, would continue. It was being made mandatory for every transporter not to transport any wild life product without proper permission. The penalties for various offences were proposed to be suitably enhanced to make them deterrent[16]. The Central Government officers as well as individuals now can also file complaints in the courts for offences under the Wildlife Protection Act, 1972. It was also proposed to provide for appointment of honorary[17] Wild Life Wardens and payment of rewards to persons helping in apprehension of offenders. The Parties to the "Convention on International Trade in Endangered Species of Wild Fauna[18] and Flora" (CITES), being greatly concerned by the decline in population of African elephant[19], the import and export of African ivory for commercial purposes has been prohibited. As a result import of ivory would no longer be possible to meet the requirements of the domestic ivory trade. If the ivory trade is allowed to continue, it will lead to large scale poaching of Indian elephants.

---

14 **Meaning of Ancillary:**

   1. Of secondary importance

   2. Auxiliary; helping

15 **Meaning of Vermin:**

   1. Various small animals or insects, such as rats or cockroaches, that are destructive, annoying, or injurious to health.

   2. Animals that prey on game, such as foxes or weasels.

16 **Meaning of Deterrent:** A retaliatory means of discouraging enemy attack

17 An **honorary** position is given as an honor, with no duties attached, and without payment.

18 **Fauna** is all of the animal life of any particular region or time. The corresponding term for plants is *flora*. Flora, fauna and other forms of life such as fungi are collectively referred to as biota

19 **African elephants** are elephants of the genus ***Loxodonta*** (from the Greek words *loxo* (oblique sided) and *donta* (tooth))[2]. The genus consists of two extant species: the African bush elephant and the smaller African forest elephant. *Loxodonta* is one of two existing genera of the family, Elephantidae. Fossil remains of *Loxodonta* have been found only in Africa, in strata as old as the middle Pliocene

Trade which is pernicious[20] can be totally banned:

The trade in ivory (word 'ivory' is used in comprehensive sense including indigenous as well as imported ivory is dangerous, subversive and pernicious as it has the potential to deplete the elephant population and to ultimately extinguish the same). It is well settled that trade which is pernicious can be totally banned without attracting Article 19(1)(g)[21] of the Constitution. There is a string of authority for the proposition that no citizen has any fundamental right[22] guaranteed under Article 19(1)(g) of the Constitution to carry on trade in any noxious[23] and dangerous goods like intoxicating drugs or intoxicating liquors. Trade and business in intoxicating drugs or liquors is only one of the noxious types of enterprises. This category does not close with drugs & intoxicating liquors. What was not considered harmful at an earlier point of time, may be discovered to be so later. Time has a way of changing norms. Several other activities being equally pernicious fall in this category too :

---

20 **Meaning of Pernicious:**

    a. Tending to cause death or serious injury; deadly

    b. Causing great harm; destructive

21 **Article 19 in The Constitution Of India 1949**

    19. Protection of certain rights regarding freedom of speech etc

    (1) All citizens shall have the right

    (a) to freedom of speech and expression;

    (b) to assemble peaceably and without arms;

    (c) to form associations or unions;

    (d) to move freely throughout the territory of India;

    (e) to reside and settle in any part of the territory of India; and

    (f) omitted

    (g) to practise any profession, or to carry on any occupation, trade or business

22 **Meaning of Fundamental Rights:** The Fundamental Rights are defined as basic human freedoms which every Indian citizen has the right to enjoy for a proper and harmonious development of personality. These rights universally apply to all citizens, irrespective of race, place of birth, religion, caste, creed, colour or gender. Aliens (persons who are not citizens) are also considered in matters like equality before law. They are enforceable by the courts, subject to certain restrictions.

23 **Meaning of Noxious:**

    Harmful to living things; injurious to health

    2. Harmful to the mind or morals; corrupting

1. Gambling,

2. Prostitution,

3. Dealing in counterfeit coins or currency notes, etc.

Activities having a baneful effect on the ecology, human and animal life etc. occupy a central position in the above category. By virtue of Section 10 of the Constitution (42 Amendment) Act, 1976, Article 48A[24] was inserted in the Constitution. Article 48A enjoins upon the State to protect and improve the environment and to safeguard the forests and the wild life of the country. Therefore, what is destructive of the environment, forest and wild life is contrary to the said directive principles of the State policy. Again by Section 11 of the Constitution (42 Amendment) Act, 1976, Article 51A[25] was incorporated in the Constitution. This Article lays down the fundamental duties[26] of the citizens. Clause (g) of Article 51A requires every citizen to protect and improve the natural environment including forests, lakes, rivers and wild life and to have compassion for living creatures. The State has the power to completely prohibit a trade

---

24 **Article 48A in The Constitution Of India 1949**

48A. Protection and improvement of environment and safeguarding of forests and wild life: The State shall endeavour to protect and improve the environment and to safeguard the forests and wild life of the country

25 **Article 51A in The Constitution Of India 1949**

51A. Fundamental duties It shall be the duty of every citizen of India (a) to abide by the Constitution and respect its ideals and institutions, the national Flag and the National Anthem;

(b) to cherish and follow the noble ideals which inspired our national struggle for freedom;

(c) to uphold and protect the sovereignty, unity and integrity of India;

(d) to defend the country and render national service when called upon to do so;

(e) to promote harmony and the spirit of common brotherhood amongst all the people of India transcending religious, linguistic and regional or sectional diversities; to renounce practices derogatory to the dignity of women;

(f) to value and preserve the rich heritage of our composite culture;

(g) to protect and improve the natural environment including forests, lakes, rivers and wild life, and to have compassion for living creatures;

(h) to develop the scientific temper, humanism and the spirit of inquiry and reform;

(i) to safeguard public property and to abjure violence;

(j) to strive towards excellence in all spheres of individual and collective activity so that the nation constantly rises to higher levels of endeavour and achievement

26 The *Fundamental Duties* are defined as the moral obligations of all citizens to help promote a spirit of patriotism and to uphold the unity of India. These duties, set out in Part IV–A of the Constitution concern individuals and the nation. Like the Directive Principles, they are not legally enforceable.

or business which has an adverse impact on the preservation of species of wild life which are on the verge of extinction both because it is inherently dangerous practice to destory such animals in terms of ecology and also because of the directive principles[27] contained in Article 48A of the Constitution. When the Legislature prohibits a pernicious, noxious or a dangerous trade or business it is in recognition of society's right of self protection.

In *M. J. Sivani v. State of Karnataka*[28], the Supreme Court was confronted with the question as to whether regulation of video games violates the fundamental right to trade or business or avocation[29] guaranteed under Articles 19(1)(g) and 21[30]. While upholding the restrictions the Apex Court held that the aforesaid trade Or business being attended with danger to the community could be totally prohibited or be permitted subject to such conditions or restrictions as would prevent the evils to the utmost.

Decision by High Court:

Court held that

(1) No citizen has a fundamental right to trade in ivory or ivory articles, whether indigenous or imported

(2) The ban on trade in imported ivory and articles made there from

---

27　The **Directive Principles of State Policy** are guidelines to the central and state governments of India, to be kept in mind while framing laws and policies. These provisions, contained in Part IV of the Constitution of India, are not enforceable by any court, but the principles laid down therein are considered fundamental in the governance of the country, making it the duty of the State to apply these principles in making laws to establish a just society in the country. The principles have been inspired by the Directive Principles given in the Constitution of Ireland and also by the principles of Gandhism; and relate to social justice, economic welfare, foreign policy, and legal and administrative matters.

28　[1995]3SCR329

29　**Meaning of Avocation:**

　　1. An activity taken up in addition to one's regular work or profession, usually for enjoyment; a hobby.

　　2. One's regular work or profession

30　**Article 21 in The Constitution Of India 1949**

　　21. Protection of life and personal liberty: No person shall be deprived of his life or personal liberty except according to procedure established by law

is not vocative[31] of Article 14[32] of the Constitution and does not suffer from any of the maladies[33], namely, unreasonableness, unfairness and arbitrariness[34].

---

31 **Meaning of Vocative:**

    1. Relating to, characteristic of, or used in calling.

    2. Of, relating to, or being a grammatical case in certain inflected languages to indicate the person or thing being addressed

32 **Article 14 in The Constitution Of India 1949**

    14. Equality before law The State shall not deny to any person equality before the law or the equal protection of the laws within the territory of India Prohibition of discrimination on grounds of religion, race, caste, sex or place of birth

33 **Meaning of Maladies:**

    1. A disease, a disorder, or an ailment.

    2. An unwholesome condition

34 **Meaning of Arbitrariness:** The trait of acting unpredictably and more from whim or caprice than from reason or judgment

18

State has to provide at least the minimum conditions ensuring human dignity[1]

Ratio Decidendi[2]: "All steps regarding public health shall be taken for improvement of public health as primary duty"

Facts in Nutshell:

Petitioner[3], who was a medical practitioner by profession preferred petition[4] by way of public interest litigation[5] annexing with the petition newspaper cuttings of to demonstrate that for want of performing the primary and obligatory duties by the Municipal Corporation, Gwalior and Public Health and Public Health Engineering Departments, in the locality of Pardi Mohalla, of State of Madhya Pradesh, due to open drain, filthy water, heaps of dirt and contaminated water and rubbish, there was spread of epidemic of cholera[6], resulting in deaths of 12 children in the year 1991 and also deaths in the year 1992. Therefore, the petitioner approached the High Court for issuance of directions to the State and the Municipal Corporation, Gwalior, to take all necessary measures to eradicate the menace.

---

1 Appellants: **Dr. K.C. Malhotra Vs.** Respondent: **State of M.P. and Ors.**

 AIR1994MP48

 Hon'ble Judges/Coram: S.K. Dubey and S.K. Chawla, JJ.

2 **Meaning of Ration Decidendi:** *Ratio decidendi* is a Latin phrase meaning "the reason" or "the rationale for the decision." The *ratio decidendi* is "the point in a case which determines the judgment" or "the principle which the case establishes."

3 **Meaning of Petitioner:** A person who presents a Petition. (**Meaning of Petition:** A formal message requesting something that is submitted to an authority)

4 **Meaning of Petition:** A formal message requesting something that is submitted to an authority

5 **Public-Interest Litigation** is litigation for the protection of the public interest. InIndian law, **Article 32** of the Indian constitution contains a tool which directly joins the public with judiciary. A PIL may be introduced in a court of law by the court itself (*suo motu*), rather than the aggrieved party or another third party. For the exercise of the court's jurisdiction, it is not necessary for the victim of the violation of his or her rights to personally approach the court. In a PIL, the right to file suit is given to a member of the public by the courts through judicial activism. The member of the public may be a non-governmental organization (NGO), an institution or an individual.

6 **Cholera** is an infection of the small intestine caused by the bacterium Vibrio cholerae.

Municipal Corporation denied the averments[7] and stated that the safai Karmacharies of the Municipal Corporation regularly clean and remove the heaps of rubbish under the supervision of the supervisory staff. Chlorine tablets were mixed up with the water and they were distributed amongst the members of the public. Municipal Corporation also contended that there was timely spraying of D.D.T.[8] and phenyle.

India is a welfare State[9]:

India is a welfare State governed by the Constitution which holds a place of pride in the hearts of its citizens. It lays a special emphasis on the protection and well-being of the weaker sections of the society and seeks to improve their economic and social status on the basis of Constitutional guarantees spelled out in its provisions. We live in an age which recognises that every person is entitled to a quality of life consistent with his human personality. The right to live with human dignity is the fundamental right[10] of every Indian citizen. And, so in the discharge of its responsibilities to the people, the State has to provide at least the minimum conditions ensuring human dignity[11]. The right to life enshrined in Article 21[12], cannot be restricted to mere animal existence. It means something much more than just physical survival. The right to life includes the right to live with human dignity and all that goes along with it, namely, the bare necessaries of life such as adequate nutrition, clothing and shelter over the head and facilities of reading, writing and-expressing oneself in diverse forms, freely moving about and mixing and

---

7   **Meaning of Averment:** The allegation of facts or claims in a Pleading

8   **DDT** (**"dichlorodiphenyltrichloroethane"**) is a colorless, crystalline, tasteless and almost odorless organochlorideknown for its insecticidal properties.

9   A **welfare state** is a concept of government in which the state plays a key role in the protection and promotion of the economic and social well-being of its citizens. It is based on the principles ofequality of opportunity, equitable distribution of wealth, and public responsibility for those unable to avail themselves of the minimal provisions for a good life. The general term may cover a variety of forms of economic and social organization.

10 **Meaning of Fundamental Rights:** The Fundamental Rights are defined as basic human freedoms which every Indian citizen has the right to enjoy for a proper and harmonious development of personality. These rights universally apply to all citizens, irrespective of race, place of birth, religion, caste, creed, colour or gender. Aliens (persons who are not citizens) are also considered in matters like equality before law. They are enforceable by the courts, subject to certain restrictions

11 See *Vikram Deo Singh Tomar v. State of Bihar,* AIR 1988 SC 1782

12 **Article 21 in The Constitution Of India 1949**

    Protection of life and personal liberty: No person shall be deprived of his life or personal liberty except according to procedure established by law

commingling with fellow human beings[13].

The term health implies more than absence of sickness:

The Supreme Court, while dealing with the case of Workers of *C.E.S.C. Limited v. Subhash Chandra Bose*[14], discussing Articles 22 to 25[15] of the Universal Declaration of Human Rights, 1948 and Articles 21 and 39(e)[16]

---

13   See, *Francis Coralie v. Administrator, Union Territory of Delhi,* 1981 AIR 746

14   (1992) 1 SCC 441 : (AIR 1992 SC 573)

15   **Articles 22 of the Universal Declaration of Human Rights, 1948**

Everyone, as a member of society, has the right to social security and is entitled to realization, through national effort and international co-operation and in accordance with the organization and resources of each State, of the economic, social and cultural rights indispensable for his dignity and the free development of his personality.

Articles 23 of the Universal Declaration of Human Rights, 1948

(1) Everyone has the right to work, to free choice of employment, to just and favourable conditions of work and to protection against unemployment.

(2) Everyone, without any discrimination, has the right to equal pay for equal work.

(3) Everyone who works has the right to just and favourable remuneration ensuring for himself and his family an existence worthy of human dignity, and supplemented, if necessary, by other means of social protection.

(4) Everyone has the right to form and to join trade unions for the protection of his interests.

Articles 24 of the Universal Declaration of Human Rights, 1948

Everyone has the right to rest and leisure, including reasonable limitation of working hours and periodic holidays with pay.

Articles 25 of the Universal Declaration of Human Rights, 1948

(1) Everyone has the right to a standard of living adequate for the health and well-being of himself and of his family, including food, clothing, housing and medical care and necessary social services, and the right to security in the event of unemployment, sickness, disability, widowhood, old age or other lack of livelihood in circumstances beyond his control.

(2) Motherhood and childhood are entitled to special care and assistance. All children, whether born in or out of wedlock, shall enjoy the same social protection.

16   **Article 39 in The Constitution Of India 1949**

39. Certain principles of policy to be followed by the State

The State shall, in particular, direct its policy towards securing

(a) that the citizens, men and women equally, have the right to an adequate means to livelihood;

(b) that the ownership and control of the material resources of the community are so distributed as best to subserve the common good;

(c) that the operation of the economic system does not result in the concentration of wealth and means of production to the common detriment;

(d) that there is equal pay for equal work for both men and women;

(e) that the health and strength of workers, men and women, and the tender age of children are not abused and that citizens are not forced by economic necessity to enter avocations unsuited to their age or strength;

of the Constitution of India, in para 32 observed, "The term health implies more than absence of sickness. Medical care and health facilities not only protect against sickness but also ensures stable manpower for economic development. Facilities of health and medical care generate devotion and dedication to give the workers' best, physically as well as mentally, in productivity. It enables the worker to enjoy the fruit of his labour, to keep him physically fit and mentally alert for leading a successful, economic, social and cultural life. The medical facilities are, therefore, part of social security and like gilt-edged[17] security, it would yield immediate return in the increased production or at any rate reduce absenteeism[18] on grounds of sickness, etc. Health is thus a state of complete physical, mental and social well being and not merely the absence of disease or infirmity. In the light of Articles 22 to 25 of the Universal Declaration of Human Rights, International Convention on Economic, Social and Cultural Rights, and in the light of socio-economic justice assured in our Constitution, **right to health is a fundamental human right to workmen.** The maintenance of health is a most imperative constitutional goal whose realisation requires interaction of many social and economic factors".

In respect of civic amenities and discharge of its primary/obligatory duties, the Supreme Court had an occasion to examine the case in *Ratlam Municipal Council v. Vardhichand*[19] arising out of the proceedings under Section 133[20], Cr.P.C. and in paras 12 and 16 of the judgment, their

---

(f) that children are given opportunities and facilities to develop in a healthy manner and in conditions of freedom and dignity and that childhood and youth are protected against exploitation and against moral and material abandonment

17 **Meaning of Gilt Edged:**

1. Having gilded edges, as the pages of a book.

2. Of the highest quality or value

18 **Meaning of absenteeism:**

1. Habitual failure to appear, especially for work or other regular duty

2. The rate of occurrence of habitual absence from work or duty

19 AIR 1980 SC 1622 : (1980 Cri LJ 1075)

20 **Section 133, Cr.P.C.**

133. Conditional order for removal of nuisance -

(1) Whenever a District Magistrate or a Sub-divisional Magistrate or any other Executive Magistrate specially empowered in this behalf by the State Government on receiving the report of a police officer or other information and on taking such evidence (if any) as he thinks fit, considers—

(a) that any unlawful obstruction or nuisance should be removed from any public place or from any way, river or channel which is or may be lawfully used by the public; or

Lordships observed that where there existed a **public nuisance**[21] in a locality due to open drains, heaps of dirt, pits and public excretion by humans for want of lavatories and consequential breeding of mosquitoes, the Court could require the Municipality under Section 133 of the Cr.P.C. to abate the nuisance by taking affirmative action on a time-bound basis.

(b) that the conduct of any trade or occupation or the keeping of any goods or merchandise; is injurious to the health or physical comfort of the community, and that in consequence such trade or occupation should be prohibited or regulated or such goods or merchandise should be removed or the keeping thereof regulated; or

(c) that the construction of any building, or the disposal of any substance, as is likely to occasion conflagration or explosion, should be prevented or stopped; or

(d) that any building, tent or structure, or any tree is in such a condition that it is likely to fall and thereby cause injury to persons living or carrying on business in the neighbourhood or passing by, and that in consequence the removal, repair or support of such building, tent or structure, or the removal or support of such tree, is necessary; or

(e) that any tank, well or excavation adjacent to any such way or public place should be fenced in such manner as to prevent danger arising to the public; or

(f) that any dangerous animal should be destroyed, confined or otherwise disposed of, such Magistrate may make a conditional order requiring the person causing such obstruction or nuisance, or carrying on such trade or occupation, or keeping any such goods or merchandise, or owning, possessing or controlling such building, tent, structure,

substance, tank, well or excavation, or owning or possessing such animal or tree, within a time to be fixed in the order—

(i) to remove such obstruction or nuisance; or

(ii) to desist from carrying on, or to remove or regulate in such manner as may be directed, such trade or occupation, or to remove such goods or merchandise, or to regulate the keeping thereof in such manner as may be directed; or (iii) to prevent or stop the construction of such building, or to alter the disposal of such substance; or

(iv) to remove, repair or support such building, tent or structure, or to remove or support such trees; or

(v) to fence such tank, well or excavation; or

(vi) to destroy, confine or dispose of such dangerous animal in the manner provided in the said order; or, if he objects so to do, to appear before himself or some other Executive Magistrate subordinate to him at a time and place

to be fixed by the order, and show cause, in the manner hereinafter provided, why the order should not be made absolute

(2) No order duly made by a Magistrate under this section shall be called in question in any civil Court

Explanation—A "public place" includes also property belonging to the State, camping grounds and grounds left unoccupied for sanitary or recreative purposes

21 **Section 268 in The Indian Penal Code**

268. Public nuisance.—A person is guilty of a public nuisance who does any act or is guilty of an illegal omission which causes any common injury, danger or annoyance to the public or to the people in general who dwell or occupy property in the vicinity, or which must necessarily cause injury, obstruction, danger or annoyance to persons who may have occasion to use any public right. A common nuisance is not excused on the ground that it causes some convenience or advantage

When such order was given, the Municipality could not take the plea that notwithstanding the public nuisance, financial inability validly exonerated it from statutory liability.

Decision by High Court:

Court held that the inhabitants[22] of the locality may be of backward class or weaker sections of the society, they have got a fundamental right under Article 21 of the Constitution entitling them to live as human beings in the area which is in the limits of the Municipal Corporation. There must be a separate sewage line from which the filthy water may flow out. The nalla must be covered and there should be proper lavatories[23] for public conservancy[24] which should be regularly cleaned. Public health and safety cannot suffer on any count and all steps are to be taken as Article 47[25] makes it a paramount principle of Government that steps are taken "for the improvement of public health as among its primary duties".

Directions by High Court:

(a) The open nalla shall be covered before the advent of the rainy season and if for the circumstances beyond the control, the nalla could not be covered within the said time, the Corporation and the P.H.E. shall take all steps to ensure that potable water[26] is not contaminated and polluted. Flow of water remains continuous from the nalla till it is covered. All necessary measures shall be taken to keep up the nalla clean.

(b) More latrines shall be constructed, to cope up with the need of the inhabitants. In any manner, all arrangement shall be done before the rainy season starts. There shall be vaccination against cholera and other

---

22 **Meaning of Inhabitants:** One that inhabits a place, especially as a permanent resident

23 **Meaning of lavatories:**

 1. A room equipped with washing and often toilet facilities; a bathroom.

 2. A washbowl or basin, especially one permanently installed with running water

24 **Meaning of conservancy:**

 Conservation, especially of natural resources

25 **Article 47 in The Constitution Of India 1949**

 Duty of the State to raise the level of nutrition and the standard of living and to improve public health: The State shall regard the raising of the level of nutrition and the standard of living of its people and the improvement of public health as among its primary duties and, in particular, the State shall endeavour to bring about prohibition of the consumption except for medicinal purposes of intoxicating drinks and of drugs which are injurious to health

26 Potable water is water which is fit for consumption by humans and other animals. It is also called drinking water

epidemic diseases, distribution of chlorine tablets and other medicines to keep up the health and safety of the inhabitants.

(c) It shall be the duty of the State and its instrumentalities to educate not only the inhabitants of the locality, but the members of the society to live with appropriate awareness and to take all measures so that **water and environment** may not be polluted.

19

State is duty bound to protect wholesome quality of water and check its pollution[1]

Ratio Decidendi[2]: "State is duty bound to protect wholesome quality of water and check its pollution"

Facts in Nutshell:

Practising advocate of the Supreme Court and General Secretary of the Indian Council for Enviro-Legal Action, a registered voluntary organization filed writ[3] application for a writ of mandamus[4] to protect the health of thousands of innocent people living in Cuttack and adjacent areas, who were suffering from pollution being caused by the Municipal Committee, Cuttack and the S.C.B. Medical College Hospital, Cuttack, Several acts of the aforesaid authorities and the State of Orissa were alleged to be in violation of Article 21[5] of the Constitution of India, the National Health Policy, the Environment (Protection) Act, 1986, and the Water (Prevention and Control of Pollution) Act, 1974. The allegations, stated in brief, are to

---

1   Appellants: **M.C. Mehta Vs.** Respondent: **State of Orissa and Ors.**

     AIR1992Ori225

     Hon'ble Judges/Coram: A. Pasayat and S.K. Mohanty, JJ.

2   **Meaning of Ration Decidendi:** *Ratio decidendi* is a Latin phrase meaning "the reason" or "the rationale for the decision." The *ratio decidendi* is "the point in a case which determines the judgment" or "the principle which the case establishes."

3   **Meaning of Writ:** A written order issued by a court, commanding the party to whom it is addressed to perform or cease performing a specified act

4   **Mandamus** is a judicial remedy in the form of an order from a superior court, to any government subordinate court,corporation, or public authority—to do (or forbear from doing) some specific act which that body is obliged under law to do (or refrain from doing)—and which is in the nature of public duty, and in certain cases one of a statutory duty. It cannot be issued to compel an authority to do something against statutory provision. For example, it cannot be used to force a lower court to reject or authorize applications that have been made, but if the court refuses to rule one way or the other then a mandamus can be used to order the court to rule on the applications.

5   **Article 21 in The Constitution Of India 1949**

     Protection of life and personal liberty: No person shall be deprived of his life or personal liberty except according to procedure established by law

the following effect:

The petitioner[6] came to visit the thousand year old silver city, Cuttack hoping to have a look at the rich and cultural heritage of the city. Instead what he found was a horrible pollution of water in the city. The petitioner visited certain areas nearby the Taladanda canal[7]. This canal was excavated about one hundred years back for the purpose of irrigation of a part of Mahanadi delta of Cuttack district. But it has become a refuse of **untreated waste-water** of the hospital and some other parts of the city. The water of the canal consequently has become highly polluted. A large section of population living in the bustees along the coast of the canal were using the water of the canal for bathing, drinking and other domestic purposes. The storm water drain which was constructed in the city for the purpose of discharge of excess water during heavy rains into the river Kathajori to avoid water stagnation[8] was intended to discharge such water through a sluice-gate. Unfortunately, the storm water drain which was expected to remain dry except during the rainy season was full throughout the year and sewage water from various parts of the city gets into it and consequently to the river. The unsanitary condition of this drain creates health problem in the city. A sewage treatment plant was contemplated for the city waste-water at Matagajpur, but the project has been abandoned mid-way. Steps were necessary to complete and upgrade the sewage treatment plant so as to stop discharge of city waste-water into the storm water drain and into the Taladanda canal by constructing appropriate sewage system for the city, and installing waste-water treatment plant at the hospital. Because of unavoidable situations the people were bound to drink contaminated water and consequentially becoming victims of water-borne diseases[9]. The authorities by their

---

6   **Meaning of Petitioner:** A person who presents a Petition. (**Meaning of Petition:** A formal message requesting something that is submitted to an authority)

7   Taladanda Canal Goes paralley to River Mahanadi From Cuttack till it drops in Bay Of Bengal in Paradeep.

8   **Water stagnation** occurs when water stops flowing. **Stagnant water** can be a major environmental hazard. it can cause mosquitoes to breed and reproduce that may lead to dengue.

9   **Waterborne diseases** are caused by pathogenic microorganisms that most commonly are transmitted in contaminated fresh water. Infection commonly results during bathing, washing, drinking, in the preparation of food, or the consumption of food thus infected. Various forms of waterborne diarrheal disease probably are the most prominent examples, and affect mainly children in developing countries; according to the World Health Organization, such diseases account for an estimated 4.1% of the total DALY global burden of disease, and cause about 1.8 million human deaths annually.

callous[10] acts have inflicted suffering and pain on the thousands of people by forcing them to drink the contaminated/polluted water instead of acting for their welfare to prevent it.

Environment Protection:

The Indian Constitution, in the 42nd Amendment[11], has laid the foundation in Articles 48A[12] and 51A (g)[13] for a jurisprudence of environmental protection. Today, the State and the citizens are under a fundamental obligation to protect and improve the environment, including forests, lakes, rivers, wildlife and to have compassion for living creatures. "Environment" includes water, air and land and the inter-relationship which exists among and between water, air and land and human beings, other living creatures, plants, microorganism and property. (Vide Section

---

10 **Meaning of Callous:** Emotionally hardened; unfeeling

11 The **Forty-second Amendment** of the Constitution of India, officially known as **The Constitution (Forty-second Amendment) Act, 1976**, was enacted during the Emergency (1975-1977) by the Congress government headed byIndira Gandhi.[1] Most provisions of the amendment came into effect on 3 January 1977, others were enforced from 1 February and Section 27 came into force on 1 April 1977. The 42nd Amendment is regarded as the most controversial constitutional amendment in Indian history. It attempted to reduce the power of the Supreme Court and High Courts to pronounce upon the constitutional validity of laws. It laid down the Fundamental Duties of Indian citizens to the nation. This amendment brought about the most widespread changes to the Constitution in its history, and is sometimes called a "mini-Constitution" or the "Constitution of India".

12 **Article 48A in The Constitution Of India 1949**

Protection and improvement of environment and safeguarding of forests and wild life: The State shall endeavour to protect and improve the environment and to safeguard the forests and wild life of the country

13 **Article 51A in The Constitution Of India 1949**

51A. Fundamental duties It shall be the duty of every citizen of India (a) to abide by the Constitution and respect its ideals and institutions, the national Flag and the National Anthem;

(b) to cherish and follow the noble ideals which inspired our national struggle for freedom;

(c) to uphold and protect the sovereignty, unity and integrity of India;

(d) to defend the country and render national service when called upon to do so;

(e) to promote harmony and the spirit of common brotherhood amongst all the people of India transcending religious, linguistic and regional or sectional diversities; to renounce practices derogatory to the dignity of women;

(f) to value and preserve the rich heritage of our composite culture;

(g) to protect and improve the natural environment including forests, lakes, rivers and wild life, and to have compassion for living creatures;

(h) to develop the scientific temper, humanism and the spirit of inquiry and reform;

(i) to safeguard public property and to abjure violence;

(j) to strive towards excellence in all spheres of individual and collective activity so that the nation constantly rises to higher levels of endeavour and achievement

2(a)[14] of the Environment (Protection) Act, 1986).

The expressions "pollution", "sewage effluent", "sewer" and "stream" are defined in the Environment (Protection) Act, 1986 as follows:

"2. **Definitions. In this Act, unless the context otherwise requires,--**

xxx xxx xxx

(e) 'pollution' means such contamination of water or such alteration of the physical, chemical or biological properties of water or such discharge of any sewage or trade effluent or of any other liquid gaseous or solid substance into water (whether directly or indirectly) as may, or is likely to create a nuisance or render such water harmful or injurious to public health or safety, or to domestic commercial, industrial, agricultural or other legitimate uses, or to the life and health of animals or plants or of acquatic organisms;

xxx xxx xxx

(g) 'sewage effluent' means effluent from any sewerage system of sewage disposal works and includes sullage from open drains;

(gg) 'sewer' means any conduit pipe or channel open or closed, carrying sewage or trade effluent;

xxx xxx xxx

(j) 'stream' includes--(i) river;

(ii) water course (whether flowing or for the time being dry);

(iii) inland water (whether natural or artificial);

(iv) sub-terranean[15] waters;

(v) sea or tidal water to such extent or as the case may be, to such point as the State Government may, by notification in the Official Gazette, specify in this behalf;

---

14 **Section 2(a) of the Environment (Protection) Act, 1986**

  (a) "environment" includes water, air and land and the inter- relationship which exists among and between water, air and land, and human beings, other living creatures, plants, micro-organism and property

15 **Meaning of Subterranean:**

  1. Situated or operating beneath the earth's surface; underground.

  2. Hidden; secret

xxx xxx xxx"

Water pollution problem:

The nature of water pollution problem has been highlighted by U.N. Mahida I.S.E. (Retd.) in the book "Water Pollution and Disposal of Waste-water on Land". It was stated as follows :

"The introduction of modern water carriage systems transferred the sewage disposal from the streets and surroundings of townships to neighbouring streams and rivers. This was the beginning of the problem of water pollution"

The urgency of the water pollution problem has been stated in the following words:

"The crucial question is not whether developing countries can afford such measures for the control of water pollution but it is whether they can afford to neglect them."

The enormity of the problem can be gauzed from the following extract of the World Health Organization (W.H.O.) report.

" One hospital bed out of four in the world is occupied by a patient who is ill because of polluted water. Provision of a safe and convenient water supply is the single most important activity that could be undertaken to improve the health of people living in rural areas of the developing world."

As stated by **Thomas Fuller in Gnomolgia,** 5451, "We never know the worth of water till the well is dry". Nature never did betray the heart that loved her. (Wordsworth in Tintern Abbey). Nature's fury when aroused have been described by Robert E. Sherwood in "The Petrified Forest", in the following words : "Nature is hitting back. Not with the old weapons -- Floods, plagues, holocausts. She's fighting back with strange instruments called neuroses[16]. She's deliberately inflicting mankind with the jilters. She's taking the world away from the intellectuals and giving it back to the apes"

---

16 **Meaning of Neuroses:** Any of various mental or emotional disorders, such as hypochondria or neurasthenia, arising from no apparent organic lesion or change and involving symptoms such as insecurity, anxiety, depression, and irrational fears, but without psychotic symptoms such as delusions or hallucinations

Decision by High Court:

Court held that the health of large number of people was at stake. Therefore, no amount of plea of helplessness or passing the buck to the other wings of the Department will be of any assistance. Court directed the State Government to immediately act on the reports relating to Pollution Load in Taladanda Canal and Water Pollution from Mass Bathing in Mahanadi during Kartik Purnima. Court further directed constitution of a committee consisting of the Executive Engineer, Public Health, Cuttack; the Chairman, Cuttack Municipality; the Collector, Cuttack; the Secretary to Government in the Urban and Housing Department; the Secretary to Government in the Health Department; the Executive Officer, Cuttack Municipality; the Vice-Chairman, Cuttack Development Authority; the Superintendent, S.C.B. Medical College Hospital; Cuttack; and such other functionaries and authorities as the State may feel necessary immediately to consider the reports, and take necessary steps to prevent and control **water pollution** and to maintain wholesomeness of water which is supplied for human consumption. Court further held that If there was necessity and desirability of having Sewage Treatment[17] Plant or Plants, the same be set up without further delay. The Storm Water Drain may be operated in such a manner as to prevent entry of sewage water through it to the rivers.

---

17 **Sewage treatment** is the process of removing contaminants from wastewater and household sewage, both runoff(effluents), domestic, commercial and institutional. It includes physical, chemical, and biological processes to remove physical, chemical and biological contaminants. Its objective is to produce an environmentally safe fluid waste stream (or treated effluent) and a solid waste (or treated sludge) suitable for disposal or reuse (usually as farm fertilizer)

20

Public Trust Doctrine[1]

Facts in Nutshell:

Court took notice of the News item appearing in the "Indian Express" dated February 25, 1996 under the caption – "Kamal Nath dares the mighty Beas to keep his dreams afloat". The relevant part or the news item is as under:

Kamal Nath's family has direct links with a private company, Span Motels Private Limited, which owns a resort - Span Resorts - for tourists in the Kullu-Manali valley. The problem is with another ambitious venture floated by the same company - Span Club.

The club represents Kamal Nath's dream of having a house on the bank of the Beas in the shadow of the snow-capped Zanskar ranges. The club was built after encroaching upon 27.12 bighas of land, including substantial forest land, in 1990. The land was later regularised and leased out to the company on April 11, 1994. The regularisation was done when Mr. Kamal Nath was Minister of Environment and Forests. The swollen Beas changed its course and engulfed the Span Club and the adjoining lawns, washing it away. The motel has constructed 190m wire crates on the bank of the river (upstream). The dredged material is piled up on the banks of the river. The dredging and channelising of the left bank has been done on a large scale with a view to keep high intensity of flow away from the motel. The dredging of the main channel of river was done by blasting the big boulders and removing the debris. The mouth of the natural relief/spill channel has been blocked by wire crates and dumping of boulders. The construction work was not done under expert advice. The construction work undertaken by the motel for channelising the main course has divided the main stream into two, one of which goes very near to the left bank because of which, according to the report, fresh land slip in future cannot be ruled out.

---

1   Appellants: **M.C. Mehta Vs.** Respondent: **Kamal Nath and Ors.**

(1997)1SCC388

Hon'ble Judges: Kuldip Singh and S. Saghir Ahmad, JJ.

The forest lands which have been given on lease to the Motel by the State Governments are situated at the bank of the river Beas. Beas is a young and dynamic river. It runs through Kullu valley between the mountain ranges of the Dhauladhar in the right bank and the Chandrakheni in the left. The river is fast - flowing, carrying large boulders, at the time of flood. When water velocity is not sufficient to carry the boulders, those are deposited in the channel often blocking the flow of water. Under such circumstances the river stream changes its course, remaining within the valley but swinging from one bank to the other. The right bank of the river Beas where motel is located mostly comes under forest, the left bank consists of plateaus, having steep - bank facing the river, where fruit orchards and cereal cultivation are predominant. The area being ecologically fragile and full of scenic-beauty should not have been permitted to be ' converted into private ownership and for commercial gains.

Doctrine of Public Trust:

The ancient Roman Empire developed a legal theory known as the "Doctrine of the Public Trust". It was founded on the ideas that certain common properties such as rivers, sea-shore, forests and the air were held by Government in trusteeship for the free and unimpeded use of the general public. Under the Roman Law these resources were either owned by no one (Res Nullious) or by every one in common (Res Communious). Under the English common law, however, the Sovereign could own these resources but the ownership was limited in nature, the Crown could not grant these properties to private owners if the effect was to interfere with the public interests in navigation of fishing. Resources that were suitable for these uses were deemed to be held in trust by the Crown for the benefit of the public, Joseph L. Sax, Professor of Law, University of Michigan proponent of the Modern Public Trust Doctrine in an erudite article "Public Trust Doctrine in natural resource law; effective judicial intervention"[2] has given the historical background of the Public Trust Doctrine as under:

The source of modern public trust law is found in a concept that received much attention in Roman and English law - the nature of property rights in rivers, the sea, and the seashore. That history has been given considerable attention in the legal literature, need not be repeated in detail here. But two points should be emphasized. First, certain interests, such as navigation and fishing, were sought to be preserved for the benefit of the public, accordingly, property used for the those purposes was distinguished from general public property which the sovereign could routinely grant to private owners. Second, while it was understood that in certain common properties - such as the seashore, highways, and running water - "perpetual use was dedicated to the public," it has never been clear whether the public had an enforceable right to prevent infringement of those interests. Although the state apparently did protect public uses, no evidence is available that public rights could be legally asserted against a recalcitrant government.

The Public Trust Doctrine primarily rests on the principle that certain resources like air, sea, waters and the forests have such a great importance to the people as a whole that it would be wholly unjustified to make them a subject of private ownership. The said resources being a gift of nature. They should be made freely available to everyone irrespective of the status in life. The doctrine enjoins upon the Government to protect the resources for the enjoyment of the general public rather than to permit then- use for private ownership or commercial purposes. According to Professor Sax the Public Trust Doctrine imposes the following restrictions on governmental authority:

Three types of restrictions on governmental authority are often thought to be imposed by the public trust: first, the property subject to the trust must not only be used for a public purpose, but it must be held available for use by the general public; second, the property may not be sold, even for a fair cash equivalent; and third, the property must be maintained for particular types of uses. Our Indian legal system-based on English Common Law - includes the public trust doctrine as part of its jurisprudence. The State is the trustee of all natural resources which are by nature meant for public use and enjoyment. Public at large is beneficiary of the sea-shore, running waters, airs, forests and ecologically fragile lands. The State as a trustee is under a legal duty to protect the natural resources. These resources meant for public use cannot be converted into private ownership.

Observation of Court (para 28):

Court observed that the issues presented in the present case illustrate the classic struggle between those members of the public who would preserve our rivers, forests, parks and open lands in their pristine purity and those charged with administrative responsibilities who, under the pressures of the changing needs of an increasing complex society, find it necessary to encroach to some extent open lands heretofore considered in-violate to change. The resolution of this conflict in any given case is for the legislature and not the courts. If there is a law made by Parliament or the State Legislature the courts can serve as an instrument of determining legislative intent in the exercise of its powers of judicial review under the Constitution. But in the absence of any legislation, the executive acting under the doctrine of public trust cannot abdicate the natural resources and convert them into private ownership or for commercial use. The esthetic use and the pres time glory of the natural resources, the environment and the eco-systems of our country cannot be permitted to be eroded for private, commercial or any other use unless the courts find it necessary in good faith, for the public good and in public interest to encroach upon the said resources.

Decision by Supreme Court:

Court held that the Himachal Pradesh Government committed patent breach of public trust by leasing the ecologically fragile land to the Motel management. Both the lease - transactions were in patent breach of the trust held by the State Government.

Court has also referred *Vellore Citizens Welfare Forum v. Union of India and Ors.*[3], explained the "Precautionary Principle" and "Polluters Pays principle" as under:

Some of the salient principles of "Sustainable Development", as culled out from Brundtland Report and other international documents, are inter-Generational Equity, Use and Conservation of Natural Resources, Environmental Protection, the Precautionary Principle, Polluter pays principle, Obligation to assist and cooperate, Eradication of Poverty and Financial Assistance to the developing countries. But courts are, however, of the view that "the Precautionary Principle" and "the Polluter Pays" principle are essential features of "Sustainable Development". The "precautionary Principle" - in the context of the municipal law - means:

(i) Environment measures - by the State Government and the statutory authorities - must anticipate, prevent and attack the causes of

---

3   AIR1996SC2715

environmental degradation.

(ii) Where there are threats of serious and irreversible damage, lack of scientific certainty should not be used as a reason for postponing measures to prevent environmental degradation.

(iii) The "Onus of proof" is on the actor or the developer/industrialist to show that his action is environmentally benign.

The Polluter Pays principle has been held to be a sound principle by Court in *Indian Council for Environ-Legal Action v. Union of India*[4]. The Court observed, "We are of the opinion that any principle evolved in this behalf should be simple, practical and suited to the conditions obtaining in this country". The Court ruled that "Once the activity carried on is hazardous or inherently dangerous, the persons carrying on such activity is liable to make good the loss caused to any other person by his activity irrespective of the fact whether he took reasonable care while carrying on his activity. The rule is premised upon the very nature of the activity carried on". Consequently the polluting industries are "absolutely liable to compensate for the harm caused by them to villagers in the affected area, to the soil and to the underground water and hence, they are bound to take all necessary measures to remove sludge and other pollutants lying in the affected areas". The "Polluter Pays" principle as interpreted by Court means that the absolute liability for harm to the environment extends not only the compensate the victims of pollution but a.lso the cost of restoring the environmental degradation. Remediation of the damaged environment is part of the process of "Sustainable Development" and as such polluter is liable to pay the cost to the individual sufferers as well as the cost of reversing the damaged ecology.

The precautionary principle and the polluter pays principle have been accepted as part of the law of the land. It is thus settled by Court that one who pollutes the environment must pay to reverse the damage caused by his acts.

Directions of the Court:

1. The public trust doctrine, is a part of the law of the land.

2. The prior approval granted by the Government of India, Ministry of Environment and Forest by the letter dated November 24, 1993 and the

---

4   [1996]2SCR503

lease-deed dated April 11, 1994 in favour of the Motel were quashed[5]. The lease granted to the Motel by the lease-deed in respect of 27 bighas and 12 biswas of area, was cancelled and set aside. The Himachal Pradesh Government was ordered by court to take over the area and restore it to its original-natural conditions.

3. The Motel shall pay compensation by way of cost for the restitution of the environment and ecology of the area. The pollution caused by various constitutions made by the Motel in the river bed and the banks on the river Beas has to be removed and reversed.

4. The Motel through its management shall show cause why pollution fine in addition be not imposed on the Motel.

5. The Motel shall construct a boundary wall at a distance of not more than 4 meters from the cluster of rooms (main building of the Motel) towards the river basin. The boundary wall shall be on the area of the Motel which is covered by the lease dated September 29, 1981. The Motel shall not encroach/cover/utilise any part of the river basin. The boundary wall shall separate the Motel building from the river basin. The river bank and the river basin shall be left open for the public use.

6. The Motel shall not discharge untreated effluent into the river.

7. The Himachal Pradesh Pollution Control Board shall not permit the discharge of untreated effluent into river Beas. The Board shall inspect all the hotels/institutions/factories in Kullu- Manali area and in case any of them are discharging untreated effluent/waste into the river, the Board shall take action in accordance with law. Court Ordered Span Motels Pvt. Ltd. to pay Rs Ten Lakh as exemplary damages[6].

---

5   **Meaning of Quash:** To set aside or annul, especially by judicial action.

6   **Meaning of Exemplary Damages: Exemplary damages are** often called punitive damages, these are damages requested and/or awarded in a lawsuit when the defendant's willful acts were malicious, violent, oppressive, fraudulent, wanton, or grossly reckless.

21

Water is the most important element of the nature[1]

Facts in Nutshell:

Petitioner[2], an active social worker filed petition[3] for the issuance of a writ[4]/order/direction in the nature of mandamus[5] to the respondents[6] restraining them from letting out the trade effluents into the river Ganga, till such time they put up necessary treatment plants for treating the trade effluents in order to arrest the pollution of water in the said river.

Water is the most important of the elements of the nature:

Water is the most important of the elements of the nature. River valleys are the cradles of civilization from the beginning of the world. Aryan civilization grew around the towns and villages on the banks of the river

---

1   Appellants: **M.C. Mehta Vs.** Respondent: **Union of India (UOI) and Ors.**

   AIR1988SC1037

   Hon'ble Judges/Coram: E.S. Venkataramiah and K.N. Singh, JJ.

2   **Meaning of Petitioner:** A person who presents a Petition. (**Meaning of Petition:** A formal message requesting something that is submitted to an authority)

3   **Meaning of Petition:** A formal message requesting something that is submitted to an authority

4   **Meaning of Writ:** An order issued by a court requiring that something be done or giving authority to do a specified act

5   **Mandamus** is a judicial remedy in the form of an order from a superior court, to any government subordinate court,corporation, or public authority—to do (or forbear from doing) some specific act which that body is obliged under law to do (or refrain from doing)—and which is in the nature of public duty, and in certain cases one of a statutory duty. It cannot be issued to compel an authority to do something against statutory provision. For example, it cannot be used to force a lower court to reject or authorize applications that have been made, but if the court refuses to rule one way or the other then a mandamus can be used to order the court to rule on the applications.

6   **Meaning of Respondent:** A **respondent** is a person who is called upon to issue a response to a communication made by another. In legal usage, this specifically refers to the defendant in a legal proceeding commenced by a petition, or to an appellee, or the opposing party, in an appeal of a decision by an initial fact-finder

Ganga[7]. Varanasi[8] which is one of the cities on the banks of the river Ganga is considered to be one of the oldest human settlements in the world. It is the popular belief that the river Ganga is the purifier of all but we are now led to the situation that action has to be taken to prevent the pollution of the water of the river Ganga since we have reached a stage that any further pollution of the river water is likely to lead to a catastrophe[9]. There are today large towns inhabited by millions of people on the banks of the river Ganga. There are also large industries on its banks. Sewage of the towns and cities on the banks of the river and the trade effluents of the factories and other industries are continuously being discharged into the river. It was the complaint of the petitioner that neither the Government nor the people were giving adequate attention to stop the pollution of the river Ganga. Steps have, therefore, to be taken for the purpose of protecting the cleanliness of the stream in the river Ganga, which was in fact the life sustainer of a large part of the northern India.

Importance of River Ganga:

The river Ganga is one of the greatest rivers of the world, although its entire course in only 1560 miles from its source in Himalaya to the sea. There are many rivers larger in shape and longer in size but no river in the world has been so great as the Ganga. It is great because to millions of people since centuries it is the most sacred river, it is called "Sursari" river of the Gods, Patitpawani' purifier of all sins and 'Ganga Ma' Mother Ganges. To millions of Hindus, it is the most sacred, most venerated river on earth. According the Hindus belief and Mythology to bathe in it is to wash away guilt, to drink the water, having bathed in it, and to carry it away in containers for those who may have not had the good fortune to make the pilgrimage, to it, is meritorious. To be cremated on its banks, or to die there, and to have one's ashes cast in its waters is the the wish of every Hindu. Many saints and sages have persued their quest for knowledge and enlightenment on the banks of the river Ganga. Its water

---

7   The **Ganges**, also **Ganga** is a trans-boundary river of Asia which flows through India and Bangladesh. The 2,525 km (1,569 mi) river rises in the western Himalayas in the Indianstate of Uttarakhand, and flows south and east through the Gangetic Plain of North India into Bangladesh, where it empties into the Bay of Bengal. It is the third largest river by discharge.

8   **Varanasi** also known as **Banaras** is an Indian city on the banks of the Ganges (Ganga) in Uttar Pradesh, 320 kilometres (200 mi) southeast of the state capital, Lucknow. It is the holiest of the seven sacred cities (*Sapta Puri*) in Hinduism and Jainism, and played an important role in the development of Buddhism. Some Hindus believe that death at Varanasi brings salvation.

9   A **catastrophe** is an extremely large-scale disaster, a horrible event

has not only purified the body and soul of the millions but it has given fertile land to the country in Uttar Pradesh and Bihar. Ganga has been used as means of water transport for trade and commerce. The Indian civilization of the Northern India thrived in the plains of Ganga and most of the important towns and places of pilgrimage are situated on its banks. The river Ganga has been part of Hindu civilization. The river Ganga is the life line of millions of people of India, Indian culture and civilization has grown around it. This great river drains of eight States of India, Himachal Pradesh, Punjab, Haryana, Uttar Pradesh, Rajasthan, Madhya Pradesh, Bihar and West Bengal. The Ganga has always been an integral part of the nation's history, cultures and environment. It has been the source of sustenance for the millions of people who have lived on its banks from time immemorial.

Why there is need for protecting our environment:

Article 48-A[10] of the Constitution provides that the State shall endeavour to protect and improve the environment and to safeguard the forests and wild life of the country. Article 51-A[11] of the Constitution imposes as one of the fundamental duties[12] on every citizen the duty to protect

---

10 **Article 48A in The Constitution Of India 1949**

   Protection and improvement of environment and safeguarding of forests and wild life: The State shall endeavour to protect and improve the environment and to safeguard the forests and wild life of the country

11 **Article 51A in The Constitution Of India 1949**

   51A. Fundamental duties It shall be the duty of every citizen of India (a) to abide by the Constitution and respect its ideals and institutions, the national Flag and the National Anthem;

   (b) to cherish and follow the noble ideals which inspired our national struggle for freedom;

   (c) to uphold and protect the sovereignty, unity and integrity of India;

   (d) to defend the country and render national service when called upon to do so;

   (e) to promote harmony and the spirit of common brotherhood amongst all the people of India transcending religious, linguistic and regional or sectional diversities; to renounce practices derogatory to the dignity of women;

   (f) to value and preserve the rich heritage of our composite culture;

   (g) to protect and improve the natural environment including forests, lakes, rivers and wild life, and to have compassion for living creatures;

   (h) to develop the scientific temper, humanism and the spirit of inquiry and reform;

   (i) to safeguard public property and to abjure violence;

   (j) to strive towards excellence in all spheres of individual and collective activity so that the nation constantly rises to higher levels of endeavour and achievement

12 The *Fundamental Duties* are defined as the moral obligations of all citizens to help promote a spirit of patriotism and to uphold the unity of India. These duties, set out in Part IV–A of the

and improve the natural environment including forests, lakes, rivers and wild life and to have compassion for living creatures. The proclamation adopted by the United Nations Conference on the Human Environment which took place at Stockholm from 5th to 16th of June, 1972 and in which the Indian delegation led by the Prime Minister of India took a leading role runs thus:

1. Man is both creature and molder of his environment which gives him physical sustenance and affords him the opportunity for intellectual, moral, social and spiritual growth. In the long and tortuous evolution of the human race on this planet a stage has been reached when through the rapid acceleration of science and technology, man has acquired the power, to transform his environment in countless ways and on an unprecedented scale. Both aspects of man's environment, the natural and the man made, are essential to his well being and to the enjoyment of basic human rights - Even the right to life itself.

2. The protection and improvement of the human environment is a major issue which affects the well-being of peoples and economic development throughout the world, it is the urgent desire of the peoples of the whole world and the duty of all Governments.

3. Man has constantly to sum up experience and go on discovering, inventing, creating and advancing. In our time man's capability to transform his surroundings, if used wisely, can bring to all peoples the benefits of development and the opportunity to enhance the quality of life. Wrongly or heedlessly applied, the same power can do incalculable harm to human beings and the human environment. We see around us growing evidence of man-made harm in many regions of the earth; dangerous levels of pollution in water, air, earth and living beings; major and undesirable disturbances to the ecological balance of the biosphere; destruction and depletion of irreplaceable resources; and gross deficiencies harmful to the physical, mental and social health of man, in the man-made environment; particularly in the living and working environment.

A point has been reached in history when we must shape our actions throughout the world with a more prudent care for their environmental consequences. Through ignorance or indifference we can do massive and irreversible harm to the earthly environment on which our life and well-

Constitution concern individuals and the nation. Like the Directive Principles, they are not legally enforceable.

being depend. Conversely, through fuller, knowledge and wiser action, we can achieve for ourselves and our posterity a better life in an environment more in keeping with human needs and hopes. There are broad vistas for the enhancement of environmental quality and the creation of a good life. What is needed is an enthusiastic but calm state of mind and intense but orderly work. For the purpose of attaining freedom in the world of nature man must use knowledge to build in collaboration with nature a better environment. To defend and improve the human environment for present and future generations has become an imperative goal for mankind a goal to be pursued together with, and in harmony with, the established and fundamental goals of peace and of world-wide economic and social development.

To achieve this environmental goal will demand the acceptance of responsibility by citizens and communities and by enterprises and institutions at every level, all sharing equitably in common efforts. Individuals in all walks of life as well as organizations in many fields, by their values and the sum of their actions, will shape the world environment of the future. Local and National Governments will bear the greatest burden for large-scale environmental policy and action within their jurisdictions. International co-operation is also needed in order to raise resources to support the developing countries carrying out their responsibilities in this field. A growing class of environmental problems, because they are regional or global in extent or because they affect the common international realm, will require extensive cooperation among nations and action by international organizations in the common interest.

Water Act, 1974:

Realising the importance of the prevention and control of pollution of water for human existence Parliament has passed the Water (Prevention and Control of Pollution) Act, 1974 (Act 6 of 1974) (hereinafter referred to as 'the Act') to provide for the prevention and control of water pollution and the maintaining or restoring of wholesomeness of water, for the establishment, with a view to carrying out the purposes aforesaid, of Boards for the prevention and control of water pollution, for conferring on and assigning to such Boards powers and functions relating thereto and for matters connected therewith. The Act, 1974 was passed pursuant to resolutions passed by all the Houses of Legislatures of the States of Assam, Bihar, Gujarat, Haryana, Himachal Pradesh, Jammu and Kashmir,

Karnataka, Kerala, Madhya Pradesh, Rajasthan, Tripura and West Bengal under Clause (1) of Article 252[13] of the Constitution to the effect that the prevention and control of **water pollution** should be regulated in those States by Parliamentary legislation. The Act has been since adopted by the State of Uttar Pradesh also by resolutions passed in that behalf by the Houses of Legislature of the said State in the year 1975 (vide notification No. 897/IX-3-100-74 dated 3-2-1975). Section 24[14] of the

---

13   **Article 252 in The Constitution Of India 1949**

    252. Power of Parliament to legislate for two or more States by consent and adoption of such legislation by any other State

    (1) If it appears to the Legislatures of two or more States to be desirable that any of the matters with respect to which Parliament has no power to make laws for the States except as provided in Articles 249 and 250 should be regulated in such States by Parliament by law, and if resolutions to that effect are passed by all the House of the Legislatures of those States, it shall be lawful for Parliament to pass an Act for regulating that matter accordingly, and any Act so passed shall apply to such States and to any other State by which it is adopted afterwards by resolution passed in that behalf by the House or, where there are two Houses, by each of the Houses of the Legislature of that State

    (2) Any Act so passed by Parliament may be amended or repealed by an Act of Parliament passed or adopted in like manner but shall not, as respects any State to which it applies, be amended or repealed by an Act of the Legislature of that State

14   **Section 24 in The Water (Prevention and Control of Pollution) Act, 1974**

    24. Prohibition on use of stream or well for disposal of polluting matter, etc.—

    (1) Subject to the provisions of this section,—

    (a) no person shall knowingly cause or permit any poisonous, noxious or polluting matter determined in accordance with such standards as may be laid down by the State Board to enter (whether directly or indirectly) into any 1[stream or well or sewer or on land]; or

    (b) no person shall knowingly cause or permit to enter into any stream any other matter which may tend, either directly or in combination with similar matters, to impede the proper flow of the water of the stream in a manner leading or likely to lead to a substantial aggravation of pollution due to other causes or of its consequences.

    (2) A person shall not be guilty of an offence under sub-section (1), by reason only of having done or caused to be done any of the following acts, namely:—

    (a) constructing, improving or maintaining in or across or on the bank or bed of any stream any building, bridge, weir, dam, sluice, dock, pier, drain or sewer or other permanent works which he has a right to construct, improve or maintain;

    (b) depositing any materials on the bank or in the bed of any stream for the purpose of reclaiming land or for supporting, repairing or protecting the bank or bed of such stream provided such materials are not capable of polluting such stream;

    (c) putting into any stream any sand or gravel or other natural deposit which has flowed from or been deposited by the current of such stream;

    (d) causing or permitting, with the consent of the State Board, the deposit accumulated in a well, pond or reservoir to enter into any stream.

    (3) The State Government may, after consultation with, or on the recommendation of, the State Board, exempt, by notification in the Official Gazette, any person from the operation of sub-section (1) subject to such conditions, if any, as may be specified in the notification and any condition so specified may by a like notification be altered, varied or amended

Act, 1974 prohibits the use of any stream or well for disposal of polluting matter etc. It provides that subject to the provisions of the said any poisonous, noxious[15] or polluting matter determined in accordance with such standards as may be laid down by the State Board to enter whether directly or indirectly into any stream or well or no person shall knowingly cause or permit to enter into any stream any other matter which may tend either directly or in combination with similar matters to impede the proper flow of the water of the stream in a manner leading or likely to lead to a substantial aggravation of pollution due to other causes or of its consequences. The expression stream is defined by Section 2(j)[16] of the Act, 1974 as including river, water course whether flowing or for the time being dry, inland water whether natural or artificial, sub-terrene waters, sea or tidal waters to such extent or as the case may be to such point as the State Government may by notification in the Official Gazette, specify in that behalf. Under the Act it is permissible to establish a Central Board and the State Boards. The functions of the Central Board and the

---

15 **Meaning of Noxious:**

1. Harmful to living things; injurious to health

2. Harmful to the mind or morals; corrupting

16 **Section 2(j) of the Water (Prevention and Control of Pollution) Act, 1974**

(j) "stream" includes —

(i) water course (whether flowing or for the time being dry);

(ii) inland water (whether natural or artificial);

(iii) subterranean waters;

(iv) sea or tidal waters to such extent or, as the case may be, to such point as the State Government may, by notification in the Official Gazette, specify in this behalf

State Boards are described in Sections 16[17] and 17[18] respectively. One of

---

17 **Section 16 of the Water (Prevention and Control of Pollution) Act, 1974**

Functions of Central Board-

(1) Subject to the provisions of this Act, the main function of the Central Board shall be to promote cleanliness of streams and wells in different areas of the States.

(2) In particular and without prejudice to the generality of the foregoing function, the Central Board may perform all or any of the following functions, namely:-

(a) advise the Central Government on any matter concerning the prevention and control of water pollution;

(b) co-ordinate the activities of the State Boards and resolve disputes among them;

(c) provide technical assistance and guidance to the State Boards, carry out and sponsor investigations and research relating to problems of water pollution and prevention, control or abatement of water pollution;

(d) plan and organise the training of persons engaged or to be engaged in programmes for the prevention, control or abatement of water pollution on such terms and conditions as the Central Board may specify;

(e) organise through mass media a comprehensive programme regarding the prevention and control of water pollution;

[33][(ee) perform such of the functions of any State Board as may be specified in an order made under sub-section (2) of section 18];

(f) collect, compile and publish technical and statistical data relating to water pollution and the measures devised for its effective prevention and control and prepare manuals, codes or guides relating to treatment and disposal of sewage and trade effluents and disseminate information connected therewith;

(g) lay down, modify or annul, in consultation with the State Government concerned, the standards for a stream or well:

Provided that different standards may be laid down for the same stream or well or for different streams or wells, having regard to the quality of water, flow characteristics of the stream or well and the nature of the use of the water in such stream or well or streams or wells;

(h) plan and cause to be executed a nation-wide programme for the prevention, control or abatement of water pollution;

(i) perform such other functions as may be prescribed.

(3) The Board may establish or recognise a laboratory or laboratories to enable the Board to perform its functions under this section efficiently, including the analysis of samples of water from any stream or well or of samples of any sewage or trade effluents.

18 **Section 17 of the Water (Prevention and Control of Pollution) Act, 1974**

Functions of State Board-

(1) Subject to the provisions of this Act, the functions of a State Board shall be-

(a) to plan a comprehensive programme for the prevention, control or abatement of pollution of streams and wells in the State and to secure the execution thereof;

(b) to advise the State Government on any matter concerning the prevention, control or abatement of water pollution;

(c) to collect and disseminate information relating to water pollution and the prevention, control or abatement thereof;

(d) to encourage, conduct and participate in investigations and research relating to problems of water pollution and prevention, control or abatement of water pollution;

the functions of the State Board is to inspect sewage or trade effluents, works and plants for the treatment of sewage and trade effluents, and to review plans, specifications or other data relating to plants set up for the treatment of water, works for the purification and the system for the disposal of sewage or trade effluents. 'Trade effluent' includes any liquid, gaseous or solid substance which is discharged from any premises used for carrying on any trade or industry, other than domestic sewage. The State Board is also entrusted with the work of laying down standards of treatment of sewage and trade effluents to be discharged into any

---

(e) to collaborate with the Central Board in organising the training of persons engaged or to be engaged in programmes relating to prevention, control or abatement of water pollution and to organise mass education programmes relating thereto;

(f) to inspect sewage or trade effluents, works and plants for the treatment of sewage and trade effluents and to review plans, specifications or other data relating to plants set up for the treatment of water, works for the purification thereof and the system for the disposal of sewage or trade effluents or in connection with the grant of any consent as required by this Act;

(g) lay down, modify or annul effluent standards for the sewage and trade effluents and for the quality of receiving waters (not being water in an inter-State stream) resulting from the discharge of effluents and to classify waters of the State;

(h) to evolve economical and reliable methods of treatment of sewage and trade effluents, having regard to the peculiar conditions of soils, climate and water resources of different regions and more especially the prevailing flow characteristics of water in streams and wells which render it impossible to attain even the minimum degree of dilution;

(i) to evolve methods of utilisation of sewage and suitable trade effluents in agriculture;

(j) to evolve efficient methods of disposal of sewage and trade effluents on land, as are necessary on account of the predominant conditions of scant stream flows that do not provide for major part of the year the minimum degree of dilution;

(k) to lay down standards of treatment of sewage and trade effluents to be discharged into any particular stream taking into account the minimum fair weather dilution available in that stream and the tolerance limits of pollution permissible in the water of the stream, after the discharge of such effluents;

(l) to make, vary or revoke any order-

(i) for the prevention, control or abatement of discharges of waste into streams or wells;
(ii) requiring any person concerned to construct new systems for the disposal of sewage and trade effluents or to modify, alter or extend any such existing system or to adopt such remedial measures as are necessary to prevent control or abate water pollution;

(m) to lay down effluent standards to be complied with by persons while causing discharge of sewage or sullage or both and to lay down, modify or annul effluent standards for the sewage and trade effluents;

(n) to advise the State Government with respect to the location of any industry the carrying on of which is likely to pollute a stream or well;

(o) to perform such other functions as may be prescribed or as may, from time to time be entrusted to it by the Central Board or the State Government

(2) The Board may establish or recognise a laboratory or laboratories to enable the Board to perform its functions under this section efficiently, including the analysis of samples of water from any stream or well or of samples of any sewage or trade effluents.

particular stream taking into account the minimum fair weather dilution available in that stream and the tolerance limits of pollution permissible in the water of the stream, after the discharge of such effluents. The State Board is also entrusted with the power of making application to courts for restraining apprehended pollution of water in streams or well.

Environment Protection Act, 1986:

Parliament has also passed the Environment (Protection) Act, 1986 (29 of 1986) which has been brought into force throughout India with effect from Nov. 19, 1986. Section 3[19] of this Act confers power on the

---

19 Section 3 of Environment Protection Act, 1986

Power of Central Government to take measures to protect and improve Environment

(1) Subject to the provisions of this Act, the Central Government, shall have the power to take all such measures as it deems necessary or expedient for the purpose of protecting and improving the quality of the environment and preventing controlling and abating environmental pollution.

(2) In particular, and without prejudice to the generality of the provisions of sub-section (1), such measures may include measures with respect to all or any of the following matters, namely:--

(i) co-ordination of actions by the State Governments, officers and other authorities--

(a) under this Act, or the rules made thereunder, or

(b) under any other law for the time being in force which is relatable to the objects of this Act;

(ii) planning and execution of a nation-wide programme for the prevention, control and abatement of environmental pollution;

(iii) laying down standards for the quality of environment in its various aspects;

(iv) laying down standards for emission or discharge of environmental pollutants from various sources whatsoever:

Provided that different standards for emission or discharge may be laid down under this clause from different sources having regard to the quality or composition of the emission or discharge of environmental pollutants from such sources;

(v) restriction of areas in which any industries, operations or processes or class of industries, operations or processes shall not be carried out or shall be carried out subject to certain safeguards;

(vi) laying down procedures and safeguards for the prevention of accidents which may cause environmental pollution and remedial measures for such accidents;

(vii) laying down procedures and safeguards for the handling of hazardous substances;

(viii) examination of such manufacturing processes, materials and substances as are likely to cause environmental pollution;

(ix) carrying out and sponsoring investigations and research relating to problems of environmental pollution;

(x) inspection of any premises, plant, equipment, machinery, manufacturing or other processes, materials or substances and giving, by order, of such directions to such authorities, officers or persons as it may consider necessary to take steps for the prevention, control and abatement of environmental pollution;

(xi) establishment or recognition of environmental laboratories and institutes to carry out the functions entrusted to such environmental laboratories and institutes under this Act;

Central Government to take all such measures as it deems necessary or expedient for the purpose of protecting and improving the quality of the environment and preventing, controlling and abating environmental pollution. Environment includes water, air and land and the inter-relationship which exists among and between water, air and land and human beings, other living creatures, plants, microorganism and property, (Vide Section 2(a)[20] of the Environment (Protection) Act, 1986). Under Section 3(2)(iv) of the said Act the Central Government may lay down standards for emission[21] or discharge of environmental pollutants from various sources whatsoever. Notwithstanding anything contained in any other law but subject to the provisions of the Environment (Protection) Act, 1986 the Central Government may under Section 5[22] of the Act, in

---

(xii) collection and dissemination of information in respect of matters relating to environmental pollution;

(xiii) preparation of manuals, codes or guides relating to the prevention, control and abatement of environmental pollution;

(xiv) such other matters as the Central Government deems necessary or expedient for the purpose of securing the effective implementation of the provisions of this Act.

(3) The Central Government may, if it considers it necessary or expedient so to do for the purpose of this Act, by order, published in the Official Gazette, constitute an authority or authorities by such name or names as may be specified in the order for the purpose of exercising and performing such of the powers and functions (including the power to issue directions under section 5) of the Central Government under this Act and for taking measures with respect to such of the matters referred to in sub-section (2) as may be mentioned in the order and subject to the supervision and control of the Central Government and the provisions of such order, such authority or authorities may exercise and powers or perform the functions or take the measures so mentioned in the order as if such authority or authorities had been empowered by this Act to exercise those powers or perform those functions or take such measures.

20 **Section 2(a) of the Environment (Protection) Act, 1986**

"environment" includes water, air and land and the inter- relationship which exists among and between water, air and land, and human beings, other living creatures, plants, micro-organism and property

21 **Meaning of Emission:**

1. The act or an instance of emitting.

2. Something emitted.

3. A substance discharged into the air, especially by an internal combustion engine.

22 **Section 5 of the Environment Protection Act, 1986:**

Power to Give Directions:

Notwithstanding anything contained in any other law but subject to the provisions of this Act, the Central Government may, in the exercise of its powers and performance of its functions under this Act, issue directions in writing to any person, officer or any authority and such person, officer or authority shall be bound to comply with such directions.[3]

Explanation--For the avoidance of doubts, it is hereby declared that the power to issue directions under this section includes the power to direct--

the exercise of its powers and performance of its functions under that Act issue directions in writing to any person, officer or authority and such authority is bound to comply with such directions. The power to issue directions under the said section includes the power to direct the closure, prohibition or regulation of any industry, operation or process or stoppage or regulation of the supply of electricity or water or any other service. Section 9[23] of the said Act imposes a duty on every person to take steps to prevent or mitigate the environmental pollution. Section 15[24] of the said Act contains provisions relating to penalties that may be imposed for the contravention of any of the provisions of the said Act or directions issued thereunder.

(a) the closure, prohibition or regulation of any industry, operation or process; or

(b) stoppage or regulation of the supply of electricity or water or any other service.

23　**Section 9 of the Environment Protection Act, 1986:**

Furnishing of Information to Authorities and Agencies in Certain Cases

(1) Where the discharge of any environmental pollutant in excess of the prescribed standards occurs or is apprehended to occur due to any accident or other unforeseen act or event, the person responsible for such discharge and the person in charge of the place at which such discharge occurs or is apprehended to occur shall be bound to prevent or mitigate the environmental pollution caused as a result of such discharge and shall also forthwith--

(a) intimate the fact of such occurrence or apprehension of such occurrence; and

(b) be bound, if called upon, to render all assistance,

to such authorities or agencies as may be prescribed.

(2) On receipt of information with respect to the fact or apprehension on any occurrence of the nature referred to in sub-section (1), whether through intimation under that sub-section or otherwise, the authorities or agencies referred to in sub-section (1) shall, as early as practicable, cause such remedial measures to be taken as necessary to prevent or mitigate the environmental pollution.

(3) The expenses, if any, incurred by any authority or agency with respect to the remedial measures referred to in sub-section (2), together with interest (at such reasonable rate as the Government may, by order, fix) from the date when a demand for the expenses is made until it is paid, may be recovered by such authority or agency from the person concerned as arrears of land revenue or of public demand.

24　**Section 15 of the Environment Protection Act, 1986:**

Penalty for Contravention of the Provisions of the act and the rules, orders and Directions

(1) Whoever fails to comply with or contravenes any of the provisions of this Act, or the rules made or orders or directions issued thereunder, shall, in respect of each such failure or contravention, be punishable with imprisonment for a term which may extend to five years with fine which may extend to one lakh rupees, or with both, and in case the failure or contravention continues, with additional fine which may extend to five thousand rupees for every day during which such failure or contravention continues after the conviction for the first such failure or contravention.

(2) If the failure or contravention referred to in sub-section (1) continues beyond a period of one year after the date of conviction, the offender shall be punishable with imprisonment for a term which may extend to seven years.

Decision by Supreme Court:

Millions of our people in the Ganga drink its water under an abiding faith and belief to purify themselves to achieve moksha[25] release from the cycle of birth and death. It is tragic that the Ganga, which has since time immemorial, purified the people is being polluted by man in numerous ways, by dumping of garbage, throwing carcass[26] of dead animals and discharge of effluents. Scientific investigations and survey reports have shown that the Ganga which serves one-third of the India's population is polluted by the discharge of municipal sewage and the industrial effluents in the river. The pollution of the river Ganga is affecting the life, health, and ecology of the Indo-Gangetic Plain. The Government as well as Parliament both have taken a number of steps to control the water pollution, but nothing substantial has been achieved. Court held that it is the sacred duty of all those who reside or carry on business around the river Ganga to ensure the purity of Ganga. Tanneries[27] have been polluting the Ganga in a big way. Court issued the directions for the closure of those tanneries which have failed to take minimum steps required for the primary treatment of industrial effluent. *Court observed that "closure of tanneries may bring unemployment, loss of revenue, but life, health and ecology have greater importance to the people".*

---

25 **Moksha** also called **vimoksha**, **vimukti** and **mukti**, means emancipation, liberation or release. In eschatological sense, it connotes freedom from *samsāra*, the cycle of death and rebirth.

26 **Meaning of Carcass:**

   1. The dead body of an animal, especially one slaughtered for food.

   2. The body of a human.

27 **Meaning of Tannery:** A place or building where skins and hides are tanned

22

Smoking in Public Places is illegal, unconstitutional and violative of Right to Life[1]

Facts in Nutshell:

Petition[2] highlighting the public health issue of the dangers of passive smoking[3] and in which prayers were made to declare that smoking of tobacco in any form, whether in the form of cigarette, cigar, beedies or otherwise in public places is illegal, unconstitutional and violative of Article 21[4] of the Constitution of India; issue a writ[5] in the nature of mandamus[6] or such other writ commanding the respondents[7] to take

---

1   Appellants: **K. Ramakrishnan and Anr. Vs.** Respondent: **State of Kerala and Ors.**

    AIR1999Ker385, ILR1999(3)Kerala383

    Hon'ble Judges/Coram: A.R. Lakshmanan, Ag. C.J. and K. Narayana Kurup, Judge

2   **Meaning of Petition:** A formal message requesting something that is submitted to an authority

3   **Passive smoking** is the inhalation of smoke, called **second-hand smoke** (**SHS**), or **environmental tobacco smoke(ETS)**, by persons other than the intended "active" smoker. It occurs when tobacco smoke permeates any environment, causing its inhalation by people within that environment. Exposure to second-hand tobacco smoke causes disease, disability, and death.

4   **Article 21 in The Constitution Of India 1949**

    Protection of life and personal liberty: No person shall be deprived of his life or personal liberty except according to procedure established by law

5   **Meaning of Writ:** A written order issued by a court, commanding the party to whom it is addressed to perform or cease performing a specified act.

6   **Mandamus** is a judicial remedy in the form of an order from a superior court, to any government subordinate court, corporation, or public authority—to do (or forbear from doing) some specific act which that body is obliged under law to do (or refrain from doing)—and which is in the nature of public duty, and in certain cases one of a statutory duty. It cannot be issued to compel an authority to do something against statutory provision. For example, it cannot be used to force a lower court to reject or authorize applications that have been made, but if the court refuses to rule one way or the other then a mandamus can be used to order the court to rule on the applications.

7   **Meaning of Respondent:** A **respondent** is a person who is called upon to issue a response to a communication made by another. In legal usage, this specifically refers to the defendant in a legal proceeding commenced by a petition, or to an appellee, or the opposing party, in an appeal of a decision by an initial fact-finder

appropriate and immediate measures to prosecute[8] and punish all persons guilty of smoking in public places treating the said act as satisfying the definition of 'public nuisance' as defined under Section 268[9] of the Indian Penal Code.

Cigarette Smoking:

One million Indians die every year from tobacco-related diseases. This is more than the number of deaths due to motor accidents, AIDS, alcohol and drug abuse put together, say the Indian Medical Association (IMA) and the Indian Academy of Paediatrics (IAP), quoting studies. Cigarette smoking is the major preventable cause of death in America, contributing to an estimated 350000 deaths annually. Epidemiologic[10] and experimental evidence has identified cigarette smoking as the primary cause of lung cancer and chronic obstructive pulmonary diseases (COPD)[11] and as a major risk factor for coronary heart disease. Smoking has been associated with other cancers, cerebrovascular and peripheral vascular diseases, and peptic ulcer disease. Smokers also suffer more acute respiratory illness. Cigarette smoke, consisting of particles dispersed in a gas phase, is a complex mixture of thousands of compounds produced by the incomplete combustion of the tobacco leaf. Smoke constituents strongly implicated in causing disease are nicotine and tar in the particulate phase and carbon monoxide in the gas phase. Smokers have a 70 per cent higher mortality rate than non smokers. The risk of dying increases with the amount and duration of smoking and is higher in smokers who inhale. Coronary heart disease is the chief contributor to the excess

---

8   Meaning of Prosecute:

    a. To initiate civil or criminal court action against.

    b. To seek to obtain or enforce by legal action.

9   Section 268 in The Indian Penal Code

    268. Public nuisance—A person is guilty of a public nuisance who does any act or is guilty of an illegal omission which causes any common injury, danger or annoyance to the public or to the people in general who dwell or occupy property in the vicinity, or which must necessarily cause injury, obstruction, danger or annoyance to persons who may have occasion to use any public right. A common nuisance is not excused on the ground that it causes some convenience or advantage

10 Meaning of Epidemiologic: The branch of medicine that deals with the study of the causes, distribution, and control of disease in populations

11 Chronic obstructive pulmonary disease (COPD), also known as chronic obstructive lung disease (COLD), and chronic obstructive airway disease (COAD), among others, is a type of obstructive lung disease characterized by chronically poor airflow. It typically worsens over time. The main symptoms include shortness of breath, cough, and sputum production. Most people with chronic bronchitis have COPD.

mortality among cigarette smokers, followed by lung cancer and chronic obstructive pulmonary disease (COPD). Life expectancy is significantly shortened by smoking cigarettes. Tobacco smoke also gets dissolved in the saliva and is swallowed, exposing the upper gastrointestinal tract to carcinogens. A strong association between smoking and lung cancer has been demonstrated in multiple prospective and retrospective epidemiologic studies, and corroborated by autopsy evidence. Lung cancer has been the leading cause of cancer death in men since the 1950s, and it surpassed breast cancer as a leading cause of cancer death in women in 1985. Male smokers have a tenfold higher risk of developing lung cancer, and the risk increases with the number of cigarettes smoked. There is also strong evidence that smoking is a major cause of cancers of the larynx[12], oral cavity anoesophagus. The risk of these cancers increases with the intensity of exposure to cigarette smoke either active or passive. Epidemiologic studies show an association between smoking and cancers of the bladder, pancreas stomach, and uterine cervix[13].

Cigarette smoking is a major independent risk factor for coronary artery disease. Retrospective and prospective epidemiologic studies have demonstrated a strong relationship between smoking and coronary morbidity and mortality in both men and women. The coronary disease death rate in smokers is 70% higher than in nonsmokers, and the risk increases with the amount of cigarette exposure. The risk of sudden death is two to four times higher in smokers. Smoking is also a risk factor for cardiac arrest and severe malignant arrythmias. In addition to increased coronary mortality, smokers have a higher risk of non fatal myocardial infraction or unstable angina. Patients with angina lower their exercise tolerance if they smoke. Women who smoke and use oral contraceptives or pot-menopausal estrogen replacement greatly increase their risk of myocardial infarction.

Autopsy studies demonstrate more atheromatous changes in smokers than nonsmokers. Carbon monoxide in cigarette smoke decreases oxygen delivery to endothelial tissues. In addition, smoking may trigger acute

---

12 **Larynx:** The part of the respiratory tract between the pharynx and the trachea, having walls of cartilage and muscle and containing the vocal cords enveloped in folds of mucous membrane.

13 The **cervix** is one of the parts of the female reproductive system that lies between the uterus and vagina. The cervix has a central canal and an internal and external opening, and is between two and three centimetres long. The ectocervix refers to the outer part of the cervix, and has an epithelia that changes from a layer of column-type cellsto multiple layers of flat cells over time. Because of this change, known as metaplasia, this part of the cervix is at increased risk of cancer.

ischemia. Carbon monoxide decreases myocardial oxygen supply, while nicotine increases myocardial demand by releasing catecholamines that raise blood pressure, heart rate, and conractility. Carbon monoxide and nicotine also induce platelet aggregation that may cause occulision of narrowed vessels. Cigarette smoking is the most important risk factor for peripheral vascular disease. In patients with intermittent claudication, smoking lowers exercise tolerance and may shorten graft survival after vascular surgery. Smokers have more aortic atherosclerosis and an increased risk of dying from a ruptured aortic aneurysm. Smokers under the age of 65 have a higher risk of dying from cerebrovascular disease and women who smoke have a greater risk of subarachnoid haemorrhage, especially if they also use oral contraceptives.

Smoking and Pulmonary Disease:

Cigarette smoking is the primary cause of chronic bronchitis and emphysema[14]. Smokers have a higher prevalence of respiratory symptoms than non smokers. Studies of pulmonary function indicate that impairment exists in asymptomatic as well as symptomatic smokers. Smokers have a higher risk of acute as well as chronic pulmonary disease. Inhaling cigarette smoke impairs pulmonary clearance mechanisms by paralyzing ciliary transport. This may explain the susceptibility to viral respiratory infections, including influenza. Smokers who develop acute respiratory infections have longer and more severe courses, with a more prolonged cough.

Other Health Consequences:

Smokers have a higher prevalence of peptic ulcer disease[15] and a higher case fatality rate. Smoking has been associated with increased osteoporosis[16] in men and post-menopausal women. Female smokers weigh less than non smokers and have an earlier age of menopause; both of these factors are associated with osteoporosis and may contribute to the relationship between smoking and osteoporosis. Moreover, smoking depresses serum estrogen levels in post-menopausal women taking

---

14 Emphysema gradually damages the air sacs (alveoli) in your lungs, making you progressively more short of breath. Emphysema is one of several diseases known collectively as chronic obstructive pulmonary disease (COPD).

15 Peptic ulcer disease refers to painful sores or ulcers in the lining of the stomach or first part of the small intestine, called the duodenum.

16 **Osteoporosis** is a progressive bone disease that is characterized by a decrease in bone mass and density which can lead to an increased risk of fracture

estrogen replacement therapy.

Passive Smoking:

Nonsmokers involuntarily inhale the smoke of nearby smokers, a phenomenon known as passive smoking. Wives, children and friends of smokers are a highly risk-prone group. Inhalation of sidestream smoke by a non-smoker is definitely more harmful to him than to the actual smoker as he inhales more toxins. This is because sidestream smoke contains three times more nicotine[17], three times more tar and about 50 times more ammonia[18]. Passive smoking (because of smoking by their fathers) could lead to severe complications in babies aged below two. It is pointed out that in India hospital admission rates are 28 per cent higher among the children of smokers. These children have acute lower respiratory infection, decreased lung function, increased eczema and asthma and increased cot deaths. Also children of heavy smokers tend to be shorter. Passive smoking is associated with an overall 23 per cent increase in risk of coronary heart disease (CHD) among men and women who had never smoked.

Maternal smoking during pregnancy increases risks to foetus and non-smokers chronically exposed to tobacco smoke will suffer health hazards. Maternal smoking during pregnancy contributes to fetal growth retardation. Infants born to mothers who smoke weigh an average of 200 gm less but have no shorter gestations than infants of non-smoking mothers. Carbon monoxide[19] in smoke may decrease oxygen availability to the fetus and account for the growth retardation. Smoking during pregnancy has also been linked with higher rates of spontaneous abortion, fetal death, and neonatal death.

When smoking occurs in enclosed areas with poor ventilation, such as in buses, bars, and conference rooms, high levels of smoke exposure can occur. Acute exposure to smoke-contaminated air decreases exercise

---

17 **Nicotine** is a potent parasympathomimetic alkaloid found in the nightshade family of plants (Solanaceae) and a stimulant drug. It is a nicotinic acetylcholine receptor agonist. It is made in the roots and accumulates in the leaves of the plants.

18 **Ammonia**, or **azane**, is a compound of nitrogen and hydrogen with the formula NH_3. It is a colourless gas with a characteristic pungent smell.

19 **Carbon monoxide** (CO) is a colorless, odorless, and tasteless gas that is slightly less dense than air. It is toxic to humans and animals when encountered in higher concentrations, although it is also produced in normal animal metabolism in low quantities, and is thought to have some normal biological functions. In the atmosphere, it is spatially variable and short lived, having a role in the formation of ground-level ozone.

capacity in healthy non-smokers and can worsen symptoms in individuals with angina, chronic obstructive pulmonary disease (COPD) or asthma. Chronic exposure to smoky air occurs in the workplace and in the homes of smokers. Non-smokers in smoky workplaces develop small-airways dysfunction similar to that observed in tight smokers. Compared to the children of non-smokers, children whose parents smoke have more respiratory infections throughout childhood, a higher risk of asthma, and alternations in pulmonary function tests. In recent studies of non-smoking women, those married to smokers had higher lung cancer rates than those married to non-smokers. Chronic smoke exposure may be associated with increased incidence of cardiopulmonary disease in nonsmokers.

Environmental tobacco smoke (ETS) also contributes to respiratory morbidity of children. Increased platelet[20] aggregation also occurs when a nonsmoker smokes or is passively exposed to smoke. Although environmental tobacco smoke (ETS) differs from "mainstream smoke" in several ways, it contains many of the same toxic substances. Infants and toddlers[21] may be especially at risk when exposed to environmental tobacco smoke (ETS). Considering the substantial morbidity, and even modality of acute respiratory illness in childhood, a doubling in risk attributable to passive smoking clearly represents a serious paediatric health problem. Exposure to environmental tobacco smoke (ETS) has been associated with increased asthma-related trips to the emergency room of hospitals. There is now sufficient evidence to conclude that passive smoking is associated with additional episodes and increased severity of asthma in children who already have the disease. Exposure to passive smoking may alter children's intelligence and behaviour and passive smoke exposure in childhood may be a risk factor for developing lung cancer as an adult. Thus, it can be safely concluded that the dangers of passive smoking are real, broader than once believed and parallel those of direct smoke.

National tobacco control strategy:

Government of India is a party to 16 or so resolutions adopted by the World Health Organisation since the 1970s, particularly the one adopted

---

20 **Platelets** are one of the three formed elements of the blood, found only in mammals, whose function, along with coagulation factors, is to stop bleeding.

21 **Meaning of Toddler:**

   1. One who toddles, especially a young child learning to walk.

   2. A size of clothing for children between the ages of about one and three years.

in 1986 which urged member-countries to formulate a comprehensive national tobacco control strategy. It was envisaged that the strategy would contain measures

(i) To ensure effective protection to non-smokers from involuntary exposure to tobacco smoke;

(ii) To promote abstention from the use of tobacco to protect children and young people from becoming addicted;

(iii) To ensure that a good example is set on all health-related premises by all health personnel;

(iv) To progressively eliminate all incentives which maintain and promote the use of tobacco;

(v) To prescribe statutory health warnings on cigarette packets and the containers of all types of tobacco products;

(vi) To establish programmes of education and public information on tobacco and health issues with the active involvement of health professionals and media;

(vii) To monitor trends in smoking and other forms of tobacco use, tobacco-related diseases and effectiveness of national smoking control action;

(viii) To promote viable economic alternatives to tobacco production, trade and taxation; and

(ix) To establish a national focal point to stimulate, support and coordinate all these activities.

Despite the fact that India is a signatory to these resolutions it is saddening to note that no significant follow-up action has been taken, except banning smoking in public places and public transport and printing a statutory warning on cigarette packets.

Right to Life:

Article 21 of the Constitution of India provides that no person shall be deprived of his life or personal liberty except according to procedure established by law. The word 'life' in this article is very significant as it covers every facet of human existence. The word 'life' has not been defined in the Constitution but it does not mean nor can it be restricted only to the vegetative or animal life or mere existence from conception to death. Life does not merely connote a continued drudgery[22] through life. The expression 'life' has a much wider meaning bringing within its sweep some of the finer graces of human civilisation which makes life worth living[23]. Life includes all such amenities and facilities which a person born in a free country is entitled to enjoy with dignity, legally and constitutionally. The apex Court has interpreted Article 21 giving wide meaning to 'life' which includes the quality of life, adequate nutrition, clothing and shelter and cannot be restricted merely to physical existence. The word 'life' in the Constitution has not been used in a limited manner. A wide meaning should be given to the expression 'life' to enable a man not only to sustain life but to enjoy it in a full measure. The sweep of right to life conferred by Article 21 of the Constitution is wide and far-reaching so as to bring within its scope the right to pollution free air and the "right to decent environment[24].

Decision by High Court:

Court held that there can be no doubt that smoking in public place will vitiate the atmosphere so as to make it noxious[25] to the health of persons who happened to be there. Therefore, smoking in a public place is an offence punishable under Section 278[26] IPC.

Directions by High court:

i) Public smoking of tobacco in any form whether in the form of cigarettes, cigars, beedies or otherwise is illegal, unconstitutional and violative of Article 21 of the Constitution of India.

ii) Tobacco smoking in public places falls within the mischief of the penal provisions relating to "public nuisance" as contained in the Indian Penal

---

22 **Meaning of Drudgery:** Tedious, menial, or unpleasant work

23 *Board of Trustees of the Port of Bombay v. D. R. Nadkarni,* AIR 1983 SC 109

24 *Shantistar Builders v. Narayan Khimalal Totame,* AIR 1990 SC 630

25 **Meaning of Noxious:**

    1. Harmful to living things; injurious to health

    2. Harmful to the mind or morals; corrupting

26 **Section 278 in The Indian Penal Code**

    Making atmosphere noxious to health: Whoever voluntarily vitiates the atmosphere in any place so as to make it noxious to the health of persons in general dwelling or carrying on business in the neighbourhood or passing along a public way, shall be punished with fine which may extend to five hundred rupees.

Code and also the definition of "air pollution" as contained in the statutes dealing with the protection and preservation of the environment, in particular the Air (Prevention and Control of Pollution) Act, 1981.

23

Noise pollution[1]

Facts in Nutshell:

Petition[2] filed by Shri Anil K. Mittal, an engineer by profession moving the Court *pro bono publico*[3]. The immediate provocation for filing the petition was that a 13 year old girl was a victim of rape (as reported in newspapers of January 3, 1998). Her cries for help sunk and went unheard due to blaring noise of music over loudspeaker in the neighbourhood. The victim girl, later in the evening, set herself ablaze and died of 100% burn injuries. The petition complains of noise created by the use of the loudspeakers being used in religious performances or singing *bhajans* and the like in busy commercial localities on the days of weekly offs. Best quality hi-fi audio systems were used. Open space, meant for use by the schools in the locality, is let out for use in marriage functions and parties wherein merry making goes on with hi-fi amplifiers and loudspeakers without any regard to timings. Modern residents of the locality organize terrace parties for socializing and use high capacity stereo systems in abundance. These are a few instances of noise pollution generated much to the chagrin of students taking examinations who find it utterly difficult to concentrate on studies before and during examinations. The noise polluters have no regard for the inconvenience and discomfort of the people in the vicinity. Noise pollution has had its victims in the past and continues to have victims today as well. The petitioner invoke the writ[4] jurisdiction

---

1   Appellants: **In**   **Re:**   **Noise**   **Pollution**   -   **Implementation**   of   the   **Laws**   for **restricting**   use   of   **loudspeakers**   and   high   volume   producing   sound   systems **WITH**   Appellants: **Forum,**   **Prevention**   of   **Envn.**   and   **Sound**   **Pollution** Vs. Respondent: **Union of India (UOI) and Anr.**

    AIR2005SC3136

    Hon'ble Judges/Coram: R.C. Lahoti, C.J. and Ashok Bhan, Judge

2   **Meaning of Petition:** A formal message requesting something that is submitted to an authority

3   ***Pro bono publico*** (English: for the public good; usually shortened to ***pro bono***) is a Latin phrase for professional work undertaken voluntarily and without payment or at a reduced fee as a public service. It is common in the legal profession and is increasingly seen in architecture, marketing, medicine, technology, and strategy consulting firms.

4   **Meaning of Writ:** A written order issued by a court, commanding the party to whom it is

of Supreme Court so that there may not be victims of noise pollution in future. The principal prayer was that the existing laws for restricting the use of loudspeakers and other high volume noise producing audio-video systems, be directed to be rigorously enforced.

Right to Life and Personal Liberty:

Article 21[5] of the Constitution guarantees life and personal liberty to all persons. It is well settled by repeated pronouncements of Supreme Court as also the High Courts that right to life enshrined in Article 21 is not of mere survival or existence. It guarantees a right of person to life with human dignity. Therein are included, all the aspects of life which go to make a person's life meaningful, complete and worth living. The human life has its charm and there is no reason why the life should not be enjoyed along with all permissible pleasures. Anyone who wishes to live in peace, comfort and quiet within his house has a right to prevent the noise as pollutant[6] reaching him. No one can claim a right to create noise even in his own premises which would travel beyond his precincts[7] and cause nuisance to neighbours or others. Any noise which has the effect of materially interfering with the ordinary comforts of life judged by the standard of a reasonable man is nuisance[8]. How and when a nuisance created by noise becomes actionable has to be answered by reference to its degree and the surrounding circumstances including the place and the time.

Those who make noise often take shelter behind Article 19(1)A[9] pleading

---

addressed to perform or cease performing a specified act

5   **Article 21 in The Constitution Of India 1949**

   Protection of life and personal liberty: No person shall be deprived of his life or personal liberty except according to procedure established by law

6   **Meaning of Pollutant:** Something that pollutes, especially a waste material that contaminates air, soil, or water.

7   **Meaning of Precincts:**

   a. A place or enclosure marked off by definite limits, such as walls.

   b. A boundary

8   **Meaning of Nuisance:** A use of property or course of conduct that interferes with the legal rights of others by causing damage, annoyance, or inconvenience.

9   **Article 19(1) in The Constitution Of India 1949**

   (1) All citizens shall have the right

   (a) to freedom of speech and expression;

   (b) to assemble peaceably and without arms;

freedom of speech and right to expression. Undoubtedly, the freedom of speech and right to expression are fundamental rights but the rights are not absolute. Nobody can claim a fundamental right[10] to create noise by amplifying the sound of his speech with the help of loudspeakers. While one has a right to speech, others have a right to listen or decline to listen. Nobody can be compelled to listen and nobody can claim that he has a right to make his voice trespass into the ears or mind of others. Nobody can indulge into aural aggression[11]. If anyone increases his volume of speech and that too with the assistance of artificial devices so as to compulsorily expose unwilling persons to hear a noise raised to unpleasant or obnoxious[12] levels then the person speaking is violating the right of others to a peaceful, comfortable and pollution-free life guaranteed by Article 21. Article 19[13] cannot be pressed into service for

---

(c) to form associations or unions;

(d) to move freely throughout the territory of India;

(e) to reside and settle in any part of the territory of India; and

(f) omitted

(g) to practise any profession, or to carry on any occupation, trade or business

10 **Meaning of Fundamental Rights:** The Fundamental Rights are defined as basic human freedoms which every Indian citizen has the right to enjoy for a proper and harmonious development of personality. These rights universally apply to all citizens, irrespective of race, place of birth, religion, caste, creed, colour or gender. Aliens (persons who are not citizens) are also considered in matters like equality before law. They are enforceable by the courts, subject to certain restrictions.

11 **Meaning of Aggression:**

1. The act of initiating hostilities or invasion

2. The practice or habit of launching attacks

3. Hostile or destructive behavior or actions

12 **Meaning of obnoxious:** Very annoying or objectionable; offensive or odious

13 **Article 19 in The Constitution Of India 1949**

19. Protection of certain rights regarding freedom of speech etc

(1) All citizens shall have the right

(a) to freedom of speech and expression;

(b) to assemble peaceably and without arms;

(c) to form associations or unions;

(d) to move freely throughout the territory of India;

(e) to reside and settle in any part of the territory of India; and

(f) omitted

(g) to practise any profession, or to carry on any occupation, trade or business

(2) Nothing in sub clause (a) of clause (1) shall affect the operation of any existing law, or prevent the State from making any law, in so far as such law imposes reasonable restrictions on the

defeating the fundamental right guaranteed by Article 21.

Noise - what it is?

The word noise is derived from the Latin term "nausea". It has been defined as "unwanted sound, a potential hazard to health and communication dumped into the environment with regard to the adverse effect it may have on unwilling ears." Noise is defined as unwanted sound. Sound which pleases the listeners is music and that which causes pain and annoyance is noise. At times, what is music for some can be noise for others. Section 2 of the Air (Prevention and Control of Pollution) Act, 1981, includes noise in the definition of 'air pollutant'.

Section 2 - "air pollutant" means any solid, liquid or gaseous substance including noise present in the atmosphere in such concentration as may be or tend to be injurious to human beings or other living creatures or plants or property or environment.

According to Encyclopaedia Britannica : "In acoustics[14] 'noise' is defined as 'any undesired sound'." According to Chambers 20th Century Dictionary,

---

exercise of the right conferred by the said sub clause in the interests of the sovereignty and integrity of India, the security of the State, friendly relations with foreign States, public order, decency or morality or in relation to contempt of court, defamation or incitement to an offence

(3) Nothing in sub clause (b) of the said clause shall affect the operation of any existing law in so far as it imposes, or prevent the State from making any law imposing, in the interests of the sovereignty and integrity of India or public order, reasonable restrictions on the exercise of the right conferred by the said sub clause

(4) Nothing in sub clause (c) of the said clause shall affect the operation of any existing law in so far as it imposes, or prevent the State from making any law imposing, in the interests of the sovereignty and integrity of India or public order or morality, reasonable restrictions on the exercise of the right conferred by the said sub clause

(5) Nothing in sub clauses (d) and (e) of the said clause shall affect the operation of any existing law in so far as it imposes, or prevent the State from making any law imposing, reasonable restrictions on the exercise of any of the rights conferred by the said sub clauses either in the interests of the general public or for the protection of the interests of any Scheduled Tribe

(6) Nothing in sub clause (g) of the said clause shall affect the operation of any existing law in so far as it imposes, or prevent the State from making any law imposing, in the interests of the general public, reasonable restrictions on the exercise of the right conferred by the said sub clause, and, in particular, nothing in the said sub clause shall affect the operation of any existing law in so far as it relates to, or prevent the State from making any law relating to,

(i) the professional or technical qualifications necessary for practising any profession or carrying on any occupation, trade or business, or

(ii) the carrying on by the State, or by a corporation owned or controlled by the State, of any trade, business, industry or service, whether to the exclusion, complete or partial, of citizens or otherwise

14 **Meaning of acoustics:** The scientific study of sound, especially of its generation, transmission, and reception.

'noise' means- sound especially of loud, harsh or confused kind; a sound of any kind; an over loud or disturbing sound; frequent or public talk. Thus, the disturbance produced in our environment by the undesirable sound of various kinds is called "noise pollution".

Noise as nuisance and health hazard:

Noise is more than just a nuisance. It constitutes a real and present danger to people's health. Day and night, at home, at work, and at play, noise can produce serious physical and psychological stress. No one is immune to this stress. Though we seem to adjust to noise by ignoring it, the ear, in fact, never closes and the body still responds-sometimes with extreme tension, as to a strange sound in the night. Noise is a type of atmospheric pollution. It is a shadowy public enemy whose growing menace has increased in the modern age of industrialization and technological advancement. Although a soft rhythmic sound in the form of music and dance stimulates brain activities, removes boredom and fatigue[15], but its excessiveness may prove detrimental to living things. Researches have proved that a loud noise during peak marketing hours creates tiredness, irritation and impairs brain activities so as to reduce thinking and working abilities. Noise pollution was previously confined to a few special areas like factory or mill, but today it engulfs every nook and corner of the globe, reaching its peak in urban areas. Industries, automobiles, rail engines, aeroplanes, radios, loudspeakers, tape recorders, lottery ticket sellers, hawkers, pop singers, etc., are the main ear contaminators of the city area and its market place. The regular rattling[16] of engines and intermittent blowing of horns emanating from the caravan of automobiles do not allow us to have any respite from irritant noise even in suburban zones.

In the modern days noise has become one of the major pollutants and it has serious effects on human health. Effects of noise depend upon sound's pitch, its frequency and time pattern and length of exposure. Noise has both auditory and non-auditory effects depending upon the intensity and the duration of the noise level. It affects sleep, hearing, communication, mental and physical health. It may even lead to the madness of people. However, noises, which are melodious, whether natural or man-made, cannot always be considered as factors leading to pollution. Noise can disturb our work, rest, sleep, and communication.

---

15 **Meaning of Fatigue:** Physical or mental weariness resulting from exertion.

16 **Meaning of Rattling:** Animated; brisk

It can damage our hearing and evoke other psychological, and possibly pathological reactions.

Sources of Noise Pollution:

Noise pollution like other pollutants is also a by-product of industrialization, urbanization and modern civilization. Broadly speaking, the noise pollution has two sources, i.e. industrial and non-industrial. The industrial source includes the noise from various industries and big machines working at a very high speed and high noise intensity. Non-industrial source of noise includes the noise created by transport/vehicular traffic and the neighbourhood noise generated by various noise pollution can also be divided into the categories, namely, natural and manmade.

Most leading noise sources will fall into the following categories: road traffic, aircraft, railroads, construction, industry, noise in buildings, and consumer products.

1. Road traffic noise

Noise from the motors and exhaust systems of large trucks provides the major portion of highway noise impact, and provides a potential noise hazard to the driver as well. In addition, noise from the interaction of tyres with the roadway is generated by trucks, buses, and private autos. In the city, the main sources of traffic noise are the motors and exhaust systems of autos, smaller trucks, buses, and motorcycles. This type of noise can be augmented by narrow streets and tall buildings, which produce a "canyon" in which traffic noise reverberates.

2. Aircraft noise

Nowadays, the problem of low-flying military aircraft has added a new dimension to community annoyance, as the nation seeks to improve its "nap-of-the-earth" warfare capabilities. In addition, the issue of aircraft operations over national parks, wilderness areas, and other areas previously unaffected by aircraft noise has claimed national attention over recent years.

3. Noise from railroads

The noise from locomotive engines, horns and whistles, and switching and shunting operations in rail yards can impact neighbouring communities and railroad workers. For example, rail car retreads can produce a high-frequency, high-level screech that can reach peak levels of 120 dB at a distance of 100 feet which translates to levels as high as 138 or 140 dB at the railroad worker's ear.

4. Construction noise

The noise from construction of highways, city streets, and buildings is a major contributor to the urban scene. Construction noise sources include pneumatic hammers, air compressors, bulldozers, loaders, dump trucks (and their back-up signals), and pavement breakers.

5. Noise in industry

Although industrial noise is one of the less prevalent community noise problems, neighbours of noisy manufacturing plants can be disturbed by sources such as fans, motors, and compressors mounted on the outside of buildings. Interior noise can also be transmitted to the community through open windows and doors, and even through building walls. These interior noise sources have significant impacts on industrial workers, among whom noise- induced hearing loss is unfortunately common.

6. Noise in buildings

Apartment dwellers are often annoyed by noise in their homes, especially when the building is not well designed and constructed. In this case, internal building noise from plumbing, boilers, generators, air conditioners, and fans, can be audible and annoying. Improperly insulated walls and ceilings can reveal the sound of amplified music, voices, footfalls, and noisy activities from neighbouring units. External noise from emergency vehicles, traffic, refuse collection, and other city noises can be a problem for urban residents, especially when windows are open or insufficiently glazed.

7. Noise from consumer products

Certain household equipment, such as vacuum cleaners and some kitchen appliances have been and continue to be noisemakers, although their contribution to the daily noise dose is usually not very large.

Noise pollution in the special context of Fireworks:

Fireworks are used all over the world to celebrate special occasions. In India, fireworks are burst on festivals like Dussehra, Diwali and on special occasions like social gatherings, marriages, Independence day, Republic day, New year day, etc. In other countries of the world, fireworks are generally burst either on the New Year day or on the birthday of their respective countries. However, bursting of firecrackers is a health hazard since it is responsible for both air pollution and noise pollution. The use of Fireworks has led to air pollution in the form of noise and smoke. Their excessive use has started to be a public hazard and violation of fundamental rights as enshrined in the Constitution of India.

It has been held in the case of *Om Birangana Religious Society v. State[17]*, that the "Freedom of speech and expression guaranteed under Article 19 of the Constitution of India includes, by necessary implication, freedom not to listen and/or to remain silent. A citizen has a right to leisure, right to sleep, right not to hear and right to remain silent. He also has the right to read and speak with others". Because of the tremendous sound and noise, the citizens cannot exercise all these fundamental rights. It has been seen that firecrackers noise is an impulsive noise and is hazardous. Bursting of a firecracker near the ear can lead sometimes to non-recoverable hearing loss. Diwali is the most important festival of India. The bursting of firecrackers during this period is a wide spread practice. The unpredictable, intermittent and impulsive noise produced by bursting of crackers all around, turns the festival of lights into cacophony of noise. People are unable to even sleep due to this excessive noise pollution. Several people are injured due to the noise produced by firecrackers every year.

Firecrackers not only increase the ambient noise level but also contribute significantly in increasing the air pollution by means of toxic gases and particles due to their blast wave resulting from a rapid release of energy.

The problem of noise pollution due to firecrackers is not only limited to India. Similar problems are being experienced in other countries as well. In fact in United Kingdom, in Nottingham the "Be Safe Not Sorry" campaign was launched after the post was inundated[18] with letters from readers to the newspaper saying they were fed up with the noise, nuisance and the distress that fireworks cause.

---

17 (1996)ILR 2Cal404

18 **Meaning of Inundated:**

    1. To cover with water, especially floodwaters.

    2. To overwhelm as if with a flood; swamp

Methodology adopted in other countries for noise pollution control:

Different countries of the World have enacted different legislations to control the noise pollution. For Example, in England there is a Noise Abetment Act, 1960. Section 2 of this Act provides that loudspeakers should not be operated between the hours of 9:00 in the evening and 8:00 in the following morning for any purpose and at any other time for purpose of advertisement and entertainment, trade or business. Control on Pollution Act of 1974, contains provisions for controlling noise pollution and it provides noise to be actionable must amount to nuisance in the ordinary legal sense. Section 62 of the English Control of Pollution Act, 1974, operates as perfect control for 'Street Noise'. This provision has been defined as a highway and any other road, footway or square or court which is for the time being open to public. In Japan, there is Anti Pollution Basic Law which helps to control the pollution including noise pollution.

A few of the notable legislations may be mentioned illustratively.

Noise Act 1996- U.K.

This Act makes provision about noise emitted from dwellings at night; about the forfeiture and confiscation of equipment used to make noise unlawfully; and for connected purposes. The kind of complaint referred to is one made by any individual present in a dwelling during night hours that excessive noise is being emitted from another dwelling. "Night hours" means the period beginning with 11p.m. and ending with 7 a.m. The Act provides for the service of a notice on the offender by the prescribed officer if he thinks that the noise being emitted is more than the permissible limits. In cases where the noise level does not come down in spite of the notice being served, the officer can seize such equipments which in his opinion are the source of such noise.

Noise and Statutory Nuisance Act 1993

An Act to make provision for noise in a street to be a statutory nuisance; to make provision with respect to the operation of loudspeakers in a street; to make provision with respect to audible intruder alarms; to make provision for expenses incurred by local authorities in abating, or preventing the recurrence of, a statutory nuisance to be a charge on the premises to which they relate; and for connected purposes.

The US Noise Pollution and Abatement Act, 1970 is an important legislation for regulating control and abatement of noise. Under this Law the environment protection agency, acting through the office of Noise Abatement and Control, holds public meetings in selected cities to compile information on noise pollution.

The Public Health And Welfare:- Chapter 65- Noise Control(US)

The Congress declares that it is the policy of the United States to promote an ennvironment for all Americans free from noise that jeopardizes their health or welfare. To that end, it is the purpose of this chapter to establish a means for effective coordination of Federal research and activities in noise control, to authorize the establishment of Federal noise emission standards for products distributed in commerce, and to provide information to the public respecting the noise emission and noise reduction characteristics of such products.

The Act further provides for -

1. Identification of major noise sources

2. Noise emission standards for products distributed in commerce

3. Labelling

4. Quiet communities, research, and public information

5. Development of low-noise-emission products

6. Motor carrier noise emission standards

Noise Regulation Law-Japan:

The purpose of this Law is to preserve living environment and contribute to protection of the people's health by regulating noise generated by the operation of factories and other types of work sites as well as construction work affecting a considerable area, and by setting maximum permissible levels of motor vehicle noise. The Prefectural Governor shall designate concentrated residential areas, school and hospital zones, and other such areas in which it is deemed necessary to protect the living environment of the residents from noise, as areas subject to the regulation of noise produced by specified factories and specified construction work. The Prefectural Governor shall be responsible for the monitoring of noise levels in designated areas.

Law of the People's Republic of China on Prevention and Control of Pollution From Environmental Noise (adopted on October 29, 1996):

This Law is enacted for the purpose of preventing and controlling environmental noise pollution, protecting and improving the living environment, ensuring human health and promoting economic and social development. For purposes of this Law, "environmental noise" means the sound that is emitted in the course of industrial production, construction, transportation and social activities and that impairs the living environment of the neighbourhood.

"Noise emission" means emission of noise from the source to the living environment of the neighbourhood. "Noise-sensitive structures" means structures that require a quiet environment such as hospitals, schools, government offices, research institutions and residential buildings. "Areas where noise-sensitive structures are concentrated" means such areas as medical treatment areas, cultural, education and research districts and areas where government offices or residential buildings constitute the main buildings. "At night" means the period from 10:00 p.m. to 6:00 a.m.

Australia

In New South Wales (NSW) no single Government authority has the responsibility or capacity to be able to minimise all forms of noise pollution. The State is excluded from control of noise in a number of areas by commonwealth legislation. These include aircraft noise, where noise limits could affect trade, and the setting standards for noise emissions from new vehicles. In areas where the State does have powers to control noise, the Environment Protection Authority (EPA) has an overall responsibility for environmental noise (as distinct from occupational noise), under the *Noise Control Act 1975*. The Act deals with the prevention, minimization and abatement of noise and vibration and empowers the EPA, the Waterways Authority, local Government and the police for these purposes.

The EPA controls noise from scheduled premises, those required by the Noise Control Act to have a licence and noise associated with rail traffic and the construction or upgrading of freeways and toll roads. The Police and local council are generally responsible for neighbourhood noise issues and have authority to issue noise abatement directions to control noise from premises and for noise from burglar alarms. Local council have an essential role in minimising the effects of excessive noise, particularly in their local residential areas, from smaller factories, non-scheduled premises and public places. The Waterways Authority has specific responsibilities in relation to noise from vessels in navigable waters.

Under the provisions of the *Noise Control Act 1975* in NSW the railway system is classified as scheduled premises and as such the EPA has a regulatory role, and seeks to achieve noise targets for rail operations throughout the State to minimise the impact on local residents. The EPA issues licences for the management of scheduled premises. When issuing a licence the EPA sets initial noise limits that are achievable with the operation of plant and equipment currently installed, operated and maintained effectively. To achieve further improvements in noise exposure to residents, negotiations with the licensed premises are carried out and can be incorporated in the licence as Pollution Reduction Programs (PRPs). The EPA is currently working with industry to reduce noise levels from major sources.

The Noise Control (Miscellaneous Articles) Regulation 1995 was introduced to cover community noise issues not covered by previous legislation. It includes limitations on burglar alarms for both residential and commercial premises. Changes have been made to the night-time control of common domestic noise sources such as power tools, air conditioners, amplified music and lawn mowers. Under the new regulation, only one warning to the offender is required and the warning is valid for 28 days. If an offence is committed within this period a fine can be issued without further warnings. The previous regulation warning was only active for 12 hours which meant it was not very effective with repetitious offences typical in suburban areas. The Noise Control (Motor Vehicles and Motor Vehicle Accessories) Regulation 1995 controls the noise of individual motor vehicles. It includes a provision to control noise from a range of accessories including horns, alarms, refrigeration units and sound systems. It also places responsibility to ensure compliance of repairs/modifications of vehicles on the vehicle repairers. In addition to the measures introduced to reduce the source and transmission of noise, measures can be undertaken to noise proof buildings thereby reducing the occupant exposure to noise.

Statutory Laws in India

Not that the Legislature and the Executive in India are completely unmindful of the menace of noise pollution. Laws have been enacted and the Rules have been framed by the Executive for carrying on the purposes of the legislation. The real issue is with the implementation of the laws. What is needed is the will to implement the laws. It would be useful to have a brief resume of some of the laws which are already available on the Statute Book. Treatment of the problem of noise pollution can be dealt under the Law of Crimes and civil Law. civil law can be divided under two heads (i) The Law of Torts and (ii) The General civil Law. The cases regarding noise have not come before the law courts in large quantity. The reason behind this is that many people in India did not consider noise as a sort of pollution and they are not very much conscious about the evil consequences of noise pollution. The level of noise pollution is relative and depends upon a person and a particular place. The law will not take care of a super sensitive person but the standard is of an average and rational human being in the society.

The Noise Pollution (Regulation and Control) Rules, 2000

In order to curb the growing problem of noise pollution, the Government of India has enacted the Noise Pollution(Regulation and Control) Rules, 2000. Prior to the enactment of these Rules noise pollution was not being dealt specifically by a particular Act.

"Whereas the increasing ambient noise levels in public places from various sources, inter-alia, industrial activity, construction activity, generator sets, loudspeakers, public address systems, music systems, vehicular horns and other mechanical devices, have deleterious effects on human health and the psychological well being of the people; it is considered necessary to regulate and control noise producing and generating sources with the objective of maintaining the ambient air quality standard in respect of noise;"

The main provisions of the Noise Pollution Rules are as under:

1. The State Government may categorize the areas into industrial, commercial, residential or silence areas/zones for the purpose of implementation of noise standards for different areas.

2. The ambient air quality standards in respect of noise for different

areas/zones has been specified for in the Schedule annexed to the Rules.

3. The State Government shall take measures for abatement of noise including noise emanating from vehicular movements and ensure that the existing noise levels do not exceed the ambient air quality standards specified under these Rules. 4. An area comprising not less than 100 meters around hospitals, educational institutions and courts may be declared as silence area/zone for the purpose of these Rules.

5. A loudspeaker or a public address system shall not be used except after obtaining written permission from the authority and the same shall not be used at night i.e. between 10.00 p.m. and 6.00 a.m.

6. A person found violating the provisions as to the maximum noise permissible in any particular area shall be liable to be punished for it as per the provisions of these Rules and any other law in force.

Indian Penal Code

Noise pollution can be dealt under Sections 268[19], 290[20] and 291[21] of the Indian Penal Code, as a public nuisance.

Criminal Procedure Code

Under Section 133[22] of the Code of Criminal Procedure, 1973 the

---

19 **Section 268 in The Indian Penal Code**

Public nuisance: A person is guilty of a public nuisance who does any act or is guilty of an illegal omission which causes any common injury, danger or annoyance to the public or to the people in general who dwell or occupy property in the vicinity, or which must necessarily cause injury, obstruction, danger or annoyance to persons who may have occasion to use any public right. A common nuisance is not excused on the ground that it causes some convenience or advantage

20 **Section 290 in The Indian Penal Code**

Punishment for public nuisance in cases not otherwise provided for: Whoever commits a public nuisance in any case not otherwise punishable by this Code, shall be punished with fine which may extend to two hundred rupees

21 **Section 291 in The Indian Penal Code**

Continuance of nuisance after injunction to discontinue: Whoever repeats or continues a public nuisance, having been enjoined by any public servant who has lawful authority to issue such injunction not to repeat or continue such nuisance, shall be punished with simple imprisonment for a term which may extend to six months, or with fine, or with both

22 **Section 133 in The Code Of Criminal Procedure, 1973**

133. Conditional order for removal of nuisance

(1) Whenever a District Magistrate or a Sub- divisional Magistrate or any other Executive Magistrate specially empowered in this of behalf by the State Government, on receiving the report of a police officer or other information and on taking such evidence (if any) as he thinks fit, considers-

magistrate has the power to make conditional order requiring the person causing nuisance to remove such nuisance.

The Factories Act, 1948

The Factories Act, 1948 does not contain any specific provision for noise control. However, under the Third Schedule [Sections 89 and 90 of the Act], 'noise induced hearing loss', is mentioned as a modifiable disease. Under Section 89[23] of the Act, any medical practitioner who detects any

(a) that any unlawful obstruction or nuisance should be removed from any public place or from any way, river or channel which is or may be lawfully used by the public; or

(b) that the conduct of any trade or occupation, or the keeping of any goods or merchandise, is injurious to the health or physical comfort of the community, and that in consequence such trade or occupation should be prohibited or regulated or such goods or merchandise should be removed or the keeping thereof regulated; or

(c) that the construction of any building, or, the disposal of any substance, as is likely to occasion configuration or explosion, should be prevented or stopped; or

(d) that any building, tent or structure, or any tree is in such a condition that it is likely to fall and thereby cause injury to persons living or carrying on business in the neighbourhood or passing by, and that in consequence the removal, repair or support of such building, tent or structure, or the removal or support of such tree, is necessary; or

(e) that any tank, well or excavation adjacent to any such way or public place should be fenced in such manner as to prevent danger arising to the public; or

(f) that any dangerous animal should be destroyed, confined or otherwise disposed of, such Magistrate may make a conditional order requiring the person causing such obstruction or nuisance, or carrying on such trade or occupation, or keeping any such goods or merchandise, or owning, possessing or controlling such building, tent, structure, substance, tank, well or excavation, or owning or possessing such animal or tree, within a time to be fixed in the order-

(i) to remove such obstruction or nuisance; or

(ii) to desist from carrying on, or to remove or regulate in such manner as may be directed, such trade or occupation, or to remove such goods or merchandise, or to regulate the keeping thereof in such manner as may be directed; or

(iii) to prevent or stop the construction of such building, or to alter the disposal of such substance; or

(iv) to remove, repair or support such building, tent or structure, or to remove or support such trees; or

(v) to fence such tank, well or excavation; or

(vi) to destroy, confine or dispose of such dangerous animal in the manner provided in the said order; or, if he objects so to do, to appear before himself or some other Executive Magistrate subordinate to him at a time and place to be fixed by the Order, and show cause, in the manner hereinafter provided, why the order should not be made absolute.

(2) No order duly made by a Magistrate under this section shall be called in question in any Civil Court. Explanation- A" public place" includes also property belonging to the State, camping grounds and grounds left unoccupied for sanitary or recreative purposes.

23 **Section 89 in The Factories Act, 1948**

Notice of certain diseases:

(1) Where any worker in a factory contracts any disease specified in [the Third Schedule], the

modifiable disease, including noise- induced hearing loss, in a worker, has to report the case to the Chief Inspector of Factories, along with all other relevant information. Failure to do so is a punishable offence.

106. Similarly, under the Model Rules, limits for noise exposure for work zone area has been prescribed.

Motor Vehicles Act, 1988, and Rules framed thereunder

Rules 119 and 120 of the Central Motor Vehicles Rules, 1989, deal with reduction of noise.

Rule 119. Horns

(1) On and after expiry of one year from the date of commencement of the Central Motor Vehicles (Amendment) Rules, 1999, every motor vehicle including construction equipment vehicle and agricultural tractor manufactured shall be fitted with an electric horn or other devices conforming to the requirements of IS: 1884?1992, specified by the Bureau of Indian Standards for use by the driver of the vehicle and capable of giving audible and sufficient warning of the approach or position of the vehicle:

Provided that on and from 1st January, 2003, the horn installation shall be as per AIS-014 specifications, as may be amended from time to time, till such time as corresponding Bureau of Indian Standards specifications are notified.

---

manager of the factory shall send notice thereof to such authorities, and in such form and within such time, as may be prescribed.

(2) If any medical practitioner attends on a person who is or has been employed in a factory, and who is, or is believed by the medical practitioner to be, suffering from any disease specified in [the Third Schedule], the medical practitioner shall without delay send a report in writing to the office of the Chief Inspector stating—

(a) the name and full postal address of the patient,

(b) the disease from which he believes the patient to be suffering, and

(c) the name and address of the factory in which the patient is, or was last, employed.

(3) Where the report under sub-section (2) is confirmed to the satisfaction of the Chief Inspector, by the certificate of certifying surgeon or otherwise, that the person is suffering from a disease specified in 1[the Third Schedule], he shall pay to the medical practitioner such fee as may be prescribed, and the fee so paid shall be recoverable as an arrear of land-revenue from the occupier of the factory in which the person contracted the disease.

(4) If any medical practitioner fails to comply with the provisions of sub-section (2), he shall be punishable with fine which may extend to [one thousand rupees]. [(5) The Central Government may, by notification in the Official Gazette, add to or alter the Third Schedule and any such addition or alteration shall have effect as if it had been made by this Act.]

(2) No motor vehicle shall be fitted with any multi-toned horn giving a succession of different notes or with any other sound-producing device giving an unduly harsh, shrill, loud or alarming noise.

Rule 120. Silencers

(1) Every motor vehicle including agricultural tractor shall be fitted with a device (hereinafter referred to as a silencer) which by means of an expansion chamber or otherwise reduces as far as practicable, the noise that would otherwise be made by the escape of exhaust gages from the engine.

(2) *Noise standards-* Every motor vehicle shall be constructed and maintained so as to conform to noise standards specified in Part E of the Schedule VI to the Environment (Protection) Rules, 1986, when tested as per IS: 3028-1998, as amended from time to time.

Law of Torts

Quietness and freedom from noise are indispensable to the full and free enjoyment of a dwelling-house. No proprietor has an absolute right to create noises upon his own land, because any right which the law gives is qualified by the condition that it must not be exercised to the nuisance of his neighbours or of the public. Noise will create an actionable nuisance only if it materially interferes with the ordinary comfort of life, judged by ordinary, plain and simple notions, and having regard to the locality; the question being one of degree in each case.

The Air (Prevention and Control of Pollution) Act, 1981

Noise was included in the definition of air pollutant in Air (Prevention and Control of Pollution) Act in 1987. Thus, the provisions of the Air Act, became applicable in respect of noise pollution, also.

The Environment (Protection) Act, 1986.

Although there is no specific provision to deal with noise pollution, the Act confers powers on Government of India to take measures to deal with various types of pollution including noise pollution.

Fireworks

The Explosives Act, 1884 regulates manufacture, possession, use, sale, transport, import & export of explosives. Firecrackers are governed by this Statute. Rule 87 of the Explosives Rule, 1983 prohibits manufacture of any explosive at any place, except in factory or premises licensed under the Rules.

In India, there is no separate Act that regulates the manufacture, possession, use, sale, manufacture and transactions in firecrackers. All this is regulated by The Explosives Act, 1884. The Noise that is produced by these fireworks is regulated by the Environmental Protection Act, 1986 and The Noise Pollution (Regulation and Control) Rules, 2000.

Decision by Supreme Court:

Court held that not only the use of loudspeakers and playing of hi-fi amplifier systems has to be regulated even the playing of high sound instruments like drums, tom-toms, trumpets, bugles and the like which create noise beyond tolerable limits need to be regulated. The law enforcing agencies must be equipped with necessary instruments and facilities out of which sound level meters conforming to Bureau of Indian Standards (BIS)[24] code are a bare necessity. Loudspeakers and amplifiers or other equipments or gadgets which produce offending noise once detected as violating the law, should be liable to be seized and confiscated by making provision in the law in that behalf. Prohibiting the sale of such firecrackers which create noise pollution by producing noise beyond permissible limits is practically unmanageable. A better option certainly is to prescribe the chemical contents and composition for each type of firecrackers to effectively curb noise pollution.

Directions by Supreme Court:

I. Firecrackers

1. The Department of Explosives (DOE) shall undertake necessary research activity for the purpose and come out with the chemical formulae for each type or category or class of firecrackers. The DOE shall specify the proportion/composition as well as the maximum permissible weight of every chemical used in manufacturing firecrackers.

2. The Department of Explosives may divide the firecrackers into two

---

24 The **Bureau of Indian Standards** (BIS) is the national Standards Body of India working under the aegis of <u>Ministry of Consumer Affairs, Food & Public Distribution, Government of India</u>. It is established by the Bureau of Indian Standards Act, 1986 which came into effect on 23 December 1986. The Minister in charge of the Ministry or Department having administrative control of the BIS is ex-officio President (Emaad Amin) of the BIS.

categories- (i) Sound emitting firecrackers, and (ii) Colour/light emitting firecrackers.

3. There shall be a complete ban on bursting sound emitting firecrackers between 10 pm and 6 am. It is not necessary to impose restrictions as to time on bursting of colour/light emitting firecrackers.

4. Every manufacturer shall on the box of each firecracker mention details of its chemical contents and that it satisfies the requirement as laid down by DOE. In case of a failure on the part of the manufacturer to mention the details or in cases where the contents of the box do not match the chemical formulae as stated on the box, the manufacturer may be held liable.

5. Firecrackers for the purpose of export may be manufactured bearing higher noise levels subject to the following conditions: (i) The manufacturer should be permitted to do so only when he has an export order with him and not otherwise;(ii) The noise levels for these firecrackers should conform to the noise standards prescribed in the country to which they are intended to be exported as per the export order; (iii) These firecrackers should have a different colour packing, from those intended to be sold in India; (iv) They must carry a declaration printed thereon something like 'not for sale in India' or 'only for export to country AB' and so on.

II. Loudspeakers

1. The noise level at the boundary of the public place, where loudspeaker or public address system or any other noise source is being used shall not exceed 10 dB(A) above the ambient noise standards for the area or 75 dB(A) whichever is lower.

2. No one shall beat a drum or tom-tom or blow a trumpet or beat or sound any instrument or use any sound amplifier at night (between 10. 00 p.m. and 6.a.m.) except in public emergencies. 3. The peripheral noise level of privately owned sound system shall not exceed by more than 5 dB(A) than the ambient air quality standard specified for the area in which it is used, at the boundary of the private place.

III. Vehicular Noise

No horn should be allowed to be used at night (between 10 p.m. and 6 a.m.) in residential areas except in exceptional circumstances.

IV. Awareness

1. There is a need for creating general awareness towards the hazardous effects of noise pollution. Suitable chapters may be added in the text-books which teach civic sense to the children and youth at the initial/early level of education. Special talks and lectures be organised in the schools to highlight the menace of noise pollution and the role of the children and younger generation in preventing it. Police and civic administration should be trained to understand the various methods to curb the problem and also the laws on the subject.

2. The State must play an active role in this process. Residents Welfare Associations, Service Clubs and Societies engaged in preventing noise pollution as a part of their projects need to be encouraged and actively involved by the local administration.

3. Special public awareness campaigns in anticipation of festivals, events and ceremonial occasions whereat firecrackers are likely to be used, need to be carried out.

V Generally

1. The States shall make provision for seizure and confiscation of loudspeakers, amplifiers and such other equipments as are found to be creating noise beyond the permissible limits.

2. Rule 3 of the Noise Pollution (Regulation and Control) Rules, 2000 makes provision for specifying ambient air quality standards in respect of noise for different areas/zones, categorization of the areas for the purpose of implementation of noise standards, authorizing the authorities for enforcement and achievement of laid down standards. The Central Government/State Governments shall take steps for laying down such standards and notifying the authorities where it has not already been done.

24

Ban use of asbestos[1]

Facts in Nutshell:

Petition[2] under Article 32[3] of the Constitution of India was filed by the Petitioner[4] Kalyaneshwari[5] (a registered Society), through its Chairman, with a prayer that a writ of mandamus[6] be issued directing the Union of India and other Respondent[7]-States to immediately ban all uses

---

1   Appellants: **Kalyaneshwari Vs.** Respondent: **Union of India (UOI) and Ors.**

    (2011)3SCC287

    Hon'ble Judges/Coram: S.H. Kapadia, C.J., K.S. Panicker Radhakrishnan and Swatanter Kumar, JJ.

2   **Meaning of Petition:** A formal message requesting something that is submitted to an authority

3   **Article 32 in The Constitution Of India 1949**

    32. Remedies for enforcement of rights conferred by this Part

    (1) The right to move the Supreme Court by appropriate proceedings for the enforcement of the rights conferred by this Part is guaranteed

    (2) The Supreme Court shall have power to issue directions or orders or writs, including writs in the nature of habeas corpus, mandamus, prohibition, quo warranto and certiorari, whichever may be appropriate, for the enforcement of any of the rights conferred by this Part

    (3) Without prejudice to the powers conferred on the Supreme Court by clause (1) and (2), Parliament may by law empower any other court to exercise within the local limits of its jurisdiction all or any of the powers exercisable by the Supreme Court under clause (2)

    (4) The right guaranteed by this article shall not be suspended except as otherwise provided for by this Constitution

4   **Meaning of Petitioner:** A person who presents a Petition. (**Meaning of Petition:** A formal message requesting something that is submitted to an authority)

5   Kalyaneshwari, a non-governmental organization, registered under the Societies Registration Act XXI of 1860. A voluntary organization allegedly promoted to serve the general public without distinction of caste or religion and working for the protection of consumers interest.

6   **Mandamus** is a judicial remedy in the form of an order from a superior court, to any government subordinate court, corporation, or public authority—to do (or forbear from doing) some specific act which that body is obliged under law to do (or refrain from doing)—and which is in the nature of public duty, and in certain cases one of a statutory duty. It cannot be issued to compel an authority to do something against statutory provision. For example, it cannot be used to force a lower court to reject or authorize applications that have been made, but if the court refuses to rule one way or the other then a mandamus can be used to order the court to rule on the applications.

7   **Meaning of Respondent:** A **respondent** is a person who is called upon to issue a response to a communication made by another. In legal usage, this specifically refers to the defendant in a legal

of asbestos[8] in any manner whatsoever; further that a committee of eminent specialists be constituted to frame a scheme for identification and certification of the workers/victims suffering from asbestosis or other asbestos related diseases or cancer. The Petitioner also prayed that the respective Governments should be directed to identify the workers/victims in the respective States and Union Territories and to provide them due treatment as well as to take measures to prevent harmful effects of asbestos in the factories or establishments where such activity is being carried out and also to initiate criminal proceedings against all the responsible persons including the owners of such factories, organizations and associations for infringing the right to life of the asbestos victims.

The Petitioner alleged that developed countries all over the world have drastically reduced the manufacture of asbestos and some of them have even banned different types of asbestos. In India, the use of carcinogenic[9] material is increasing every year approximately at the rate of 12% and the Petitioner drew attention of the concerned authorities towards this issue and requested them to take stringent actions, but to no effect. The World Trade Organisation considered this aspect in the EC-Asbestos case, [WT/DS135/ ABR] adopted on 5th April, 2001 where its appellate body observed that available scientific data reveals that a high mortality rate persists despite the so called 'safe' use of Chrysolite Asbestos. Surveys carried out more than 30 years after the introduction of controlled use policy in United Kingdom indicate a significant increase in deaths from Lung Cancer and Mesothelioma[10], not only among the workers but even to the families residing nearby such plants. Citing the example of some countries and the measures being taken by different organizations, request was made for banning import, manufacture and use of asbestos and it was averred[11] that 'controlled use' is hardly workable. It was also averred by the

---

proceeding commenced by a petition, or to an appellee, or the opposing party, in an appeal of a decision by an initial fact-finder

8   **Asbestos** is a set of six naturally occurring silicate minerals which all have in common their eponymous asbestiform habit: long (roughly 1:20 aspect ratio), thin fibrous crystals.

9   **Meaning of carcinogenic:** A cancer-causing substance or agent.

10 **Mesothelioma** (or, more precisely, **malignant mesothelioma**) is a rare form of cancer that develops from cells of the mesothelium, the protective lining that covers many of the internal organs of the body. Mesothelioma is most commonly caused by exposure to asbestos

11 **Meaning of averred:**

    a. To assert formally as a fact

    b. To justify or prove

Petitioner that in most parts of the world, there was a drastic reduction in manufacture and use of asbestos. In fact, efforts were being made to ban on use of asbestos in any form. On the contrary, in India, use of asbestos was permitted indiscriminately on the premise that its controlled use is absolutely safe. There is a large number of victims in India who are suffering from various effects of asbestos in one form or the other. The Petitioner claimed to have identified five hundred plus victims from five different States, namely, West Bengal, Rajasthan, Jharkhand, Andhra Pradesh and Tamil Nadu. The Petitioner claimed that in order to find out the exact health scenario of asbestos workers, it got 14 direct workers of an asbestos unit examined by qualified occupational health doctors and the results were shocking, inasmuch as 13 workers were suffering from asbestosis with five workers being in advanced stage. Though these workers were covered under State (Employment State Insurance) ESI Scheme, no proper and adequate treatment was being provided to them. Thousands of poor and ignorant people in Udaipur District in Rajasthan were engaged in asbestos mining before the Ministry of Mines decided in the year 1996 not to issue or renew any asbestos mining licenses in India. Still today, some of them were engaged in illegal mining, which they do at the instance of local asbestos products manufacturers. It was also averred by the Petitioner that there is complete failure on the part of the manufacturers in providing safety equipments to workers, regular health checkup, monitoring air borne dust and maintaining health register of the workmen. Despite overwhelming evidence, asbestos which has been banned in other countries is still being manufactured, imported and used in India and the Government has failed to take proper action which compelled the Petitioner to approach Supreme Court by filing the Writ Petition[12] in larger public interest as there was apparent violation of

---

12 **Meaning of Writ Petition:** Under the Indian legal system, jurisdiction to issue 'prerogative writs' is given to the Supreme Court, and to the High Courts of Judicature of all Indian states. Parts of the law relating to writs are set forth in the Constitution of India. The Supreme Court, the highest in the country, may issue writs under Article 32 of the Constitution for enforcement of Fundamental Rights and under Articles 139 for enforcement of rights other than Fundamental Rights, while High Courts, the superior courts of the States, may issue writs under Articles 226. 'Writ' is eminently designed by the makers of the Constitution, and in the same way it is developed very widely and efficiently by the courts in India. The Constitution broadly provides for five kinds of "prerogative" writs, namely, Habeas Corpus, Certiorari, Mandamus, Quo Warranto and Prohibition.

Articles 14[13] and 21[14] of the Constitution of India.

Decision by Supreme Court:

Court held that Government had introduced the White Asbestos (Ban on Use and Import) Bill, 2009 (hereinafter referred to as, 'the Bill'), which is pending in the Upper House[15]. Thus, there could be no doubt that it was a matter which squarely falls in the domain of the legislature and the legislature in its wisdom has taken steps in the direction of enacting necessary law. Court observed that Issuance of any direction or formulation of any further policy will be a futile exercise. There could hardly be any justification for banning, completely or partially, of the activity of manufacturing of asbestos and allied products in face of the above admitted position.

Directions by Supreme Court:

A. Court directed the Union of India and the States to review safeguards in relation to primary as well as secondary exposure to asbestos.

b. Further court directed that if Union of India considers it proper and in public interest, after consulting the States where there are large number of asbestos industries in existence, it should constitute a regulatory body[16] to exercise proper control and supervision over manufacturing of asbestos activities while ensuring due regard to the aspect of health care of the workmen involved in such activity. It may even constitute a Committee of such experts as it may deem appropriate to effectively

---

13 **Article 14 in The Constitution Of India 1949**

   Equality before law: The State shall not deny to any person equality before the law or the equal protection of the laws within the territory of India Prohibition of discrimination on grounds of religion, race, caste, sex or place of birth

14 **Article 21 in The Constitution Of India 1949**

   Protection of life and personal liberty: No person shall be deprived of his life or personal liberty except according to procedure established by law

15 The **Parliament of India,** also popularly known as *Sansad*, is the supreme legislative body in India. The Parliament comprises the President of India and the two Houses—Lok Sabha (House of the People) and Rajya Sabha (Council of States). The President has the power to summon and prorogue either House of Parliament or to dissolve Lok Sabha.

16 A **regulatory agency** (also **regulatory authority, regulatory body** or **regulator**) is a public authority or government agency responsible for exercising autonomous authority over some area of human activity in a regulatory or supervisory capacity. An independent regulatory agency is a regulatory agency that is independent from other branches or arms of the government.

prevent and control its hazardous effects on the health of the workmen.

c. The concerned authorities under the provisions of Environment (Protection) Act, 1986 should ensure that all the appropriate and protective steps to meet the specified standards were taken by the industry before or at the time of issuance of environmental clearance.

25

Illegal Mining[1]

Facts in Nutshell:

Writ petitions[2] which have been filed by way of public interest litigation[3], highlight issues of grave environmental and ecological degradation due to large scale illegal, un-authorised, un-scientific and un-systematic mining activities being undertaken in violation of the provisions of various enactments, rules framed and notifications issued thereunder, and the orders of the Supreme Court and Jaipur High court. Petition[4] filed by one Ashwani Chobisa, who was a practicing lawyer, in the Rajasthan High Court and claims himself to be a public spirited and keenly interested person in protecting the environment and water resources. He has focused on the aspects of large scale illegal un-systematic, haphazard and un-scientific mining taking place in the entire State of Rajasthan and operation of stone crushers at various places in the State and their benefit repercussions[5] on

---

1 Appellants: **Ashwani Chobisa Vs.** Respondent: **Union of India (UOI) and Ors.**

   RLW2005(1)Raj389

   Hon'ble Judges/Coram: Anil Dev Singh, C.J. and Harbans Lal, Judge

2 **Meaning of Writ Petition:** Under the Indian legal system, jurisdiction to issue 'prerogative writs' is given to the Supreme Court, and to the High Courts of Judicature of all Indian states. Parts of the law relating to writs are set forth in the Constitution of India. The Supreme Court, the highest in the country, may issue writs under Article 32 of the Constitution for enforcement of Fundamental Rights and under Articles 139 for enforcement of rights other than Fundamental Rights, while High Courts, the superior courts of the States, may issue writs under Articles 226. 'Writ' is eminently designed by the makers of the Constitution, and in the same way it is developed very widely and efficiently by the courts in India. The Constitution broadly provides for five kinds of "prerogative" writs, namely, Habeas Corpus, Certiorari, Mandamus, Quo Warranto and Prohibition.

3 **Public-Interest Litigation** is litigation for the protection of the public interest. In Indian law, **Article 32** of the Indian constitution contains a tool which directly joins the public with judiciary. A PIL may be introduced in a court of law by the court itself (*suo motu*), rather than the aggrieved party or another third party. For the exercise of the court's jurisdiction, it is not necessary for the victim of the violation of his or her rights to personally approach the court. In a PIL, the right to file suit is given to a member of the public by the courts through judicial activism. The member of the public may be a non-governmental organization (NGO), an institution or an individual.

4 **Meaning of Petition:** A formal message requesting something that is submitted to an authority

5 **Meaning of repercussions:**

the ecology.

According to the petitioner (Ashwini Chobisa), the State and its functionaries have been complacent[6] in not strictly enforcing environmental laws and notifications. He has referred to Article 21[7] of the Constitution, which guarantees the protection of life and personal liberty to an individual. Article 48-A[8] enjoins the State to make every endeavor[9] to protect and improve the environment and to safeguard the forest and wild life of the country. Article 51-A(g)[10] provides that it shall be the duty of the every citizen of India to protect and improve the natural environment including forest, lakes, rivers, wild life and to have compassion for living creatures.

---

1. An often indirect effect, influence, or result that is produced by an event or action.

2. A recoil, rebounding, or reciprocal motion after impact.

3. A reflection, especially of sound.

6 **Meaning of Complacent:**

Contented to a fault; self-satisfied and unconcerned Eager to please; complaisant

7 **Article 21 in The Constitution Of India 1949**

Protection of life and personal liberty: No person shall be deprived of his life or personal liberty except according to procedure established by law

8 **Article 48A in The Constitution Of India 1949**

48A. Protection and improvement of environment and safeguarding of forests and wild life: The State shall endeavour to protect and improve the environment and to safeguard the forests and wild life of the country

9 **Meaning of endeavor:**

1. A conscientious or concerted effort toward an end; an earnest attempt.

2. Purposeful or industrious activity; enterprise.

10 **Article 51A in The Constitution Of India 1949**

51A. Fundamental duties It shall be the duty of every citizen of India (a) to abide by the Constitution and respect its ideals and institutions, the national Flag and the National Anthem;

(b) to cherish and follow the noble ideals which inspired our national struggle for freedom;

(c) to uphold and protect the sovereignty, unity and integrity of India;

(d) to defend the country and render national service when called upon to do so;

(e) to promote harmony and the spirit of common brotherhood amongst all the people of India transcending religious, linguistic and regional or sectional diversities; to renounce practices derogatory to the dignity of women;

(f) to value and preserve the rich heritage of our composite culture;

(g) to protect and improve the natural environment including forests, lakes, rivers and wild life, and to have compassion for living creatures;

(h) to develop the scientific temper, humanism and the spirit of inquiry and reform;

(i) to safeguard public property and to abjure violence;

(j) to strive towards excellence in all spheres of individual and collective activity so that the nation constantly rises to higher levels of endeavour and achievement

Articles 48A and 51A have been inserted in the Constitution through constitutional Amendment Act, 1976. Prior to insertion of these provisions in the Constitution, there have been several legislations on the subject including the Water (Prevention and Control of Pollution) Act, 1974, The Air (Protection and Control of Pollution) Act, 1981. The constitutional and statutory provisionsa are aimed at protecting the individual's rights to fresh air, clean water and pollution free environment. The petition was filed to highlight the serious environmental degradation[11] being caused by excessive mining activity and industrial operations and indiscriminate felling of trees.

Environment Protection:

It is well settled that the pollution of environment, air and water tantamounts[12] to violation of the right to life guaranteed by Article 21 of the Constitution of India as without these generous gifts of nature, it is not possible to enjoy life. In this regard the Supreme Court in *Virender Gaur and Ors. v. State of Haryana Ors.*[13], has held as follows:

"The word 'environment' is of broad spectrum which brings within its ambit "hygienic atmosphere and ecological balance." It is, therefore, not only the duty of the State but also the duty of every citizen to maintain hygienic environment. The State in particular has duty in that behalf and to shed its extravagant unbridled sovereign power and to forge in its policy to maintain ecological balance and hygienic environment. Article 21 protects right to life as a fundamental right[14]. Enjoyment of life and its attainment includes the right to life with human dignity encompasses within its ambit, the protection and preservation of environment, ecological balance free from pollution of air and water, sanitation without which life cannot be enjoyed. Any contra acts or action would cause environmental pollution. Environmental, ecological, air, water, pollution etc. should be regarded

---

11 **Environmental degradation** is the deterioration of the environment through depletion of resources such as air, water and soil; the destruction of ecosystems and the extinction of wildlife. It is defined as any change or disturbance to the environment perceived to be deleterious or undesirable

12 **Meaning of tantamount:** Equivalent in effect or value

13 (1995)2SCC577

14 **Meaning of Fundamental Rights:** The Fundamental Rights are defined as basic human freedoms which every Indian citizen has the right to enjoy for a proper and harmonious development of personality. These rights universally apply to all citizens, irrespective of race, place of birth, religion, caste, creed, colour or gender. Aliens (persons who are not citizens) are also considered in matters like equality before law. They are enforceable by the courts, subject to certain restrictions.

as amounting to violation of Article 21 of Constitution. Therefore, hygienic environment is an integral facet of right to healthy life and it would be impossible to live with human dignity without a humane and healthy environment. Environmental protection, therefore, has now become a matter of grave concern for human existence. Promoting environmental protection implies maintenance of the environment as a constitutional imperative on the State Government and the municipalities, not only to ensure and safeguard proper environment but also an imperative duty to take adequate measures to promote, protect and improve both the man-made and the natural environment."

The UN Conference on Human Environment at Stockhom, declared that man has fundamental right to freedom, quality and adequate conditions of life in an environment of quality and he bears a solemn responsibility to protect and improve the environment. It urged the nation-states to preserve the natural resources of the Earth including Air, Water, Land, Flora[15] and Fauna. Rio de Janerio Earth Summit[16] (1992) is also of great significance as it declared two extremely important principles. They are-Concept of Sustainable Development[17] and Inter-generational Equity[18].

It has been observed in the case of *Mahavir Nagar Vikas Samiti, Pali v. State of Rajasthan and Ors.*[19], by a Division Bench of High court:

"In Indian civilization man never considered himself to be an overlord and every other creation to be subservient to his interest. His activities did not disturb ecological balance. In ancient India it was an offence to tinker with

---

15 **Flora** is the plant life occurring in a particular region or time, generally the naturally occurring or indigenous—native plant life. The corresponding term for animal life is fauna. *Flora, fauna* and other forms of life such as fungi are collectively referred to as biota.

16 The **United Nations Conference on Environment and Development (UNCED)**, also known as the Rio Summit, Rio Conference, and Earth Summit was a major United Nations conference held inRio de Janeiro from 3 to 14 June 1992

17 The United Nations World Commission on Environment and Development (WCED) in its 1987 report Our Common Futuredefines sustainable development: "Development that meets the needs of the present without compromising the ability of future generations to meet their own needs."

18 **Intergenerational equity** in economic, psychological, and sociological contexts, is the concept or idea of fairness or justice in relationships between children, youth,adults and seniors, particularly in terms of treatment and interactions. It has been studied in environmental and sociological settings

19 2004(1) ILR 187

nature by defiling, destroying and desecrating it. Kautilya[20] Arthashastra is testimony to the respect which was paid to the trees. Felling of trees was made severely punishable. This is reflected in the following Shloka of the Arthashastra:-

'Vrikshachhedaney dandaparushyan viddat.'

The natural resources such as air, water and soil cannot be utilized in a manner that results in irreversible damage to them.

Mining activities and Environment Degradation:

It is their (people involved in illegal Mining) uncontrollable greed which goads[21] them to exploit the ecology by inflicting a permanent injury upon it. It is evident by looking at the areas where mining is being undertaken that how the hills have been cut to exploit the minerals. In some of the cases small hills have been plundered to the point of no return. The exploiters forget that hills cannot be re-created once destroyed. Destruction of hills is an ecological disaster and is irreversible. Even the mining at the cost of trees and vegetation is equally disastrous. But the mines operators' are unmindful of the consequence as they are interested in making as much money as possible by exploiting the nature. Articles 21, 48A and 51A(g) of the Constitution lay down the foundation for the environmental jurisprudence with a view to protect, preserve and improve ecology. Articles 21, 48A and 51A(g) echo the principle of inter-generational equity. They create right of the unborn to the preservation of ecology for his survival. The present generation cannot be allowed to rob the nature and deprive the future generation of its bounties. That means, the present generation must act in consonance with the principles of sustainable development, a development which is not at the cost of environment but is compatible with it.

Most of our environmental problems would be solved in case the State and the people acquire kind and reverential attitude towards the nature.

---

20 Chanakya is traditionally identified as **Kautilya** or **Vishnu Gupta**, who authored the ancient Indian political treatise called *Arthasastra (Economics)*. As such, he is considered as the pioneer of the field of economics and political science in India, and his work is thought of as an important precursor to classical economics

21 The **goad** is a traditional farming implement, used to spur or guide life stock, usually oxen, which are pulling a plough or a cart; used also to round up cattle. It is a type of a long stick with a pointed end, also known as the cattle prod. Though many people are unfamiliar with them today, goads have been common throughout the world.

In ancient India, mountains were venerated[22], they being sources of rivers, flora, fauna and various other life-sustaining materials, and habitats for birds and animals. People were aware of the great usefulness of the mountains in helping cloud formation and ultimate breaking of rains over parched lands, rendering them fertile to satisfy the need of the human beings and animals, for food. In the past, man understood nature better. He preserved and protected the same. For its kindness, he used to prostrate[23] before it. Gratitude was expressed by feeling of love and admiration for nature. Today, nature is being plundered[24] for short term gains, the kindness of mountains is being returned by denuding them of trees, fauna and flora. Birds and animals are being killed. Man is not mindful of the fact that trees are the very life line of human existence.

Directions by High Court:

(1) The State and its functionaries shall ensure that the mining activities in the State of Rajasthan are carried on after obtaining proper consent/ clearance from the concerned authorities and in accordance with the provisions of the law and the rules and also the orders of the Supreme Court and High court issued from time to time.

(2) The State shall ensure that illegal un-scientific and un-systematic mining operations shall not be permitted to be carried on unless mining lease holders adopt and adhere to the norms prescribed under the law and the rules.

(3) The State shall ensure that the stone crushers comply with the norms laid down under the Environmental Protection Act, 1986.

(4) The State shall take effective steps for reclamation of abandoned mines by having them filled up by over burden, waste and fly ash from the thermal power plants.

(5) Mines from which water is being discharged should be closed to

---

22 **Meaning of Venerate:** To regard with respect, reverence, or heartfelt deference

23 Meaning of Prostrate:

   1. To put or throw flat with the face down, as in submission or adoration

   2. To cause to lie flat

   3. To reduce to extreme weakness or incapacitation; overcome

24 **Meaning of Plundered:**

   1. The act or practice of plundering.

   2. Property stolen by fraud or force; booty.

prevent wastage of water and depleting of ground water.

(6) All efforts should be made for plantation of trees in the mining areas as well as where trees have been cut in large number for widening of the road. The number and variety of trees, vegetation and shrubs to be planted in the mining areas shall be as per the advice of the Forest Department. No mining activity shall take place before planting of trees, shrubs and vegetation in accordance with the advice of the Forest Department and acing thereupon.

(7) The mine owners shall not be allowed to increase their production without receiving the permission from the Ministry of Environment and consent from the Rajasthan Pollution Control Board.

26

Animals are born with an equal claim for life[1]

Facts in Nutshell:

Petitioners[2] who claimed to be animal lovers and engaged in welfare of animals, in educating the general public concerning the necessity of treating all animals with compassion and to be the activist interested in ensuring that all laws concerning prevention of cruelty to the animals are enforced, have approached High Court of Bombay (Panaji Bench) with the complaint that the statutory authorities are either hesitant or negligent in taking appropriate steps to prevent the cruelty to the animals that is being inflicted in the course of the game of bull fights taking place in the State of Goa. According to the petitioners, bull fights are in contravention of section 11(1)[3] of the Prevention of Cruelty to Animals Act, 1968, hereinafter called as "the said Act'. It was the contention of the petitioners that inspite of their efforts to bring this fact to the notice of the authorities concerned, such illegalities are being committed in the State of Goa and further that inspite of requests to such authorities to take appropriate steps in the matter to prevent the same, no action was taken by the respondents[4] and the bull fights continued tp take place in Goa. It was further contended by the petitioners that the immediate occasion for the

---

1   Appellants: **People for Animals through Mrs. Norma Alvares and Anr. Vs.** Respondent: **The State of Goa through its Chief Secretary and Ors.**

    1997(4)BomCR271

    Hon'ble Judges/Coram: R.K. Batta and R.M.S. Khandeparkar, JJ.

2   **Meaning of Petitioner:** A person who presents a Petition. (**Meaning of Petition:** A formal message requesting something that is submitted to an authority)

3   **Sections 11(1)(a) of Prevention of Cruelty to Animals Act, 1960**

    11. Treating animals cruelly : (1) If any person (a) beats, kicks, over-rides, over-drives, over-loads, tortures or otherwise treats any animal so as to subject it to unnecessary pain or suffering or causes, or being the owner permits, any animal to be so treated

4   **Meaning of Respondent:** A **respondent** is a person who is called upon to issue a response to a communication made by another. In legal usage, this specifically refers to the defendant in a legal proceeding commenced by a petition, or to an appellee, or the opposing party, in an appeal of a decision by an initial fact-finder.

petitioners to approach High Court is the incident of killing of a person in a most brutal fashion by a violent bull at one of such bull fights organized at Fatorda near Margao on 17th September 1996.

The petitioners claimed that the bull fights are recent introduction in the State of Goa and though initially, no money or gambling was associated with it, in the recent times, due to the patronage of local politicians, the frequency of bull fights have increased enormously and they have become completely commercialised. Newspapers' advertisements of bull fights are openly published to attract more and more spectators. On any given day, there would be fights between 6 to 10 bulls and in the process, bulls get severely hurt and wounded and further they also become insane. Specific procedures are utilised by the bull owners to instigate[5] the bulls to fight with each other. Accordingly, two bulls or buffaloes specially trained and bred for this game only fight against each other, with their owner or trainer standing behind them goading them on. At regular intervals, either mud is rubbed on the back of the animal or water is poured on its back. This is done to agitate or cool down the animal as the need may be. It was further contended by the petitioners that several social evils have sprung up and are associated with events of bull fights and they include large scale of illegal betting relating to the fortunes and fate of the individual bull. It was stated that the situation gets worse when the defeated bull starts running away from the field and the victor charges him. Such bull fights are locally known as 'dhirio' and they are in direct contravention of the provisions contained in section 11(1)(m)[6] and section 11(1)(n)[7] of the Prevention of Cruelty to Animals Act, 1968 and that the authorities are duty-bound to take action against the said offenders.

The petitioners, therefore approached the High Court for necessary directions to the respondents (State Government) to take appropriate steps to stop the practice of bull fights in Goa.

---

5   **Meaning of Instigate:** To urge on to some drastic or inadvisable action

6   **Section 11(1)(m), Prevention of Cruelty to Animals Act, 1960:**

    11. Treating animals cruelly : (1) If any person

    (m)solely with a view to providing entertainment

7   **Section 11(1)(n), Prevention of Cruelty to Animals Act, 1960:**

    (1) If any person

    (n) organises, keeps uses or acts in the management or, any place for animal fighting or for the purpose of baiting any animal or permits or offers any place to be so used or receives money for the admission of any other person to any place kept or used for any such purposes

Bull Fight:

A bull fight consists of a fight between two bulls or two buffaloes or a bull and a buffalo. Such fights are organized in an open field and the same is witnessed by the crowd of spectators which spread all around the arena or the ground where such fights are arranged. The organizers of the bull fights collect fees from the spectators who witness such bull fights. The crowd of spectators range anywhere between 500 to 5000 depending upon the bulls and buffaloes arranged for such fights. The bulls or buffaloes are specially maintained for such fights by some of the people in the State of Goa. The fight begins when two bulls or buffaloes specially trained and bred for the fight are brought against each other with their owner or trainer standing behind them goading them on. At regular intervals, either mud is rubbed on the back of the animals or water is poured on its back. This is done either to agitate or to cool down the animal as the need may arise. In the process of such fight, the animals are goaded and incited not only by the owners or trainers who stand behind such bulls but almost the entire crowd participate in inciting the animals to fight. Before the actual fight begins, the bulls with their eyes turned red glare at each other and sometimes try to scare their opponent by scything their horns in the ground, flinging mud up into the air. Then suddenly they dash at each other, locking horns, pushing each other. They move back and forth intermittently charging and retreating. It all depends on the strength of the bull and its stamina. Pushing each other sometimes they even try their force on the spectators while the crowd scrambles for safety. The bull that gets pushed out of the arena first or turns and runs away, loses the fight. One fight could go on as long as an hour or get over within two or three minutes. On some occasions the bull runs away from the field without even locking horns. In the process the animals suffer injuries. At times, the bull can get gored and have to be put to sleep. Normally the defeated animal runs away from the field with the victor chasing it and on such occasions it can even run towards the spectators causing injuries to them.

In brief the bull fight involves fight between two bulls or buffaloes without any restrictions to be observed in such fights & without any control of human being as regards the nature of the fight which can take place between such bulls and in the result the animals are injured and at times go insane and also can inflict injuries to the spectators of such bull fights.

Decision of the High Court:

Court held that all animals are born with an equal claim for life without any cruelty to them. The bull fights or 'dhirios' are in contravention of the provisions of the Prevention of Cruelty to Animals Act, 1968 & therefore, illegal & cannot be permitted to be organized. Court directed the respondents (State Government) to take immediate steps to ban all types of animal fights including bull fights and 'dhirios' in the State of Goa and to see to it that the direction is fully complied with in letter and spirit which the Act seeks to achieve.

Education, Students and Examination

Right to Education:

In *Mohini Jain v. State of Kamataka & Ors.[1], Court* held the preamble[2] promises to secure justice "social, economic and political for the citizens. A peculiar feature of the Indian Constitution is that it combines social and economic rights along with political and justiciable[3] legal rights. The preamble embodies the goal which the State has to achieve in order to establish social justice and to make the masses free in the positive sense. The securing of social justice has been specifically enjoined an object of the State under Article 38[4] of the Constitution. Can the objective which has been so prominently pronounced in the preamble and Article 38 of the Constitution be achieved without providing education to the large majority of citizens who are illiterate. The objectives flowing from the preamble cannot be achieved and shall remain on paper unless the people in this country are educated. The three pronged justice promised by the preamble is only an illusion to the teaming-million who are illiterate. It is only the education which equips a citizen to participate in achieving the objective enshrined in the preamble. The preamble further assures the dignity of the individual. The Constitution seeks to achieve this object by guaranteeing fundamental rights[5] to each individual which he can

---

1   1992 4 JT 292

2   The **preamble to the Constitution of India** is a brief introductory statement that sets out the guiding purpose and principles of the document.

3   **Meaning of justiciable:**

   1. Appropriate for or subject to court trial

   2. That can be settled by law or a court of law

4   **Article 38 in The Constitution Of India 1949**

   State to secure a social order for the promotion of welfare of the people

   (1) The State shall strive to promote the welfare of the people by securing and protecting as effectively as it may a social order in which justice, social, economic and political, shall inform all the institutions of the national life

   (2) The State shall, in particular, strive to minimize the inequalities in income, and endeavor to eliminate inequalities in status, facilities and opportunities, not only amongst individuals but also amongst groups of people residing in different areas or engaged in different vocations

5   **Meaning of Fundamental Rights:** The Fundamental Rights are defined as basic human freedoms which every Indian citizen has the right to enjoy for a proper and harmonious development of personality. These rights universally apply to all citizens, irrespective of race,

enforce through Court of law if necessary. The directive principles[6] in Part IV of the Constitution are also within the same objective. The dignity of man is inviolable[7]. It is the duty of the State to respect and protect the same. It is primarily the education which brings forth the dignity of a man. The framers of the Constitution were aware that more than seventy per cent of the people, to whom they were giving the Constitution of India, were illiterate. They were also hopeful that within a period of ten years illiteracy would be wiped out from the country. It was with that hope that Articles 41[8] and 45[9] were brought in Chapter IV of the Constitution. An individual cannot be assured of human dignity unless his personality is developed and the only way to do that is to educate him. This is why the Universal Declaration of Human Rights, 1948 emphasises "Education shall be directed to the full development of the human personality." Article 41 in Chapter IV of the Constitution recognises an individual's "right to education". It says that "the State shall, within the limits of its economic capacity and development, make effective provision for securing the right to education." The directive principles which are fundamental in the governance of the country cannot be isolated from the fundamental rights guaranteed under Part III. These principles have to be read into the fundamental rights. Both are supplementary to each

---

place of birth, religion, caste, creed, colour or gender. Aliens (persons who are not citizens) are also considered in matters like equality before law. They are enforceable by the courts, subject to certain restrictions.

6   The **Directive Principles of State Policy** are guidelines to the central and state governments of India, to be kept in mind while framing laws and policies. These provisions, contained in Part IV of the Constitution of India, are not enforceable by any court, but the principles laid down therein are considered fundamental in the governance of the country, making it the duty of the State[1] to apply these principles in making laws to establish a just society in the country. The principles have been inspired by the Directive Principles given in the Constitution of Ireland and also by the principles of Gandhism; and relate to social justice, economic welfare, foreign policy, and legal and administrative matters.

7   **Meaning of Inviolable:**

   1. Secure from violation or profanation

   2. Impregnable to assault or trespass; invincible

8   **Article 41 in The Constitution Of India 1949**

   Right to work, to education and to public assistance in certain cases: The State shall, within the limits of its economic capacity and development, make effective provision for securing the right to work, to education and to public assistance in cases of unemployment, old age, sickness and disablement, and in other cases of undeserved want

9   **Article 45 in The Constitution Of India 1949**

   Provision for free and compulsory education for children: The State shall endeavour to provide, within a period of ten years from the commencement of this Constitution, for free and compulsory education for all children until they complete the age of fourteen years

other. The State is under a constitutional mandate to create conditions in which the fundamental rights guaranteed to the individuals under Part III could be enjoyed by all. Without making "right to education" under Article 41 of the Constitution a reality the fundamental rights under Chapter III shall remain beyond the reach of large majority which is illiterate."

27

What level of education is necessary to make the life meaningful[1]?

Facts in Nutshell:

Petition[2] filed by the petitioners[3] who secured 47.75 per cent marks and 46 per cent marks respectively in their graduate examination conducted by the University of Delhi. The respondent[4]-Faculty of Law, University of Delhi issued an advertisement declaring that admission to the LL.B. three years degree course for the academic year 1992-93 would be on the basis of entrance test conducted by the respondents-Faculty of Law, University of Delhi. Advertisement further said that the test was open only to the candidates who had passed Master/B.A. Degree examination securing at least **50 per cent** marks in the aggregate. The petitioners submitted their application forms and they contended that eligibility of 50 per cent marks for appearing in the entrance examination was illegal, arbitrary and irrational. By virtue of the interim orders the petitioners were allowed to take the examination provisionally subject to the final determination of the writ petition[5].

---

1 Appellants: **Jayshree Ravi and Anr. Vs.** Respondent: **University of Delhi and Anr.**

   AIR1993Delhi171

   Hon'ble Judges/Coram: C.L. Choudhary, V.K. Jain and Arun Madan, JJ.

2 **Meaning of Petition:** A formal message requesting something that is submitted to an authority

3 **Meaning of Petitioner:** A person who presents a Petition. (**Meaning of Petition:** A formal message requesting something that is submitted to an authority)

4 **Meaning of Respondent:** A **respondent** is a person who is called upon to issue a response to a communication made by another. In legal usage, this specifically refers to the defendant in a legal proceeding commenced by a petition, or to an appellee, or the opposing party, in an appeal of a decision by an initial fact-finder.

5 **Meaning of Writ Petition:** Under the Indian legal system, jurisdiction to issue 'prerogative writs' is given to the Supreme Court, and to the High Courts of Judicature of all Indian states. Parts of the law relating to writs are set forth in the Constitution of India. The Supreme Court, the highest in the country, may issue writs under Article 32 of the Constitution for enforcement of Fundamental Rights and under Articles 139 for enforcement of rights other than Fundamental Rights, while High Courts, the superior courts of the States, may issue writs under Articles 226. 'Writ' is eminently designed by the makers of the Constitution, and in the same way it is developed very widely and efficiently by the courts in India. The Constitution broadly provides for

Decision by Division Bench[6] of Delhi High Court:

The Division Bench of Delhi High Court (Mahinder Narain and Jaspal Singh JJ.) took divergent views while Mahinder Narain Judge allowed the writ petition and declared that the prescription of minimum 50 per cent marks in B.A. as a condition precedent[7] for taking the entrance examination was arbitrary, unreasonable and the same being vocative[8] of provisions of Articles 14[9] and 21[10] of the Constitution of India and on this ground struck the eligibility criteria of 50 per cent and quashed[11] the same while another member of the Division Bench (Jaspal Singh Judge) held that eligibility condition was not in violation of Article 14 of the Constitution of India and, therefore, disagreed with the view taken by Mahinder Narain Judge. In view of the difference of opinion between two Judges a reference was made by the said Division Bench to refer the matter to a third Judge to the following effect:-

"IS the eligibility condition of obtaining at least 50% marks in the Graduate/ Post Graduate examination for appearing in the entrance test for admission to the first year of LL.B. course a valid consideration, keeping in view the provisions of Articles 14 and 21 of the Constitution of India ?"

Third Judge (C.L. Chaudhry Judge) who vide his order dated 22nd January, 1993 issued directions to the University to declare the result of the petitioners and grant them provisional admission to appear in

---

five kinds of "prerogative" writs, namely, Habeas Corpus, Certiorari, Mandamus, Quo Warranto and Prohibition.

6   A **Division Bench** is a term in judicial system in India in which a case is heard and judged by *at least* two judges. However, if the bench during the hearing of any matter feels that the matter needs to be considered by a larger bench, such a matter is referred to a larger bench

7   **Meaning of Precedent:** An act or instance that may be used as an example in dealing with subsequent similar instances.

8   **Meaning of Vocative:**

   1. of or designating a grammatical case, as in Latin, used to indicate that a noun or pronoun refers to the person or thing being addressed.

   2. of or used in calling or addressing.

9   **Article 14 in The Constitution Of India 1949**

   Equality before law: The State shall not deny to any person equality before the law or the equal protection of the laws within the territory of India Prohibition of discrimination on grounds of religion, race, caste, sex or place of birth

10 **Article 21 in The Constitution Of India 1949**

   21. Protection of life and personal liberty: No person shall be deprived of his life or personal liberty except according to procedure established by law

11 **Meaning of Quash:** To set aside or annul, especially by judicial action.

the First Semester Examination of the LL.B. Course. On hearing the parties C.L. Chaudhry Judge, allowed the applications and directed the University to declare the result of the petitioners within 3 days and in case they secure more marks than the last candidate who was given admission by the University of Delhi, the petitioners would also be given admission provisionally and they will be allowed to take the 1st Semester Examination. However, it was made clear in that order that the grant of provisional admission and taking of the 1st Semester Examination shall not confer any right in favor of the petitioners in case they ultimately fail in the writ petition. Aggrieved by the order, the University filed the appeal[12] before the Supreme Court by way of Special Leave Petition[13].

Decision by Supreme Court:

The Supreme Court while disposing[14] of the special leave petition made the following order that the learned Chief Justice of Delhi High Court should constitute a larger Bench for hearing of the writ petitions. **Thereafter, Full Bench was constituted by Delhi High court and matter was referred again to Full Bench of Delhi High Court.**

Right to Education:

In *Mohini Jain v. State of Kamataka & Ors.[15]*, Court held the preamble[16]

---

12 **Meaning of Appeal:** In law, an **appeal** is a process for requesting a formal change to an official decision. Very broadly speaking there are appeals on the record and *de novo* appeals. In *de novo* appeals, a new decision maker re-hears the case without any reference to the prior decision maker. In appeals on the record, the decision of the prior decision maker is challenged by arguing that he or she misapplied the law, came to an incorrect factual finding, acted in excess of his jurisdiction, abused his powers, was biased, considered evidence which he should not have considered or failed to consider evidence that he should have considered.

13 **Article 136 in The Constitution Of India 1949**

   Special leave to appeal by the Supreme Court

   (1) Notwithstanding anything in this Chapter, the Supreme Court may, in its discretion, grant special leave to appeal from any judgment, decree, determination, sentence or order in any cause or matter passed or made by any court or tribunal in the territory of India

   (2) Nothing in clause (1) shall apply to any judgment, determination, sentence or order passed or made by any court or tribunal constituted by or under any law relating to the Armed Forces

14 **Meaning of Disposing:**

   1. To place or set in a particular order; arrange.

   2. To put (business affairs, for example) into correct, definitive, or conclusive form.

   3. To put into a willing or receptive frame of mind; incline.

15 1992 4 JT 292

16 The **preamble to the Constitution of India** is a brief introductory statement that sets out the guiding purpose and principles of the document.

promises to secure justice "social, economic and political for the citizens. A peculiar feature of the Indian Constitution is that it combines social and economic rights along with political and justiciable[17] legal rights. The preamble embodies the goal which the State has to achieve in order to establish social justice and to make the masses free in the positive sense. The securing of social justice has been specifically enjoined an object of the State under Article 38[18] of the Constitution. Can the objective which has been so prominently pronounced in the preamble and Article 38 of the Constitution be achieved without providing education to the large majority of citizens who are illiterate. The objectives flowing from the preamble cannot be achieved and shall remain on paper unless the people in this country are educated. The three pronged justice promised by the preamble is only an illusion to the teaming-million who are illiterate. It is only the education which equips a citizen to participate in achieving the objective enshrined in the preamble. The preamble further assures the dignity of the individual. The Constitution seeks to achieve this object by guaranteeing fundamental rights[19] to each individual which he can enforce through Court of law if necessary. The directive principles[20] in Part IV of the Constitution are also within the same objective. The dignity

---

17 **Meaning of justiciable:**

    1. Appropriate for or subject to court trial

    2. That can be settled by law or a court of law

18 **Article 38 in The Constitution Of India 1949**

    State to secure a social order for the promotion of welfare of the people

    (1) The State shall strive to promote the welfare of the people by securing and protecting as effectively as it may a social order in which justice, social, economic and political, shall inform all the institutions of the national life

    (2) The State shall, in particular, strive to minimize the inequalities in income, and endeavor to eliminate inequalities in status, facilities and opportunities, not only amongst individuals but also amongst groups of people residing in different areas or engaged in different vocations

19 **Meaning of Fundamental Rights:** The Fundamental Rights are defined as basic human freedoms which every Indian citizen has the right to enjoy for a proper and harmonious development of personality. These rights universally apply to all citizens, irrespective of race, place of birth, religion, caste, creed, colour or gender. Aliens (persons who are not citizens) are also considered in matters like equality before law. They are enforceable by the courts, subject to certain restrictions.

20 The **Directive Principles of State Policy** are guidelines to the central and state governments of India, to be kept in mind while framing laws and policies. These provisions, contained in Part IV of the Constitution of India, are not enforceable by any court, but the principles laid down therein are considered fundamental in the governance of the country, making it the duty of the State[1] to apply these principles in making laws to establish a just society in the country. The principles have been inspired by the Directive Principles given in the Constitution of Ireland and also by the principles of Gandhism; and relate to social justice, economic welfare, foreign policy, and legal and administrative matters.

of man is inviolable[21]. It is the duty of the State to respect and protect the same. It is primarily the education which brings forth the dignity of a man. The framers of the Constitution were aware that more than seventy per cent of the people, to whom they were giving the Constitution of India, were illiterate. They were also hopeful that within a period of ten years illiteracy would be wiped out from the country. It was with that hope that Articles 41[22] and 45[23] were brought in Chapter IV of the Constitution. An individual cannot be assured of human dignity unless his personality is developed and the only way to do that is to educate him. This is why the Universal Declaration of Human Rights, 1948 emphasises "Education shall be directed to the full development of the human personality." Article 41 in Chapter IV of the Constitution recognises an individual's "right to education". It says that "the State shall, within the limits of its economic capacity and development, make effective provision for securing the right to education." The directive principles which are fundamental in the governance of the country cannot be isolated from the fundamental rights guaranteed under Part III. These principles have to be read into the fundamental rights. Both are supplementary to each other. The State is under a constitutional mandate to create conditions in which the fundamental rights guaranteed to the individuals under Part III could be enjoyed by all. Without making "right to education" under Article 41 of the Constitution a reality the fundamental rights under Chapter III shall remain beyond the reach of large majority which is illiterate."

Decision by High Court of Delhi (Full Bench):

Court held that the fixation of 50% as a precondition for taking the entrance test is vocative[24] of Article 14 of the Constitution of India.

---

21 **Meaning of Inviolable:**

    1. Secure from violation or profanation

    2. Impregnable to assault or trespass; invincible

22 **Article 41 in The Constitution Of India 1949**

    Right to work, to education and to public assistance in certain cases: The State shall, within the limits of its economic capacity and development, make effective provision for securing the right to work, to education and to public assistance in cases of unemployment, old age, sickness and disablement, and in other cases of undeserved want

23 **Article 45 in The Constitution Of India 1949**

    Provision for free and compulsory education for children: The State shall endeavour to provide, within a period of ten years from the commencement of this Constitution, for free and compulsory education for all children until they complete the age of fourteen years

24 **Meaning of Vocative:**

The criteria to select students who are 'best amongst the best' can be achieved without such precondition, on the basis of performance and relative merits in the entrance test, otherwise there is no object of providing entrance test. Court further held that petitioners have right to education. The State cannot limit or take away the right of the petitioners to take legal education. Laying down the criteria of minimum 50% marks in BA /MA examinations for LL.B. 1st year entrance test was irrational, improper and arbitrary and deserved to be struck down. Court issued writ of mandamus[25] to the University of Delhi and allowed the writ petition by petitioners.

Court observed that the right to education means that a citizen has a right to call upon the State to provide educational facilities to him within the limits of its economic capacity and development. Education is enlightenment. It is the one that lends dignity to a man as was rightly observed by Gajendragarkar, Judge in *University of Delhi v. Ram Nath*[26] "EDUCATION seeks to built up; the personality of the pupil by assisting his physical, intellectual, moral and emotional development."

Higher education calls heavily on national economic resources. The right to it must necessarily be limited in any given country by its economic and social circumstances. The State's obligation to provide it is, therefore, not absolute and immediate but relative and progressive.

---

1. Relating to, characteristic of, or used in calling.

2. Of, relating to, or being a grammatical case in certain inflected languages to indicate the person or thing being addressed.

25 **Mandamus** is a judicial remedy in the form of an order from a superior court, to any government subordinate court,corporation, or public authority—to do (or forbear from doing) some specific act which that body is obliged under law to do (or refrain from doing)—and which is in the nature of public duty, and in certain cases one of a statutory duty. It cannot be issued to compel an authority to do something against statutory provision. For example, it cannot be used to force a lower court to reject or authorize applications that have been made, but if the court refuses to rule one way or the other then a mandamus can be used to order the court to rule on the applications.

26 (1963)IILLJ335SC

28

Right of Examinee[1] to Inspect answer sheet[2]

Facts in Nutshell:

The petitioner[3] obtained 91.6 per cent in his Madhyamik (Class X) Examinations and 80.8 per cent in his Higher Secondary (Class XII) and got himself enrolled for the mathematics honours course of the Calcutta University in Presidency College where admission itself is an acknowledgment of merit. In 2006, the petitioner took his Part I Bachelor's degree examinations and secured a somewhat modest 52 per cent score. In the following year he appeared for his Part II Examinations and secured 208 marks out of a maximum of 400. The petitioner was particularly aggrieved by his being awarded 28 out of 100 in the fifth paper. The petitioner applied for a post publication scrutiny, seeking re-evaluation of his answer scripts in the fifth and sixth papers in accordance with the rules prescribed by the University. On view, the marks awarded to him in the fifth paper increased by four and a fresh, corrected mark sheet was issued to him. The petitioner claimed that he was called for an interview for the integrated Ph.D. programme in mathematics at the Tata Institute of Fundamental Research, Bangalore Centre after clearing the written examination there for. He claimed that his poor marks in the second leg of his Bachelor's course led to his exclusion from the final list. The petitioner averred[4] that the poor marks stand in the way of his obtaining admission for the master's programme in any of the better universities.

---

1   **Meaning of Examinee: One that is examined**

2   Appellants: **Pritam Rooj Vs.** Respondent: University **of Calcutta and Ors.**

   AIR2008Cal118

   Hon'ble Judges/Coram: Sanjib Banerjee, Judge

3   **Meaning of Petitioner:** A person who presents a Petition. (**Meaning of Petition:** A formal message requesting something that is submitted to an authority)

4   **Meaning of Averred:**

   a. To assert formally as a fact.

   b. To justify or prove.

The petitioner cleared the written examination for the integrated doctoral programme in mathematical sciences at the Indian Institute of Science, Bangalore and following the interview, was placed eighth on the merit list. The petitioner's provisional application fell through as he failed to obtain a first class in his Bachelor's course.

On August 14, 2007 the petitioner made a request to obtain his University answerscript in appropriate format to the State Public Information Officer under the Right to Information Act, 2005. Such officer rejected the application by a writing of September 17, 2007 which was the subject matter of the challenge before the High Court. The letter appeared to be on a printed format where there was a blank left for the date at the top; there was a space left for the examinee's name and address being inserted; and the date of the application was also left open to be filled up. The officer used his pen to fill up the date of the letter, the name and address of the examine, the date of the application and has inserted the word "been" as there was an obvious mistake in the printed form. The officer acknowledged the receipt of an application under the said RTI Act, 2005 but did not deal with the application in the manner provided by the said RTI Act, 2005 and it was such action and the stereo typed decision from the letter of rejection that prompted the writ petition[5] to be entertained by High Court, rather than requiring the petitioner to exhaust the alternative remedy ordinarily available under the RTI Act, 2005.

Section 7[6] of the said RTI Act, 2005 lays down the manner of disposal

---

5   **Meaning of Writ Petition:** Under the Indian legal system, jurisdiction to issue 'prerogative writs' is given to the Supreme Court, and to the High Courts of Judicature of all Indian states. Parts of the law relating to writs are set forth in the Constitution of India. The Supreme Court, the highest in the country, may issue writs under Article 32 of the Constitution for enforcement of Fundamental Rights and under Articles 139 for enforcement of rights other than Fundamental Rights, while High Courts, the superior courts of the States, may issue writs under Articles 226. 'Writ' is eminently designed by the makers of the Constitution, and in the same way it is developed very widely and efficiently by the courts in India. The Constitution broadly provides for five kinds of "prerogative" writs, namely, Habeas Corpus, Certiorari, Mandamus, Quo Warranto and Prohibition

6   **Section 7 in The Right To Information Act, 2005**

Disposal of request

(1) Subject to the proviso to sub-section (2) of section 5 or the proviso to sub-section (3) of section 6, the Central Public Information Officer or State Public Information Officer, as the case may be on receipt of a request under section 6 shall, as expeditiously as possible, and in any case within thirty days of the receipt of the request, either provide the information on payment of such fee as may be prescribed or reject the request for any of the reasons specified in sections 8 and 9.

Disposal of request.—(1) Subject to the proviso to sub-section (2) of section 5 or the proviso to sub-section (3) of section 6, the Central Public Information Officer or State Public Information Officer, as the case may be on receipt of a request under section 6 shall, as expeditiously as possible, and in any case within thirty days of the receipt of the request, either provide the information on payment of such fee as may be prescribed or reject the request for any of the reasons specified in sections 8 and 9" Provided that where the information sought for concerns the life or liberty of a person, the same shall be provided within forty-eight hours of the receipt of the request. tc "Provided that where the information sought for concerns the life or liberty of a person, the same shall be provided within forty-eight hours of the receipt of the request."

(2) If the Central Public Information Officer or State Public Information Officer, as the case may be fails to give decision on the request for information within the period specified under sub-section (1), the Central Public Information Officer or State Public Information Officer, as the case may be shall be deemed to have refused the request. "(2) If the Central Public Information Officer or State Public Information Officer, as the case may be fails to give decision on the request for information within the period specified under sub-section (1), the Central Public Information Officer or State Public Information Officer, as the case may be shall be deemed to have refused the request."

(3) Where a decision is taken to provide the information on payment of any further fee representing the cost of providing the information, the Central Public Information Officer or State Public Information Officer, as the case may be shall send an intimation to the person making the request, giving— "(3) Where a decision is taken to provide the information on payment of any further fee representing the cost of providing the information, the Central Public Information Officer or State Public Information Officer, as the case may be shall send an intimation to the person making the request, giving—"

(a) the details of further fees representing the cost of providing the information as determined by him, together with the calculations made to arrive at the amount in accordance with fee prescribed under sub-section (1), requesting him to deposit that fees, and the period intervening between the despatch of the said intimation and payment of fees shall be excluded for the purpose of calculating the period of thirty days referred to in that sub-section; " (a) the details of further fees representing the cost of providing the information as determined by him, together with the calculations made to arrive at the amount in accordance with fee prescribed under sub-section (1), requesting him to deposit that fees, and the period intervening between the despatch of the said intimation and payment of fees shall be excluded for the purpose of calculating the period of thirty days referred to in that sub-section;"

(b) information concerning his or her right with respect to review the decision as to the amount of fees charged or the form of access provided, including the particulars of the appellate authority, time limit, process and any other forms. (b) information concerning his or her right with respect to review the decision as to the amount of fees charged or the form of access provided, including the particulars of the appellate authority, time limit, process and any other forms."

(4) Where access to the record or a part thereof is required to be provided under this Act and the person to whom access is to be provided is sensorily disabled, the Central Public Information Officer or State Public Information Officer, as the case may be shall provide assistance to enable access to the information, including providing such assistance as may be appropriate for the inspection. tc "(4) Where access to the record or a part thereof is required to be provided under this Act and the person to whom access is to be provided is sensorily disabled, the Central Public Information Officer or State Public Information Officer, as the case may be shall provide assistance to enable access to the information, including providing such assistance as may be appropriate for the inspection."

(5) Where access to information is to be provided in the printed or in any electronic format, the applicant shall, subject to the provisions of sub-section (6), pay such fee as may be prescribed: tc "(5) Where access to information is to be provided in the printed or in any electronic format, the applicant shall, subject to the provisions of sub-section (6), pay such fee as may be prescribed\:" Provided that the fee prescribed under sub-section (1) of section 6 and sub-sections (1) and (5)

of request for obtaining information received under the RTI Act, 2005. Sub-section (8) of Section 7 stipulates that where a request has been rejected under Sub-section (1), the relevant officer shall communicate to the person making the request, the reasons for such rejection; the period within which an appeal against such rejection may be preferred; and, the particulars of the appellate authority. The letter of rejection of September 17, 2007 was lacking on all three counts. It does not convey any reason for the rejection. It does not inform the petitioner of his right to appellate authority. The rejection was wholly without jurisdiction and in contravention of the mandate under Section 7(8) of the RTI Act, 2005 and per se contrary to the principles of natural justice[7]. When the order is assessed to be of such poor quality that it fails to comply with the

---

of section 7 shall be reasonable and no such fee shall be charged from the persons who are of below poverty line as may be determined by the appropriate Government. tc "Provided that the fee prescribed under sub-section (1) of section 6 and sub-sections (1) and (5) of section 7 shall be reasonable and no such fee shall be charged from the persons who are of below poverty line as may be determined by the appropriate Government."

(6) Notwithstanding anything contained in sub-section (5), the person making request for the information shall be provided the information free of charge where a public authority fails to comply with the time limits specified in sub-section (1). tc "(6) Notwithstanding anything contained in sub-section (5), the person making request for the information shall be provided the information free of charge where a public authority fails to comply with the time limits specified in sub-section (1)."

(7) Before taking any decision under sub-section (1), the Central Public Information Officer or State Public Information Officer, as the case may be shall take into consideration the representation made by a third party under section 11. (7) Before taking any decision under sub-section (1), the Central Public Information Officer or State Public Information Officer, as the case may be shall take into consideration the representation made by a third party under section 11."

(8) Where a request has been rejected under sub-section (1), the Central Public Information Officer or State Public Information Officer, as the case may be shall communicate to the person making the request,— (8) Where a request has been rejected under sub-section (1), the Central Public Information Officer or State Public Information Officer, as the case may be shall communicate to the person making the request,—"

(i) the reasons for such rejection; (i) the reasons for such rejection;"

(ii) the period within which an appeal against such rejection may be preferred; and (ii) the period within which an appeal against such rejection may be preferred; and"

(iii) the particulars of the appellate authority. (iii) the particulars of the appellate authority."

(9) An information shall ordinarily be provided in the form in which it is sought unless it would disproportionately divert the resources of the public authority or would be detrimental to the safety or preservation of the record in question. (9) An information shall ordinarily be provided in the form in which it is sought unless it would disproportionately divert the resources of the public authority or would be detrimental to the safety or preservation of the record in question."

7   In English law, **natural justice** is technical terminology for the rule against bias (*nemo iudex in causa sua*) and the right to a fair hearing (*audi alteram partem*). While the term *natural justice* is often retained as a general concept, it has largely been replaced and extended by the general "duty to act fairly".

statutory requirements, a petition[8] challenging the order may be filed in Court under Article 226[9] of the Constitution.

Question before the High Court:

Whether an examinee has access to his evaluated answerscript under the Right to Information Act, 2005.

Right to Know:

In *Union of India v. Association for Democratic Rights*[10] where the Supreme Court held that in a democratic form of Government voters are of utmost importance and voters have a right to know the antecedents[11] of a candidate. Relying on the International Covenant on Civil and Political Rights the Supreme Court held as follows:

---

8   **Meaning of Petition:** A formal message requesting something that is submitted to an authority

9   **Article 226 in The Constitution Of India 1949**

     Power of High Courts to issue certain writs

     (1) Notwithstanding anything in Article 32 every High Court shall have powers, throughout the territories in relation to which it exercise jurisdiction, to issue to any person or authority, including in appropriate cases, any Government, within those territories directions, orders or writs, including writs in the nature of habeas corpus, mandamus, prohibitions, quo warranto and certiorari, or any of them, for the enforcement of any of the rights conferred by Part III and for any other purpose

     (2) The power conferred by clause (1) to issue directions, orders or writs to any Government, authority or person may also be exercised by any High Court exercising jurisdiction in relation to the territories within which the cause of action, wholly or in part, arises for the exercise of such power, notwithstanding that the seat of such Government or authority or the residence of such person is not within those territories

     (3) Where any party against whom an interim order, whether by way of injunction or stay or in any other manner, is made on, or in any proceedings relating to, a petition under clause (1), without

     (a) furnishing to such party copies of such petition and all documents in support of the plea for such interim order; and

     (b) giving such party an opportunity of being heard, makes an application to the High Court for the vacation of such order and furnishes a copy of such application to the party in whose favour such order has been made or the counsel of such party, the High Court shall dispose of the application within a period of two weeks from the date on which it is received or from the date on which the copy of such application is so furnished, whichever is later, or where the High Court is closed on the last day of that period, before the expiry of the next day afterwards on which the High Court is open; and if the application is not so disposed of, the interim order shall, on the expiry of that period, or, as the case may be, the expiry of the aid next day, stand vacated

     (4) The power conferred on a High Court by this article shall not be in derogation of the power conferred on the Supreme court by clause (2) of Article 32

10   [2002]3SCR696

11   **Meaning of Antecedents:** A person's past history

The right to get information in democracy is recognised all throughout and it is a natural right flowing from the concept of democracy. Article 19(1) and (2) of the International Covenant on Civil and Political Rights are as follows:

(1) Everyone shall have the right to hold opinions without interference.

(2) Everyone shall have the right to freedom of expression; this right shall include freedom to seek, receive and Impart information and Ideas of all kinds, regardless of frontiers, either orally, in writing or in print, in the form of art, or through any other media of his choice.

Knowledge is the plinth[12] on which a polity is built and which it draws from for its sustenance. Access to information is at the foundation of a democracy, for what is a choice if it is uninformed. Education is part of the process of empowerment that the Constitution mandates the State to strive for. The freedom of speech and expression that the Constitution guarantees to all citizens is considerably larger than the words used in

---

12 **Meaning of Plinth:**

   1. A block or slab on which a pedestal, column, or statue is placed.

   2. The base block at the intersection of the baseboard and the vertical trim around an opening.

   3. A continuous course of stones supporting a wall

Article 19(1)(a)[13] of the Constitution. The promise held out in Article 38[14]

---

13 **Article 19 in The Constitution Of India 1949**

Protection of certain rights regarding freedom of speech etc

(1) All citizens shall have the right

(a) to freedom of speech and expression;

(b) to assemble peaceably and without arms;

(c) to form associations or unions;

(d) to move freely throughout the territory of India;

(e) to reside and settle in any part of the territory of India; and

(f) omitted

(g) to practise any profession, or to carry on any occupation, trade or business

(2) Nothing in sub clause (a) of clause (1) shall affect the operation of any existing law, or prevent the State from making any law, in so far as such law imposes reasonable restrictions on the exercise of the right conferred by the said sub clause in the interests of the sovereignty and integrity of India, the security of the State, friendly relations with foreign States, public order, decency or morality or in relation to contempt of court, defamation or incitement to an offence

(3) Nothing in sub clause (b) of the said clause shall affect the operation of any existing law in so far as it imposes, or prevent the State from making any law imposing, in the interests of the sovereignty and integrity of India or public order, reasonable restrictions on the exercise of the right conferred by the said sub clause

(4) Nothing in sub clause (c) of the said clause shall affect the operation of any existing law in so far as it imposes, or prevent the State from making any law imposing, in the interests of the sovereignty and integrity of India or public order or morality, reasonable restrictions on the exercise of the right conferred by the said sub clause

(5) Nothing in sub clauses (d) and (e) of the said clause shall affect the operation of any existing law in so far as it imposes, or prevent the State from making any law imposing, reasonable restrictions on the exercise of any of the rights conferred by the said sub clauses either in the interests of the general public or for the protection of the interests of any Scheduled Tribe

(6) Nothing in sub clause (g) of the said clause shall affect the operation of any existing law in so far as it imposes, or prevent the State from making any law imposing, in the interests of the general public, reasonable restrictions on the exercise of the right conferred by the said sub clause, and, in particular, nothing in the said sub clause shall affect the operation of any existing law in so far as it relates to, or prevent the State from making any law relating to,

(i) the professional or technical qualifications necessary for practising any profession or carrying on any occupation, trade or business, or

(ii) the carrying on by the State, or by a corporation owned or controlled by the State, of any trade, business, industry or service, whether to the exclusion, complete or partial, of citizens or otherwise

14 **Article 38 in The Constitution Of India 1949**

State to secure a social order for the promotion of welfare of the people

(1) The State shall strive to promote the welfare of the people by securing and protecting as effectively as it may a social order in which justice, social, economic and political, shall inform all the institutions of the national life

(2) The State shall, in particular, strive to minimize the inequalities in income, and endeavor to eliminate inequalities in status, facilities and opportunities, not only amongst individuals but also amongst groups of people residing in different areas or engaged in different vocations

of Constitution is for a social order to be brought in, in which Justice, social, economic and political shall inform all the institutions of national life. The State, the Constitution directs, shall strive to eliminate inequalities in status, facilities and opportunities. From the first days of its taking upon the burden of balancing, the Supreme Court has read a word into what is expressly recognised in Article 19(1)(a) of the Constitution. Beginning the judgment in the Romesh Thappar case[15], the Supreme Court found the freedom of discussion to be included in Article19(1)(a) and the freedom of press to be an aspect of the freedom of discussion so that members of a democratic society should be sufficiently informed to "be able to form their own beliefs and communicate. The fundamental principle is the people's right to know".

The right to know has been seen to be at the base of the democratic process and in the cases of Sakal Papers (P) Ltd.[16], Bennett Coleman and Co. 1972)[17], and Indian Express Newspapers (Bombay) P. Ltd.[18], the view expressed in the Romesh Thappar judgment has been echoed and amplified. Be it the case of a magazine being banned in a locality or in quality newsprint being made more difficult to obtain or in Government advertisements being released in more favoured publications, Courts have discerned in several executive actions an attempt to stifle[19] the press; and unmuzzled[20] the right of expression on the touchstone of the larger societal interest to inform and to be kept informed. It is now beyond question that the community has a right to be supplied with information; and the Government has a duty to educate the people within the limits of its resources. Such right and the corresponding obligation is found in Article 41[21] of the Constitution.

---

15 1950 SCR 594 : AIR 1950 SC 124

16 1962 (3) SCR 842 : AIR 1962 SC 305

17 2 SCC 788 : AIR 1973 SC 106

18 (1985) 1 SCC 641 : AIR 1986 SC 515

19 **Meaning of Stifle:**

   1. To interrupt or cut off (the voice, for example)

   2. To keep in or hold back; repress

20 **Meaning of Unmuzzled:** To free from control or censorship

21 **Article 41 in The Constitution Of India 1949**

   Right to work, to education and to public assistance in certain cases: The State shall, within the limits of its economic capacity and development, make effective provision for securing the right to work, to education and to public assistance in cases of unemployment, old age, sickness and disablement, and in other cases of undeserved want

Information which is exempted from Disclosure:

Section 8(1)(j)[22] of RTI Act, 2005 provides that personal information the

---

22   Section 8 in The Right To Information Act, 2005

8. Exemption from disclosure of information

(1) Notwithstanding anything contained in this Act, there shall be no obligation to give any citizen,— tc "8. Exemption from disclosure of information.—(1) Notwithstanding anything contained in this Act, there shall be no obligation to give any citizen,—"

(a) information, disclosure of which would prejudicially affect the sovereignty and integrity of India, the security, strategic, scientific or economic interests of the State, relation with foreign State or lead to incitement of an offence; tc" (a) information, disclosure of which would prejudicially affect the sovereignty and integrity of India, the security, strategic, scientific or economic interests of the State, relation with foreign State or lead to incitement of an offence;"

(b) information which has been expressly forbidden to be published by any court of law or tribunal or the disclosure of which may constitute contempt of court; tc" (b) information which has been expressly forbidden to be published by any court of law or tribunal or the disclosure of which may constitute contempt of court;"

(c) information, the disclosure of which would cause a breach of privilege of Parliament or the State Legislature; tc" (c) information, the disclosure of which would cause a breach of privilege of Parliament or the State Legislature;"

(d) information including commercial confidence, trade secrets or intellectual property, the disclosure of which would harm the competitive position of a third party, unless the competent authority is satisfied that larger public interest warrants the disclosure of such information; tc" (d) information including commercial confidence, trade secrets or intellectual property, the disclosure of which would harm the competitive position of a third party, unless the competent authority is satisfied that larger public interest warrants the disclosure of such information;"

(e) information available to a person in his fiduciary relationship, unless the competent authority is satisfied that the larger public interest warrants the disclosure of such information; tc" (e) information available to a person in his fiduciary relationship, unless the competent authority is satisfied that the larger public interest warrants the disclosure of such information;"

(f) information received in confidence from foreign government; tc" (f) information received in confidence from foreign government;"

(g) information, the disclosure of which would endanger the life or physical safety of any person or identify the source of information or assistance given in confidence for law enforcement or security purposes; tc" (g) information, the disclosure of which would endanger the life or physical safety of any person or identify the source of information or assistance given in confidence for law enforcement or security purposes;"

(h) information which would impede the process of investigation or apprehension or prosecution of offenders; tc" (h) information which would impede the process of investigation or apprehension or prosecution of offenders;"

(i) cabinet papers including records of deliberations of the Council of Ministers, Secretaries and other officers: tc" (i) cabinet papers including records of deliberations of the Council of Ministers, Secretaries and other officers\:" Provided that the decisions of Council of Ministers, the reasons thereof, and the material on the basis of which the decisions were taken shall be made public after the decision has been taken, and the matter is complete, or over: tc" Provided that the decisions of Council of Ministers, the reasons thereof, and the material on the basis of which the decisions were taken shall be made public after the decision has been taken, and the matter is complete, or over\:" Provided further that those matters which come under the exemptions specified in this section shall not be disclosed; tc" Provided further that those matters which come under the exemptions specified in this section shall not be disclosed;"

disclosure of which has no relationship to any public activity or interest, or which would cause unwarranted invasion of the privacy of the individual shall not be disclosed unless the Central Public Information Officer or the State Public Information Officer or the Appellate Authority is satisfied, that the larger public interest justifies the disclosure of such information.

Decision by High Court:

Education is more than just reading prescribed texts and taking examinations in a given format, it is more than a garnering of degrees, certificates and diplomas. Any real education requires the amassing of knowledge that may or may not be in the prescription for an examination. An educated human being may also strive to create a new body of knowledge that is outside the purview of prescriptions. There can be no education if limits are imposed on the amount and type of knowledge an individual may gather or create. A democracy can only be functional in all its aspects, extents and senses when there is an informed citizenry.

An examining authority has every right to judge the student's knowledge and expression of that knowledge, but it cannot take away the examinee's right to know the methodology of and the criteria for its evaluation. An examinee who has written hurried answers and solved problems under examination conditions several months before, when gets the marksheet does not really "know" his answers. His memory of what he wrote will not be complete or accurate. He may not even have a clear recollection of what he has recorded in his answers. Alternatively, he may feel that he has written something that he actually has not. His silly mistakes, graphical or grammatical errors and oversights may not be obvious to him. A look at his evaluated answer script can serve the wonderful purpose of pointing out his mistakes - whether or not the evaluated paper marks such mistakes -- clarifying his doubts and helping him to know once and for all, what he wrote and what he did not.

(j) information which relates to personal information the disclosure of which has not relationship to any public activity or interest, or which would cause unwarranted invasion of the privacy of the individual unless the Central Public Information Officer or the State Public Information Officer or the appellate authority, as the case may be, is satisfied that the larger public interest justifies the disclosure of such information: tc" (j) information which relates to personal information the disclosure of which has not relationship to any public activity or interest, or which would cause unwarranted invasion of the privacy of the individual unless the Central Public Information Officer or the State Public Information Officer or the appellate authority, as the case may be, is satisfied that the larger public interest justifies the disclosure of such information\:" Provided that the information, which cannot be denied to the Parliament or a State Legislature shall not be denied to any person. tc "Provided that the information, which cannot be denied to the Parliament or a State Legislature shall not be denied to any person."

Court held that if inspection of answer scripts is denied to the examinee, the spirit of the Constitutional right to expression and information may be lost. The knowledge-builder's -the University's bid to perpetuate the draconian[23], elitist[24], one-sided right to know and judge and rule without being open to question or accountable to the examinee cannot be encouraged. For a system to foster meaningful proliferation[25] of knowledge, it must itself be crystal clear to its core. Access to answer scripts may have the desirable side-effect of ensuring that there is no loss of any of the papers. Court ordered the University to immediately offer inspection of the paper that the petitioner seeks and issued Writ of Mandamus[26] in that regard.

---

23 **Meaning of Draconian:** Exceedingly harsh; very severe

24 **Meaning of Elitist:** Someone who believes in rule by an elite group

25 **Meaning of Proliferation:** To increase or spread at a rapid rate

26 **Mandamus** is a judicial remedy in the form of an order from a superior court, to any government subordinate court, corporation, or public authority—to do (or forbear from doing) some specific act which that body is obliged under law to do (or refrain from doing)—and which is in the nature of public duty, and in certain cases one of a statutory duty. It cannot be issued to compel an authority to do something against statutory provision. For example, it cannot be used to force a lower court to reject or authorize applications that have been made, but if the court refuses to rule one way or the other then a mandamus can be used to order the court to rule on the applications.

29

Ban on Political activities in College Campus[1]

Facts in Nutshell:

Petitioner[2], a second year B. A. Degree student of St. Thomas College, Palai with politics as Main and History and Economics as subsidiaries. He was a College Union member and Editor of the College Magazine and Area Committee member of the Students Federation of India. He preferred an application for appearing for the second year B.A. Degree examination during March/April 2003 along with various other applicants. Applications received from the students were forwarded to the University by the Principal in January 2003. When the application forms were forwarded to the University the number of attendance of candidates was not taken into consideration since classes were not over. University after affixing the seal returned all the hall tickets to the college with a direction to issue the same to the candidates after verifying the attendance and progress certificates. In the forwarding letter dated 26.2.2003 Controller of Examinations had informed the college authorities to withhold the hall tickets of those who had not fulfilled the necessary requirements. Principal informed the petitioner that he would not be allowed to write the examination due to lack of attendance. Petitioner then submitted a representation to the Controller of Examinations who made endorsement[3] in the representation on 3.3.2003 to admit the petitioner provisionally. Principal did not admit the petitioner to the second year B.A. Degree examination since he did not have sufficient attendance as per rules and regulations.

---

1   Appellants: **Sojan Francis Vs.** Respondent: **M.G. University**

      AIR2003Ker290

      Hon'ble Judges/Coram: K.S. Radhakrishnan and K. Padmanabhan Nair , JJ.

2   **Meaning of Petitioner:** A person who presents a Petition. (**Meaning of Petition:** A formal message requesting something that is submitted to an authority)

3   **Meaning of Endorsement:** The signature on a check, contract, instrument, or other document endorsing it

Petitioner then approached High Court for a writ[4] of mandamus[5] directing the Management and the Principal to allow him to write the examination or in the alternative to hold a special examination of Politics Main for the second year B.A. degree examination. He also sought for a writ of mandamus directing the Management and the Principal to pay a compensation of Rs. 25,000/- by way of damages to the petitioner for illegally preventing him from writing the Politics Main Examination scheduled on 4.3.2003 and for causing mental agony and loss of reputation. The complaint raised against the Principal by the Petitioner is as follows:

(i) Principal did not allow the petitioner to write the second year B.A. Degree examination provisionally in spite of the direction given by the Controller of Examinations. The action of the Principal was illegal and mala fide[6].

(ii) Petitioner stated that the action of the Principal was politically motivated so as to curb the activities of Students Federation of India (S.F.I.) in the college campus.

(iii) The Principal's decision not to allow the petitioner to write the examination has caused mental agony, loss of reputation and irreparable loss and the Management and the Principal be directed to pay Rs. 25,000/- by way of compensation.

Question before the High Court:

Whether an educational institution has got the freedom to prohibit political activities within the college campus and forbid the student from organising or attending meetings other than official ones within the college campus and whether such a restriction would violate Article 19(1) (a)[7] and 19(1)(c) of the Constitution of India.

---

4   **Meaning of Writ:** A written order issued by a court, commanding the party to whom it is addressed to perform or cease performing a specified act

5   **Mandamus** is a judicial remedy in the form of an order from a superior court, to any government subordinate court, corporation, or public authority—to do (or forbear from doing) some specific act which that body is obliged under law to do (or refrain from doing)—and which is in the nature of public duty, and in certain cases one of a statutory duty. It cannot be issued to compel an authority to do something against statutory provision. For example, it cannot be used to force a lower court to reject or authorize applications that have been made, but if the court refuses to rule one way or the other then a mandamus can be used to order the court to rule on the applications.

6   **Meaning of Malafide:** In bad faith

7   **Article 19 in The Constitution Of India 1949**

       Protection of certain rights regarding freedom of speech etc

Decision by Learned Single Judge of High Court:

Learned single Judge of High court dismissed the Writ Petition[8]. Aggrieved by the same appeal[9] was field by petitioner in High Court before Division Bench.

Authority and importance given to the Principal of an educational institution:

A Division Bench[10] of High Court *Unni Raja v. Principal, Medical College[11]* held that the head of an education like the Principal occupies a preeminent[12] position and at the same time, now a days an unenviable one. Principal is answerable to the authorities and to the public for the discipline in the institution. Time was when his authority was never questioned but with passage of time, when educational institutions became the arena of activities by political and political forces, there was a deterioration

---

(1) All citizens shall have the right

(a) to freedom of speech and expression;

(b) to assemble peaceably and without arms;

(c) to form associations or unions;

(d) to move freely throughout the territory of India;

(e) to reside and settle in any part of the territory of India; and

(f) omitted

(g) to practise any profession, or to carry on any occupation, trade or business

8   **Meaning of Writ Petition:** Under the Indian legal system, jurisdiction to issue 'prerogative writs' is given to the Supreme Court, and to the High Courts of Judicature of all Indian states. Parts of the law relating to writs are set forth in the Constitution of India. The Supreme Court, the highest in the country, may issue writs under Article 32 of the Constitution for enforcement of Fundamental Rights and under Articles 139 for enforcement of rights other than Fundamental Rights, while High Courts, the superior courts of the States, may issue writs under Articles 226. 'Writ' is eminently designed by the makers of the Constitution, and in the same way it is developed very widely and efficiently by the courts in India. The Constitution broadly provides for five kinds of "prerogative" writs, namely, Habeas Corpus, Certiorari, Mandamus, Quo Warranto and Prohibition

9   **Meaning of Appeal:** In law, an **appeal** is a process for requesting a formal change to an official decision. Very broadly speaking there are appeals on the record and *de novo* appeals. In *de novo* appeals, a new decision maker re-hears the case without any reference to the prior decision maker. In appeals on the record, the decision of the prior decision maker is challenged by arguing that he or she misapplied the law, came to an incorrect factual finding, acted in excess of his jurisdiction, abused his powers, was biased, considered evidence which he should not have considered or failed to consider evidence that he should have considered

10   A **Division Bench** is a term in judicial system in India in which a case is heard and judged by *at least* two judges.

11   (1983 (2) ILR Ker 754)

12   **Meaning of Preeminent:** Superior to or notable above all others; outstanding

of values cherished for long and an invasion on his powers. Hence it is necessary to unto him what is his. The Division Bench concluded that the essence of the matter is the Head of the Institution should in law be presumed to possess an inherent right of such acts as are necessary in his opinion to maintain discipline in the institution. This right is incapable of an exhaustive identification. To limit it within defined confines would be to erode into his authority and fetter his discretion. To deny this right to the Head of the Institution would be to sound the death knell of discipline in the institution which is already a casualty, by the combination of diverse forces, from within and from without.

Again in *Manu Vilson v. Sree Narayana College*[13] court held that for maintaining the discipline in educational institutions, it has become necessary to strengthen the hands of the Heads of the Institutions and to arm them with sufficient powers, so that those who are keen to study and to improve their career should not be made the victims of a handful of persons who are found to spoil the academic atmosphere by indulging in anti-social activities. It was also held that the Principal, the Head of the Institution, in consultation with the College Council, should have the primary authority to initiate appropriate action against the students for maintenance of discipline.

Bane[14] of campus politics:

Supreme Court in *Haripal Singh v. Devinder Singh*[15] highlighted the bane of campus politics which resulted in the death of a student studying in the final year M.A. Economics. While dealing with the case, Apex Court held as follows:

"It is a malady[16] in our country that political parties allure young students through their student wings. They do so because it is an easy method for enlisting support and participation of student population in their political programmes. Students, particularly in the adolescent age, are easily swayable by political parties without much effort or cost as young and tender minds are susceptible to easy persuasiveness by party

---

13   (1996 (1) KLT 788)

14   **Meaning of Bane:** Ruin or distress

15   1997 (6) SCC 660

16   **Meaning of Malady:**

   1. A disease, a disorder, or an ailment.

   2. An unwholesome condition

leaders. But the disturbing aspect is that most of the political leaders do not mind their student supporters developing hospitality towards their fellow students belonging to rival political wings. What happened in this case perhaps was only the tip of the iceberg as campus rivalry has now deteriorated[17] into a bane for the country. The print media is now replete with reports of such calamitous[18] instances in the campus atmosphere. While at the top layer leaders belonging to different political parties dine together and socialise with each other without any personal acrimony[19] as between themselves, it is a pity that they do not encourage that healthy attitude to percolate down to the grassroot level. Tender minds get galvanised on minor issues, frenzy flares up even on trivialities, young children and adolescents unaware of the disastrous consequences befalling their own future indulge in vandalism[20], mayhem[21] and killing spree against their own fellow students.

Decision by Division Bench of High Court:

Court held that it is open to the educational institutions to prohibit political activities within the college campus and forbid students from organizing or attending meetings other than the official ones within the college campus and such a restriction would not violate Article 19(1) (a) or (c) of the Constitution of India.

---

17 **Meaning of Deteriorate:**

To diminish or impair in quality, character, or value

18 **Meaning of Calamitous:** Causing or involving calamity; disastrous

19 **Meaning of Acrimony:** Bitter, sharp animosity, especially as exhibited in speech or behavior.

20 **Meaning of Vandalism:** Willful or malicious destruction of public or private property

21 **Meaning of Mayhem:** The offense of willfully maiming or crippling a person

30

Career of Student cannot be allowed to be sacrificed[1]

Facts in Nutshell:

Petitioner[2] was final year M.B.A. student of the Osmania University, Hyderabad. The examinations for the IV semester were conducted in the month of September and October 1987. According to the time-table, the last examination in the IV semester was to be held on 3-10-1987. But the University decided to postpone the holding of the examination and shifted the date to 5-10-1987. For that purpose, it had put up a notice on the notice-board on 2-10-1987 informing the examinees[3] that the postponed examination would be held on 5-10-1987. But it realized that notice might not be sufficient or adequate to all the examinees. It has therefore, sent the same notification for publication in the local newspapers like the Udayam, the News Time, the Indian Express and the Deccan Chronicle. This notification of the University was published correctly in all the newspapers on 4-10-1987 informing the postponed examination would be held on 5-10-1987. But unfortunately the newspaper Deccan Chronicle had wrongly printed the notification. According to notification printed in the Deccan Chronicle, postponed examination would be held on 6-10-1987. The petitioner contended that by the notification published by the University in the Deccan Chronicle, he had been misled and, therefore, could not appear for the examination held on 5-10-1987. The consequence of this would be to deny the petitioner to pass the examination in one attempt and to get a first class.

---

1 Appellants: **M. Venkatesham Vs.** Respondent: **Controller of Examinations, Osmania University, Hyderabad and Ors.**

AIR1989AP198

Hon'ble Judges: P.A. Chowdary, Judge

2 **Meaning of Petitioner:** A person who presents a Petition. (**Meaning of Petition:** A formal message requesting something that is submitted to an authority)

3 **Meaning of Examinee:** One that is examined

Therefore, Petitioner approached High Court under article 226[4] of the Constitution of India by filing a petition[5].

Decision by High Court:

Court held that the University was responsible for the wrong printing in the Deccan Chronicle for the reason that it was the University that has deliberately chosen the media of Deccan Chronicle for publication of its notification. Court observed that career of the Student cannot be allowed to be sacrificed. Court ordered the university to permit the petitioner to appear for the sixth paper, Marketing Research, in the supplementary examination and treating the petitioner as a regular candidate and publishing the results on the basis of his performance in all the papers.

---

4   Article 226 in The Constitution Of India 1949

Power of High Courts to issue certain writs

(1) Notwithstanding anything in Article 32 every High Court shall have powers, throughout the territories in relation to which it exercise jurisdiction, to issue to any person or authority, including in appropriate cases, any Government, within those territories directions, orders or writs, including writs in the nature of habeas corpus, mandamus, prohibitions, quo warranto and certiorari, or any of them, for the enforcement of any of the rights conferred by Part III and for any other purpose

(2) The power conferred by clause (1) to issue directions, orders or writs to any Government, authority or person may also be exercised by any High Court exercising jurisdiction in relation to the territories within which the cause of action, wholly or in part, arises for the exercise of such power, notwithstanding that the seat of such Government or authority or the residence of such person is not within those territories

(3) Where any party against whom an interim order, whether by way of injunction or stay or in any other manner, is made on, or in any proceedings relating to, a petition under clause (1), without

(a) furnishing to such party copies of such petition and all documents in support of the plea for such interim order; and

(b) giving such party an opportunity of being heard, makes an application to the High Court for the vacation of such order and furnishes a copy of such application to the party in whose favour such order has been made or the counsel of such party, the High Court shall dispose of the application within a period of two weeks from the date on which it is received or from the date on which the copy of such application is so furnished, whichever is later, or where the High Court is closed on the last day of that period, before the expiry of the next day afterwards on which the High Court is open; and if the application is not so disposed of, the interim order shall, on the expiry of that period, or, as the case may be, the expiry of the aid next day, stand vacated

(4) The power conferred on a High Court by this article shall not be in derogation of the power conferred on the Supreme court by clause (2) of Article 32

5   **Meaning of Petition:** A formal message requesting something that is submitted to an authority

31

Authority shall not deny appointment to candidate based on scheme which is arbitrary and illegal[1]

Ratio Decidendi[2]: *"Authority shall not deny appointment to candidate based on scheme/ policy/ eligibility criteria which is arbitrary and illegal."*

Facts in Nutshell:

The petitioner[3], a topper of her batch. She pursued her studies in law at the Army Institute of Law, situated at Mohali (i.e., respondent[4] no. 2). Respondent no. 2, is affiliated to the Punjabi University, at Patiala, and is recognized by the Bar Council of India. The petitioner, approached Delhi High Court for redressal of her grievance, which stems from the stand taken by respondent No. 1 (i.e. The Registrar General, Supreme Court of India) to not, consider her application, for appointment as a Law CLerk-cum-Research Assistant (in short LCRA) for the year 2013-14, inter alia[5], on the following grounds. First, that respondent No. 2 (i.e Army Institute of Law, situated at Mohali) is not empanelled with it. Second, that the petitioner's application has not been forwarded by respondent No. 2 (i.e. Army Institute of Law, situated at Mohali).

---

1   Appellants: **Phaguni Nilesh Lal** Vs. Respondent: **The Registrar General, Supreme Court of India & Anr.**

   2014(141)DRJ229

   Hon'ble Judges/Coram: Rajiv Shakdher, Juudge

2   **Meaning of Ration Decidendi:** *Ratio decidendi* is a Latin phrase meaning "the reason" or "the rationale for the decision." The *ratio decidendi* is "the point in a case which determines the judgment" or "the principle which the case establishes"

3   **Meaning of Petitioner:** A person who presents a Petition. (**Meaning of Petition:** A formal message requesting something that is submitted to an authority)

4   **Meaning of Respondent:** A **respondent** is a person who is called upon to issue a response to a communication made by another. In legal usage, this specifically refers to the defendant in a legal proceeding commenced by a petition, or to an appellee, or the opposing party, in an appeal of a decision by an initial fact-finder

5   **Meaning of Inter alia:** Among other things

The Supreme Court, on its administrative side issued a communication dated 03.12.2012, addressed to the Registrar, National Law University, Dwarka, New Delhi (in short NLU, Delhi), whereby it invited applications from LL.B. (Final Year)/Semester/Trimester students, who were likely to graduate in May-June, 2013, to consider them for selection as LCRAs in respect of, assignments commencing from 01.07.2013 and ending in the summer of 2014. A request was made that the recommendations should be supported by signed applications, in the format specified, accompanied by passport size attested photographs along with attested photocopies of mark-sheets/grade-cards and other testimonials of eligible candidates. The recommendations, with indicated enclosures, were required to reach respondent No. 1(i.e. The Registrar General, Supreme Court of India), latest by 31.01.2013. The opening paragraph of the aforementioned communication dated 03.12.2012, clearly indicated that, the applications for consideration for short-term assignment as LCRA were being called from National Law Schools/Universities on the "approved panel", and in the "stand-by-category". Since, NLU, Delhi was evidently empanelled; applications were invited from its students.

The petitioner, who had joined the law course with respondent no. 2 (i.e Army Institute of Law, situated at Mohali) in 2008, and was likely to graduate in 2013, approached respondent no. 1, (i.e. The Registrar General, Supreme Court of India) to know the procedure for making an application for being considered for appointment as a LCRA, in the Supreme Court. The petitioner was told that, students of only those National Law Schools could apply, which were placed on the approved panel of the Supreme Court. The petitioner was aggrieved, which made her approach the then Hon'ble the Chief Justice of India (CJI) vide communication dated 11.01.2013. The petitioner, claimed that she did not receive a response to her communication.

Consequently, the petitioner filed an application under the Right to Information Act, 2005 (in short the RTI Act) with the Additional Registrar/ Central Public Information Officer (CPIO) of the Supreme Court on 14.01.2013. No information was supplied with regard to the queries raised by the petitioner, vide her application dated 14.01.2013. The petitioner approached High court of Delhi by instituting a writ[6] under

---

6   **Meaning of Writ:** A written order issued by a court, commanding the party to whom it is addressed to perform or cease performing a specified act

Article 226[7] of the Constitution.

Decision by High Court:

Court held that, the fact that the engagement as a Law CLerk-cum-Research Assistant (LCRA) is for assistance of Judges, does not make it a personal engagement. The terms of engagement of LCRAs require admittedly payment of a stipend/honorarium[8], which is paid out of public money, in the form of funds provided by the Government of India through the consolidated fund of India. The right to be considered for engagement as a LCRA by a State authority has thus a public law character.

Court further held that the scheme/policy/eligibility criteria which favours candidates of only empanelled law colleges to apply for LCRA was both discriminatory and arbitrary, and thus, violative of the equality clause engrafted in Article 14[9] of the Constitution. Sourcing of candidates only

---

7   **Article 226 in The Constitution Of India 1949**

     Power of High Courts to issue certain writs

     (1) Notwithstanding anything in Article 32 every High Court shall have powers, throughout the territories in relation to which it exercise jurisdiction, to issue to any person or authority, including in appropriate cases, any Government, within those territories directions, orders or writs, including writs in the nature of habeas corpus, mandamus, prohibitions, quo warranto and certiorari, or any of them, for the enforcement of any of the rights conferred by Part III and for any other purpose

     (2) The power conferred by clause (1) to issue directions, orders or writs to any Government, authority or person may also be exercised by any High Court exercising jurisdiction in relation to the territories within which the cause of action, wholly or in part, arises for the exercise of such power, notwithstanding that the seat of such Government or authority or the residence of such person is not within those territories

     (3) Where any party against whom an interim order, whether by way of injunction or stay or in any other manner, is made on, or in any proceedings relating to, a petition under clause (1), without

     (a) furnishing to such party copies of such petition and all documents in support of the plea for such interim order; and

     (b) giving such party an opportunity of being heard, makes an application to the High Court for the vacation of such order and furnishes a copy of such application to the party in whose favour such order has been made or the counsel of such party, the High Court shall dispose of the application within a period of two weeks from the date on which it is received or from the date on which the copy of such application is so furnished, whichever is later, or where the High Court is closed on the last day of that period, before the expiry of the next day afterwards on which the High Court is open; and if the application is not so disposed of, the interim order shall, on the expiry of that period, or, as the case may be, the expiry of the aid next day, stand vacated

     (4) The power conferred on a High Court by this article shall not be in derogation of the power conferred on the Supreme court by clause (2) of Article 32

8   **Meaning of Honorarium:** A payment given to a professional person for services for which fees are not legally or traditionally required

9   **Article 14 in The Constitution Of India 1949**

from empanelled Law Colleges and Universities was illegal. Court directed the respondent no. 1 (i.e. The Registrar General, Supreme Court of India) to consider the petitioner's application for engagement as a LCRA, notwithstanding the fact that respondent no. 2 (i.e Army Institute of Law, situated at Mohali) was not on the panel maintained by respondent no. 1, and that, the petitioner's application was not sponsored by respondent no. 2.

Equality before law: The State shall not deny to any person equality before the law or the equal protection of the laws within the territory of India Prohibition of discrimination on grounds of religion, race, caste, sex or place of birth

Miscellaneous

Meaning of Surrogacy:

The question of becoming parents through surrogacy came to be considered by the Supreme Court in a judgment in *Baby Manji Yamada v. Union of India*[1]. In that case various forms of surrogacy were discussed from paragraph 8 to 16 and it was stated as follows:

8. Surrogacy is a well-known method of reproduction whereby a woman agrees to become pregnant for the purpose of gestating[2] and giving birth to a child she will not raise but hand over to a contracted party. She may be the child's genetic mother (the more traditional form for surrogacy) or she may be, as a gestational carrier, carry the pregnancy to delivery after having been implanted with an embryo. In some cases surrogacy is the only available option for parents who wish to have a child that is biologically related to them.

9. The word surrogate, from Latin subrogate, means appointed to act in the place of. The intended parent(s) is the individual or couple who intends to rear the child after its birth.

10. In traditional surrogacy (also known as the Straight method) the surrogate is pregnant with her own biological child, but this child was conceived[3] with the intention of relinquishing[4] the child to be raised by others; by the biological father and possibly his spouse or partner, either male or female. The child may be conceived via home artificial insemination using fresh or frozen sperm or impregnated via IUI (intrauterine insemination), or ICI (intracervical insemination) which is

---

1   (2008) 13 SCC 518

2   **Meaning of Gestate:**

    1. To carry within the uterus from conception to delivery.

    2. To conceive and develop in the mind

3   **Meaning of Conceived:** To become pregnant with (offspring)

4   **Meaning of relinquishing:**

    1. To retire from; give up or abandon.

    2. To put aside or desist from (something practiced, professed, or intended).

performed at a fertility clinic.

11. In gestational surrogacy (also known as the Host method) the surrogate becomes pregnant via embryo transfer with a child of which she is not the biological mother. She may have made an arrangement to relinquish it to the biological mother or father to raise, or to a parent who is themselves unrelated to the child (e.g. because the child was conceived using egg donation, germ donation or is the result of a donated embryo). The surrogate mother may be called the gestational carrier.

12. Altruistic surrogacy is a situation where the surrogate receives no financial reward for her pregnancy or the relinquishment of the child (although usually all expenses related to the pregnancy and birth are paid by the intended parents such as medical expenses, maternity clothing, and other related expenses).

13. Commercial surrogacy is a form of surrogacy in which a gestational carrier is paid to carry a child to maturity in her womb and is usually resorted to by well-off infertile couples who can afford the cost involved or people who save and borrow in order to complete their dream of being parents. This medical procedure is legal in several countries including in India where due to excellent medical infrastructure, high international demand and ready availability of poor surrogates it is reaching industry proportions. Commercial surrogacy is sometimes referred to by the emotionally charged and potentially offensive terms wombs for rent, outsourced pregnancies or baby farms.

14. Intended parents may arrange a surrogate pregnancy because a woman who intends to parent is infertile in such a way that she cannot carry a pregnancy to term. Examples include a woman who has had a hysterectomy, has a uterine malformation, has had recurrent pregnancy loss or has a health condition that makes it dangerous for her to be pregnant. A female intending parent may also be fertile and healthy, but unwilling to undergo pregnancy.

15. Alternatively, the intended parent may be a single male or a male homosexual couple.

16. Surrogates may be relatives, friends, or previous strangers. Many surrogate arrangements are made through agencies that help match up intended parents with women who want to be surrogates for a fee. The agencies often help manage the complex medical and legal aspects *involved. Surrogacy arrangements can also be made independently. In compensated surrogacies the amount a surrogate receives varies widely from almost nothing above expenses to over $30,000. Careful screening is needed to assure their health as the gestational carrier incurs potential obstetrical risks.*

Contempt of Court:

The Common Law definition of contempt of Court is: 'An act or omission[5] calculated to interfere with the due administration of justice.'[6] The contempt of court as defined by the Contempt of Courts Act, 1971 includes civil and criminal contempt. Criminal contempt as defined by the Act: 'Means the publication whether by words, spoken or written, or by signs, or by visible representations, or otherwise of any matter or the doing of any other act whatsoever which scandalizes[7] or tends to scandalize, or lowers or tends to lower the authority of, any court; or prejudices, or interferes or tends or to interfere with, the due course of any judicial proceeding; or interferes, or tends to interfere with, or obstructs or tends to obstruct, the administration of justice in any other manner.' The definition of criminal contempt is wide enough to include any act by a person which would tend to interfere with the administration of justice or which would lower the authority of court. The public have a vital stake in effective and orderly administration of justice. The Court has the duty of protecting, the interest-of the community in the due administration of justice and, so, it is entrusted with the power to commit for contempt of court, not to protect the dignity of the Court against insult or injury, but, to protect and vindicate the right of the public so that the administration of justice is not perverted, prejudiced, obstructed or interfered with. "It is a mode of vindicating the majesty of law, in its active manifestation against obstruction and outrage."[8] The object and purpose of punishing contempt for interference with the administration of justice is not to safeguard or protect the dignity of the Judge or the Magistrate, but the purpose is to preserve the authority of the courts to ensure an ordered

---

5   **Meaning of Omission:**

     1. The act or an instance of omitting.

     2. The state of having been omitted.

     3. Something omitted or neglected

6   Bowen L.J. in *Helmore v. Smith*[1886]35 Ch. D. 436

7   **Meaning of scandalize:** To offend the moral sensibilities of

8   Frank Furter, J. in Offuttv. U.S. [1954] 348 US 11

life in society. In *Attorney-General v. Times Newspapers*[9] the necessity for the law of contempt was summarised by Lord Morris as:

In an ordered community courts are established for the pacific settlement of disputes and for the maintenance of law and order. In the general interests of the community it is imperative that the authority of the courts should not be imperilled and that recourse to them should not be subject to unjustifiable interference. When such unjustifiable interference is suppressed it is not because those charged with the responsibilities of administering justice are concerned for their own dignity: it is because the very structure of ordered life is at risk if the recognised courts of the land are so flouted and their authority wanes and is supplanted.

"The summary power of punishment for contempt has been conferred on the courts to keep a blaze of glory around them, to deter people from attempting to render them contemptible in the eyes of the public. These powers are necessary to keep the course of justice free, as it is of great importance to society."[10] The power to punish contempt is vested in the Judges not for their personal protection only, but for the protection of public justice, whose interest, requires that decency and decorum is preserved in Courts of Justice. Those who have to discharge duty in a Court of Justice are protected by the law, and shielded in the discharge of their duties, any deliberate interference with the discharge of such duties either in court or outside the court by attacking the presiding officers of the court, would amount to criminal contempt and the courts must take serious cognizance of such conduct.

Gender Identity and Sexual Orientation:

Gender identity is one of the most-fundamental aspects of life which refers to a person's intrinsic[11] sense of being male, female or transgender or transsexual[12] person. A person's sex is usually assigned at birth, but a relatively small group of persons may born with bodies which incorporate both or certain aspects of both male and female physiology[13]. At times,

---

9   [1974] A.C. 273

10 Oswald on Contempt of Court

11 **Meaning of Intrinsic:** Of or relating to the essential nature of a thing; inherent.

12 **Meaning of Transsexual:**

   1. One who wishes to be considered by society as a member of the opposite sex.

   2. One who has undergone a sex change

13 **Meaning of Physiology:**

genital[14] anatomy problems may arise in certain persons, their innate perception of themselves, is not in conformity with the sex assigned to them at birth and may include pre and post-operative transsexual persons and also persons who do not choose to undergo or do not have access to operation and also include persons who cannot undergo successful operation. Countries, all over the world, including India, are grappled[15] with the question of attribution of gender to persons who believe that they belong to the opposite sex. Few persons undertake surgical and other procedures to alter their bodies and physical appearance to acquire gender characteristics of the sex which conform to their perception of gender, leading to legal and social complications since official record of their gender at birth is found to be at variance with the assumed gender identity. Gender identity refers to each person's deeply felt internal and individual experience of gender, which may or may not correspond with the sex assigned at birth, including the personal sense of the body which may involve a freely chosen, modification of bodily appearance or functions by medical, surgical or other means and other expressions of gender, including dress, speech and mannerisms. Gender identity, therefore, refers to an individual's self-identification as a man, woman, transgender or other identified category.

Sexual orientation refers to an individual's enduring physical, romantic and/or emotional attraction to another person. Sexual orientation includes transgender and gender-variant people with heavy sexual orientation and their sexual orientation may or may not change during or after gender transmission, which also includes homosexuals[16], bisexuals[17],

---

1. The biological study of the functions of living organisms and their parts.

2. All the functions of a living organism or any of its parts

14 **Meaning of Genital:**

1. Of or relating to biological reproduction.

2. Of or relating to the genitals

15 **Meaning of Grappled:**

a. A struggle or contest in which the participants attempt to clutch or grip each other.

b. A struggle for superiority or dominance

16 **Homosexuality** is romantic attraction, sexual attraction or sexual behavior between members of the same sex or gender

17 **Bisexuality** is romantic attraction, sexual attraction or sexual behavior toward both males and females. The term is mainly used in the context of human attraction to denote romantic or sexual feelings toward both men and women.

heterosexuals[18], asexual[19] etc. Gender identity and sexual orientation, as already indicated, are different concepts. Each person's self-defined sexual orientation and gender identity is integral to their personality and is one of the most basic aspects of self-determination, dignity and freedom and no one shall be forced to undergo medical procedures, including SRS, sterilization or hormonal therapy, as a requirement for legal recognition of their gender identity.

United Nations and other Human Rights Bodies on Gender Identity and Sexual Orientation:

United Nations has been instrumental in advocating the protection and promotion of rights of sexual minorities, including transgender persons. Article 6[20] of the Universal Declaration of Human Rights, 1948 and Article 16[21] of the International Covenant on Civil and Political Rights, 1966 (ICCPR) recognize that every human being has the inherent right to live and this right shall be protected by law and that no one shall be arbitrarily[22] denied of that right. Everyone shall have a right to recognition, everywhere as a person before the law. Article 17[23] of the ICCPR states that no one shall be subjected to arbitrary or unlawful interference with his privacy, family, home or correspondence, nor to unlawful attacks on his honour and reputation and that everyone has the right to protection of law against such interference or attacks. International Commission

---

18 **Heterosexuality** is romantic attraction, sexual attraction or sexual behavior between persons of opposite sex or gender in the gender binary. As a sexual orientation, heterosexuality refers to "an enduring pattern of or disposition to experience sexual, affectionate, physical or romantic attractions to persons of the opposite sex"; it also refers to "a person's sense of identity based on those attractions, related behaviors, and membership in a community of others who share those attractions"

19 **Meaning of Asexual:**

   1. Having no evident sex or sex organs; sexless.

   2. Relating to, produced by, or involving reproduction that occurs without the union of male and female gametes, as in binary fission or budding

20 **Article 6 of the Universal Declaration of Human Rights, 1948:**

   Everyone has the right to recognition everywhere as a person before the law

21 **Article 16 of the International Covenant on Civil and Political Rights, 1966 (ICCPR):**

   Everyone shall have the right to recognition everywhere as a person before the law

22 **Meaning of Arbitrary:** In a random manner

23 **Article 17 of the ICCPR:**

   1. No one shall be subjected to arbitrary or unlawful interference with his privacy, family, home or correspondence, nor to unlawful attacks on his honour and reputation.

   2. Everyone has the right to the protection of the law against such interference or attacks

of Jurists and the International Service for Human Rights on behalf of a coalition of human rights organizations, took a project to develop a set of international legal principles on the application of international law to human rights violations based on sexual orientation and sexual identity to bring greater clarity and coherence to State's human rights obligations. A distinguished group of human rights experts has drafted, developed, discussed and reformed the principles in a meeting held at Gadjah Mada University in Yogyakarta, Indonesia from 6 to 9 November, 2006, which is unanimously adopted the Yogyakarta Principles on the application of International Human Rights Law in relation to Sexual Orientation and Gender Identity. Yogyakarta Principles address a broad range of human rights standards and their application to issues of sexual orientation gender identity.

Marriage and Marital Relationship:

Marriage is often described as one of the basic civil rights of man/woman, which is voluntarily undertaken by the parties in public in a formal way, and once concluded, recognizes the parties as husband and wife. Three elements of common law marriage are (1) agreement to be married (2) living together as husband and wife, (3) holding out to the public that they are married. Sharing a common household and duty to live together form part of the 'Consortium Omnis Vitae" which obliges spouses[24] to live together, afford each other reasonable marital privileges and rights and be honest and faithful to each other. One of the most important invariable consequences of marriage is the reciprocal support and the responsibility of maintenance of the common household, jointly and severally. Marriage as an institution has great legal significance and various obligations and duties flow out of marital relationship, as per law, in the matter of inheritance of property, successionship, etc. Marriage, therefore, involves legal requirements of formality, publicity, exclusivity and all the legal consequences flow out of that relationship.

Marriages in India take place either following the personal Law of the Religion to which a party is belonged or following the provisions of the Special Marriage Act. Marriage, as per the Common Law, constitutes a contract between a man and a woman, in which the parties undertake to live together and support each other. Marriage, as a concept, is also nationally and internationally recognized. O'Regan, Judge, in *Dawood and*

---

24 **Meaning of Spouses:** A marriage partner; a husband or wife.

Anr. v. Minister of Home Affairs and Ors.[25] noted as follows:

Marriage and the family are social institutions of vital importance. Entering into and sustaining a marriage is a matter of intense private significance to the parties to that marriage for they make a promise to one another to establish and maintain an intimate relationship for the rest of their lives which they acknowledge obliges them to support one another, to live together and to be faithful to one another. Such relationships are of profound significance to the individuals concerned. But such relationships have more than personal significance at least in part because human beings are social beings whose humanity is expressed through their relationships with others. Entering into marriage therefore is to enter into a relationship that has public significance as well.

The institutions of marriage and the family are important social institutions that provide for the security, support and companionship of members of our society and bear an important role in the rearing of children. The celebration of a marriage gives rise to moral and legal obligations, particularly the reciprocal duty of support placed upon spouses and their joint responsibility for supporting and raising children born of the marriage. These legal obligations perform an important social function. This importance is symbolically acknowledged in part by the fact that marriage is celebrated generally in a public ceremony, often before family and close friends.

---

25   2000 (3) SA 936 (CC)

32

Woman employee[1] entitled to avail maternity leave even in case where she gets the child through arrangement by Surrogate parents[2]

Facts in Nutshell:

The petitioner[3] was working as an Assistant Superintendent in the Traffic department of the Chennai Port Trust. She had put in 24 years of service. She was married. Her son (Shyam Sundar) aged 20 years died due to road accident on 31.01.2009. After his birth, the petitioner has removed her uterus[4] due to some problem on 30.04.2008. Therefore, she in order to have a child had entered into an arrangement with Prashanth Multi Speciality hospital, Chennai to have a baby through surrogate procedure. Finally with the consent of her husband and his cooperation, a female baby was born on 08.02.2011 through a host mother. She had incurred substantial expenditure towards treatment. In order to look after the newly born baby, she had applied for maternity leave. But she was informed that she was not entitled for maternity leave (post delivery) for having a child through surrogate procedure though such a rejection was not possible in case of a person adopting a child. The petitioner, therefore, requested for sanction of maternity leave to look after the newly born girl child and reimburse the medical expenses and also to issue the FMI Card incorporating the newly born child through her representation, dated 17.6.2011. She sent a reminder on 13.8.2011. However, by proceedings,

---

1   **Meaning of Employee:** A person who works for another in return for financial or other compensation

2   Appellants: **K. Kalaiselvi Vs.** Respondent: **Chennai Port Trust**

 2013(2)CTC400, [2013(138)FLR55], 2013(2)KLT567

 Hon'ble Judges/Coram: K. Chandru, Judge

3   **Meaning of Petitioner:** A person who presents a Petition. (**Meaning of Petition:** A formal message requesting something that is submitted to an authority)

4   A hollow muscular organ located in the pelvic cavity of female mammals in which the fertilized egg implants and develops. Also called *womb*.

dated 22.11.2011, she was informed that the Chairman of the Port Trust had granted her two months period leave as a special case, which will be treated as an eligible leave. But the leave granted on 17.9.2011 for a period of 59 days from 08.02.2011 to 07.04.2011 vide medical certificate dated 17.09.2011 was subsequently cancelled. Her request for inclusion of the female child in the FMI card was also rejected. She was informed by a letter dated 05.12.2011 that inclusion of her daughter name G.K. Sharanya in the FMI Card does not arise. The petitioner produced before the respondent[5] Port Trust all documents relating to surrogate arrangement, hospital expenditures incurred by her as well as the birth certificate given by the Corporation of Chennai evidencing that the female child was born on 08.02.2011. It was under these circumstances, writ petition[6] was filed in High Court seeking to set aside the order dated 05.12.2011 and for a consequential direction to the Chennai Port Trust to grant leave to the petitioner on equal footing in terms of Rule 3-A[7] of the Madras Port Trust (Leave) Regulations, 1987, which benefit was granted to adoptive parents.

---

5   **Meaning of Respondent:** A **respondent** is a person who is called upon to issue a response to a communication made by another. In legal usage, this specifically refers to the defendant in a legal proceeding commenced by a petition, or to an appellee, or the opposing party, in an appeal of a decision by an initial fact-finder

6   **Meaning of Writ Petition:** Under the Indian legal system, jurisdiction to issue ⊠prerogative writs⊠ is given to the Supreme Court, and to the High Courts of Judicature of all Indian states. Parts of the law relating to writs are set forth in the Constitution of India. The Supreme Court, the highest in the country, may issue writs under Article 32 of the Constitution for enforcement of Fundamental Rights and under Articles 139 for enforcement of rights other than Fundamental Rights, while High Courts, the superior courts of the States, may issue writs under Articles 226. ⊠Writ⊠ is eminently designed by the makers of the Constitution, and in the same way it is developed very widely and efficiently by the courts in India. The Constitution broadly provides for five kinds of "prerogative" writs, namely, Habeas Corpus, Certiorari, Mandamus, Quo Warranto and Prohibition

7   **Rule 3A, which reads as follows:**

   3-A. Leave to female employees on adoption of a child:

   A female employee on her adoption a child may be granted leave of the kind and admissible (including commuted leave without production of medical certificate for a period not exceeding 60 days and leave not due) upto one year subject to the following conditions:

   (i) the facility will not be available to an adoptive mother already having two living children at the time of adoption;

   (ii) the maximum admissible period of leave of the kind due and admissible will be regulated as under:

   (a) If the age of the adopted child is less than one month, leave upto one year may be allowed.

   (b) If the age of the child is six months or more, leave upto six months may be allowed.

   (c) If the age of the child is nine months or more leave upto three months may be allowed

Question before the High Court:

Whether a woman employee working in the Chennai Port Trust was entitled to avail maternity leave even in case where she gets the child through arrangement by Surrogate parents?

Meaning of Surrogacy:

The question of becoming parents through surrogacy came to be considered by the Supreme Court in a judgment in *Baby Manji Yamada v. Union of India*[8]. In that case various forms of surrogacy were discussed from paragraph 8 to 16 and it was stated as follows:

8. Surrogacy is a well-known method of reproduction whereby a woman agrees to become pregnant for the purpose of gestating[9] and giving birth to a child she will not raise but hand over to a contracted party. She may be the child's genetic mother (the more traditional form for surrogacy) or she may be, as a gestational carrier, carry the pregnancy to delivery after having been implanted with an embryo. In some cases surrogacy is the only available option for parents who wish to have a child that is biologically related to them.

9. The word surrogate, from Latin subrogate, means appointed to act in the place of. The intended parent(s) is the individual or couple who intends to rear the child after its birth.

10. In traditional surrogacy (also known as the Straight method) the surrogate is pregnant with her own biological child, but this child was conceived[10] with the intention of relinquishing[11] the child to be raised by others; by the biological father and possibly his spouse or partner, either male or female. The child may be conceived via home artificial insemination using fresh or frozen sperm or impregnated via IUI (intrauterine insemination), or ICI (intracervical insemination) which is performed at a fertility clinic.

---

8   (2008) 13 SCC 518

9   **Meaning of Gestate:**

   1. To carry within the uterus from conception to delivery.

   2. To conceive and develop in the mind

10   **Meaning of Conceived:** To become pregnant with (offspring)

11   **Meaning of relinquishing:**

   1. To retire from; give up or abandon.

   2. To put aside or desist from (something practiced, professed, or intended).

11. *In gestational surrogacy (also known as the Host method) the surrogate becomes pregnant via embryo transfer with a child of which she is not the biological mother. She may have made an arrangement to relinquish it to the biological mother or father to raise, or to a parent who is themselves unrelated to the child (e.g. because the child was conceived using egg donation, germ donation or is the result of a donated embryo). The surrogate mother may be called the gestational carrier.*

12. *Altruistic surrogacy is a situation where the surrogate receives no financial reward for her pregnancy or the relinquishment of the child (although usually all expenses related to the pregnancy and birth are paid by the intended parents such as medical expenses, maternity clothing, and other related expenses).*

13. *Commercial surrogacy is a form of surrogacy in which a gestational carrier is paid to carry a child to maturity in her womb and is usually resorted to by well-off infertile couples who can afford the cost involved or people who save and borrow in order to complete their dream of being parents. This medical procedure is legal in several countries including in India where due to excellent medical infrastructure, high international demand and ready availability of poor surrogates it is reaching industry proportions. Commercial surrogacy is sometimes referred to by the emotionally charged and potentially offensive terms wombs for rent, outsourced pregnancies or baby farms.*

14. *Intended parents may arrange a surrogate pregnancy because a woman who intends to parent is infertile in such a way that she cannot carry a pregnancy to term. Examples include a woman who has had a hysterectomy, has a uterine malformation, has had recurrent pregnancy loss or has a health condition that makes it dangerous for her to be pregnant. A female intending parent may also be fertile and healthy, but unwilling to undergo pregnancy.*

15. *Alternatively, the intended parent may be a single male or a male homosexual couple.*

16. *Surrogates may be relatives, friends, or previous strangers. Many surrogate arrangements are made through agencies that help match up intended parents with women who want to be surrogates for a fee. The agencies often help manage the complex medical and legal aspects involved. Surrogacy arrangements can also be made independently. In*

compensated surrogacies the amount a surrogate receives varies widely from almost nothing above expenses to over $30,000. Careful screening is needed to assure their health as the gestational carrier incurs potential obstetrical risks.

Beijing Declaration and Platform for Action Fourth World Conference on Women (Dated 15.09.1995) wherein the right of all women to control all aspects of their health, in particular their own fertility is basic to their empowerment was reaffirmed. **Articles 17 and 33 reads as follows:**

17. The explicit recognition and reaffirmation of the right of all women to control all aspects of their health, in particular their own fertility, is basic "to their empowerment.

33. Ensure respect for "international law, including humanitarian law, in order to protect women and girls in particular.

All India Services (Leave) Rules, 1955: Wherein the Central Government had recognised even paternity leave[12] to be granted. Rule 18(D) was introduced with effect from 21.09.2011. The child care leave is given to a female member of the service.

Rule 18(D) reads as follows:

18(D) Child Care Leave to a female member of the Service--(1) A female member of the Service having minor children below the age of eighteen years may be granted child care leave by the competent authority for a maximum of 730 days during her entire service for taking care of upto two children.

(2) During the period of child care leave, such member shall be paid leave salary equal to the pay drawn immediately before proceeding on leave.

(3) Child care leave may be combined with leave of the kind due and admissible.

(4) Child care leave may be availed in more than one spell.

(5) Child care leave shall not be debited[13] against the leave account of the

---

12 **Parental leave** is an employee benefit that provides paid or unpaid time off work to care for a child or make arrangements for the child's welfare. The term "parental leave" includes maternity, paternity, and adoption leave. Often, the minimum benefits are stipulated by law

13 **Meaning of Debit:**

member of the Service.

Decision by High Court:

Court directed the respondent Chennai Port Trust to grant leave to the petitioner in terms of Rule 3-A of the Madras Port Trust (Leave) Regulations, 1987 recognizing the child obtained through surrogate procedure. Court further directed the respondent to include the name of the child G.K. Sharanya, as a member of the petitioner's family and also include her name in the FMI card by relying on the judgment referred by petitioner counsel of the Supreme Court of California (Anna Johnson Vs. Mark Calvert et al., reported in 5 Cal 4th 84), wherein the court affirmed the judgment of the lower court that genetic parents were the natural parents of child gestated through surrogate.

---

a. An item of debt as recorded in an account.

b. The left-hand side of an account or accounting ledger where bookkeeping entries are made.

c. An entry of a sum in the left-hand side of an account

33

Distribution of free gifts by the political parties[1]

Facts in Nutshell:

The case relates to distribution of free gifts by the political parties (popularly known as 'freebies'[2]). The Dravida Munnetra Kazhagam (DMK) - Respondent[3] No. 8 while releasing the election manifesto[4] for the Assembly Elections 2006, announced a Scheme of free distribution of Colour Television Sets (CTVs) to each and every household. The Party justified the decision of distribution of free CTVs for the purpose of providing recreation and general knowledge to the household women, more particularly, those living in the rural areas. In pursuance of the same, follow up actions by way of enlisting the households which did not have a TV set and door to door identification and distribution of application forms were initiated.

This Scheme was challenged by one S. Subramaniam Balaji-the Appellant[5] by way of filing writ petition[6] before the High Court on the

---

1   Appellants: **S. Subramaniam Balaji Vs.** Respondent: **The Government of Tamil Nadu and Ors.**

    (2013)9SCC659

    Hon'ble Judges/Coram: P. Sathasivam and Ranjan Gogoi, JJ.

2   **Meaning of Freebies:** An article or service given free

3   **Meaning of Respondent:** A **respondent** is a person who is called upon to issue a response to a communication made by another. In legal usage, this specifically refers to the defendant in a legal proceeding commenced by a petition, or to an appellee, or the opposing party, in an appeal of a decision by an initial fact-finder

4   A **manifesto** is a published verbal declaration of the intentions, motives, or views of the issuer, be it an individual, group, political party or government. A manifesto usually accepts a previously published opinion or public consensus and/or promotes a new idea with prescriptive notions for carrying out changes the author believes should be made. It often is political or artistic in nature, but may present an individual's life stance. Manifestos relating to religious belief are generally referred to as creeds.

5   **Meaning of Appellant:** A person who dissatisfied with the judgment rendered in a lawsuit decided in a lower court or the findings from a proceeding before an Administrative Agency, asks a superior court to review the decision

6   **Meaning of Writ Petition:** Under the Indian legal system, jurisdiction to issue 'prerogative writs'

ground that the expenditure to be incurred by the State Government for its implementation out of the State Exchequer was unauthorized, impermissible and *ultra vires*[7] of the Constitutional mandates. The Appellant filed a complaint dated 24.04.2006 to the Election Commission of India seeking initiation of action in respect of the said promise under Section 123[8] of the Representation of People Act, 1951 (in short 'the RP

---

is given to the Supreme Court, and to the High Courts of Judicature of all Indian states. Parts of the law relating to writs are set forth in the Constitution of India. The Supreme Court, the highest in the country, may issue writs under Article 32 of the Constitution for enforcement of Fundamental Rights and under Articles 139 for enforcement of rights other than Fundamental Rights, while High Courts, the superior courts of the States, may issue writs under Articles 226. 'Writ' is eminently designed by the makers of the Constitution, and in the same way it is developed very widely and efficiently by the courts in India. The Constitution broadly provides for five kinds of "prerogative" writs, namely, Habeas Corpus, Certiorari, Mandamus, Quo Warranto and Prohibition

7   **Meaning of Ultra Vires:** Beyond the legal power or authority of a person, corporation, agent, etc

8   **Section 123 of the Representation of People Act, 1951**

Corrupt practices

The following shall be deemed to be corrupt practices for the purposes of this Act

[(1) "Bribery", that is to say—

(A) any gift, offer or promise by a candidate or his agent or by any other person with the consent of a candidate or his election agent of any gratification, to any person whomsoever, with the object, directly or indirectly of inducing—

(a) a person to stand or not to stand as, or [to withdraw or not to withdraw] from being a candidate at an election, or

(b) an elector to vote or refrain from voting at an election, or as a reward to—

(i) a person for having so stood or not stood, or for [having withdrawn or not having withdrawn] his candidature; or

(ii) an elector for having voted or refrained from voting;

(B) the receipt of, or agreement to receive, any gratification, whether as a motive or a reward—

(a) by a person for standing or not standing as, or for [withdrawing or not withdrawing] from being, a candidate; or

(b) by any person whomsoever for himself or any other person for voting or refraining from

voting, or inducing or attempting to induce any elector to vote or refrain from voting, or any candidate [to withdraw or not to withdraw] his candidature.

(2) Undue influence, that is to say, any direct or indirect interference or attempt to interfere on the part of the

candidate or his agent, or of any other person [with the consent of the candidate or his election agent], with the free

exercise of any electoral right:

Provided that—

(a) without prejudice to the generality of the provisions of this clause any such person as is referred to therein who—

(i) threatens any candidate or any elector, or any person in whom a candidate or an elector is

Act'). The Appellant also forwarded the complaint to the Chief Election Officer, Tamil Nadu.

The DMK and its political allies emerged victorious in the State Assembly Election held in the month of May, 2006. In pursuit of fulfilling the promise made in the election manifesto, a policy decision was taken by the then government to provide one 14 inch TV to all eligible families in the State. It was further decided by the Government to implement the Scheme in a phased manner and a provision of Rs. 750 crores was made in the budget for implementing the same. A Committee was constituted, headed by the then Chief Minister and eight other legislative members of various political parties, in order to ensure transparency in the matter of implementation of the Scheme. For implementing the first phase of the Scheme, the work of procurement of around 30,000 TVs was entrusted to Electronic Corporation of Tamil Nadu Ltd. (ELCOT), a State owned Corporation. The first phase of the Scheme was implemented on 15/17th September, 2006 by distributing around 30,000 TVs to the identified families in all the districts of the State of Tamil Nadu. Being aggrieved by the implementation of the Scheme, the Appellant filed another complaint to the Chief Secretary and the Revenue Secretary pointing out the unconstitutionality of the Scheme. He also preferred Writ Petition before the Madurai Bench of the High Court of Madras alleging the Scheme a corrupt practice to woo[9] the gullible[10] electorates with an eye on the vote bank. The grievance of the Appellant was that the public resources were being used for the benefit of individuals.

Decision by High Court:

By order dated 25.06.2007, the High Court dismissed the writ petitions

---

interested, with injury of any kind including social ostracism and ex-communication or expulsion from any caste or community; or

(ii) induces or attempts to induce a candidate or an elector to believe that he, or any person in whom he is interested, will become or will be rendered an object of divine displeasure or spiritual censure, shall be deemed to interfere with the free exercise of the electoral right of such candidate or elector within the meaning of this clause;

(b) a declaration of public policy, or a promise of public action, or the mere exercise of a legal right without intent to interfere with an electoral right, shall not be deemed to be interference within the meaning of this clause.

9   **Meaning of Woo:**

  a. To seek to achieve; try to gain.

  b. To tempt or invite

10 **Meaning of Gullible:** Easily deceived or duped.

filed by the Appellant holding that the action of the Government in distributing free TVs cannot be branded as a waste of exchequer[11]. Being aggrieved, the Appellant preferred appeal[12] by way of special leave[13] before Supreme Court.

Question before the Supreme Court:

(i) Whether the promises made by the political parties in the election manifesto would amount to 'corrupt practices' as per Section 123 of the RP Act?

(ii) Whether the schemes under challenge are within the ambit of public purpose and if yes, is it violative of Article 14 of the Constitution?

Contentions by Learned Counsel for Appellant:

Learned Counsel for the Appellant pointed out that the right to equality under Article 14[14] of the Constitution requires that the State must make a reasonable classification based on intelligible[15] differentia, and such classification must have a nexus with the object of the law. In making free distributions, the State, therefore, must show that it has identified the class of persons to whom such distributions are sought to be made using intelligible differentia, and that such differentia has a rational

---

11 **Meaning of Exchequer:** A treasury, as of a state or nation.

12 **Meaning of Appeal:** In law, an **appeal** is a process for requesting a formal change to an official decision. Very broadly speaking there are appeals on the record and *de novo* appeals. In *de novo* appeals, a new decision maker re-hears the case without any reference to the prior decision maker. In appeals on the record, the decision of the prior decision maker is challenged by arguing that he or she misapplied the law, came to an incorrect factual finding, acted in excess of his jurisdiction, abused his powers, was biased, considered evidence which he should not have considered or failed to consider evidence that he should have considered

13 **Article 136 in The Constitution Of India 1949**

Special leave to appeal by the Supreme Court

(1) Notwithstanding anything in this Chapter, the Supreme Court may, in its discretion, grant special leave to appeal from any judgment, decree, determination, sentence or order in any cause or matter passed or made by any court or tribunal in the territory of India

(2) Nothing in clause (1) shall apply to any judgment, determination, sentence or order passed or made by any court or tribunal constituted by or under any law relating to the Armed Forces

14 **Article 14 in The Constitution Of India 1949**

Equality before law: The State shall not deny to any person equality before the law or the equal protection of the laws within the territory of India Prohibition of discrimination on grounds of religion, race, caste, sex or place of birth

15 **Meaning of intelligible:**

1. Capable of being understood

2. Capable of being apprehended by the intellect alone

nexus with the object of the distribution. As held in **Union of India and Anr.** v. **International Trading Co. and Anr.**[16], article 14 applies to matters of government policy and such policy or action would be unconstitutional if it fails to satisfy the test of reasonableness. In **K.T. Moopil Nair** v. **State of Kerala,**[17] court held that a statute[18] can offend Article 14 if it groups together persons who are dissimilar. In that case, a flat tax of Rs. 2 per acre was levied on land without ascertaining the income earning potential of such land, which was struck down as unconstitutional.

According to Learned Counsel in the present case on hand, the colour televisions, mixies and grinders were being distributed to all persons having ration card. While the distribution of these goods is supposedly being made to help people who cannot afford these items, the State has not made any attempt to find out if such persons already own a colour television, a mixie or a grinder. Further, the differentia of a ration card has no rational nexus with the object of free distribution of the items since a ration card does not indicate the income of the family or whether they already own these goods. Similarly, in another Scheme, the State has promised to distribute free laptops to all the students studying in the State Board. Again, this classification was arbitrary since there were numerous similarly placed students in Central Board schools who were being excluded by this Scheme. The Scheme also excludes commerce, law and medical college students and violates Article 14 by not providing intelligible differentia having a nexus with such distribution.

Promises of free distribution of non-essential commodities in election manifesto amounts to an electoral bribe under Section 123 of the RP Act.

Learned Counsel for the appellant pointed out that under Section 123(1)(A) of the RP Act, any "gift, offer or promise" by a candidate or his agent or by any other person, with the object of inducing a person to vote at an election amounts to "bribery", which is a "corrupt practice" under the said section. The key element in this section is that the voter must be

---

16 2003 (5) SCC 437

17 AIR 1961 SC 552

18 **Meaning of Statue:**

   1. A law enacted by a legislature.

   2. A decree or edict, as of a ruler.

   3. An established law or rule, as of a corporation

influenced to vote in a particular manner.

Whether the promises made by the political parties in their election manifestos would amount to 'corrupt practices' as per Section 123 of the Representation of the People Act, 1951?

The purpose of incorporating Section 123 of the RP Act is to ensure that elections are held in a free and fair manner. The object of provisions relating to corrupt practices was elucidated[19] by Supreme Court in ***Patangrao Kadam*** v. ***Prithviraj Sayajirao Yadav Deshmukh and Ors.***[20] as follows:

Fair and free elections are essential requisites to maintain the purity of election and to sustain the faith of the people in election itself in a democratic set up. Clean, efficient and benevolent administration are the essential features of good governance which in turn depends upon persons of competency and good character. Hence those indulging in corrupt practices at an election cannot be spared and allowed to pollute the election process and this purpose is sought to be achieved by these provisions contained in the RP Act.

The manifesto of a political party is a statement of its policy. The question of implementing the manifesto arises only if the political party forms a Government. It is the promise of a future Government. It is not a promise of an individual candidate. Section 123 and other relevant provisions, upon their true construction, contemplate corrupt practice by individual candidate or his agent. Moreover, such corrupt practice is directly linked to his own election irrespective of the question whether his party forms a Government or not. The provisions of the RP Act clearly draw a distinction between an individual candidate put up by a political party and the political party as such. The provisions of the said Act prohibit an individual candidate from resorting to promises, which constitute a corrupt practice within the meaning of Section 123 of the RP Act. The provisions of the said Act place no fetter[21] on the power of the political parties to make promises in the election manifesto. The provisions relating to corrupt practice are penal in nature and, therefore, the rule of

---

19 **Meaning of Elucidated:** To make clear or plain, especially by explanation; clarify.

20 (2001) 3 SCC 594

21 **Meaning of Fetter:**

   1. A chain or shackle for the ankles or feet.

   2. Something that serves to restrict; a restraint

strict interpretation must apply and hence, promises by a political party cannot constitute a corrupt practice on the part of the political party as the political party is not within the sweep of the provisions relating to corrupt practices. As the rule of strict interpretation applies, there is no scope for applying provisions relating to corrupt practice contained in the said Act to the manifesto of a political party.

Decision by Supreme Court:

Court held that the promises in the election manifesto cannot be read into Section 123 of RP Act, 1951 for declaring it to be a corrupt practice. Thus, promises in the election manifesto do not constitute as a corrupt practice under the prevailing law. In *Prof. Ramchandra G. Kapse* v. *Haribansh Ramakbal Singh*[22] Supreme Court held that "Ex facie[23] contents of a manifesto, by itself, cannot be a corrupt practice committed by a candidate of that party." Further, it has been decided that the schemes challenged in the present writ petition falls within the realm of fulfilling the Directive Principles of State Policy[24] thereby falling within the scope of public purpose. The mandate of the Constitution provides various checks and balances before a Scheme can be implemented. Therefore, as long as the schemes come within the realm of public purpose and monies withdrawn for the implementation of schemes by passing suitable Appropriation Bill, the court has limited jurisdiction to interfere in such schemes. Judicial interference is permissible only when the action of the government is unconstitutional or contrary to a statutory provision and not when such action is not wise or that the extent of expenditure is not for the good of the State. Court further asserted that the schemes challenged under the present petition[25] were in consonance with Article 14 of the Constitution.

---

22 (1996) 1 SCC 206

23 **Meaning of Ex-Facie: Ex facie** is a legal term typically used to note that a document's explicit terms are defective without further investigation

24 The **Directive Principles of State Policy** are guidelines to the central and state governments of India, to be kept in mind while framing laws and policies. These provisions, contained in Part IV of the Constitution of India, are not enforceable by any court, but the principles laid down therein are considered fundamental in the governance of the country, making it the duty of the State to apply these principles in making laws to establish a just society in the country. The principles have been inspired by the Directive Principles given in the Constitution of Ireland and also by the principles of Gandhism; and relate to social justice, economic welfare, foreign policy, and legal and administrative matters

25 **Meaning of Petition:** A formal message requesting something that is submitted to an authority

Directions by Supreme Court:

Although, the law is obvious that the promises in the election manifesto cannot be construed as 'corrupt practice' under Section 123 of RP Act, the reality cannot be ruled out that distribution of freebies of any kind, undoubtedly, influences all people. It shakes the root of free and fair elections to a large degree. Court directed the Election Commission to frame guidelines in consultation with all the recognized political parties for general conduct of the candidates, meetings, processions, polling day, party in power etc. In the similar way, a separate head for guidelines for election manifesto released by a political party can also be included in the Model Code of Conduct for the Guidance of Political Parties & Candidates. Generally political parties release their election manifesto before the announcement of election date, in that scenario the Election Commission will not have the authority to regulate any act which is done before the announcement of the date.

34

Guidelines to be followed in the case of arrest and detention of a Judicial Officer[1]

Facts in Nutshell:

On 25th September, 1989, a horrendus[2] incident took place in the town of Nadiad, District Kheda in the State of Gujarat, which exhibited the berserk[3] behaviour of Police undermining the dignity and independence of judiciary. S.R. Sharma, Inspector of Police, with 25 years of service posted at the Police Station, Nadiad, arrested, assaulted[4] and handcuffed N.L. Patel, Chief Judicial Magistrate, Nadiad and tied him with a thick rope like an animal and made a public exhibition of it by sending him in the same condition to the Hospital for medical examination on an alleged charge of having consumed liquor in breach of the prohibition law enforced in the State of Gujarat. The Inspector S.R. Sharma got the Chief Judicial Magistrate photographed in handcuffs with rope tied around his body which were published in the news papers all over the country. This led to tremors[5] in the Bench and the Bar throughout the whole country.

---

1   Appellants: Delhi Judicial **Service Association, Tis Hazaro Court, Delhi Vs.** Respondent: State **of Gujarat and others**

    AIR1991SC2176

    Hon'ble Judges/Coram: K.N. Singh, Kuldip Singh and N.M. Kasliwal, JJ.

2   **Meaning of Horrendus:** Shockingly dreadful; horrible

3   **Meaning of Berserk:**

    1. Destructively or frenetically violent

    2. Mentally or emotionally upset; deranged

4   **Meaning of Assault:**

    a. An unlawful threat or attempt to do bodily injury to another.

    b. The act or an instance of unlawfully threatening or attempting to injure another

5   **Meaning of Tremors:**

    1. an involuntary shudder or vibration, as from illness, fear, shock, etc

    2. any trembling or quivering movement

    3. a vibrating or trembling effect, as of sound or light

The incident undermined the dignity of courts in the country, Judicial Officers, Judges and Magistrates all over the country were in a state of shock, they felt insecure and humiliated[6] and it appeared that instead of Rule of Law there was Police Raj in Gujarat. A number of Bar Associations passed Resolutions and went on strike. The Delhi Judicial Service Association, the All India Judges Association, Bar Council of Uttar Pradesh, Judicial Service of Gujarat and many others approached the Apex Court (Supreme Court) by means of telegrams and petitions[7] under Article 32[8] of the Constitution of India for Saving the dignity and honour of the judiciary. On 29.9.1989, Supreme Court took cognizance[9] of the matter by issuing notices to the State of Gujarat and other Police Officers. The Court appealed to the Members of the Bar and Judiciary to resume work to avoid inconvenience to the litigant public. Subsequently, a number of petitions were filed under Article 32 of the Constitution of India for taking action against the Police Officers and also for quashing[10] the criminal proceedings initiated by the Police against N.L. Patel, Chief Judicial Magistrate. A number of Bar Associations, Bar Councils and individuals appeared as interveners[11] condemning[12] the action of the police and urging the Court for taking action against the Police Officers.

---

6   **Meaning of Humiliated:** To lower the pride, dignity, or self-respect of

7   **Meaning of Petition:** A formal message requesting something that is submitted to an authority

8   **Article 32 in The Constitution Of India 1949**

Remedies for enforcement of rights conferred by this Part

(1) The right to move the Supreme Court by appropriate proceedings for the enforcement of the rights conferred by this Part is guaranteed

(2) The Supreme Court shall have power to issue directions or orders or writs, including writs in the nature of habeas corpus, mandamus, prohibition, quo warranto and certiorari, whichever may be appropriate, for the enforcement of any of the rights conferred by this Part

(3) Without prejudice to the powers conferred on the Supreme Court by clause (1) and (2), Parliament may by law empower any other court to exercise within the local limits of its jurisdiction all or any of the powers exercisable by the Supreme Court under clause (2)

(4) The right guaranteed by this article shall not be suspended except as otherwise provided for by this Constitution

9   **Meaning of Cognizance:** Acknowledgment, recognition, or jurisdiction; the assumption of jurisdiction in a case

10 **Meaning of Quash:** To set aside or annul, especially by judicial action

11 **Meaning of Interveners:** To interpose and become a party to a legal action between others, esp in order to protect one's interests

12 **Meaning of Condemn:** To express strong disapproval of

Contempt of Court:

The Common Law definition of contempt of Court is: 'An act or omission[13] calculated to interfere with the due administration of justice.'[14] The contempt of court as defined by the Contempt of Courts Act, 1971 includes civil and criminal contempt. Criminal contempt as defined by the Act: 'Means the publication whether by words, spoken or written, or by signs, or by visible representations, or otherwise of any matter or the doing of any other act whatsoever which scandalizes[15] or tends to scandalize, or lowers or tends to lower the authority of, any court; or prejudices, or interferes or tends or to interfere with, the due course of any judicial proceeding; or interferes, or tends to interfere with, or obstructs or tends to obstruct, the administration of justice in any other manner.' The definition of criminal contempt is wide enough to include any act by a person which would tend to interfere with the administration of justice or which would lower the authority of court. The public have a vital stake in effective and orderly administration of justice. The Court has the duty of protecting, the interest-of the community in the due administration of justice and, so, it is entrusted with the power to commit for contempt of court, not to protect the dignity of the Court against insult or injury, but, to protect and vindicate the right of the public so that the administration of justice is not perverted, prejudiced, obstructed or interfered with. "It is a mode of vindicating the majesty of law, in its active manifestation against obstruction and outrage."[16] The object and purpose of punishing contempt for interference with the administration of justice is not to safeguard or protect the dignity of the Judge or the Magistrate, but the purpose is to preserve the authority of the courts to ensure an ordered life in society. In *Attorney-General v. Times Newspapers*[17] the necessity for the law of contempt was summarised by Lord Morris as:

In an ordered community courts are established for the pacific settlement of disputes and for the maintenance of law and order. In the general interests of the community it is imperative that the authority of the courts

---

13 **Meaning of Omission:**

   1. The act or an instance of omitting.

   2. The state of having been omitted.

   3. Something omitted or neglected

14 Bowen L.J. in *Helmore v. Smith*[1886]35 Ch. D. 436

15 **Meaning of scandalize:** To offend the moral sensibilities of

16 Frank Furter, J. in Offuttv. U.S. [1954] 348 US 11

17 [1974] A.C. 273

should not be imperilled and that recourse to them should not be subject to unjustifiable interference. When such unjustifiable interference is suppressed it is not because those charged with the responsibilities of administering justice are concerned for their own dignity: it is because the very structure of ordered life is at risk if the recognised courts of the land are so flouted and their authority wanes and is supplanted.

"The summary power of punishment for contempt has been conferred on the courts to keep a blaze of glory around them, to deter people from attempting to render them contemptible in the eyes of the public. These powers are necessary to keep the course of justice free, as it is of great importance to society."[18] The power to punish contempt is vested in the Judges not for their personal protection only, but for the protection of public justice, whose interest, requires that decency and decorum is preserved in Courts of Justice. Those who have to discharge duty in a Court of Justice are protected by the law, and shielded in the discharge of their duties, any deliberate interference with the discharge of such duties either in court or outside the court by attacking the presiding officers of the court, would amount to criminal contempt and the courts must take serious cognizance of such conduct.

Decision by Supreme Court:

Court held that the Chief Judicial Magistrate is head of the Magistracy in the District who administers justice to ensure, protect and safeguard the rights of citizens. The subordinate courts at the district level cater to the need of the masses in administering justice at the base level. By and large the majority of the people get their disputes adjudicated in subordinate courts. It is in the general interest of the community that the authority of subordinate courts is protected. If the CJM is led into trap by unscrupulous[19] Police Officers and if he is assaulted, handcuffed and roped, the public is bound to lose faith in courts, which would be destructive of basic structure of an ordered society. Viewed in this perspective the incident was not a case of physical assault on an individual judicial officer, instead it was an onslaught on the institution of the judiciary itself. The incident was a clear interference with the administration of justice, lowering its judicial authority. Its effect was not confined to one District or State, it had a tendency to affect the entire judiciary in the country. The incident highlights a dangerous trend that if the Police is annoyed with

---

18 Oswald on Contempt of Court

19 **Meaning of unscrupulous:** Devoid of scruples; oblivious to or contemptuous of what is right or honorable

the orders of a presiding officer of a court, he would be arrested on flimsy manufactured charges, to humiliate him publicly as has been done in the instant case. The conduct of Police Officers in assaulting and humiliate the CJM brought the authority and administration of justice into disrespect, affecting the public confidence in the institution of justice. The Police has power to arrest a person even without obtaining a warrant[20] of arrest from a court. The amplitude[21] of this power casts an obligation on the Police to take maximum care in exercising that power, The Police must bear in mind, as held by Supreme Court that if a person is arrested for a crime, his constitutional and fundamental rights[22] must not be violated[23].

In the present case, Patel, CJM, was assaulted, arrested and handcuffed by Police inspector Sharma and other Police Officers. The Police Officers were not content with this, they tied him with a thick rope round his arms and body as if N.L. Patel (CJM) was a wild animal. Supreme Court awarded simple imprisonment to S.R. Sharma, the then Police Inspector, Nadiad for a period of six months and directed him to pay a fine of Rs. 2,000.

Supreme Court Guidelines which should be followed in the case of arrest and detention of a Judicial Officer:

No person whatever his rank, or designation may be, is, above law. A Magistrate, Judge or any other Judicial Officer is liable to criminal prosecution[24] for an offence like any other citizen Court issued following guidelines:

(A) If a judicial officer is to be arrested for some offence, it should be done under intimation to the District Judge or the High Court as the case may be.

---

20 **Meaning of Warrant:** A judicial writ authorizing an officer to make a search, seizure, or arrest or to execute a judgment.

21 **Meaning of Amplitude:**

    1. Greatness of size; magnitude.

    2. Fullness; copiousness.

    3. Breadth or range, as of intelligence

22 **Meaning of Fundamental Rights:** The Fundamental Rights are defined as basic human freedoms which every Indian citizen has the right to enjoy for a proper and harmonious development of personality. These rights universally apply to all citizens, irrespective of race, place of birth, religion, caste, creed, colour or gender. Aliens (persons who are not citizens) are also considered in matters like equality before law. They are enforceable by the courts, subject to certain restrictions

23 See: *Sunil Batra v. Delhi Administration and Ors.*, 1978CriLJ1741

24 **Meaning of Criminal Prosecution:** The institution and conduct of legal proceedings against a defendant for criminal behavior

(B) If facts and circumstances necessitate the immediate arrest of a judicial officer of the subordinate judiciary, a technical or formal arrest may be effected.

(C) The facts of such arrest should be immediately communicated to the District and Sessions Judge of the concerned District and the Chief Justice of the High Court.

(D)The Judicial Officer so arrested shall not be taken to a police station, without the prior order or directions of the District & Sessions Judge of the concerned District, if available.

(E) Immediate facilities shall be provided to the Judicial Officer for communication with his family members, legal advisers and Judicial Officers, including the District & Sessions Judge.

(F) No statement of a Judicial Officer who is under arrest be recorded nor any panchnama[25] be drawn up nor any medical tests be conducted except in the presence of the Legal Adviser of the Judicial Officer concerned or another Judicial Office of equal or higher rank, if available.

(G) There should be no handcuffing of a Judicial Officer. If, however, violent resistance to arrest is offered or there is imminent need to effect physical arrest in order to avert danger to life and limb, the person resisting arrest may be over-powered and handcuffed. In such case, immediate report shall be made to the District & Sessions Judge concerned and also to the Chief Justice of the High Court. But the burden would be on the Police to establish necessity for effecting physical arrest and handcuffing the Judicial Officer and if it be established that the physical arrest and handcuffing of the Judicial Officer was unjustified, the Police Officers causing or responsible for such arrest and hand cuffing would be guilty of misconduct and would also be personally liable for compensation and/or damages as may be summarily determined by the High Court.

Court opined that no Judicial Officer should visit a Police Station on his own except in connection with his official and judicial duties and functions. If it is necessary for a Judicial Officer or a Subordinate Judicial Officer to visit the Police Station in connection with his official duties, he must do so with prior intimation of his visit to the District & Sessions Judge.

---

25 **Meaning of Panchnama:** A first listing of the evidence and findings that a police officer makes at the scene of a crime. The document has to be signed by the investigating officer and two supposedly impartial witnesses.

35

Hijras[1] as third gender[2]

Facts in Nutshell:

Case concerned with the grievances[3] of the members of Transgender Community (for short 'TG community') who seek a legal declaration of their gender identity than the one assigned to them (male or female) at the time of birth and their prayer was that non-recognition of their gender identity violates Articles 14[4] and 21[5] of the Constitution of India. Hijras/Eunuchs[6], who also fall in that group, claim legal status as a third gender with all legal and constitutional protection.

The National Legal Services Authority, constituted under the Legal Services Authority Act, 1997, to provide free legal services to the weaker and other marginalized sections of the society came forward to advocate their cause, by filing Writ Petition[7] in Supreme Court. Poojaya Mata Nasib

---

1   *Hijras*, also known as *chhakka* in Kannada *kojja* in Telugu, is a term used to refer to individuals in South Asia who are transsexual or transgender

2   Appellants: **National Legal Services Authority Vs.** Respondent: **Union of India (UOI) and Ors.**

    MANU/SC/0309/2014

    Hon'ble Judges/Coram: K.S. Panicker Radhakrishnan and A.K. Sikri, JJ.

3   **Meaning of Grievance:**

    a. An actual or supposed circumstance regarded as just cause for complaint.

    b. A complaint or protestation based on such a circumstance

4   **Article 14 in The Constitution Of India 1949**

    Equality before law: The State shall not deny to any person equality before the law or the equal protection of the laws within the territory of India Prohibition of discrimination on grounds of religion, race, caste, sex or place of birth

5   **Article 21 in The Constitution Of India 1949**

    Protection of life and personal liberty: No person shall be deprived of his life or personal liberty except according to procedure established by law

6   A **eunuch** is a man who (by the common definition of the term) may have been castrated, typically early enough in his life for this change to have major hormonal consequences. In some ancient texts, "eunuch" may refer to a man who is not castrated but who is impotent, celibate, or otherwise not inclined to marry and procreate.

7   **Meaning of Writ Petition:** Under the Indian legal system, jurisdiction to issue 'prerogative writs' is given to the Supreme Court, and to the High Courts of Judicature of all Indian states. Parts

Kaur Ji Women Welfare Society, a registered association also preferred Writ Petition, seeking similar reliefs in respect of Kinnar community, a TG community. Laxmi Narayan Tripathy, claimed to be a Hijra said that non-recognition of the identity of Hijras, a TG community, as a third gender, denies them the right of equality before the law and equal protection of law guaranteed Under Article 14 of the Constitution and violates the rights guaranteed to them Under Article 21 of the Constitution of India.

Question before the Supreme Court:

(a) Whether a person who is born as a male with predominantly[8] female orientation (or vice-versa), has a right to get himself to be recognized as a female as per his choice moreso, when such a person after having undergone operational procedure, changes his/her sex as well

(b) Whether transgender (TG), who are neither males nor females, have a right to be identified and categorized as a "third gender"?

Meaning of Transgender:

Transgender is generally described as an umbrella term for persons whose gender identity, gender expression or behavior does not conform to their biological sex. TG may also take in persons who do not identify with their sex assigned at birth, which include Hijras/Eunuchs who describe themselves as "third gender" and they do not identify as either male or female. Hijras are not men by virtue of anatomy[9] appearance and

---

of the law relating to writs are set forth in the Constitution of India. The Supreme Court, the highest in the country, may issue writs under Article 32 of the Constitution for enforcement of Fundamental Rights and under Articles 139 for enforcement of rights other than Fundamental Rights, while High Courts, the superior courts of the States, may issue writs under Articles 226. 'Writ' is eminently designed by the makers of the Constitution, and in the same way it is developed very widely and efficiently by the courts in India. The Constitution broadly provides for five kinds of "prerogative" writs, namely, Habeas Corpus, Certiorari, Mandamus, Quo Warranto and Prohibition.

8 **Meaning of Predominant:**

   1. Having greatest ascendancy, importance, influence, authority, or force.

   2. Most common or conspicuous; main or prevalent

9 **Meaning of Anatomy:**

   1. The bodily structure of a plant or an animal or of any of its parts.

   2. The science of the shape and structure of organisms and their parts.

   3. A treatise on anatomic science

psychologically[10], they are also not women, though they are like women with no female reproduction organ and no menstruation[11]. Since Hijras do not have reproduction capacities as either men or women, they are neither men nor women and claim to be an institutional "third gender". Among Hijras, there are emasculated[12] (castrated, nirvana) men, non-emasculated men (not castrated/akva/akka) and inter-sexed persons (hermaphrodites[13]). TG also includes persons who intend to undergo Sex Re-Assignment Surgery[14] (SRS) or have undergone SRS to align their biological sex with their gender identity in order to become male or female. They are generally called transsexual persons. Further, there are persons who like to cross-dress in clothing of opposite gender, i.e. transvestites[15]. Resultantly, the term "transgender", in contemporary usage, has become an umbrella term that is used to describe a wide range of identities and experiences, including but not limited to pre-operative, post-operative and non-operative transsexual people, who strongly identify with the gender opposite to their biological sex; male and female.

Historical Background of Transgenders in India:

TG Community comprises of Hijras, eunuchs, Kothis, Aravanis, Jogappas, Shiv-Shakthis etc. and they, as a group, have got a strong historical presence in our country in the Hindu mythology and other religious texts. The Concept of tritiya prakrti or napunsaka has also been an integral part of vedic and puranic literatures. The word 'napunsaka' has been used to denote absence of procreative capability. Lord Rama, in the epic Ramayana, was leaving for the forest upon being banished from the

---

10 **Meaning of Psychological**: Of, relating to, or arising from the mind or emotions

11 **Meaning of Menstruation**: The periodic discharge of blood and mucosal tissue from the uterus, occurring approximately monthly from puberty to menopause in nonpregnant women and females of other primate species.

12 **Meaning of Emasculate:**

    1. To castrate.

    2. To deprive of strength or vigor; weaken

13 **Meaning of hermaphrodites:**

    1. An animal or plant exhibiting hermaphroditism.

    2. Something that is a combination of disparate or contradictory elements

14 **Sex reassignment surgery** (initialized as **SRS**; also known as **gender reassignment surgery (GRS), genital reconstruction surgery, sex affirmation surgery** or **sex realignment surgery**) is a term for the surgical procedures by which a person's physical appearance and function of their existing sexual characteristics are altered to resemble that of the other sex.

15 **Meaning of transvestites**: A person who dresses and acts in a style or manner traditionally associated with the opposite sex.

kingdom for 14 years, turns around to his followers and asks all the 'men and women' to return to the city. Among his followers, the hijras alone do not feel bound by this direction and decide to stay with him. Impressed with their devotion, Rama sanctions them the power to confer blessings on people on auspicious occasions like childbirth and marriage, and also at inaugural functions which, it is believed set the stage for the custom of badhai in which hijras sing, dance and confer blessings.

Aravan, the son of Arjuna and Nagakanya in Mahabharata, offers to be sacrificed to Goddess Kali to ensure the victory of the Pandavas in the Kurukshetra war, the only condition that he made was to spend the last night of his life in matrimony. Since no woman was willing to marry one who was doomed to be killed, Krishna assumes the form of a beautiful woman called Mohini and marries him. The Hijras of Tamil Nadu consider Aravan their progenitor[16] and call themselves Aravanis. Jain Texts also make a detailed reference to TG which mentions the concept of 'psychological sex'. Hijras also played a prominent role in the royal courts of the Islamic world, especially in the Ottaman empires[17] and the Mughal rule[18] in the Medieval India.

Though historically, Hijras/transgender persons had played a prominent role, with the onset of colonial rule from the 18th century onwards, the situation had changed drastically. During the British rule, a legislation was enacted to supervise the deeds of Hijras/TG community, called the Criminal Tribes Act, 1871, which deemed the entire community of Hijras persons as innately 'criminal' and 'addicted to the systematic commission of non-bailable offences'. The Act provided for the registration, surveillance[19] and control of certain criminal tribes and eunuchs and had penalized eunuchs, who were registered, and appeared to be dressed or ornamented like a woman, in a public street or place, as well as those

---

16 **Meaning of Progenitor:**

   1. a direct ancestor

   2. an originator or founder of a future development; precursor

17 The **Ottoman Empire** historically also referred to as the **Turkish Empire** or **Turkey**, was an empire founded by Oghuz Turks underOsman Bey in northwestern Anatolia in 1299

18 The **Mughal Empire** self-designated as **Gurkani** was an empire extending over large parts of the Indian subcontinent and ruled by a dynasty ofTurkic-Mongol origin

19 **Meaning of Surveillance:**

   1. Close observation of a person or group, especially one under suspicion.

   2. The act of observing or the condition of being observed

who danced or played music in a public place. Such persons also could be arrested without warrant[20] and sentenced to imprisonment up to two years or fine or both. Under the Act, the local government had to register the names and residence of all eunuchs residing in that area as well as of their properties, who were reasonably suspected of kidnapping or castrating[21] children, or of committing offences under Section 377[22] of the Indian Penal Code, or of abetting[23] the commission of any of the said offences. Under the Act, the act of keeping a boy under 16 years in the charge of a registered eunuch was made an offence punishable with imprisonment up to two years or fine and the Act also denuded[24] the registered eunuchs of their civil rights by prohibiting them from acting as guardians[25] to minors, from making a gift deed or a will, or from adopting a son. Act has, however, been repealed in August 1949.

Section 377 of the Indian Penal Code, 1860:

Section 377 of the Indian Penal Code found a place in the Indian Penal Code, 1860, prior to the enactment of Criminal Tribes Act that criminalized all penile-non-vaginal sexual acts between persons, including anal sex and oral sex, at a time when transgender persons were also typically associated with the prescribed sexual practices. Reference may be made to the judgment of the Allahabad High Court in *Queen Empress v. Khairati*[26], wherein a transgender person was arrested and prosecuted[27]

---

20 **Meaning of Warrant:**

   A judicial writ authorizing an officer to make a search, seizure, or arrest or to execute a judgment

21 **Meaning of Castrating:**

   1. To remove the testicles of (a male); geld or emasculate.

   2. To remove the ovaries of (a female); spay.

   3. To deprive of virility or spirit; emasculate.

22 **Section 377 in The Indian Penal Code**

   377. Unnatural offences: Whoever voluntarily has carnal intercourse against the order of nature with any man, woman or animal, shall be punished with 1[imprisonment for life], or with imprisonment of either description for a term which may extend to ten years, and shall also be liable to fine. Explanation.—Penetration is sufficient to constitute the carnal intercourse necessary to the offence described in this section

23 **Meaning of Abet:** To assist or encourage, esp in crime or wrongdoing

24 **Meaning of Denuded:** Without the natural or usual covering; "a bald spot on the lawn"; "bare hills"

25 **Meaning of Guardian:** One who is legally responsible for the care and management of the person or property of an incompetent or a minor.

26 (1884) ILR 6 All 204

27 **Meaning of Prosecute:**

under Section 377 on the suspicion that he was a 'habitual sodomite[28]' and was later acquitted[29] on appeal[30]. In that case, while acquitting him, the Sessions Judge stated as follows:

This case relates to a person named Khairati, over whom the police seem to have exercised some sort of supervision, whether strictly regular or not, as a eunuch. The man is not a eunuch in the literal sense, but he was called for by the police when on a visit to his village, and was found singing dressed as a woman among the women of a certain family. Having been subjected to examination by the Civil Surgeon (and a subordinate medical man), he is shown to have the characteristic mark of a habitual catamite[31]-the distortion of the orifice of the anus into the shape of a trumpet and also to be affected with syphilis[32] in the same region in a manner which distinctly points to unnatural intercourse within the last few months.

Even though, he was acquitted on appeal, this case would demonstrate that Section 377, though associated with specific sexual acts, highlighted certain identities, including Hijras and was used as an instrument of harassment and physical abuse against Hijras and transgender persons.

Wide range of transgender related identities, cultures or experiences are as follows:

Hijras: Hijras are biological males who reject their 'masculine' identity in due course of time to identify either as women, or "not-men", or "in-between man and woman", or "neither man nor woman". Hijras can be

---

a. To initiate civil or criminal court action against.

b. To seek to obtain or enforce by legal action

28 **Meaning of Sodomite:** One who engages in sodomy (Any of various forms of sexual intercourse held to be unnatural or abnormal, especially anal intercourse or bestiality)

29 **Meaning of Acquit:** To free or clear from a charge or accusation

30 **Meaning of Appeal:** In law, an **appeal** is a process for requesting a formal change to an official decision. Very broadly speaking there are appeals on the record and *de novo* appeals. In *de novo* appeals, a new decision maker re-hears the case without any reference to the prior decision maker. In appeals on the record, the decision of the prior decision maker is challenged by arguing that he or she misapplied the law, came to an incorrect factual finding, acted in excess of his jurisdiction, abused his powers, was biased, considered evidence which he should not have considered or failed to consider evidence that he should have considered

31 **Meaning of Catamite:** A boy who has a sexual relationship with a man.

32 **Meaning of syphilis:** A chronic infectious disease caused by a spirochete *(Treponema pallidum)*, either transmitted by direct contact, usually in sexual intercourse, or passed from mother to child in utero, and progressing through three stages characterized respectively by local formation of chancres, ulcerous skin eruptions, and systemic infection leading to general paresis

considered as the western equivalent of transgender/transsexual (male-to-female) persons but Hijras have a long tradition/culture and have strong social ties formalized through a ritual called "reet" (becoming a member of Hijra community). There are regional variations in the use of terms referred to Hijras. For example, Kinnars (Delhi) and Aravanis (Tamil Nadu). Hijras may earn through their traditional work: 'Badhai' (clapping their hands and asking for alms), blessing new-born babies, or dancing in ceremonies. Some proportion of Hijras engage in sex work for lack of other job opportunities, while some may be self-employed or work for non-governmental organisations."[33]

Eunuch: Eunuch refers to an emasculated male and intersexed to a person whose genitals are ambiguously male-like at birth, but this is discovered the child previously assigned to the male sex, would be recategorized as intesexexd-as a Hijra.

"Aravanis and 'Thirunangi'-Hijras in Tamil Nadu identify as "Aravani". Tamil Nadu Aravanigal Welfare Board, a state government's initiative under the Department of Social Welfare defines Aravanis as biological males who self-identify themselves as a woman trapped in a male's body. Some Aravani activists want the public and media to use the term 'Thirunangi' to refer to Aravanis.

Kothi-Kothis are a heterogeneous[34] group. 'Kothis' can be described as biological males who show varying degrees of 'femininity'-which may be situational. Some proportion of Kothis have bisexual behavior and get married to a woman. Kothis are generally of lower socioeconomic status and some engage in sex work for survival. Some proportion of Hijra-identified people may also identify themselves as 'Kothis'. But not all Kothi identified people identify themselves as transgender or Hijras.

Jogtas/Jogappas: Jogtas or Jogappas are those persons who are dedicated to and serve as a servant of goddess Renukha Devi (Yellamma) whose temples are present in Maharashtra and Karnataka. 'Jogta' refers to male servant of that Goddess and 'Jogti' refers to female servant (who is also sometimes referred to as 'Devadasi'). One can become a 'Jogta' (or Jogti) if it is part of their family tradition or if one finds a 'Guru' (or 'Pujari') who

---

33 See UNDP India Report (December, 2010)

34 **Meaning of Heterogenous:**

    1. composed of unrelated or differing parts or elements

    2. not of the same kind or type

accepts him/her as a 'Chela' or 'Shishya' (disciple). Sometimes, the term 'Jogti Hijras' is used to denote those male-to-female transgender persons who are devotees/servants of Goddess Renukha Devi and who are also in the Hijra communities. This term is used to differentiate them from 'Jogtas' who are heterosexuals and who may or may not dress in woman's attire when they worship the Goddess. Also, that term differentiates them from 'Jogtis' who are biological females dedicated to the Goddess. However, 'Jogti Hijras' may refer to themselves as 'Jogti' (female pronoun) or Hijras, and even sometimes as 'Jogtas'.

Shiv-Shakthis: Shiv-Shakthis are considered as males who are possessed by or particularly close to a goddess and who have feminine gender expression. Usually, Shiv-Shakthis are inducted into the Shiv-Shakti community by senior gurus, who teach them the norms, customs, and rituals to be observed by them. In a ceremony, Shiv-Shakthis are married to a sword that represents male power or Shiva (deity). Shiv-Shakthis thus become the bride of the sword. Occasionally, Shiv-Shakthis cross-dress and use accessories and ornaments that are generally/socially meant for women. Most people in this community belong to lower socio-economic status and earn for their living as astrologers, soothsayers, and spiritual healers; some also seek alms."[35]

Gender Identity and Sexual Orientation:

Gender identity is one of the most-fundamental aspects of life which refers to a person's intrinsic[36] sense of being male, female or transgender or transsexual[37] person. A person's sex is usually assigned at birth, but a relatively small group of persons may born with bodies which incorporate both or certain aspects of both male and female physiology[38]. At times, genital[39] anatomy problems may arise in certain persons, their innate

---

35 See Serena Nanda, Wadsworth Publishing Company, Second Edition (1999)

36 **Meaning of Intrinsic:** Of or relating to the essential nature of a thing; inherent.

37 **Meaning of Transsexual:**

   1. One who wishes to be considered by society as a member of the opposite sex.

   2. One who has undergone a sex change

38 **Meaning of Physiology:**

   1. The biological study of the functions of living organisms and their parts.

   2. All the functions of a living organism or any of its parts

39 **Meaning of Genital:**

   1. Of or relating to biological reproduction.

perception of themselves, is not in conformity with the sex assigned to them at birth and may include pre and post-operative transsexual persons and also persons who do not choose to undergo or do not have access to operation and also include persons who cannot undergo successful operation. Countries, all over the world, including India, are grappled[40] with the question of attribution of gender to persons who believe that they belong to the opposite sex. Few persons undertake surgical and other procedures to alter their bodies and physical appearance to acquire gender characteristics of the sex which conform to their perception of gender, leading to legal and social complications since official record of their gender at birth is found to be at variance with the assumed gender identity. Gender identity refers to each person's deeply felt internal and individual experience of gender, which may or may not correspond with the sex assigned at birth, including the personal sense of the body which may involve a freely chosen, modification of bodily appearance or functions by medical, surgical or other means and other expressions of gender, including dress, speech and mannerisms. Gender identity, therefore, refers to an individual's self-identification as a man, woman, transgender or other identified category.

Sexual orientation refers to an individual's enduring physical, romantic and/or emotional attraction to another person. Sexual orientation includes transgender and gender-variant people with heavy sexual orientation and their sexual orientation may or may not change during or after gender transmission, which also includes homosexuals[41], bisexuals[42], heterosexuals[43], asexual[44] etc. Gender identity and sexual

---

2. Of or relating to the genitals

40 **Meaning of Grappled:**

    a. A struggle or contest in which the participants attempt to clutch or grip each other.

    b. A struggle for superiority or dominance

41 **Homosexuality** is romantic attraction,sexual attraction or sexual behavior between members of the same sex or gender

42 **Bisexuality** is romantic attraction, sexual attraction or sexual behavior toward both males and females. The term is mainly used in the context of human attraction to denote romantic or sexual feelings toward both men and women.

43 **Heterosexuality** is romantic attraction, sexual attraction or sexual behavior between persons of opposite sex or genderin the gender binary. As a sexual orientation, heterosexuality refers to "an enduring pattern of or disposition to experience sexual, affectionate, physical or romantic attractions to persons of the opposite sex"; it also refers to "a person's sense of identity based on those attractions, related behaviors, and membership in a community of others who share those attractions"

44 **Meaning of Asexual:**

orientation, as already indicated, are different concepts. Each person's self-defined sexual orientation and gender identity is integral to their personality and is one of the most basic aspects of self-determination, dignity and freedom and no one shall be forced to undergo medical procedures, including SRS, sterilization or hormonal therapy, as a requirement for legal recognition of their gender identity.

United Nations and other Human Rights Bodies on Gender Identity and Sexual Orientation:

United Nations has been instrumental in advocating the protection and promotion of rights of sexual minorities, including transgender persons. Article 6[45] of the Universal Declaration of Human Rights, 1948 and Article 16[46] of the International Covenant on Civil and Political Rights, 1966 (ICCPR) recognize that every human being has the inherent right to live and this right shall be protected by law and that no one shall be arbitrarily[47] denied of that right. Everyone shall have a right to recognition, everywhere as a person before the law. Article 17[48] of the ICCPR states that no one shall be subjected to arbitrary or unlawful interference with his privacy, family, home or correspondence, nor to unlawful attacks on his honour and reputation and that everyone has the right to protection of law against such interference or attacks. International Commission of Jurists and the International Service for Human Rights on behalf of a coalition of human rights organizations, took a project to develop a set of international legal principles on the application of international law to human rights violations based on sexual orientation and sexual identity to bring greater clarity and coherence to State's human rights obligations. A distinguished group of human rights experts has drafted, developed,

---

1. Having no evident sex or sex organs; sexless.

2. Relating to, produced by, or involving reproduction that occurs without the union of male and female gametes, as in binary fission or budding

45 **Article 6 of the Universal Declaration of Human Rights, 1948:**

Everyone has the right to recognition everywhere as a person before the law

46 **Article 16 of the International Covenant on Civil and Political Rights, 1966 (ICCPR):**

Everyone shall have the right to recognition everywhere as a person before the law

47 **Meaning of Arbitrary:** In a random manner

48   **Article 17 of the ICCPR:**

1. No one shall be subjected to arbitrary or unlawful interference with his privacy, family, home or correspondence, nor to unlawful attacks on his honour and reputation.

2. Everyone has the right to the protection of the law against such interference or attacks

discussed and reformed the principles in a meeting held at Gadjah Mada University in Yogyakarta, Indonesia from 6 to 9 November, 2006, which is unanimously adopted the Yogyakarta Principles on the application of International Human Rights Law in relation to Sexual Orientation and Gender Identity. Yogyakarta Principles address a broad range of human rights standards and their application to issues of sexual orientation gender identity. Reference to few Yogyakarta Principles would be useful.

Yogyakarta Principles:

Principle 1 Which deals with the right to the universal enjoyment of human rights, reads as follows:

1. The Right to the Universal Enjoyment of Human Rights

All human beings are born free and equal in dignity and rights. Human beings of all sexual orientations and gender identities are entitled to the full enjoyment of all human rights.

States shall:

A. Embody the principles of the universality, interrelatedness, interdependence and indivisibility of all human rights in their national constitutions or other appropriate legislation and ensure the practical realisation of the universal enjoyment of all human rights;

B. Amend any legislation, including criminal law, to ensure its consistency with the universal enjoyment of all human rights;

C. Undertake programmes of education and awareness to promote and enhance the full enjoyment of all human rights by all persons, irrespective of sexual orientation or gender identity;

D. Integrate within State policy and decision-making a pluralistic approach that recognises and affirms the interrelatedness and indivisibility of all aspects of human identity including sexual orientation and gender identity.

2. The Right to Equality and Non-Discrimination

Everyone is entitled to enjoy all human rights without discrimination on the basis of sexual orientation or gender identity. Everyone is entitled to equality before the law and the equal protection of the law without any such discrimination whether or not the enjoyment of another human right is also affected. The law shall prohibit any such discrimination and guarantee to all persons equal and effective protection against any such discrimination.

Discrimination on the basis of sexual orientation or gender identity includes any distinction, exclusion, restriction or preference based on sexual orientation or gender identity which has the purpose or effect of nullifying or impairing equality before the law or the equal protection of the law, or the recognition, enjoyment or exercise, on an equal basis, of all human rights and fundamental freedoms. Discrimination based on sexual orientation or gender identity may be, and commonly is, compounded by discrimination on other grounds including gender, race, age, religion, disability, health and economic status.

States shall:

A. Embody the principles of equality and non-discrimination on the basis of sexual orientation and gender identity in their national constitutions or other appropriate legislation, if not yet incorporated therein, including by means of amendment and interpretation, and ensure the effective realisation of these principles;

B. Repeal criminal and other legal provisions that prohibit or are, in effect, employed to prohibit consensual sexual activity among people of the same sex who are over the age of consent, and ensure that an equal age of consent applies to both same-sex and different- sex sexual activity;

C. Adopt appropriate legislative and other measures to prohibit and eliminate discrimination in the public and private spheres on the basis of sexual orientation and gender identity;

D. Take appropriate measures to secure adequate advancement of persons of diverse sexual orientations and gender identities as may be necessary to ensure such groups or individuals equal enjoyment or exercise of human rights. Such measures shall not be deemed to be discriminatory;

E. In all their responses to discrimination on the basis of sexual orientation or gender identity, take account of the manner in which such discrimination may intersect with other forms of discrimination;

F. Take all appropriate action, including programmes of education and training, with a view to achieving the elimination of prejudicial or discriminatory attitudes or behaviours which are related to the idea of the inferiority or the superiority of any sexual orientation or gender identity or gender expression.

The Right to Recognition before the Law:

Everyone has the right to recognition everywhere as a person before the law. Persons of diverse sexual orientations and gender identities shall enjoy legal capacity in all aspects of life. Each person's self-defined sexual orientation and gender identity is integral to their personality and is one of the most basic aspects of self-determination[49], dignity and freedom. No one shall be forced to undergo medical procedures, including sex reassignment surgery, sterilisation or hormonal therapy, as a requirement for legal recognition of their gender identity. No status, such as marriage or parenthood, may be invoked as such to prevent the legal recognition of a person's gender identity. No one shall be subjected to pressure to conceal, suppress or deny their sexual orientation or gender identity.

States shall:

A. Ensure that all persons are accorded legal capacity in civil matters, without discrimination on the basis of sexual orientation or gender identity, and the opportunity to exercise that capacity, including equal rights to conclude contracts, and to administer, own, acquire (including through inheritance), manage, enjoy and dispose of property;

B. Take all necessary legislative, administrative and other measures to fully respect and legally recognise each person's self-defined gender identity;

C. Take all necessary legislative, administrative and other measures to ensure that procedures exist whereby all State-issued identity papers which indicate a person's gender/sex -- including birth certificates, passports, electoral records and other documents -- reflect the person's profound self-defined gender identity;

D. Ensure that such procedures are efficient, fair and non-discriminatory, and respect the dignity and privacy of the person concerned;

---

49 The right of nations to **self-determination** or in short form, the right to self-determination is the cardinal principle in modern international law (*jus cogens*), binding, as such, on the United Nations as authoritative interpretation of the Charter's norms. It states that nations based on respect for the principle of equal rights and fair equality of opportunity have the right to freely choose their sovereignty and international political status with no external compulsion or interference which can be traced back to the Atlantic Charter, signed on 14 August 1941, by Franklin D. Roosevelt, President of the United States of America, and Winston Churchill, Prime Minister of the United Kingdom who pledged The Eight Principal points of the Charter

E. Ensure that changes to identity documents will be recognised in all contexts where the identification or disaggregation of persons by gender is required by law or policy;

F. Undertake targeted programmes to provide social support for all persons experiencing gender transitioning or reassignment.

The Right to Life:

Everyone has the right to life. No one shall be arbitrarily deprived of life, including by reference to considerations of sexual orientation or gender identity. The death penalty shall not be imposed on any person on the basis of consensual sexual activity among persons who are over the age of consent or on the basis of sexual orientation or gender identity.

States shall:

A. Repeal[50] all forms of crime that have the purpose or effect of prohibiting consensual sexual activity among persons of the same sex who are over the age of consent and, until such provisions are repealed, never impose the death penalty on any person convicted under them;

B. Remit sentences of death and release all those currently awaiting execution for crimes relating to consensual sexual activity among persons who are over the age of consent;

C. Cease any State-sponsored or State-condoned attacks on the lives of persons based on sexual orientation or gender identity, and ensure that all such attacks, whether by government officials or by any individual or group, are vigorously investigated, and that, where appropriate evidence is found, those responsible are prosecuted, tried and duly punished.

The Right to Privacy:

Everyone, regardless of sexual orientation or gender identity, is entitled to the enjoyment of privacy without arbitrary or unlawful interference, including with regard to their family, home or correspondence as well as to protection from unlawful attacks on their honour and reputation. The right to privacy ordinarily includes the choice to disclose or not to disclose information relating to one's sexual orientation or gender

---

50 **Meaning of Repeal:**

    1. To revoke or rescind, especially by an official or formal act.

    2. *Obsolete* To summon back or recall, especially from exile.

identity, as well as decisions and choices regarding both one's own body and consensual sexual and other relations with others.

States shall:

A. Take all necessary legislative, administrative and other measures to ensure the right of each person, regardless of sexual orientation or gender identity, to enjoy the private sphere, intimate decisions, and human relations, including consensual sexual activity among persons who are over the age of consent, without arbitrary interference;

B. Repeal all laws that criminalise consensual sexual activity among persons of the same sex who are over the age of consent, and ensure that an equal age of consent applies to both same-sex and different-sex sexual activity;

C. Ensure that criminal and other legal provisions of general application are not applied to de facto criminalise consensual sexual activity among persons of the same sex who are over the age of consent;

D. Repeal any law that prohibits or criminalises the expression of gender identity, including through dress, speech or mannerisms, or that denies to individuals the opportunity to change their bodies as a means of expressing their gender identity;

E. Release all those held on remand or on the basis of a criminal conviction, if their detention is related to consensual sexual activity among persons who are over the age of consent, or is related to gender identity;

F. Ensure the right of all persons ordinarily to choose when, to whom and how to disclose information pertaining to their sexual orientation or gender identity, and protect all persons from arbitrary or unwanted disclosure, or threat of disclosure of such information by others

The Right to Treatment with Humanity while in Detention[51]

Everyone deprived of liberty shall be treated with humanity and with respect for the inherent dignity of the human person. Sexual orientation and gender identity are integral to each person's dignity.

---

51 **Meaning of Detention:** Maintenance of a person in custody or confinement, as while awaiting a court decision.

States shall:

A. Ensure that placement in detention avoids further marginalising persons on the basis of sexual orientation or gender identity or subjecting them to risk of violence, ill-treatment or physical, mental or sexual abuse;

B. Provide adequate access to medical care and counseling appropriate to the needs of those in custody, recognising any particular needs of persons on the basis of their sexual orientation or gender identity, including with regard to reproductive health, access to HIV/AIDS information and therapy and access to hormonal or other therapy as well as to gender-reassignment treatments where desired;

C. Ensure, to the extent possible, that all prisoners participate in decisions regarding the place of detention appropriate to their sexual orientation and gender identity;

D. Put protective measures in place for all prisoners vulnerable to violence or abuse on the basis of their sexual orientation, gender identity or gender expression and ensure, so far as is reasonably practicable, that such protective measures involve no greater restriction of their rights than is experienced by the general prison population;

E. Ensure that conjugal visits, where permitted, are granted on an equal basis to all prisoners and detainees, regardless of the gender of their partner;

F. Provide for the independent monitoring of detention facilities by the State as well as by non-governmental organisations including organisations working in the spheres of sexual orientation and gender identity;

G. Undertake programmes of training and awareness-raising for prison personnel and all other officials in the public and private sector who are engaged in detention facilities, regarding international human rights standards and principles of equality and non-discrimination, including in relation to sexual orientation and gender identity.

Protection from Medical Abuses:

No person may be forced to undergo any form of medical or psychological treatment, procedure, testing, or be confined to a medical facility, based on sexual orientation or gender identity. Notwithstanding any classifications to the contrary, a person's sexual orientation and gender identity are not, in and of themselves, medical conditions and are not to be treated, cured or suppressed[52].

States shall:

A. Take all necessary legislative, administrative and other measures to ensure full protection against harmful medical practices based on sexual orientation or gender identity, including on the basis of stereotypes, whether derived from culture or otherwise, regarding conduct, physical appearance or perceived gender norms;

B. Take all necessary legislative, administrative and other measures to ensure that no child's body is irreversibly altered by medical procedures in an attempt to impose a gender identity without the full, free and informed consent of the child in accordance with the age and maturity of the child and guided by the principle that in all actions concerning children, the best interests of the child shall be a primary consideration;

C. Establish child protection mechanisms whereby no child is at risk of, or subjected to, medical abuse;

D. Ensure protection of persons of diverse sexual orientations and gender identities against unethical or involuntary medical procedures or research, including in relation to vaccines, treatments or microbicides for HIV/AIDS or other diseases;

E. Review and amend any health funding provisions or programmes, including those of a development-assistance nature, which may promote, facilitate or in any other way render possible such abuses;

F. Ensure that any medical or psychological treatment or counseling does not, explicitly or implicitly, treat sexual orientation and gender identity as medical conditions to be treated, cured or suppressed.

The Right to Freedom of Opinion and Expression:

Everyone has the right to freedom of opinion and expression, regardless of sexual orientation or gender identity. This includes the expression of identity or personhood through speech, deportment, dress, bodily

---

52 **Meaning of Suppressed:**

    1. To put an end to forcibly; subdue.

    2. To curtail or prohibit the activities of.

    3. To keep from being revealed, published, or circulated.

characteristics, choice of name, or any other means, as well as the freedom to seek, receive and impart information and ideas of all kinds, including with regard to human rights, sexual orientation and gender identity, through any medium and regardless of frontiers.

States shall:

A. Take all necessary legislative, administrative and other measures to ensure full enjoyment of freedom of opinion and expression, while respecting the rights and freedoms of others, without discrimination on the basis of sexual orientation or gender identity, including the receipt and imparting of information and ideas concerning sexual orientation and gender identity, as well as related advocacy for legal rights, publication of materials, broadcasting, organisation of or participation in conferences, and dissemination of and access to safer-sex information;

B. Ensure that the outputs and the organisation of media that is State-regulated is pluralistic and non-discriminatory in respect of issues of sexual orientation and gender identity and that the personnel recruitment and promotion policies of such organisations are non-discriminatory on the basis of sexual orientation or gender identity;

C. Take all necessary legislative, administrative and other measures to ensure the full enjoyment of the right to express identity or personhood, including through speech, deportment, dress, bodily characteristics, choice of name or any other means;

D. Ensure that notions of public order, public morality, public health and public security are not employed to restrict, in a discriminatory manner, any exercise of freedom of opinion and expression that affirms diverse sexual orientations or gender identities;

E. Ensure that the exercise of freedom of opinion and expression does not violate the rights and freedoms of persons of diverse sexual orientations and gender identities;

F. Ensure that all persons, regardless of sexual orientation or gender identity, enjoy equal access to information and ideas, as well as to participation in public debate.

UN bodies, Regional Human Rights Bodies, National Courts, Government Commissions and the Commissions for Human Rights, Council of Europe, etc. have endorsed the Yogyakarta Principles and have considered them as an important tool for identifying the obligations of States to respect, protect and fulfill the human rights of all persons, regardless of their gender identity.

Article 14 of the Constitution and Transgenders:

Article 14 of the Constitution of India states that the State shall not deny to "any person" equality before the law or the equal protection of the laws within the territory of India. Equality includes the full and equal enjoyment of all rights and freedom. Right to equality has been declared as the basic feature of the Constitution and treatment of equals as unequals or unequals as equals will be violative of the basic structure of the Constitution. Article 14 of the Constitution also ensures equal protection and hence a positive obligation on the State to ensure equal protection of laws by bringing in necessary social and economic changes, so that everyone including TGs may enjoy equal protection of laws and nobody is denied such protection. Article 14 does not restrict the word 'person' and its application only to male or female. Hijras/transgender persons who are neither male/female fall within the expression 'person' and, hence, entitled to legal protection of laws in all spheres of State activity, including employment, healthcare, education as well as equal civil and citizenship rights, as enjoyed by any other citizen of this country.

Non-recognition of the identity of Hijras/transgender persons denies them equal protection of law, thereby leaving them extremely vulnerable to harassment, violence and sexual assault in public spaces, at home and in jail, also by the police. Sexual assault, including molestation, rape, forced anal and oral sex, gang rape and stripping is being committed with impunity and there are reliable statistics and materials to support such activities. Further, non-recognition of identity of Hijras/transgender persons results in them facing extreme discrimination in all spheres of society, especially in the field of employment, education, healthcare etc. Hijras/ transgender persons face huge discrimination in access to public spaces like restaurants, cinemas, shops, malls etc. Further, access to public toilets is also a serious problem they face quite often. Since, there are no separate toilet facilities for Hijras/transgender persons, they have to use male toilets where they are prone to sexual assault and harassment. Discrimination on the ground of sexual orientation or gender identity, therefore, impairs equality before law and equal protection of law and violates Article 14 of the Constitution of India.

Articles 15[53] & 16[54] of the Constitution and Transgenders:

Articles 15 and 16 prohibit discrimination against any citizen on certain enumerated[55] grounds, including the ground of 'sex'. In fact, both the Articles prohibit all forms of gender bias and gender based discrimination.

Article 15 states that the State shall not discriminate against any citizen, inter alia, on the ground of sex, with regard to

(a) access to shops, public restaurants, hotels and places of public

---

53 **Article 15 in The Constitution Of India 1949**

15. Prohibition of discrimination on grounds of religion, race, caste, sex or place of birth

(1) The State shall not discriminate against any citizen on grounds only of religion, race, caste, sex, place of birth or any of them

(2) No citizen shall, on grounds only of religion, race, caste, sex, place of birth or any of them, be subject to any disability, liability, restriction or condition with regard to

(a) access to shops, public restaurants, hotels and palaces of public entertainment; or

(b) the use of wells, tanks, bathing ghats, roads and places of public resort maintained wholly or partly out of State funds or dedicated to the use of the general public

(3) Nothing in this article shall prevent the State from making any special provision for women and children

(4) Nothing in this article or in clause (2) of Article 29 shall prevent the State from making any special provision for the advancement of any socially and educationally backward classes of citizens or for the Scheduled Castes and the Scheduled Tribes

54 **Article 16 in The Constitution Of India 1949**

16. Equality of opportunity in matters of public employment

(1) There shall be equality of opportunity for all citizens in matters relating to employment or appointment to any office under the State

(2) No citizen shall, on grounds only of religion, race, caste, sex, descent, place of birth, residence or any of them, be ineligible for, or discriminated against in respect or, any employment or office under the State

(3) Nothing in this article shall prevent Parliament from making any law prescribing, in regard to a class or classes of employment or appointment to an office under the Government of, or any local or other authority within, a State or Union territory, any requirement as to residence within that State or Union territory prior to such employment or appointment

(4) Nothing in this article shall prevent the State from making any provision for the reservation of appointments or posts in favor of any backward class of citizens which, in the opinion of the State, is not adequately represented in the services under the State

(5) Nothing in this article shall affect the operation of any law which provides that the incumbent of an office in connection with the affairs of any religious or denominational institution or any member of the governing body thereof shall be a person professing a particular religion or belonging to a particular denomination

55 **Meaning of Enumerat:**

1. To count off or name one by one

2. To determine the number of; count.

entertainment; or

(b) use of wells, tanks, bathing ghats, roads and places of public resort maintained wholly or partly out of State funds or dedicated to the use of the general public.

The requirement of taking affirmative action for the advancement of any socially and educationally backward classes of citizens is also provided in this Article.

Article 16 states that there shall be equality of opportunities for all the citizens in matters relating to employment or appointment to any office under the State. Article 16(2) of the Constitution of India reads as follows:

16(2). No citizen shall, on grounds only of religion, race, caste, sex, descent, place of birth, residence or any of them, be ineligible for, or discriminated against in respect or, any employment or office under the State.

Article 16 not only prohibits discrimination on the ground of sex in public employment, but also imposes a duty on the State to ensure that all citizens are treated equally in matters relating to employment and appointment by the State.

Articles 15 and 16 sought to prohibit discrimination on the basis of sex, recognizing that sex discrimination is a historical fact and needs to be addressed. Constitution makers, it can be gathered, gave emphasis to the fundamental right[56] against sex discrimination so as to prevent the direct or indirect attitude to treat people differently, for the reason of not being in conformity with stereotypical[57] generalizations of binary genders. Both gender and biological attributes constitute distinct components of sex. Biological characteristics, of course, include genitals, chromosomes[58] and secondary sexual features, but gender attributes

---

56 **Meaning of Fundamental Rights:** The Fundamental Rights are defined as basic human freedoms which every Indian citizen has the right to enjoy for a proper and harmonious development of personality. These rights universally apply to all citizens, irrespective of race, place of birth, religion, caste, creed, colour or gender. Aliens (persons who are not citizens) are also considered in matters like equality before law. They are enforceable by the courts, subject to certain restrictions

57 **Meaning of stereotypical:**

   1. A conventional, formulaic, and oversimplified conception, opinion, or image.

   2. One that is regarded as embodying or conforming to a set image or type

58 **Meaning of chromosomes:** one of a set of threadlike structures, composed of DNA and a protein, that form in the nucleus when the cell begins to divide and that carry the genes which determine an individual's hereditary traits.

include one's self image, the deep psychological or emotional sense of sexual identity and character. The discrimination on the ground of 'sex' under Articles 15 and 16, therefore, includes discrimination on the ground of gender identity. The expression 'sex' used in Articles 15 and 16 is not just limited to biological sex of male or female, but intended to include people who consider themselves to be neither male or female.

TGs have been systematically denied the rights under Article 15(2) that is not to be subjected to any disability, liability, restriction or condition in regard to access to public places. TGs have also not been afforded special provisions envisaged Under Article 15(4) for the advancement of the socially and educationally backward classes (SEBC) of citizens, which they are, and hence legally entitled and eligible to get the benefits of SEBC. State is bound to take some affirmative action for their advancement so that the injustice done to them for centuries could be remedied. TGs are also entitled to enjoy economic, social, cultural and political rights without discrimination, because forms of discrimination on the ground of gender are violative of fundamental freedoms and human rights. TGs have also been denied rights under Article 16(2) and discriminated against in respect of employment or office under the State on the ground of sex. TGs are also entitled to reservation in the matter of appointment, as envisaged Under Article 16(4) of the Constitution. State is bound to take affirmative action to give them due representation in public services.

Articles 15(2) to (4) and Article 16(4) read with the Directive Principles of State Policy[59] and various international instruments to which Indian is a party, call for social equality, which the TGs could realize, only if facilities and opportunities are extended to them so that they can also live with dignity and equal status with other genders.

---

59 The **Directive Principles of State Policy** are guidelines to the central and state governments of India, to be kept in mind while framing laws and policies. These provisions, contained in Part IV of the Constitution of India, are not enforceable by any court, but the principles laid down therein are considered fundamental in the governance of the country, making it the duty of the State to apply these principles in making laws to establish a just society in the country. The principles have been inspired by the Directive Principles given in the Constitution of Ireland and also by the principles of Gandhism; and relate to social justice, economic welfare, foreign policy, and legal and administrative matters.

Article 19(1)(a)[60] of the Constitution and Transgenders:

Article 19(1) of the Constitution guarantees certain fundamental rights, subject to the power of the State to impose restrictions from exercise of those rights. The rights conferred by Article 19 are not available to any person who is not a citizen of India. Article 19(1) guarantees those great basic rights which are recognized and guaranteed as the natural rights inherent in the status of the citizen of a free country. Article 19(1)(a) of

---

60   **Article 19 in The Constitution Of India 1949**

19. Protection of certain rights regarding freedom of speech etc

(1) All citizens shall have the right

(a) to freedom of speech and expression;

(b) to assemble peaceably and without arms;

(c) to form associations or unions;

(d) to move freely throughout the territory of India;

(e) to reside and settle in any part of the territory of India; and

(f) omitted

(g) to practise any profession, or to carry on any occupation, trade or business

(2) Nothing in sub clause (a) of clause (1) shall affect the operation of any existing law, or prevent the State from making any law, in so far as such law imposes reasonable restrictions on the exercise of the right conferred by the said sub clause in the interests of the sovereignty and integrity of India, the security of the State, friendly relations with foreign States, public order, decency or morality or in relation to contempt of court, defamation or incitement to an offence

(3) Nothing in sub clause (b) of the said clause shall affect the operation of any existing law in so far as it imposes, or prevent the State from making any law imposing, in the interests of the sovereignty and integrity of India or public order, reasonable restrictions on the exercise of the right conferred by the said sub clause

(4) Nothing in sub clause (c) of the said clause shall affect the operation of any existing law in so far as it imposes, or prevent the State from making any law imposing, in the interests of the sovereignty and integrity of India or public order or morality, reasonable restrictions on the exercise of the right conferred by the said sub clause

(5) Nothing in sub clauses (d) and (e) of the said clause shall affect the operation of any existing law in so far as it imposes, or prevent the State from making any law imposing, reasonable restrictions on the exercise of any of the rights conferred by the said sub clauses either in the interests of the general public or for the protection of the interests of any Scheduled Tribe

(6) Nothing in sub clause (g) of the said clause shall affect the operation of any existing law in so far as it imposes, or prevent the State from making any law imposing, in the interests of the general public, reasonable restrictions on the exercise of the right conferred by the said sub clause, and, in particular, nothing in the said sub clause shall affect the operation of any existing law in so far as it relates to, or prevent the State from making any law relating to,

(i) the professional or technical qualifications necessary for practising any profession or carrying on any occupation, trade or business, or

(ii) the carrying on by the State, or by a corporation owned or controlled by the State, of any trade, business, industry or service, whether to the exclusion, complete or partial, of citizens or otherwise

the Constitution states that all citizens shall have the right to freedom of speech and expression, which includes one's right to expression of his self-identified gender. Self-identified gender can be expressed through dress, words, action or behavior or any other form. No restriction can be placed on one's personal appearance or choice of dressing, subject to the restrictions contained in Article 19(2) of the Constitution.

Gender identity, therefore, lies at the core of one's personal identity, gender expression and presentation and, therefore, it will have to be protected Under Article 19(1)(a) of the Constitution of India. A transgender's personality could be expressed by the transgender's behavior and presentation. State cannot prohibit, restrict or interfere with a transgender's expression of such personality, which reflects that inherent personality. Often the State and its authorities either due to ignorance or otherwise fail to digest the innate character and identity of such persons. Values of privacy, self-identity, autonomy and personal integrity are fundamental rights guaranteed to members of the transgender community Under Article 19(1)(a) of the Constitution of India and the State is bound to protect and recognize those rights.

Article 21 of the Constitution and the Transgenders:

Article 21 of the Constitution of India reads as follows:

21. Protection of life and personal liberty-No person shall be deprived of his life or personal liberty except according to procedure established by law.

Article 21 is the heart and soul of the Indian Constitution, which speaks of the rights to life and personal liberty. Right to life is one of the basic fundamental rights and not even the State has the authority to violate or take away that right. Article 21 takes all those aspects of life which go to make a person's life meaningful. Article 21 protects the dignity of human life, one's personal autonomy, one's right to privacy, etc. Right to dignity has been recognized to be an essential part of the right to life and accrues to all persons on account of being humans. In *Francis Coralie Mullin v. Administrator, Union Territory of Delhi*[61] Court held that the right to dignity forms an essential part of our constitutional culture which seeks to ensure the full development and evolution of persons and includes "expressing oneself in diverse forms, freely moving about and mixing and

---

61   (1981) 1 SCC 608

commingling with fellow human beings". Recognition of one's gender identity lies at the heart of the fundamental right to dignity. Gender constitutes the core of one's sense of being as well as an integral part of a person's identity. Legal recognition of gender identity is, therefore, part of right to dignity and freedom guaranteed under our Constitution.

Legal Recognition of Third/Transgender Identity:

Self-identified gender can be either male or female or a third gender. Hijras are identified as persons of third gender and are not identified either as male or female. Gender identity refers to a person's internal sense of being male, female or a transgender, for example Hijras do not identify as female because of their lack of female genitalia or lack of reproductive capability. This distinction makes them separate from both male and female genders and they consider themselves neither man nor woman, but a "third gender". Hijras, therefore, belong to a distinct socio-religious and cultural group and have, therefore, to be considered as a "third gender", apart from male and female. State of Punjab has treated all TGs as male which is not legally sustainable. State of Tamil Nadu has taken lot of welfare measures to safeguard the rights of TGs, which we have to acknowledge. Few States like Kerala, Tripura, Bihar have referred TGs as "third gender or sex". Certain States recognize them as "third category". Few benefits have also been extended by certain other States. Our neighbouring countries have also upheld their fundamental rights and right to live with dignity.

The Supreme Court of Nepal in *Sunil Babu Pant and Ors. v. Nepal Government*[62] spoke on the rights of Transgenders as follows:

The homosexuals and third gender people are also human beings as other men and women, and they are the citizens of this country as well. Thus, the people other than 'men' and 'women', including the people of 'third gender' cannot be discriminated. The State should recognize the existence of all natural persons including the people of third gender other than the men and women.

The Supreme Court of Pakistan in *Dr. Mohammad Aslam Khaki and Anr. v. Senior Superintendent of Police (Operation) Rawalpindi and Ors.*[63], had occasion to consider the rights of eunuchs and held as follows:

The Government functionaries both at federal and provincial levels are

---

62   Writ Petition No. 917 of 2007 decided on 21st December, 2007

63   (Constitution Petition No. 43 of 2009) decided on 22nd March, 2011

bound to provide them (Eunuchs) protection of life and property and secure their dignity as well, as is done in case of other citizens.

Directions by Supreme Court:

Court directed that:

(1) Hijras, Eunuchs, apart from binary gender, be treated as "third gender" for the purpose of safeguarding their rights under Part III of our Constitution and the laws made by the Parliament and the State Legislature.

(2) Transgender persons' right to decide their self-identified gender was also upheld and the Centre and State Governments were directed to grant legal recognition of their gender identity such as male, female or as third gender.

(3) Court directed the Centre and the State Governments to take steps to treat them (TGs) as socially and educationally backward classes of citizens and extend all kinds of reservation in cases of admission in educational institutions and for public appointments.

(4) Centre and State Governments were directed to operate separate HIV Sero-surveillance Centres since Hijras/Transgenders face several sexual health issues.

(5) Centre and State Governments were directed to seriously address the problems being faced by Hijras/Transgenders such as fear, shame, gender dysphoria[64], social pressure, depression, suicidal tendencies, social stigma, etc. and any insistence for SRS for declaring one's gender is immoral and illegal.

(6) Centre and State Governments were directed to take proper measures to provide medical care to TGs in the hospitals and also provide them separate public toilets and other facilities.

(7) Centre and State Governments were directed to take steps for framing various social welfare schemes for their betterment.

(8) Centre and State Governments were directed to create public awareness so that TGs will feel that they are also part and parcel of the social life and be not treated as untouchables.

---

64 **Meaning of dysphoria:** An emotional state characterized by anxiety, depression, or unease.

(9) Centre and the State Governments were directed to take measures to regain their respect (TGs) and place in the society which once they enjoyed in our cultural and social life.

36

Cinemas cannot run without obtaining license from the Licensing Authority[1]

Ratio Decidendi[2]: "There must be close or direct proximity[3] to acts of Licensing Authority and fire accident and death/injuries of victims to pay compensation to its claimant[4] must be granted according to facts and circumstances of case"

Facts in Nutshell:

During the matinee show[5] of a newly released film on 13.6.1997, Fire breakout at Uphaar Cinema Theatre in Green Park, South Delhi, resulting in the death of 59 patrons[6] and injury to 103 patrons. Shortly after the interval, a transformer of Delhi Vidyut Board installed in the ground floor parking area of Uphaar Cinema caught fire. The oil from the transformer leaked and found its way to the passage outside where many cars were parked. Two cars were parked immediately adjoining the entrance of the transformer room. The burning oil spread the fire to nearby cars and from then to the other parked cars. The burning of (i) the transformer oil (ii) the diesel and petrol from the parked vehicles (iii) the upholstery material,

---

1   Appellants: **Municipal Corporation of Delhi, Delhi Vs.** Respondent: **Association of Victims of Uphaar Tragedy and Ors.**

    AIR2012SC100

    Hon'ble Judges/Coram: R.V. Raveendran and K.S. Panicker Radhakrishnan, JJ.

2   **Meaning of Ration Decidendi:** *Ratio decidendi* is a Latin phrase meaning "the reason" or "the rationale for the decision." The *ratio decidendi* is "the point in a case which determines the judgment" or "the principle which the case establishes."

3   **Meaning of Proximity:** The state, quality, sense, or fact of being near or next; closeness

4   **Meaning of Claimant:** A party that makes a claim

5   **Meaning of Matinee Show:** An entertainment, such as a dramatic performance or movie, presented in the daytime, usually in the afternoon

6   **Meaning of Patron:**

    1. One that supports, protects, or champions someone or something, such as an institution, event, or cause; a sponsor or benefactor

    2. A customer, especially a regular customer

paint and other chemicals of the vehicles and (iv) foam and other articles stored in the said parking area generated huge quantity of fumes and smoke which consisted of carbon monoxide[7] and several poisonous gases. As the ground floor parking was covered all round by walls, and the air was blowing in from the entry and exit points, the smoke and noxious fumes/smoke could not find its way out into open atmosphere and was blown towards the staircase leading to the balcony exit. On account of the chimney effect, the smoke travelled up. Smoke also travelled to the air-conditioner ducts and was sucked in and released into the auditorium. The smoke and the noxious fumes stagnated in the upper reaches of the auditorium, particularly in the balcony area. By then the electricity went off and the exit signs were also not operating or visible. The patrons in the balcony, who were affected by the fumes, were groping[8] in the dark to get out. The central gangway[9] in the balcony that led to the Entrance foyer[10] could have been an effective and easy exit, but it was closed and bolted from outside, as that door was used only for entry into the balcony from the foyer. The patrons therefore groped through towards the only exit situated on the left side top corner of the balcony. The staircase outside the balcony exit which was the only way out was also full of noxious[11] fumes and smoke. They could not get out of the staircase into the foyer as the door was closed and locked. This resulted in death of 59 persons in the balcony and stairwell due to asphyxiation[12] by inhaling the noxious fumes/smoke. 103 patrons were also injured in trying to get out.

First Respondent[13], an association of the victims of Uphaar Tragedy (for

---

7   **Carbon monoxide** (CO) is a colorless, odorless, and tasteless gas that is slightly less dense than air. It is toxic to humans and animals when encountered in higher concentrations, although it is also produced in normal animal metabolism in low quantities, and is thought to have some normal biological functions.

8   **Meaning of Groping:** Acting with uncertainty or hesitance or lack of confidence

9   **Meaning of Gangway:** A raised platform or walkway providing a passage.

10 **Meaning of Foyer:**

    1. A lobby or anteroom, as of a theater or hotel.

    2. An entrance hall; a vestibule

11 **Meaning of Noxious:**

    1. Harmful to living things; injurious to health

    2. Harmful to the mind or morals; corrupting

12 **Meaning of asphyxiation:** The condition of being deprived of oxygen

13 **Meaning of Respondent:** A **respondent** is a person who is called upon to issue a response to a communication made by another. In legal usage, this specifically refers to the defendant in a legal proceeding commenced by a petition, or to an appellee, or the opposing party, in an appeal of a

short the 'Victims Association' or 'Association'). The members of the Association were either those who were injured in the fire or were relatives/legal heirs of those who were killed in the fire. The Association filed a writ petition[14] before the Delhi High Court. They highlighted the shocking state of affairs existing in the cinema building at the time of the incident and the inadequate safety arrangements made by the owners. They described the several violations by the owners of the statutory obligations placed on theatre owners under law, for prevention of fire hazards in public places. They highlighted the acts of omission[15] and commission by the public authorities concerned namely Delhi Vidyut Board ('DVB' for short), MCD Fire Force and the Licensing Authority. They alleged that these authorities not only failed in the discharge of their statutory obligations, but acted in a manner which was prejudicial to public interest by failing to observe the standards set under the statute[16] and the rules framed for the purpose of preventing fire hazards; that they issued licenses and permits in complete disregard of the mandatory conditions of inspection which were required to ensure that the minimum safeguards were provided in the cinema theatre. They pointed out that most of the cinema theatres were and are being permitted to run without any proper inspection and many a time without the required licenses, permissions and clearances. They therefore, sought adequate compensation for the victims of the tragedy and punitive damages against the theatre owner, DVB, MCD, Fire Force and the Licensing Authority

---

decision by an initial fact-finder

14 **Meaning of Writ Petition:** Under the Indian legal system, jurisdiction to issue 'prerogative writs' is given to the Supreme Court, and to the High Courts of Judicature of all Indian states. Parts of the law relating to writs are set forth in the Constitution of India. The Supreme Court, the highest in the country, may issue writs under Article 32 of the Constitution for enforcement of Fundamental Rights and under Articles 139 for enforcement of rights other than Fundamental Rights, while High Courts, the superior courts of the States, may issue writs under Articles 226. 'Writ' is eminently designed by the makers of the Constitution, and in the same way it is developed very widely and efficiently by the courts in India. The Constitution broadly provides for five kinds of "prerogative" writs, namely, Habeas Corpus, Certiorari, Mandamus, Quo Warranto and Prohibition

15 **Meaning of Omission:**

1. The act or an instance of omitting.

2. The state of having been omitted.

3. Something omitted or neglected

16 **Meaning of Statue:**

1. A law enacted by a legislature.

2. A decree or edict, as of a ruler

for showing callous[17] disregard to their statutory obligations and to the fundamental and indefeasible[18] rights guaranteed under Article 21[19] of the Constitution of India, of the theatre going public, in failing to provide safe premises, free from reasonably foreseeable hazards. They claimed compensation and other relief's as under:

(a) award damages of Rs. 11.8 crores against the Respondents, jointly and severally, to the legal heirs of the victims who lost their lives through the Association with the direction to equally distribute the same to the first degree heirs of all the victims

(b) award damages of Rs. 10.3 crores against the Respondents, jointly and severally, to the injured to be distributed evenly or in such manner as may be considered just and proper

(c) award punitive damages[20] of Rs. 100 crores to the association for setting up and running a Centralized Accident and Trauma Services and other allied services in the city of Delhi; and to direct Union of India to create a fund for that purpose;

(d) to monitor the investigation from time to time, to ensure that no person guilty of any of the offences is able to escape the clutches[21] of law and that the investigation is carried out as expeditiously as possible in a free and fair manner; and

(e) direct the Union of India to ensure that no cinema hall in the country is allowed to run without license granted after strictly observing all the

---

17 **Meaning of Callous:**

    1. Having calluses; toughened

    2. Emotionally hardened; unfeeling

18 **Meaning of indefeasible:**

    That cannot be annulled or made void

19 **Article 21 in The Constitution Of India 1949**

    Protection of life and personal liberty: No person shall be deprived of his life or personal liberty except according to procedure established by law

20 **Punitive damages** or **exemplary damages** are damages intended to reform or deter the defendant and others from engaging in conduct similar to that which formed the basis of the lawsuit. Although the purpose of punitive damages is not to compensate the plaintiff, the plaintiff will receive all or some portion of the punitive damage award. Punitive damages are often awarded where compensatory damages are deemed an inadequate remedy

21 **Meaning of Clutch:**

    1. To grasp and hold tightly

    2. To seize; snatch

mandatory conditions prescribed under the laws and to further direct them to stop the operation of all cinema halls and to permit the operation only after verification of the existence of a valid license/permit by the licensing authority, under the Cinematograph Act, 1952.

Decision by High Court:

The High Court allowed the writ petition by order dated 24.4.2003. In the said order, the High Court identified the causes that led to the calamity and persons responsible therefore. It was held by High Court that the theatre owner, DVB, MCD and the Licensing Authority were responsible for the fire tragedy. It exonerated[22] the Delhi Fire Force.

Acts/omissions by Delhi Vidyut Board (DVB):

DVB violated several provisions of the Electricity Act and the Rules. It had not obtained the approval of the Electrical Inspector for installation of the transformer as required under the Rules. The Rules required that the floor of the transformer room should be at a higher level than the surrounding areas and there should be a channel for draining of oil with a pit so that any leaking oil would not spread outside, increasing the fire hazard, and also to ensure that water did not enter the transformer. The transformer had to be checked periodically and subjected to regular maintenance and should have appropriate covers. The connecting of wires should be by crimping and not by hammering. The negligence on the part of DVB in maintaining the transformers and repairs led to the root cause of the incident, namely the starting of the fire.

Acts/Omissions of owner

Though the starting of the fire in the transformer happened due to the negligence of DVB, but if the owner had taken the necessary usual precautions and security measures expected of a theatre owner, even if the transformer had caught fire, it would not have spread to nearby cars or other stored articles nor would the balcony and staircases become a death trap on account of the fumes.

The High Court held that the theatre owner (Licencee), DVB, MCD and Licensing Authority being responsible for the incident were jointly and

---

22 **Meaning of exonerate:**

   1. To free from blame.

   2. To free from a responsibility, obligation, or task.

severally liable to compensate the victims. The High Court directed payment of compensation to the legal heirs of 59 patrons who died, and also to the 103 persons who were injured. The High Court determined a uniform compensation of Rs. 18 lakhs payable in the case of deceased[23] who were aged more than 20 years, and 15 lakhs each in the case of those deceased who were less than 20 years of age. It also awarded a compensation of Rs. 1,00,000 to each of the 103 injured. The High Court directed that the Licensee shall pay Rs. 2,50,00,000/- (Rupees two and half crores) as punitive damages. The said amount was ordered to be paid to Union of India for setting up a Central Accident Trauma Centre. The Delhi Vidyut Board accepted the judgment and deposited 15% of the total compensation. The theatre owner, Delhi Police and MCD have not accepted the judgment and have filed appeals[24] in Supreme Court denying there liability.

Decision by Supreme Court:

Supreme Court reduced the punitive damages awarded by High Court of Delhi from Rs. 2.5 crores to Rs. 25 lakhs. Court rejected the writ petition filed by the Victims Association on behalf of the victims, to the extent it seeks compensation from MCD and Licensing Authority. The licensee and Delhi Vidyut Board were held jointly and severally liable to compensate the victims of the Uphaar fire tragedy. Though their liability was joint and several, as between them, the liability shall be 85% on the part the licensee and 15% on the part of DVB. The compensation awarded by the High Court in the case of death was reduced from Rs. 18 lacs to Rs. 10 lacs (in the case of those aged more than 20 years) and Rs. 15 lacs to Rs. 7.5 lacs (in the case of those aged 20 years and less). The said sum was payable to legal representatives of the deceased to be determined by a brief and summary enquiry by the Registrar General (or nominee of learned Chief Justice/Acting Chief Justice of the Delhi High Court).The compensation of Rs. One lakh awarded by the High Court in the case of each of the 103 injured persons was affirmed. Court further held that the injured victims who were not satisfied with the award of Rs. One lakh as compensation, may approach the civil court.

---

23 **Meaning of Deceased:** No longer living; dead.

24 **Meaning of Appeal:** In law, an **appeal** is a process for requesting a formal change to an official decision. Very broadly speaking there are appeals on the record and *de novo* appeals. In *de novo* appeals, a new decision maker re-hears the case without any reference to the prior decision maker. In appeals on the record, the decision of the prior decision maker is challenged by arguing that he or she misapplied the law, came to an incorrect factual finding, acted in excess of his jurisdiction, abused his powers, was biased, considered evidence which he should not have considered or failed to consider evidence that he should have considered.

General observations and suggestions by Supreme Court:

The Parliament has enacted the Disaster Management Act, 2005. Section 1(3) the Disaster Management Act, 2005 thereof provides that it shall come into force on such dates as the Central Government may by notification in the Official Gazette appoint; and different dates may be appointed for different provisions of the Act for different States, and any reference to commencement in any provisions of the Act in relation to any State shall be construed as a reference to the commencement of that provision in that State. All the provisions of the Act have not been brought into effect in all the States. Having regard to the object of the Act, bringing the Act into force promptly would be in public interest. In so far as Delhi is concerned, by notification dated 19.3.2008, the Government of NCT of Delhi has established the Delhi Disaster Management Authority for the national capital territory of Delhi. A disaster management helpline number has been made operational. Emergency operating centre and relief centres have been established. A State Disaster Response Force has been established. Several volunteers have been given training in disaster management. Attempts are being made to hold regular mockdrills in regard to various types of disasters (like earthquakes, flood, fire, road accidents, industrial and chemical disasters, terrorists attacks, gas leaks etc.). Steps are taken to contact the public in regard to several natural and man-made disasters. The key to successfully meeting the consequences of disasters is preparedness. There can be no complacency. Human tendency is to be awake and aware in the immediate aftermath of a disaster. But as the days pass, slowly the disaster management equipment and disaster management personnel allowed to slip away from their readiness. Only when the next disaster takes place, there is sudden awakening. In regard to preparedness to meet disasters there could be no let up in the vigil. The expenditure required for maintaining a high state of alert and readiness to meet disasters may appear to be high and wasteful regarding 'non-disaster periods' but the expenditure and readiness is absolutely must. Be that as it may.

Supreme Court suggestions to the government for consideration and implementation:

(i) Every licensee (cinema theatre) shall be required to draw up an emergency evacuation plan and get it approved by the licensing authority.

(ii) Every cinema theatre shall be required to screen a short documentary during every show showing the exits, emergency escape routes and instructions as to what to do and what not to do in the case of fire or other hazards.

(iii) The staff/ushers in every cinema theatre should be trained in fire drills and evacuation procedures to provide support to the patrons in case of fire or other calamity.

(iv) While the theatres are entitled to regulate the exit through doors other than the entry door, under no circumstances, the entry door (which can act as an emergency exit) in the event of fire or other emergency) should be bolted from outside. At the end of the show, the ushers may request the patrons to use the exit doors by placing a temporary barrier across the entry gate which should be easily movable.

(v) There should be mandatory half yearly inspections of cinema theatres by a senior officer from the Delhi Fire Services, Electrical Inspectorate and the Licensing Authority to verify whether the electrical installations and safety measures are properly functioning and take action wherever necessary.

(vi) As the cinema theatres have undergone a change in the last decade with more and more multiplexes coming up, separate rules should be made for Multiplex Cinemas whose requirements and concerns are different from stand-alone cinema theatres.

(vii) An endeavour should be made to have a single point nodal agency/licensing authority consisting of experts in structural Engineering/building, fire prevention, electrical systems etc. The existing system of police granting licences should be abolished.

(viii) Each cinema theatre, whether it is a multiplex or stand-alone theatre should be given a fire safety rating by the Fire Services which can be in green (fully compliant), yellow (satisfactorily compliant), red (poor compliance). The rating should be prominently displayed in each theatre so that there is awareness among the patrons and the building owners.

(ix) The Delhi Disaster Management Authority, established by the Government of NCT of Delhi may expeditiously evolve standards to manage the disasters relating to cinema theatres and the guidelines in regard to ex gratia assistance. It should be directed to conduct mock drills in each cinema theatre at least once in a year.

37

All live-in-relationships are not relationships in the nature of marriage[1]

Facts in Nutshell:

Appellant[2] and Respondent[3] were working together in a private company. The Respondent, (V.K.V. Sarma) who was working as a Personal Officer of the Company, was a married person having two children and the Appellant (Indra Sarma), aged 33 years, was unmarried. Constant contacts between them developed intimacy and in the year 1992, Appellant left the job from the above-mentioned Company and started living with the Respondent in a shared household. Appellant's family members, including her father, brother and sister, and also the wife of the Respondent, opposed that live-in-relationship. After some time, the Respondent shifted the business to his residence and continued the business with the help of his son, thereby depriving her (Indra Sarma) right of working and earning. Appellant (Indra Sarma) also stated that both of them (V.K.V Sarma and Indra Sarma) lived together in a shared household and, due to their relationship, Appellant (Indra Sarma) became pregnant on three occasions, though all resulted in abortion. Appellant (Indra Sarma) also stated that respondent (V.K.V Sarma) forced her to take contraceptive methods to avoid pregnancy. Further, it was also stated that the Respondent (V.K.V. Sarma) took a sum of Rs. 1,00,000/- from the Appellant (Indra Sarma) stating that he would buy a land in her name, but the same was not done. Appellant (Indra Sarma) also alleged that, during the year 2006, Respondent (V.K.V

---

1   Appellants: **Indra Sarma Vs.** Respondent: **V.K.V. Sarma**

2013(14)SCALE448, 2014(1)BomCR(Cri)496

Hon'ble Judges/Coram: K.S. Panicker Radhakrishnan and Pinaki Chandra Ghose, JJ.

2   **Meaning of Appellant:** A person who dissatisfied with the judgment rendered in a lawsuit decided in a lower court or the findings from a proceeding before an Administrative Agency, asks a superior court to review the decision

3   **Meaning of Respondent:** A **respondent** is a person who is called upon to issue a response to a communication made by another. In legal usage, this specifically refers to the defendant in a legal proceeding commenced by a petition, or to an appellee, or the opposing party, in an appeal of a decision by an initial fact-finder

Sarma) took a loan of Rs. 2,50,000/- from her and had not returned. Further, it was also stated that the Respondent (V.K.V Sarma), all along, was harassing the Appellant (Indra Sarma) by not exposing her as his wife publicly, or permitting to suffix his name after the name of the Appellant. Respondent's (V.K.V Sarma) family constantly opposed their live-in relationship and ultimately forced him to leave the company of the Appellant (Indra Sarma) and it was alleged that he (V.K.V Sarma) left the company of the Appellant (Indra Sarma) without maintaining her. Appellant (Indra Sarma) then preferred petition[4] Under Section 12[5] of

---

4   **Meaning of Petition:** A formal message requesting something that is submitted to an authority

5   **Section 12 in The Protection of Women from Domestic Violence Act, 2005**

12. Application to Magistrate:

(1) An aggrieved person or a Protection Officer or any other person on behalf of the aggrieved person may present an application to the Magistrate seeking one or more reliefs under this Act: tc "12. Application to Magistrate.—(1) An aggrieved person or a Protection Officer or any other person on behalf of the aggrieved person may present an application to the Magistrate seeking one or more reliefs under this Act\:" Provided that before passing any order on such application, the Magistrate shall take into consideration any domestic incident report received by him from the Protection Officer or the service provider. tc "Provided that before passing any order on such application, the Magistrate shall take into consideration any domestic incident report received by him from the Protection Officer or the service provider."

(2) The relief sought for under sub-section (1) may include a relief for issuance of an order for payment of compensation or damages without prejudice to the right of such person to institute a suit for compensation or damages for the injuries caused by the acts of domestic violence committed by the respondent: tc "(2) The relief sought for under sub-section (1) may include a relief for issuance of an order for payment of compensation or damages without prejudice to the right of such person to institute a suit for compensation or damages for the injuries caused by the acts of domestic violence committed by the respondent\:" Provided that where a decree for any amount as compensation or damages has been passed by any court in favour of the aggrieved person, the amount, if any, paid or payable in pursuance of the order made by the Magistrate under this Act shall be set off against the amount payable under such decree and the decree shall, notwithstanding anything contained in the Code of Civil Procedure, 1908 (5 of 1908), or any other law for the time being in force, be executable for the balance amount, if any, left after s uch set off. tc "Provided that where a decree for any amount as compensation or damages has been passed by any court in favour of the aggrieved person, the amount, if any, paid or payable in pursuance of the order made by the Magistrate under this Act shall be set off against the amount payable under such decree and the decree shall, notwithstanding anything contained in the Code of Civil Procedure, 1908 (5 of 1908), or any other law for the time being in force, be executable for the balance amount, if any, left after such set off."

(3) Every application under sub-section (1) shall be in such form and contain such particulars as may be prescribed or as nearly as possible thereto. tc "(3) Every application under sub-section (1) shall be in such form and contain such particulars as may be prescribed or as nearly as possible thereto."

(4) The Magistrate shall fix the first date of hearing, which shall not ordinarily be beyond three days from the date of receipt of the application by the court. tc "(4) The Magistrate shall fix the first date of hearing, which shall not ordinarily be beyond three days from the date of receipt of the application by the court."

(5) The Magistrate shall endeavour to dispose of every application made under sub-section (1) within a period of sixty days from the date of its first hearing. tc "(5) The Magistrate shall

the Domestic Violence Act, 2005 (DV, Act, 2005) before the III Additional Chief Metropolitan Magistrate, Bangalore.

Decision by Learned Additional Chief Metropolitan Magistrate and Appellate Court:

The learned Magistrate found proof that the parties had lived together for a considerable period of time, for about 18 years, and then the Respondent (V.K.V Sarma) left the company of the Appellant (Indra Sarma) without maintaining her. Learned Magistrate took the view that the plea of "domestic violence" had been established, due to the non-maintenance of the Appellant (Indra Sarma) and passed the order directing the Respondent (V.K.V Sarma) to pay an amount of Rs. 18,000/- per month towards maintenance from the date of the petition.

Respondent (V.K.V Sarma), aggrieved by the said order of the learned Magistrate, filed an appeal[6] before the Sessions Court under Section 29[7] of the DV Act, 2005. The Appellate Court, after having noticed that the Respondent (V.K.V Sarma) had admitted the relationship with Appellant for over a period of 14 years, took the view that, due to their live-in relationship for a considerable long period, non-maintenance of the Appellant would amount to domestic violence within the meaning of Section 3[8] of the DV Act, 2005. The appellate Court also concluded

---

endeavour to dispose of every application made under sub-section (1) within a period of sixty days from the date of its first hearing."

6   **Meaning of Appeal:** In law, an **appeal** is a process for requesting a formal change to an official decision. Very broadly speaking there are appeals on the record and *de novo* appeals. In *de novo* appeals, a new decision maker re-hears the case without any reference to the prior decision maker. In appeals on the record, the decision of the prior decision maker is challenged by arguing that he or she misapplied the law, came to an incorrect factual finding, acted in excess of his jurisdiction, abused his powers, was biased, considered evidence which he should not have considered or failed to consider evidence that he should have considered

7   **Section 29 in The Protection of Women from Domestic Violence Act, 2005**

     Appeal: There shall lie an appeal to the Court of Session within thirty days from the date on which the order made by the Magistrate is served on the aggrieved person or the respondent, as the case may be, whichever is later. tc "29. Appeal.—There shall lie an appeal to the Court of Session within thirty days from the date on which the order made by the Magistrate is served on the aggrieved person or the respondent, as the case may be, whichever is later."

8   **Section 3 in The Protection of Women from Domestic Violence Act, 2005**

     3. Definition of domestic violence.—For the purposes of this Act, any act, omission or commission or conduct of the respondent shall constitute domestic violence in case it— tc "3. Definition of domestic violence.—For the purposes of this Act, any act, omission or commission or conduct of the respondent shall constitute domestic violence in case it—"

     (a) harms or injures or endangers the health, safety, life, limb or well-being, whether mental or physical, of the aggrieved person or tends to do so and includes causing physical abuse, sexual abuse, verbal and emotional abuse and economic abuse; or tc" (a) harms or injures or endangers the health, safety, life, limb or well-being, whether mental or physical, of the aggrieved person or tends to do so and includes causing physical abuse, sexual abuse, verbal and emotional abuse and economic abuse; or"

(b) harasses, harms, injures or endangers the aggrieved person with a view to coerce her or any other person related to her to meet any unlawful demand for any dowry or other property or valuable security; or tc" (b) harasses, harms, injures or endangers the aggrieved person with a view to coerce her or any other person related to her to meet any unlawful demand for any dowry or other property or valuable security; or"

(c) has the effect of threatening the aggrieved person or any person related to her by any conduct mentioned in clause (a) or clause (b); or tc" (c) has the effect of threatening the aggrieved person or any person related to her by any conduct mentioned in clause (a) or clause (b); or"

(d) otherwise injures or causes harm, whether physical or mental, to the aggrieved person. tc" (d) otherwise injures or causes harm, whether physical or mental, to the aggrieved person." Explanation I.—For the purposes of this section,— tc "Explanation I.—For the purposes of this section,—"

(i) "physical abuse" means any act or conduct which is of such a nature as to cause bodily pain, harm, or danger to life, limb, or health or impair the health or development of the aggrieved person and includes assault, criminal intimidation and criminal force; tc" (i) "physical abuse" means any act or conduct which is of such a nature as to cause bodily pain, harm, or danger to life, limb, or health or impair the health or development of the aggrieved person and includes assault, criminal intimidation and criminal force;"

(ii) "sexual abuse" includes any conduct of a sexual nature that abuses, humiliates, degrades or otherwise violates the dignity of woman; tc" (ii) "sexual abuse" includes any conduct of a sexual nature that abuses, humiliates, degrades or otherwise violates the dignity of woman;"

(iii) "verbal and emotional abuse" includes— tc" (iii) "verbal and emotional abuse" includes—"

(a) insults, ridicule, humiliation, name calling and insults or ridicule specially with regard to not having a child or a male child; and tc" (a) insults, ridicule, humiliation, name calling and insults or ridicule specially with regard to not having a child or a male child; and"

(b) repeated threats to cause physical pain to any person in whom the aggrieved person is interested. tc" (b) repeated threats to cause physical pain to any person in whom the aggrieved person is interested."

(iv) "economic abuse" includes— tc" (iv) "economic abuse" includes—"

(a) deprivation of all or any economic or financial resources to which the aggrieved person is entitled under any law or custom whether payable under an order of a court or otherwise or which the aggrieved person requires out of necessity including, but not limited to, household necessities for the aggrieved person and her children, if any, stridhan, property, jointly or separately owned by the aggrieved person, payment of rental related to the shared household and maintenance; tc" (a) deprivation of all or any economic or financial resources to which the aggrieved person is entitled under any law or custom whether payable under an order of a court or otherwise or which the aggrieved person requires out of necessity including, but not limited to, household necessities for the aggrieved person and her children, if any, stridhan, property, jointly or separately owned by the aggrieved person, payment of rental related to the shared household and maintenance;"

(b) disposal of household effects, any alienation of assets whether movable or immovable, valuables, shares, securities, bonds and the like or other property in which the aggrieved person has an interest or is entitled to use by virtue of the domestic relationship or which may be reasonably required by the aggrieved person or her children or her stridhan or any other property jointly or separately held by the aggrieved person; and tc" (b) disposal of household effects, any alienation of assets whether movable or immovable, valuables, shares, securities, bonds and the like or other property in which the aggrieved person has an interest or is entitled to use by

that the Appellant (Indra Sarma) has no source of income and that the Respondent (V.K.V Sarma) was legally obliged to maintain her and confirmed the order passed by the learned Magistrate.

Decision by High Court:

The Respondent (V.K.V Sarma) took up the matter in appeal before the High Court. It was contended before the High Court that the Appellant (Indra Sarma) was aware of the fact that the Respondent was a married person having two children, yet she developed a relationship, in spite of the opposition raised by the wife of the Respondent (V.K.V Sarma) and also by the Appellant's (Indra Sarma) parents. The High Court held that the relationship between the parties would not fall within the ambit of "relationship in the nature of marriage". Consequently, the High Court allowed the appeal and set aside the order passed by the Courts i.e Learned Magistrate court and Appellate Court. Aggrieved by the same Appellant (Indra Sarma) preferred appeal before Supreme Court.

Question before the Supreme Court:

Whether a "live-in relationship" would amount to a "relationship in the nature of marriage" falling within the definition of "domestic relationship" Under Section 2(f)[9] of the Protection of Women from Domestic Violence Act, 2005 (for short "the DV Act") and the disruption of such a relationship by failure to maintain a women involved in such a relationship amounts to "domestic violence" within the meaning of Section 3 of the DV Act.

---

virtue of the domestic relationship or which may be reasonably required by the aggrieved person or her children or her stridhan or any other property jointly or separately held by the aggrieved person; and"

(c) prohibition or restriction to continued access to resources or facilities which the aggrieved person is entitled to use or enjoy by virtue of the domestic relationship including access to the shared household. tc" (c) prohibition or restriction to continued access to resources or facilities which the aggrieved person is entitled to use or enjoy by virtue of the domestic relationship including access to the shared household." Explanation II.—For the purpose of determining whether any act, omission, commission or conduct of the respondent constitutes "domestic violence" under this section, the overall facts and circumstances of the case shall be taken into consideration.

9   Section 2(f) in The Protection of Women from Domestic Violence Act, 2005

(f) "domestic relationship" means a relationship between two persons who live or have, at any point of time, lived together in a shared household, when they are related by consanguinity, marriage, or through a relationship in the nature of marriage, adoption or are family members living together as a joint family; tc" (f) "domestic relationship" means a relationship between two persons who live or have, at any point of time, lived together in a shared household, when they are related by consanguinity, marriage, or through a relationship in the nature of marriage, adoption or are family members living together as a joint family"

Domestic Violence Act, 2005:

The Domestic Violence Act, 2005 has been enacted to provide a remedy in Civil Law for protection of women from being victims of domestic violence and to prevent occurrence of domestic violence in the society. The DV Act, 2005 has been enacted also to provide an effective protection of the rights of women guaranteed under the Constitution, who are victims of violence of any kind occurring within the family.

"Domestic Violence" is undoubtedly a human rights issue, which was not properly taken care of in this country even though the Vienna Accord 1994 and the Beijing Declaration and Platform for Action (1995) had acknowledged that domestic violence was undoubtedly a human rights issue. UN Committee on Convention on Elimination of All Forms of Discrimination against Women in its general recommendations had also exhorted the member countries to take steps to protect women against violence of any kind, especially that occurring within the family, a phenomenon widely prevalent in India. Presently, when a woman is subjected to cruelty by husband or his relatives, it is an offence punishable Under Section 498A[10] Indian Penal Code. The Civil Law, it was noticed, did not address this phenomenon in its entirety. Consequently, the Parliament, to provide more effective protection of rights of women

---

10 **Section 498A in The Indian Penal Code**

Husband or relative of husband of a woman subjecting her to cruelty: Whoever, being the husband or the relative of the husband of a woman, subjects such woman to cruelty shall be punished with imprisonment for a term which may extend to three years and shall also be liable to fine. Explanation.—For the purpose of this section, "cruelty" means—

(a) any wilful conduct which is of such a nature as is likely to drive the woman to commit suicide or to cause grave injury or danger to life, limb or health (whether mental or physical) of the woman; or

(b) harassment of the woman where such harassment is with a view to coercing her or any person related to her to meet any unlawful demand for any property or valuable security or is on account of failure by her or any person related to her to meet such demand

guaranteed under the Constitution under Articles 14[11], 15[12] and 21[13], who are victims of violence of any kind occurring in the family, enacted the DV Act, 2005. Chapter IV is the heart and soul of the DV Act, which provides various reliefs to a woman who has or has been in domestic relationship with any adult male person and seeks one or more reliefs provided under the Act. The Magistrate, while entertaining an application from an aggrieved person Under Section 12 of the DV Act, 2005 can grant the following reliefs:

(1) Payment of compensation or damages without prejudice[14] to the right of such person to institute a suit for compensation or damages for injuries caused by the acts of domestic violence committed by the adult male member, with a prayer for set off against the amount payable under a decree obtained in Court

(2) The Magistrate, Under Section 18[15] of the DV Act, 2005 can pass a

---

11 **Article 14 in The Constitution Of India 1949**

   Equality before law: The State shall not deny to any person equality before the law or the equal protection of the laws within the territory of India Prohibition of discrimination on grounds of religion, race, caste, sex or place of birth

12 **Article 15 in The Constitution Of India 1949**

   Prohibition of discrimination on grounds of religion, race, caste, sex or place of birth

   (1) The State shall not discriminate against any citizen on grounds only of religion, race, caste, sex, place of birth or any of them

   (2) No citizen shall, on grounds only of religion, race, caste, sex, place of birth or any of them, be subject to any disability, liability, restriction or condition with regard to

   (a) access to shops, public restaurants, hotels and palaces of public entertainment; or

   (b) the use of wells, tanks, bathing ghats, roads and places of public resort maintained wholly or partly out of State funds or dedicated to the use of the general public

   (3) Nothing in this article shall prevent the State from making any special provision for women and children

   (4) Nothing in this article or in clause (2) of Article 29 shall prevent the State from making any special provision for the advancement of any socially and educationally backward classes of citizens or for the Scheduled Castes and the Scheduled Tribes

13 **Article 21 in The Constitution Of India 1949**

   Protection of life and personal liberty: No person shall be deprived of his life or personal liberty except according to procedure established by law

14   **Meaning of prejudice:**

   a. An adverse judgment or opinion formed beforehand or without knowledge or examination of the facts.

   b. A preconceived preference or idea

15 **Section 18 in The Protection of Women from Domestic Violence Act, 2005**

   18. Protection orders.—The Magistrate may, after giving the aggrieved person and the

"protection order" in favour of the aggrieved person and prohibit the Respondent from:

(a) committing any act of domestic violence;

(b) aiding or abetting[16] in the commission of acts of domestic violence;

(c) entering the place of employment of the aggrieved person or, if the person aggrieved is a child, its school or any other place frequented by the aggrieved person;

(d) attempting to communicate in any form, whatsoever, with the aggrieved person, including personal, oral or written or electronic or telephonic contact;

---

respondent an opportunity of being heard and on being prima facie satisfied that domestic violence has taken place or is likely to take place, pass a protection order in favour of the aggrieved person and prohibit the respondent from— tc "18. Protection orders.—The Magistrate may, after giving the aggrieved person and the respondent an opportunity of being heard and on being prima facie satisfied that domestic violence has taken place or is likely to take place, pass a protection order in favour of the aggrieved person and prohibit the respondent from—"

(a) committing any act of domestic violence; tc" (a) committing any act of domestic violence;"

(b) aiding or abetting in the commission of acts of domestic violence; tc" (b) aiding or abetting in the commission of acts of domestic violence;"

(c) entering the place of employment of the aggrieved person or, if the person aggrieved is a child, its school or any other place frequented by the aggrieved person; tc" (c) entering the place of employment of the aggrieved person or, if the person aggrieved is a child, its school or any other place frequented by the aggrieved person;"

(d) attempting to communicate in any form, whatsoever, with the aggrieved person, including personal, oral or written or electronic or telephonic contact; tc" (d) attempting to communicate in any form, whatsoever, with the aggrieved person, including personal, oral or written or electronic or telephonic contact;"

(e) alienating any assets, operating bank lockers or bank accounts used or held or enjoyed by both the parties, jointly by the aggrieved person and the respondent or singly by the respondent, including her stridhan or any other property held either jointly by the parties or separately by them without the leave of the Magistrate; tc" (e) alienating any assets, operating bank lockers or bank accounts used or held or enjoyed by both the parties, jointly by the aggrieved person and the respondent or singly by the respondent, including her stridhan or any other property held either jointly by the parties or separately by them without the leave of the Magistrate;"

(f) causing violence to the dependants, other relatives or any person who give the aggrieved person assistance from domestic violence; tc" (f) causing violence to the dependants, other relatives or any person who give the aggrieved person assistance from domestic violence;"

(g) committing any other act as specified in the protection order. tc" (g) committing any other act as specified in the protection order."

16 **Meaning of Abet:**

   1. To approve, encourage, and support (an action or a plan of action); urge and help on.

   2. To urge, encourage, or help (a person)

(e) alienating[17] any assets, operating bank lockers or bank accounts used or held or enjoyed by both the parties, jointly by the aggrieved person and the Respondent or singly by the Respondent, including her stridhan or any other property held either jointly by the parties or separately by them without the leave of the Magistrate;

(f) causing violence to the dependants, other relatives or any person who give the aggrieved person assistance from domestic violence;

(g) committing any other act as specified in the protection order.

(3) The Magistrate, while disposing of an application Under Section 12(1) of the DV Act, 2005 can pass a "residence order" Under Section 19[18] of the

---

17 **Meaning of alienating:** To transfer (property or a right) to the ownership of another, especially by an act of the owner rather than by inheritance.

18 Section 19 in The Protection of Women from Domestic Violence Act, 2005

19. Residence orders

(1) While disposing of an application under sub-section (1) of section 12, the Magistrate may, on being satisfied that domestic violence has taken place, pass a residence order— tc "19. Residence orders.—(1) While disposing of an application under sub-section (1) of section 12, the Magistrate may, on being satisfied that domestic violence has taken place, pass a residence order—"

(a) restraining the respondent from dispossessing or in any other manner disturbing the possession of the aggrieved person from the shared household, whether or not the respondent has a legal or equitable interest in the shared household; tc" (a) restraining the respondent from dispossessing or in any other manner disturbing the possession of the aggrieved person from the shared household, whether or not the respondent has a legal or equitable interest in the shared household;"

(b) directing the respondent to remove himself from the shared household; tc" (b) directing the respondent to remove himself from the shared household;"

(c) restraining the respondent or any of his relatives from entering any portion of the shared household in which the aggrieved person resides; tc" (c) restraining the respondent or any of his relatives from entering any portion of the shared household in which the aggrieved person resides;"

(d) restraining the respondent from alienating or disposing of the shared household or encumbering the same; tc" (d) restraining the respondent from alienating or disposing of the shared household or encumbering the same;"

(e) restraining the respondent from renouncing his rights in the shared household except with the leave of the Magistrate; or tc" (e) restraining the respondent from renouncing his rights in the shared household except with the leave of the Magistrate; or"

(f) directing the respondent to secure same level of alternate accommodation for the aggrieved person as enjoyed by her in the shared household or to pay rent for the same, if the circumstances so require: tc" (f) directing the respondent to secure same level of alternate accommodation for the aggrieved person as enjoyed by her in the shared household or to pay rent for the same, if the circumstances so require\:" Provided that no order under clause (b) shall be passed against any person who is a woman. tc "Provided that no order under clause (b) shall be passed against any person who is a woman."

(2) The Magistrate may impose any additional conditions or pass any other direction which he may deem reasonably necessary to protect or to provide for the safety of the aggrieved person or

DV Act, 2005.

Marriage and Marital Relationship:

Marriage is often described as one of the basic civil rights of man/woman, which is voluntarily undertaken by the parties in public in a formal way, and once concluded, recognizes the parties as husband and wife. Three elements of common law marriage are (1) agreement to be married (2) living together as husband and wife, (3) holding out to the public that they are married. Sharing a common household and duty to live together form part of the 'Consortium Omnis Vitae" which obliges spouses[19] to live together, afford each other reasonable marital privileges and rights and be honest and faithful to each other. One of the most important invariable consequences of marriage is the reciprocal support and the responsibility of maintenance of the common household, jointly and

---

any child of such aggrieved person. tc "(2) The Magistrate may impose any additional conditions or pass any other direction which he may deem reasonably necessary to protect or to provide for the safety of the aggrieved person or any child of such aggrieved person."

(3) The Magistrate may require from the respondent to execute a bond, with or without sureties, for preventing the commission of domestic violence. tc "(3) The Magistrate may require from the respondent to execute a bond, with or without sureties, for preventing the commission of domestic violence."

(4) An order under sub-section (3) shall be deemed to be an order under Chapter VIII of the Code of Criminal Procedure, 1973 (2 of 1974) and shall be dealt with accordingly. tc "(4) An order under sub-section (3) shall be deemed to be an order under Chapter VIII of the Code of Criminal Procedure, 1973 (2 of 1974) and shall be dealt with accordingly."

(5) While passing an order under sub-section (1), sub-section (2) or sub-section (3), the court may also pass an order directing the officer-in-charge of the nearest police station to give protection to the aggrieved person or to assist her or the person making an application on her behalf in the implementation of the order. tc "(5) While passing an order under sub-section (1), sub-section (2) or sub-section (3), the court may also pass an order directing the officer-in-charge of the nearest police station to give protection to the aggrieved person or to assist her or the person making an application on her behalf in the implementation of the order."

(6) While making an order under sub-section (1), the Magistrate may impose on the respondent obligations relating to the discharge of rent and other payments, having regard to the financial needs and resources of the parties. tc "(6) While making an order under sub-section (1), the Magistrate may impose on the respondent obligations relating to the discharge of rent and other payments, having regard to the financial needs and resources of the parties."

(7) The Magistrate may direct the officer-in-charge of the police station in whose jurisdiction the Magistrate has been approached to assist in the implementation of the protection order. tc "(7) The Magistrate may direct the officer-in-charge of the police station in whose jurisdiction the Magistrate has been approached to assist in the implementation of the protection order."

(8) The Magistrate may direct the respondent to return to the possession of the aggrieved person her stridhan or any other property or valuable security to which she is entitled to. tc "(8) The Magistrate may direct the respondent to return to the possession of the aggrieved person her stridhan or any other property or valuable security to which she is entitled to."

19 **Meaning of Spouses:** A marriage partner; a husband or wife.

severally. Marriage as an institution has great legal significance and various obligations and duties flow out of marital relationship, as per law, in the matter of inheritance of property, successionship, etc. Marriage, therefore, involves legal requirements of formality, publicity, exclusivity and all the legal consequences flow out of that relationship.

Marriages in India take place either following the personal Law of the Religion to which a party is belonged or following the provisions of the Special Marriage Act. Marriage, as per the Common Law, constitutes a contract between a man and a woman, in which the parties undertake to live together and support each other. Marriage, as a concept, is also nationally and internationally recognized. O'Regan, Judge, in *Dawood and Anr. v. Minister of Home Affairs and Ors.*[20] noted as follows:

Marriage and the family are social institutions of vital importance. Entering into and sustaining a marriage is a matter of intense private significance to the parties to that marriage for they make a promise to one another to establish and maintain an intimate relationship for the rest of their lives which they acknowledge obliges them to support one another, to live together and to be faithful to one another. Such relationships are of profound significance to the individuals concerned. But such relationships have more than personal significance at least in part because human beings are social beings whose humanity is expressed through their relationships with others. Entering into marriage therefore is to enter into a relationship that has public significance as well.

The institutions of marriage and the family are important social institutions that provide for the security, support and companionship of members of our society and bear an important role in the rearing of children. The celebration of a marriage gives rise to moral and legal obligations, particularly the reciprocal duty of support placed upon spouses and their joint responsibility for supporting and raising children born of the marriage. These legal obligations perform an important social function. This importance is symbolically acknowledged in part by the fact that marriage is celebrated generally in a public ceremony, often before family and close friends.

Article 23 of the International Covenant on Civil and Political Rights, 1966 (ICCPR) provides that:

---

20   2000 (3) SA 936 (CC)

1. The family is the natural and fundamental group unit of society and is entitled to protection by society and the State.

2. The right of men and women of marriageable age to marry and to found a family shall be recognized.

3. No marriage shall be entered into without the free and full consent of the intending spouses.

4. States Parties to the present Covenant shall take appropriate steps to ensure equality of rights and responsibilities of spouses as to marriage, during marriage and at its dissolution. In the case of dissolution, provision shall be made for the necessary protection of any children.

Article 16 of the Universal Declaration of Human Rights, 1948 provides that:

1. Men and women of full age, without any limitation due to race, nationality or religion, have the right to marry and to found a family. They are entitled to equal rights as to marriage, during marriage and at it dissolution.

2. Marriage shall be entered into only with the free and full consent of the intending spouses.

3. The family is the natural and fundamental group unit of society and is entitled to protection by society and the State.

Conditions for a Hindu marriage:

"Conditions for a Hindu marriage" are dealt with in Section 5 of the Hindu Marriage Act which reads as under:

Section 5: Conditions for a Hindu marriage-A marriage may be solemnized[21] between any two hindus, if the following conditions are fulfilled, namely:

(i) neither party has a spouse living at the time of the marriage

(ii) at the time of the marriage, neither party-

(a) is incapable of giving a valid consent to it in consequence of

---

21 **Meaning of Solemnized:**

   1. To celebrate or observe with dignity and gravity

   2. To perform with formal ceremony

unsoundness of mind; or

(b) though capable of giving a valid consent, has been suffering from mental disorder of such a kind or to such an extent as to be unfit for marriage and the procreation of children; or

(c) has been subject to recurrent attacks of insanity;

(iii) the bridegroom has completed the age of twenty- one years and the bride the age of eighteen years at the time of the marriage;

(iv) the parties are not within the degrees of prohibited relationship unless the custom or usage governing each of them permits of a marriage between the two;

(v) the parties are not sapindas of each other, unless the custom or usage governing each of them permits of a marriage between the two.

Ceremonies for a Hindu marriage:

Section 7 of the Hindu Marriage Act deals with the "Ceremonies for a Hindu marriage" and reads as follows:

Section 7: Ceremonies for a Hindu marriage.-

(1) A Hindu marriage may be solemnized in accordance with the customary rites and ceremonies of either party thereto.

(2) Where such rites and ceremonies include the saptapadi[22] (that is, the taking of seven steps by the bridegroom and the bride jointly before the sacred fire), the marriage becomes complete and binding when the seventh step is taken.

A live-in relationship will fall within the expression "relationship in the nature of marriage" under following circumstances:

(1) Pooling of Resources and Financial Arrangements

Supporting each other, or any one of them, financially, sharing bank accounts, acquiring immovable properties in joint names or in the name of the woman, long term investments in business, shares in separate and joint names, so as to have a long standing relationship, may be a guiding factor.

---

22 **Saptapadi** is the most important rite of a Hindu marriage ceremony. The word, **Saptapadi** means "Seven steps". After tying the Mangalsutra, the newly wed couple take seven steps around the holy fire, that is called Saptapadi.

(2) Domestic Arrangements

Entrusting the responsibility, especially on the woman to run the home, do the household activities like cleaning, cooking, maintaining or up keeping the house, etc. is an indication of a relationship in the nature of marriage.

(3) Sexual Relationship

Marriage like relationship refers to sexual relationship, not just for pleasure, but for emotional and intimate relationship, for procreation of children, so as to give emotional support, companionship and also material affection, caring etc.

(4) Children

Having children is a strong indication of a relationship in the nature of marriage. Parties, therefore, intend to have a long standing relationship. Sharing the responsibility for bringing up and supporting them is also a strong indication.

(5) Socialization in Public

Holding out to the public and socializing with friends, relations and others, as if they are husband and wife is a strong circumstance to hold the relationship is in the nature of marriage.

(6) Intention and conduct of the parties

Common intention of parties as to what their relationship is to be and to involve, and as to their respective roles and responsibilities, primarily determines the nature of that relationship.

Decision by Supreme Court:

Court held that since the Appellant (Indra Sarma) was aware that the Respondent (V.K.V Sarma) was a married person even before the commencement of their relationship, hence the status of the Appellant (Indra Sarma) was that of a concubine[23] or a mistress, who cannot enter into relationship in the nature of a marriage. Court observed that appellant (Indra Sarma) had entered into relationship knowing well that the Respondent (V.K.V Sarma) was a married person and encouraged

---

23 **Meaning of Concubine:** A woman who cohabits with a man without being legally married to him.

bigamous[24] relationship. By entering into such a relationship, the Appellant (Indra Sarma) has committed an intentional tort[25], i.e. interference in the marital relationship with intentionally alienating[26] Respondent (V.K.V Sarma) from his family, i.e. his wife and children.

Court was of the view that the Appellant (Indra Sarma) having been fully aware of the fact that the Respondent (V.K.V Sarma) was a married person, could not have entered into a live-in relationship in the nature of marriage. All live-in-relationships are not relationships in the nature of marriage. Appellant's and the Respondent's relationship was therefore, not a "relationship in the nature of marriage" because it has no inherent or essential characteristic of a marriage, but a relationship other than "in the nature of marriage" and the Appellant's (Indra Sarma) status was lower than the status of a wife and that relationship would not fall within the definition of "domestic relationship" Under Section 2(f) of the DV Act, 2005.

---

24 **Meaning of Bigamous:** Having two wives or husbands at the same time.

25 An **intentional tort** is a category of torts that describes a civil wrong resulting from an intentional act on the part of thetortfeasor. The term negligence, on the other hand, pertains to a tort that simply results from the failure of the tortfeasor to take sufficient care in fulfilling a duty owed, while strict liability torts refers to situations where a party is liable for injuries no matter what precautions were taken. In leyman's terms, an unintentional tort occurs when someone does not provide proper care for another person. This is generally referred to as: negligence. An example would be someone running a red light and crashing into your car.

26 **Meaning of Alienate:** To transfer (property or a right) to the ownership of another, especially by an act of the owner rather than by inheritance.

38

Registration of FIR is mandatory, if the information discloses commission of a cognizable offence [1]

Facts in Nutshell:

Writ petition[2] under Article 32[3] of the Constitution was filed by one Lalita Kumari (minor[4]) through her father, viz., Shri Bhola Kamat for the issuance of a writ of *Habeas Corpus*[5] or direction(s) of like nature against

---

1   Appellants: **Lalita Kumari Vs.** Respondent: **Govt. of U.P. and Ors.**

     2013(13)SCALE559, 2014 (1) SCJ 68

     Hon'ble Judges/Coram: P. Sathasivam, C.J.I., Balbir Singh Chauhan, Ranjana Prakash Desai, Ranjan Gogoi and Sharad Arvind Bobde, JJ.

2   **Meaning of Writ Petition:** Under the Indian legal system, jurisdiction to issue 'prerogative writs' is given to the Supreme Court, and to the High Courts of Judicature of all Indian states. Parts of the law relating to writs are set forth in the Constitution of India. The Supreme Court, the highest in the country, may issue writs under Article 32 of the Constitution for enforcement of Fundamental Rights and under Articles 139 for enforcement of rights other than Fundamental Rights, while High Courts, the superior courts of the States, may issue writs under Articles 226. 'Writ' is eminently designed by the makers of the Constitution, and in the same way it is developed very widely and efficiently by the courts in India. The Constitution broadly provides for five kinds of "prerogative" writs, namely, Habeas Corpus, Certiorari, Mandamus, Quo Warranto and Prohibition

3   **Article 32 in The Constitution Of India 1949**

     32. Remedies for enforcement of rights conferred by this Part

     (1) The right to move the Supreme Court by appropriate proceedings for the enforcement of the rights conferred by this Part is guaranteed

     (2) The Supreme Court shall have power to issue directions or orders or writs, including writs in the nature of habeas corpus, mandamus, prohibition, quo warranto and certiorari, whichever may be appropriate, for the enforcement of any of the rights conferred by this Part

     (3) Without prejudice to the powers conferred on the Supreme Court by clause (1) and (2), Parliament may by law empower any other court to exercise within the local limits of its jurisdiction all or any of the powers exercisable by the Supreme Court under clause (2)

     (4) The right guaranteed by this article shall not be suspended except as otherwise provided for by this Constitution

4   In law, a *minor* is a person under a certain age—usually the age of majority—which legally demarcates childhood from adulthood. The age of majority depends upon jurisdiction and application, but is generally 18 years

5   A writ of *habeas corpus* is a writ (court order) that requires a person under arrest to be brought

the Respondents[6] i.e. Government of U.P. for the protection of his minor daughter who has been kidnapped. The grievance in the said writ petition was that on 11.05.2008, a written report was submitted by the Petitioner[7] before the officer in-charge of the police station concerned who did not take any action on the same. Thereafter, when the Superintendent of Police was moved, an FIR was registered. According to the Petitioner, even thereafter, steps were not taken either for apprehending the accused[8] or for the recovery of the minor girl child.

Question before the Supreme Court:

The important issue which aroused for consideration in the matter was whether "a police officer is bound to register a First Information Report (FIR) upon receiving any information relating to commission of a cognizable offence[9] under Section 154[10] of the Code of Criminal Procedure, 1973 (in short 'the Code') or the police officer has the power

---

before a judge or into court.

6   Meaning of Respondent: A **respondent** is a person who is called upon to issue a response to a communication made by another. In legal usage, this specifically refers to the defendant in a legal proceeding commenced by a petition, or to an appellee, or the opposing party, in an appeal of a decision by an initial fact-finder

7   **Meaning of Petitioner:** A person who presents a Petition. (**Meaning of Petition:** A formal message requesting something that is submitted to an authority)

8   **Meaning of Accused:** A person charged with a criminal offense, or the state of being so charged

9   Generally, cognizable offence means a police officer has the authority to make an arrest without a warrant. The police is also allowed to start an investigation with or without the permission of a court. Whereas in case of a non-cognizable offence, a police officer doesn't have the authority to make an arrest without a warrant and an investigation cannot be initiated without a court order.

10   **Section 154 in The Code Of Criminal Procedure, 1973**

Information in cognizable cases.

(1) Every information relating to the commission of a cognizable offence, if given orally to an officer in charge of a police station, shall be reduced to writing by him or under his direction, and be read Over to the informant; and every such information, whether given in writing or reduced to writing as aforesaid, shall be signed by the person giving it, and the substance thereof shall be entered in a book to be kept by such officer in such form as the State Government may prescribe in this behalf.

(2) A copy of the information as recorded under sub- section (1) shall be given forthwith, free of cost, to the informant.

(3) Any person aggrieved by a refusal on the part of an officer in charge of a police station to record the information referred to in subsection (1) may send the substance of such information, in writing and by post, to the Superintendent of Police concerned who, if satisfied that such information discloses the commission of a cognizable offence, shall either investigate the case himself or direct an investigation to be made by any police officer subordinate to him, in the manner provided by this Code, and such officer shall have all the powers of an officer in charge of the police station in relation to that offence.

to conduct a "preliminary inquiry" in order to test the veracity[11] of such information before registering the same?"

Significance and Compelling reasons for registration of FIR at the earliest:

The object sought to be achieved by registering the earliest information as FIR is inter alia[12] two fold: *one that the criminal process is set into motion and is well documented from the very start; and second, that the earliest information received in relation to the commission of a cognizable offence is recorded so that there cannot be any embellishment etc., later.* Principles of democracy and liberty demand a regular and efficient check on police powers. One way of keeping check on authorities with such powers is by documenting every action of theirs. Accordingly, under the Code, actions of the police etc., are provided to be written and documented. For example, in case of arrest under Section 41(1)(b)[13] of

---

11 **Meaning of Veracity:**

   1. Adherence to the truth; truthfulness.

   2. Conformity to fact or truth; accuracy or precision

12 **Meaning of Inter Alia:** Among other things

13 **Section 41of the Code of Criminal Procedure:**

   41.When police may arrest without warrant

   (1) Any police officer may without an order from a Magistrate and without a warrant, arrest any person-

   (a) who has been concerned in any cognizable offence, or against whom a reasonable complaint has been made, or credible information has been received, or a reasonable suspicion exists, of his having been so concerned; or

   (b) who has in his possession without lawful excuse, the burden of proving which excuse shall lie on such person, any implement of house-breaking; or

   (c) who has been proclaimed as an offender either under this Code or by order of the State Government; or

   (d) in whose possession anything is found which may reasonably be suspected to be stolen property and who may reasonably be suspected of having committed an offence with reference to such thing; o

   (e) who obstructs a police officer while in the execution of his duty, or who has escaped, or attempts to escape, from lawful custody; or

   (f) who is reasonably suspected of being a deserter from any of the Armed Forces of the Union; or

   (g) who has been concerned in, or against whom a reasonable complaint has been made, or credible information has been received, or a reasonable suspicion exists, of his having been concerned in, any act committed at any place out of India which, if committed in India, would have been punishable as an offence, and for which he is, under any law relating to extradition, or otherwise, liable to be apprehended or detained in custody in India; or

   (h) who, being a released convict, commits a breach of any rule made under sub-section (5) of

the Code of Criminal Procedure arrest memo along with the grounds has to be in writing mandatorily; under Section 55[14] of the Code, if an officer is deputed to make an arrest, then the superior officer has to write down and record the offence etc., for which the person is to be arrested; under Section 91[15] of the Code, a written order has to be passed by the concerned officer to seek documents; under Section 160[16] of the Code,

---

section 356; or

(l) for whose arrest any requisition, whether written or oral, has been received from another police officer, provided that the requisition specifies the person to be arrested and the offence or other cause for which the arrest is to be made and it appears therefrom that the person might lawfully be arrested without a warrant by the officer who issued the requisition.

(2) Any officer in charge of a police station may, in like manner, arrest or cause to be arrested any person, belonging to one or more of the categories of persons specified in section 109 or section 110

14 **Section 55 of the Code of Criminal Procedure**

Procedure when police officer deputes subordinate to arrest without warrant.-

(1) When any officer in charge of a police station or any police officer making an investigation under Chapter XII requires any officer subordinate to him to arrest without a warrant (otherwise than in his presence) any person who may lawfully be arrested without a warrant, he shall deliver to the officer required to make the arrest an order in writing, specifying the person to be arrested and the offence or other cause for which the arrest is to be made and the officer so required shall, before making the arrest, notify to the person to be arrested the substance of the order and, if so required by such person, shall show him the order.

(2) Nothing in sub-section (1) shall affect the power of a police officer to arrest a person under section 41

15 **Section 91of the Code of Criminal Procedure:**

Summons to produce document or other thing.-

(1) Whenever any Court or any officer in charge of a police station considers that the production of any document or other thing is necessary or desirable for the purposes of any investigation, inquiry, trial or other proceeding under this Code by or before such Court or officer, such Court may issue a summons, or such officer a written order, to the person in whose possession or power such document or thing is believed to be, requiring him to attend and produce it, or to produce it, at the time and place stated in the summons or order.

(2) Any person required under this section merely to produce a document or other thing shall be deemed to have complied with the requisition if he causes such document or thing to be produced instead of attending personally to produce the same.

(3) Nothing in this section shall be deemed-

(a) to affect sections 123 and 124 of the Indian Evidence Act, 1872,(1 of 1872) or the Bankers' Books Evidence Act, 1891,(13 of 1891) or

(b) to apply to a letter, postcard, telegram, or other document or any parcel or thing in the custody of the postal or telegraph authority.

16 **Section 160 of the Code of Criminal Procedure:**

160.Police officers power to require attendance of witnesses.-

(1) Any police officer making an investigation under this Chapter may, by order in writing, require the attendance before himself of any person being within the limits of his own or any adjoining station who, from the information given or otherwise, appears to be acquainted with the facts

a written notice has to be issued to the witness so that he can be called for recording of his/her statement, seizure memo/panchnama has to be drawn for every article seized etc.

The police is required to maintain several records including Case Diary as provided under Section 172[17] of the Code, General Diary as provided under Section 44[18] of the Police Act etc., which helps in documenting every information collected, spot visited and all the actions of the police officers so that their activities can be documented. Moreover, every information received relating to commission of a non-cognizable offence[19] also has to be registered under Section 155[20] of the Code.

---

and circumstances of the case; and such person shall attend as so required:

Provided that no male person under the age of fifteen years or woman shall be required to attend at any place other than the place in which such male person or woman resides.

(2) The State Government may, by rules made in this behalf, provide for the payment by the police officer of the reasonable expenses of every person, attending under sub-section (1) at any place other than his residence.

17 **Section 172 of the Code of Criminal Procedure:**

Diary of proceedings in investigation.-

(1) Every police officer making an investigation under this Chapter shall day by day enter his proceedings in the investigation in a diary, setting forth the time at which the information reached him, the time at which he began and closed his investigation, the place or places visited by him, and a statement of the circumstances ascertained through his investigation.

(2) Any Criminal Court may send for the police diaries of a case under inquiry or trial in such Court, and may use such diaries, not as evidence in the case, but to aid it in such inquiry or trial.

(3) Neither the accused nor his agents shall be entitled to call for such diaries, nor shall he or they be entitled to see them merely because they are referred to by the Court; but, if they are used by the police officer who made them to refresh his memory, or if the Court uses them for the purpose of contradicting such police officer, the provisions of section 161 or section 145 as the case may be, of the Indian Evidence Act, 1872, (1 of 1872) shall apply.

18 **Section 44 in [The Police Act, 1861]**

Police- officers to keep diary: It shall be the duty of every officer in charge of a police- station to keep a general diary in such form shall, from time to time, be prescribed by the State Government and to record therein all complaints and charges preferred, the names of all persons arrested, the names of the complainants, the offences charged against them, the weapons or property that shall have been taken from their possession or otherwise, and the names of the witnesses who shall have been examined. The Magistrate of the district shall be at liberty to call for and inspect such diary

19 Generally, cognizable offence means a police officer has the authority to make an arrest without a warrant. The police is also allowed to start an investigation with or without the permission of a court. Whereas in case of a non-cognizable offence, a police officer doesn't have the authority to make an arrest without a warrant and an investigation cannot be initiated without a court order.

20 **Section 155 of the Code of Criminal Procedure:**

Information as to non-cognizable cases and investigation of such cases.-

(1) When information is given to an officer in charge of a police station of the commission within the limits of such station of a non-cognizable offence, he shall enter or cause to be entered

The underpinnings of compulsory registration of FIR is not only to ensure transparency in the criminal justice delivery system but also to ensure 'judicial oversight'. Section 157(1)[21] deploys the word 'forthwith'. Thus, any information received under Section 154(1)[22] or otherwise has to

---

the substance of the information in a book to be kept by such officer in such form as the State Government may prescribe in this behalf, and refer the informant to the Magistrate.

(2) No police officer shall investigate a non-cognizable case without the order of a Magistrate having power to try such case or commit the case for trial.

(3) Any police officer receiving such order may exercise the same powers in respect of the investigation (except the power to arrest without warrant) as an officer in charge of a police station may exercise in a cognizable case.

(4) Where a case relates to two or more offences of which at least one is cognizable, the case shall be deemed to be a cognizable case, not-withstanding that the other offences are non-cognizable.

21 **Section 157 of the Code of Criminal Procedure**

Procedure for investigation.-

(1) If, from information received or otherwise, an officer in charge of a police station has reason to suspect the commission of an offence which he is empowered under section 156 to investigate, he shall forthwith send a report of the same to a Magistrate empowered to take cognizance of such offence upon a police report and shall proceed in person, or shall depute one of his subordinate officers not being below such rank as the State Government may, by general or special order, prescribe in this behalf, to proceed, to the spot, to investigate the facts and circumstances of the case, and, if necessary, to take measures for the discovery and arrest of the offender:

Provided that-

(a) when information as to the commission of any such offence is given against any person by name and the case is not of a serious nature, the officer in charge of a police station need not proceed in person or depute a subordinate officer to make an investigation on the spot;

(b) if it appears to the officer in charge of a police station that there is no sufficient ground for entering on an investigation, he shall not investigate the case.

(2) In each of the cases mentioned in clauses (a) and (b) of the proviso to sub-section (1), the officer in charge of the police station shall state in his report his reasons for not fully complying with the requirements of that sub-section, and, in the case mentioned in clause (b) of the said proviso, the officer shall also forthwith notify to the informant, if any, in such manner as may be prescribed by the State Government, the fact that he will not investigate the case or cause it to be investigated.

22 **Section 154 of the Code of Criminal Procedure**

154.Information in cognizable cases.-

(1) Every information relating to the commission of a cognizable offence, if given orally to an officer in charge of a police station, shall be reduced to writing by him or under his direction, and be read over to the informant; and every such information, whether given in writing or reduced to writing as aforesaid, shall be signed by the person giving it, and the substance thereof shall be entered in a book to be kept by such officer in such form as the State Government may prescribe in this behalf.

(2) A copy of the information as recorded under sub-section (1) shall be given forthwith, free of cost, to the informant.

(3) Any person aggrieved by a refusal on the part of an officer in charge of a police station to record the information referred to in sub-section (1) may send the substance of such information, in writing and by post, to the Superintendent of Police concerned who, if satisfied that such

be duly informed in the form of a report to the Magistrate. Thus, the commission of a cognizable offence is not only brought to the knowledge of the investigating agency but also to the subordinate judiciary.

The Code contemplates two kinds of FIRs. The duly signed FIR under Section 154(1) is by the informant to the concerned officer at the police station. The second kind of FIR could be which is registered by the police itself on any information received or other than by way of an informant [Section 157(1)] and even this information has to be duly recorded and the copy should be sent to the Magistrate forthwith.

The registration of FIR either on the basis of the information furnished by the informant under Section 154(1) of the Code or otherwise under Section 157(1) of the Code is obligatory. The obligation to register FIR has inherent advantages:

a) It is the first step to 'access to justice' for a victim.

b) It upholds the 'Rule of Law' inasmuch as the ordinary person brings forth the commission of a cognizable crime in the knowledge of the State.

c) It also facilitates swift investigation and sometimes even prevention of the crime. In both cases, it only effectuates the regime of law.

d) It leads to less manipulation in criminal cases and lessens incidents of 'ante-dates' FIR or deliberately delayed FIR.

First information report in a criminal case is an extremely vital and valuable piece of evidence for the purpose of corroborating[23] the oral evidence adduced[24] at the trial. The importance of the above report can hardly be overestimated from the standpoint of the accused. The object of insisting upon prompt lodging of the report to the police in respect of commission of an offence is to obtain early information regarding the circumstances in which the crime was committed, the names of the actual culprits and the part played by them as well as the names of eyewitnesses present at the scene of occurrence. Delay in lodging the first information report quite often results in embellishment which is a creature of afterthought.

---

information discloses the commission of a cognizable offence, shall either investigate the case himself or direct an investigation to be made by any police officer subordinate to him, in the manner provided by this Code, and such officer shall have all the powers of an officer in charge of the police station in relation to that offence.

23 **Meaning of Corroborate:** To strengthen or support with other evidence; make more certain

24 **Meaning of Adduced:** To cite as an example or means of proof in an argument

On account of delay, the report not only gets bereft[25] of the advantage of spontaneity, danger creeps in of the introduction of coloured version, exaggerated account or concocted story as a result of deliberation and consultation. It is, therefore, essential that the delay in the lodging of the first information report should be satisfactorily explained.[26]

Decision by Supreme Court:

Court held that if no cognizable offence was made out in the information given, then the FIR need not be registered immediately and perhaps the police can conduct a sort of preliminary verification or inquiry for the limited purpose of ascertaining as to whether a cognizable offence has been committed. But, if the information given clearly mentions the commission of a cognizable offence, there is no other option but to register an FIR forthwith. *Other considerations are not relevant at the stage of registration of FIR, such as, whether the information is falsely given, whether the information is genuine, whether the information is credible etc.* These are the issues that have to be verified during the investigation[27] of the FIR. At the stage of registration of FIR, what is to be seen is merely whether the information given ex facie[28] discloses the commission of a cognizable offence. If, after investigation, the information given is found to be false, there is always an option to prosecute the complainant for filing a false FIR.

Court observed that while registration of FIR is mandatory, arrest of the accused immediately on registration of FIR is not at all mandatory. In fact, registration of FIR and arrest of an accused person are two entirely different concepts under the law, and there are several safeguards available against arrest. An accused person also has a right to apply for "anticipatory bail"[29] under the provisions of Section 438[30] of the Code

---

25 **Meaning of bereft:** Unhappy in love; suffering from unrequited love

26 *Thulia Kali v. State of Tamil Nadu,* (1972) 3 SCC 393

27 **Meaning of Investigation:**

   1. The act or process of investigating.

   2. A detailed inquiry or systematic examination

28 **Meaning of Ex-Facie: Ex facie** is a legal term typically used to note that a document's explicit terms are defective without further investigation.

29 Under Indian criminal law, there is a provision for **anticipatory bail** under Section 438 of the Criminal Procedure Code. This provision allows a person to seek bail in anticipation of an arrest on accusation of having committed a non-bailable offence

30 **Section 438 of the Code of Criminal Procedure**

if the conditions mentioned therein are satisfied. Thus, in appropriate cases, he can avoid the arrest under that provision by obtaining an order from the Court.

Directions by Supreme Court:

(i) Registration of FIR is mandatory under Section 154 of the Code, if the information discloses commission of a cognizable offence and no preliminary inquiry is permissible in such a situation.

(ii) If the information received does not disclose a cognizable offence but indicates the necessity for an inquiry, a preliminary inquiry may be conducted only to ascertain whether cognizable offence is disclosed or not.

(iii) If the inquiry discloses the commission of a cognizable offence, the

---

438. Direction for grant of bail to person apprehending arrest:---(1) When any person has reason to believe that he may be arrested on an accusation of having committed a non-bailable offence, he may apply to the High Court or the Court of Sessions for a direction under this section, and that Court may, if it thinks fit, direct that in the event of such arrest, he shall be released on bail.

(2) When the High Court or the Court of Sessions makes a direction under sub-section (1), it may include such conditions in such direction in the light of the facts of the particular case, as it may think fit, including-

(i) a condition that the person shall make himself available for interrogation by a police officer as and

when required;

(ii) a condition that the person shall not, directly or indirectly, make any inducement, threat or promise

to any person acquainted with the facts of the case so as to dissuade him from disclosing such facts to the

Court or to any police officer;

(iii) a condition that the person shall not leave India without the previous permission of the Court;

(iv) such other condition as may be imposed under sub-section (3) of section 437, as if the bail were

granted under that section.

(2) If such person is thereafter arrested without warrant by an officer in charge of a police station on such

accusation, and is prepared either at the time of arrest or at any time while in the custody of such officer to

give bail, he shall be released on bail, and if a Magistrate taking cognizance of such offence decides that a

warrant should be issued in the first instance against that person, he shall issue a bailable warrant in

confirmity with the direction of the Court under sub-section (1).

FIR must be registered. In cases where preliminary inquiry ends in closing the complaint, a copy of the entry of such closure must be supplied to the first informant forthwith and not later than one week. It must disclose reasons in brief for closing the complaint and not proceeding further.

(iv) The police officer cannot avoid his duty of registering offence if cognizable offence is disclosed. Action must be taken against erring officers who do not register the FIR if information received by him discloses a cognizable offence.

(v) The scope of preliminary inquiry is not to verify the veracity or otherwise of the information received but only to ascertain whether the information reveals any cognizable offence.

(vi)   As to what type and in which cases preliminary inquiry is to be conducted will depend on the facts and circumstances of each case. The category of cases in which preliminary inquiry may be made are as under:

(a) Matrimonial disputes/family disputes

(b) Commercial offences

(c) Medical negligence cases

(d) Corruption cases

(e) Cases where there is abnormal delay/laches in initiating criminal prosecution, for example, over 3 months delay in reporting the matter without satisfactorily explaining the reasons for delay.

The aforesaid are only illustrations and not exhaustive of all conditions which may warrant preliminary inquiry.

(vii) While ensuring and protecting the rights of the accused and the complainant, a preliminary inquiry should be made time bound and in any case it should not exceed 7 days. The fact of such delay and the causes of it must be reflected in the General Diary entry.

(viii) Since the General Diary/Station Diary/Daily Diary is the record of all information received in a police station, court directed that all information relating to cognizable offences, whether resulting in registration of FIR or leading to an inquiry, must be mandatorily and meticulously reflected in the said Diary and the decision to conduct a preliminary inquiry must also be reflected.

39

Guidelines regarding Dishonour of cheque[1]

Facts in Nutshell:

Writ Petition[2] under Article 32[3] of the Constitution of India was preferred by the Indian Banks' Association (IBA) along with Punjab National Bank and another, seeking the following relief:

Laying down appropriate guidelines/directions to be followed by all Courts within the territory of India competent to try a complaint under Section 138[4] of the Negotiable Instruments Act, 1881.

---

1 Appellants: **Indian Bank Association and Ors. Vs.** Respondent: **Union of India (UOI) and Anr.**

   MANU/SC/0387/2014

   Hon'ble Judges/Coram: K.S. Panicker Radhakrishnan and Vikramajit Sen, JJ.

2 **Meaning of Writ Petition:** Under the Indian legal system, jurisdiction to issue 'prerogative writs' is given to the Supreme Court, and to the High Courts of Judicature of all Indian states. Parts of the law relating to writs are set forth in the Constitution of India. The Supreme Court, the highest in the country, may issue writs under Article 32 of the Constitution for enforcement of Fundamental Rights and under Articles 139 for enforcement of rights other than Fundamental Rights, while High Courts, the superior courts of the States, may issue writs under Articles 226. 'Writ' is eminently designed by the makers of the Constitution, and in the same way it is developed very widely and efficiently by the courts in India. The Constitution broadly provides for five kinds of "prerogative" writs, namely, Habeas Corpus, Certiorari, Mandamus, Quo Warranto and Prohibition

3 **Article 32 in The Constitution Of India 1949**

   32. Remedies for enforcement of rights conferred by this Part

   (1) The right to move the Supreme Court by appropriate proceedings for the enforcement of the rights conferred by this Part is guaranteed

   (2) The Supreme Court shall have power to issue directions or orders or writs, including writs in the nature of habeas corpus, mandamus, prohibition, quo warranto and certiorari, whichever may be appropriate, for the enforcement of any of the rights conferred by this Part

   (3) Without prejudice to the powers conferred on the Supreme Court by clause (1) and (2), Parliament may by law empower any other court to exercise within the local limits of its jurisdiction all or any of the powers exercisable by the Supreme Court under clause (2)

   (4) The right guaranteed by this article shall not be suspended except as otherwise provided for by this Constitution

4 **Section 138 in The Negotiable Instruments Act, 1881**

   Dishonour of cheque for insufficiency, etc., of funds in the account: Where any cheque drawn by a person on an account maintained by him with a banker for payment of any amount of

The first Petitioner[5], which is an Association of Persons with 174 banks/ financial institutions as its members, is a voluntary association of banks and functions as think tank for banks in the matters of concern for the whole banking industry. The Petitioners submitted that the issue raised was of considerable national importance owing to the reason that in the era of globalization and rapid technological developments, financial trust and commercial interest have to be restored. The Petitioners submitted that the banking industry has been put to a considerable disadvantage due to the delay in disposing of the cases relating to Negotiable Instruments Act. The Petitioner banks being custodian of public funds find it difficult to expeditiously recover huge amount of public fund which are blocked in cases pending Under Section 138 of the Negotiable Instruments Act, 1881. Petitioners submitted that, in spite of the fact, Chapter XIV has been introduced in the Negotiable Instruments Act by Section 4 of the Banking, Public Financial Institutions and Negotiable Instruments Laws (Amendment) Act, 1988, to enhance the acceptability of cheques in settlement of liability by making the drawer liable for penalties in case of bouncing of cheques due to insufficiency of funds, the desired object of the Amendment Act has not achieved.

Legislature has noticed that the introduction of Sections 138 to 142 of the Act has not achieved desired result for dealing with dishonoured cheques, hence, it inserted new Sections 143 to 147 in the Negotiable

---

money to another person from out of that account for the discharge, in whole or in part, of any debt or other liability, is returned by the bank unpaid, either because of the amount of money standing to the credit of that account is insufficient to honour the cheque or that it exceeds the amount arranged to be paid from that account by an agreement made with that bank, such person shall be deemed to have committed an offence and shall, without prejudice to any other provisions of this Act, be punished with imprisonment for [19] [a term which may be extended to two years], or with fine which may extend to twice the amount of the cheque, or with both: Provided that nothing contained in this section shall apply unless—

(a) the cheque has been presented to the bank within a period of six months from the date on which it is drawn or within the period of its validity, whichever is earlier;

(b) the payee or the holder in due course of the cheque, as the case may be, makes a demand for the payment of the said amount of money by giving a notice in writing, to the drawer of the cheque, [within thirty days] of the receipt of information by him from the bank regarding the return of the cheque as unpaid; and

(c) the drawer of such cheque fails to make the payment of the said amount of money to the payee or, as the case may be, to the holder in due course of the cheque, within fifteen days of the receipt of the said notice.

Explanation.— For the purposes of this section, "debt or other liability" means a legally enforceable debt or other liability.]

5   **Meaning of Petitioner:** A person who presents a Petition. (**Meaning of Petition:** A formal message requesting something that is submitted to an authority)

Instruments Act vide Negotiable Instruments (Amendment and Miscellaneous Provisions) Act, 2002 for speedy disposal of cases relating to dishonour of cheques through summary trial as well as making the offence compoundable. But, no uniform practice is seen followed by the various Magistrate Courts in the country, as a result of which, the object and purpose for which the amendments were incorporated, have not been achieved.

Directions by Supreme Court:

(1) Metropolitan Magistrate/Judicial Magistrate (MM/JM), on the day when the complaint Under Section 138 of the Act is presented, shall scrutinize the complaint and, if the complaint is accompanied by the affidavit[6], and the affidavit and the documents, if any, are found to be in order, take cognizance and direct issuance of summons[7].

(2) MM/JM should adopt a pragmatic and realistic approach while issuing summons. Summons must be properly addressed and sent by post as well as by e-mail address got from the complainant. Court, in appropriate cases, may take the assistance of the police or the nearby Court to serve notice to the accused[8]. For notice of appearance, a short date be fixed. If the summons is received back un-served, immediate follow up action be taken.

(3) Court may indicate in the summon that if the accused makes an application for compounding of offences at the first hearing of the case and, if such an application is made, Court may pass appropriate orders at the earliest.

(4) Court should direct the accused, when he appears to furnish a bail bond, to ensure his appearance during trial and ask him to take notice under Section 251[9] Code of Criminal Procedure to enable him to

---

6   An **affidavit** is a written sworn statement of fact voluntarily made by an *affiant* or *deponent* under an oath or affirmation administered by a person authorized to do so by law. Such statement is witnessed as to the authenticity of the affiant's signature by a taker of oaths, such as a notary public or commissioner of oaths.

7   Legally, a **summons** is a legal document issued by a court (a *judicial summons*) or by an administrative agency of government (an *administrative summons*) for various purposes

8   **Meaning of Accused:** A person charged with a criminal offense, or the state of being so charged

9   **Sections 251 of Code of Criminal Procedure, 1973**

   Substance of accusation to be stated.-

   When in a summons-case the accused appears or is brought before the Magistrate, the particulars of the offence of which he is accused shall be stated to him, and he shall be asked whether he

enter his plea of defence and fix the case for defence evidence, unless an application is made by the accused for re-calling a witness for cross-examination[10].

(5) The Court concerned must ensure that examination-in-chief[11], cross-examination and reexamination[12] of the complainant must be conducted within three months of assigning the case. The Court has option of accepting affidavits of the witnesses, instead of examining them in Court. Witnesses to the complaint and accused must be available for cross-examination as and when there is direction to this effect by the Court.

---

pleads guilty or has any defence to make, but it shall not be necessary to frame a formal charge

10 **Section 137 of Evidence Act, 1872**

   Cross-examination: The examination of a witness by the adverse party shall be called his cross-examination

11 **Section 137 of Evidence Act, 1872**

   Examination-in-chief: The examination of witness by the party who calls him shall be called his examination-in-chief

12 **Section 137 of Evidence Act, 1872**

   Re-examination: The examination of a witness, subsequent to the cross-examination by the party who called him, shall be called his re-examination

Glossary of Common Legal Terms

Advocate

A person authorized to appear in a litigation on behalf of a party. An advocate possesses a law degree and is enrolled with a Bar Council, as prescribed by the Advocates Act, 1961. Advocates are the only class of persons legally entitled to practise law. They provide legal advice. After being authorized to appear in a case by a client who has signed a vakalat, advocates prepare cases and argue them in Court. In the Bombay and Calcutta High Courts there is a separate class of legal practitioners, known as solicitors, who prepare the case, but do not argue in Court. When appearing in a courtroom, an advocate usually dresses in black and white, and wears a band and gown. Any complaint against an advocate is made to the Bar Council of India. See junior advocate, advocate-on-record, senior advocate, amicus curiae, vakalath.

Advocate-on-record (AOR)

An advocate who has passed a qualifying examination conducted by the Supreme Court. The examination is taken by an advocate who has been enrolled with a Bar Council for at least five years and has completed one year"s training with an AOR of not less than five years standing. Only an AOR can file a vakalath, a petition, an affidavit or any other application on behalf of a party in the Supreme Court. All the procedural aspects of a case are dealt with by the AOR, with the assistance of a registered clerk. It is the AOR"s name that appears on the cause list. The AOR is held accountable, by the Court, for the conduct of the case. Any notices and correspondence from the Court are sent to the AOR, and not to the party.

Advocate's fees

There are no standardized fees charged for the various tasks performed by an advocate. Some advocates charge a lump sum amount for dealing with an entire case, others charge separate fees for each task - e.g., drafting, filing, legal advice, arguing. Senior advocates generally charge a separate fee for every hearing. In the majority of PIL cases, these fees have been waived by the advocates. When appearing on behalf of a legal aid committee, an advocate receives expenses and nominal fees, at no cost to the party. In some PIL cases the Court has awarded costs to the party.

Affidavit

This is a sworn statement made by a party, in writing, made in the presence of an oath commissioner or a notary public which is used either in support of applications to the Court or as evidence in court proceedings. In writ jurisdiction, cases are generally disposed of on the basis of affidavits. An affidavit in reply to a petition, filed by a respondent, is called a counter affidavit. The petitioner's response to this counter, is called a rejoinder affidavit. All affidavits are verified as to the truth of their contents.

Amicus curiae

Translated from the Latin as 'friend of the Court'. An advocate appears in this capacity when asked to help with the case by the Court or on volunteering services to the Court.

Appeal

The correctness of the decision of a lower court or tribunal is questioned by way of an appeal in a higher court.

Cognizable offence

An offence in which arrest can be made without a warrant.

Commission

A commission is appointed by a court to ascertain or investigate facts needed to decide a case. A commission is usually given specific terms of reference. Members of a commission have been chosen from amongst experts, academics, social activists/workers, advocates, judges and others. Costs of the commission are usually borne by the State. Such commissions have often been appointed in PILs.

Court Fees

These are mandatory charges payable by affixing judicial stamps on petitions, applications and various kinds of documents before they are filed in a court. It is only in legal aid matters that the petitioners are exempt from paying these fees.

Court Master

An officer of the court who occupies a seat just below the judges' dias and assists in the conduct of proceedings.

Decree

The formal expression of an adjudication which, so far as regards the Court expressing it, conclusively determines the rights of the parties with regard to all or any of the matters in controversy in the suit and may be either preliminary or final.

Decree –holder

A person in whose favour a decree has been passed or an order capable of execution has been made.

High Court

Article 214 of the Constitution provides that each state shall have a High Court. This is the highest court in a state and is subordinate only to the Supreme Court of India. The powers of the High Court are broadly categorized as judicial and administrative. In its judicial function the High Court can be approached directly (eg. writ petitions), or in appeals or revisions—both civil and criminal. In its administrative function the High Court supervises the functioning of the lower judiciary in the State. In the civil side, in an ascending order of hierarchy, is the Civil Judge (Junior Division), Civil Judge (Senior Division), the Additional District Judge and the District Judge; the criminal side includes Metropolitan Magistrates, Chief Metropolitan Magistrates, Additional Sessions Judges and the Sessions Judge. The powers of a High Court do not extend beyond the territory of the State. While every decision of the Supreme Court is binding on the High Courts, the decisions of one High Court is not binding on the other. The High Court is a court of record.

Judgment

The final order of a court in a case which, while giving reasons, conclusively decides the rights of parties in the case, resolves the dispute and grants reliefs. See bench, order.

Judgment-debtor

Any person against whom a decree has been passed or an order capable of execution has been made

Judicial Review

A term that describes the function of the judiciary being able to examine and correct the actions of all the organs of State—the executive, the legislature and the judiciary itself. Judicial review is part of the basic structure of the Indian Constitution.

Junior Advocate

Any advocate who wants to practise law, enrols with a Bar Council and generally begins work in the office of a practising advocate.

Jurisdiction

This indicates the scope and extent of a court's powers. For instance, a court only has territorial jurisdiction within the territory over which its powers extend. Jurisdiction is also used to describe the nature of the proceedings in the Court, for example: civil original jurisdiction, criminal appellate jurisdiction. A court's decision can always be challenged on the ground that while deciding a case it has exceeded its jurisdiction, i.e. powers, or that it has exercised a jurisdiction it does not possess.

Legal Aid

A system by which legal services are rendered at government cost to those in financial need and who cannot afford the cost of litigation. This is mandated by Article 39A of the Constitution. In Delhi, the Delhi High Court Legal Services Committee (DHCLSC) and the Delhi Legal Services Authority (DLSA) provide legal aid on behalf of the State.

Legal Representative

A person who in law represents the estate of a deceased person, and includes any person who intermeddles with the estate of the deceased and where a party sues or is sued in a representative character the person on whom the estate devolves on the death of the party so suing or sued

Locus Standi

Translated from Latin as 'place of standing', locus standi gives the right to pursue a litigation. Under this rule, only a person or group of persons affected by the issue may petition the Court. A petition may be dismissed on the preliminary ground that the petitioner lacks locus standi. However, in PIL, the locus standi of public spirited persons to petition on behalf of others has been recognized. This relaxation of the rule of standing is an important feature of PIL—for instance, journalists, lawyers, politicians, social activists, students, or any 'concerned individual' not acting for personal interest or gain, and not as a 'busy body', have been given standing.

Mesne-profits

Those profits which the person in wrongful possession of such property actually received or might with ordinary diligence have received therefrom, together with interest on such profits, but shall not include profits due to improvements made by the person in wrongful possession

Notification

Notice, information or announcement published in the official gazette notifying, for instance, the coming into effect of a changed law.

Obiter dicta

Remarks of a judge, which are said by the way and are not directly relevant to the case at hand.

Ratio decidendi

The reason behind or crux of a judicial decision.

Res Judicata

A legal principle which prevents a party to a case which has been finally decided from bringing an action on the same issue. For example, a case is barred by res judicata if an earlier case between the same parties has decided upon the same points. This is embodied in Section 11 of the Code of Civil Procedure, 1908.

Respondent

A party against whom a petition is filed. A proforma respondent is a party against whom no relief is sought.

Review

A court has the power to review its orders on specified grounds, as provided by law. Generally the same court which passed the order or judgement in a case reviews its decision. There is, however, no inherent power in a court to review its decisions. The power has to be given by statute or be found in the Constitution.

Revision

Orders that cannot be appealed against can be revised by the High Court on specific grounds, as provided in S 115 of the Code of Civil Procedure, 1908 and Ss. 397 and 401 of the Code of Criminal Procedure, 1973.

Supreme Court

The highest court in the country constituted under Article 124 of the Constitution. Its decisions are law under Article 141 and are binding on all lower courts. It has unlimited powers to do complete justice. It exercises original as well as appellate jurisdiction. Under Article 143 the President of India can ask the Supreme Court for an opinion on questions of law or fact. States can file suits against each other or against the Union of India under Article 131. The Supreme Court can transfer cases to itself from the High Courts or from one High Court to another under Article 139A of the Constitution. It can also transfer civil cases from one Court to another under S 25 of the Code of Civil Procedure, 1908, and likewise criminal cases under S 406 of the Code of Criminal Procedure, 1973. Apart from special leave petitions, in certain instances, appeals can be filed directly against the judgments of lower courts and tribunals. Petitions challenging the election of the President or Vice-President of India are also filed directly in the Supreme Court. The chairperson of a public service commission may be removed only after an inquiry by the Supreme Court. The Supreme Court has a sanctioned strength of 31 judges, headed by the Chief Justice of India. The seat of the Supreme Court is New Delhi and its language is English.

Void

One that law regards as never having taken place.

Writ

A writ is a direction that the Court issues, which is to be obeyed by the authority/person to whom it is issued.

Writ Petition

A petition seeking issuance of a writ is a writ petition. Pits in the first instance in the High Courts and the Supreme Court are writ petitions.

A writ of habeas corpus is issued to an authority or person to produce in court a person who is either missing or kept in illegal custody. Where the detention is found to be without authority of law, the Court may order compensation to the person illegally detained.

A writ of mandamus is a direction to an authority to either do or refrain from doing a particular act. For instance, a writ to the Pollution Control Board to strictly enforce the Pollution Control Acts. For a mandamus to be issued, it must be shown:

a) That the authority was under obligation, statutory or otherwise to act in a particular manner;

b) that the said authority failed in performing such obligation; c) that such failure has resulted in some specific violation of a fundamental right of either the petitioner or an indeterminate class of persons.

A writ of certiorari is a direction to an authority to produce before the Court the records on the basis of which a decision under challenge in the writ petition has been taken. By looking into those records, the Court will examine whether the authority applied its mind to the relevant materials before it took the decision. If the Court finds that no reasonable person could come to the decision in question, it will set aside (quash) that decision and give a further direction to the authority to consider the matter afresh.

For instance, the permission given by an authority to operate a distillery next to a school can be challenged by filing a petition asking for a writ of certiorari.

A writ of prohibition issues to prevent a judicial authority subordinate to the High Court from exercising jurisdiction over a matter pending before it. This could be on the ground that the authority lacks jurisdiction and further that prejudice would be caused if the authority proceeds to decide the matter. Where the authority is found to be biased and refuses to rescue, a writ of prohibition may issue.

A petition seeking a writ of quo warranto questions the legal basis and authority of a person appointed to public office. For instance, the appointment of a member of a Public Service Commission not qualified to hold the post can be questioned by a writ of quo warranto and appointment nullified if found to be illegal.

A writ of declaration issues to declare an executive, legislative or quasi-judicial act to be invalid in law. For instance, a court could declare S. 81 of the Mental Health Act, 1987 that permits use of mentally ill patients for experimentation to be violative of the fundamental rights of the mentally ill and therefore illegal and void. A petition seeking such declaratory relief must also necessarily seek certain consequential reliefs. For instance, immediate discontinuance of the illegal practice and appropriate remedial compensation.

These apart, a writ petition could seek other writs, orders and directions which the Court may fashion in response to the facts placed before it.

Where The Mind Is Without Fear

Where the mind is without fear and the head is held high

Where knowledge is free

Where the world has not been broken up into fragments

By narrow domestic walls

Where words come out from the depth of truth

Where tireless striving stretches its arms towards perfection

Where the clear stream of reason has not lost its way

Into the dreary desert sand of dead habit

Where the mind is led forward by thee

Into ever-widening thought and action

Into that heaven of freedom, my Father, let my country awake

- Rabindranath Tagore

www.ingramcontent.com/pod-product-compliance
Lightning Source LLC
Chambersburg PA
CBHW061135220326
41599CB00025B/4236